The Cool Knife

SMITHSONIAN SERIES IN ETHNOGRAPHIC INQUIRY

William L. Merrill and Ivan Karp, Series Editors

Ethnography as fieldwork, analysis, and literary form is the distinguishing feature of modern anthropology. Guided by the assumption that anthropological theory and ethnography are inextricably linked, this series is devoted to exploring the ethnographic enterprise.

ADVISORY BOARD

Richard Bauman (Indiana University), Gerald Berreman (University of California, Berkeley), James Boon (Princeton University), Stephen Gudeman (University of Minnesota), Shirley Lindenbaum (City University of New York), George Marcus (Rice University), David Parkin (University of Oxford), Roy Rappaport (University of Michigan), Renato Rosaldo (Stanford University), Annette Weiner (New York University), and Norman Whitten (University of Illinois).

The Cool Knife

Imagery of Gender, Sexuality, and Moral Education in Kaguru Initiation Ritual

T. O. BEIDELMAN

SMITHSONIAN INSTITUTION PRESS

Washington and London

Copy editor: Susan A. Warga
Production editor: Duke Johns
Designer: Kathleen Sims

Library of Congress Cataloging-in-Publication Data
Beidelman, T. O. (Thomas O.), 1931–
    The cool knife : imagery of gender, sexuality, and moral education in Kaguru initiation
ritual / T. O. Beidelman.
        p. cm.
    Includes bibliographical references and index.
    ISBN 1-56098-713-8 (cloth : alk. paper). — ISBN 1-56098-714-6 (pbk. : alk. paper)
      1. Kaguru (African people)—Rites and ceremonies.   2. Initiation rites—Tanzania.
3. Kaguru (African people)—Ethnic identity.   4. Kaguru (African people)—Psychology.
5. Adolescence—Tanzania.   6. Sex role—Tanzania.   7. Tanzania—Social conditions.
I. Title.
DT443.3.K33B43   1997
306'.089'96391—dc20   96-43928

British Library Cataloguing-in-Publication Data is available

Manufactured in the United States of America
04 03 02 01 00 99 98 97 5 4 3 2 1

♾ The paper used in this publication meets the minimum requirements of the American
National Standard for Information Sciences—Permanence of Paper for Printed Library
Materials, ANSI Z39.48-1984.

For permission to reproduce illustrations appearing in this book, please correspond directly
with the author. The Smithsonian Institution Press does not retain reproduction rights for
these illustrations individually, or maintain a file of addresses for photo sources.

To the Kaguru
and to the memory of
Arnold van Gennep

In other words, one might begin a book on anthropology in this way: when we watch the life and behavior of men all over the earth we see that apart from what we might call animal activities, taking food, etc., etc., men also carry out actions that bear a peculiar character and might be called ritualistic.

Ludwig Wittgenstein, "Remarks on Frazer's *Golden Bough*"

The men of the first generation who lived cowardly or immoral lives were, it is reasonable to suppose, reborn in the second generation as women; and it was therefore at that point of time that the gods produced sexual love, constructing in us and in women a living creature itself instinct with life. This is how they did it. What we drink makes its way through the lung to the kidneys and thence to the bladder from which it is expelled by air pressure. From this channel they pierced a hole into the column of marrow which extends from the head down through the neck along the spine and which we have already referred to as "seed"; this marrow, being instinct with life, completed the process and finding an outlet caused there a vital appetite for emission, the desire for sexual reproduction. So a man's genitals are naturally disobedient and self-willed, like a creature that will not listen to reason, and will do any-thing in their mad lust for possession. Much the same is true of the matrix of the womb in women which is a living creature within them which longs to bear children. And if it is left unfertilized long beyond the normal time, it causes extreme unrest, strays about the body, blocks the channels of the breath and causes in consequence acute distress and disorders of all kinds. This goes on until the woman's longing and the man's desire meet and pick the fruit from the tree, as it were, sowing the ploughland of the womb with seeds as yet unformed and too small to be seen, which take shape and grow big within until they are born into the light of day as a complete living creature.

Plato, *Timaeus* 49

Contents

Preface

Each of us then is the mere broken tally of a human, the result of a bisection which has reduced us to a condition like that of flat fish, and each of us is perpetually in search of his corresponding tally.

Plato, Aristophanes's speech in the *Symposium*

I am not a psychiatrist but I am convinced that sex is not as important as we tend to make it.

Xaviera Hollander, *The Happy Hooker*

You complain about fucking being "monotonous." There's a very simple remedy: stop doing it.

Gustave Flaubert,
letter to Guy de Maupassant (August 1878)

Love, bumping its head blindly against the obstacles of civilization.

George Sand, *Indiana*

Perhaps men are nothing but a freakish variety of women, or women only a freakish variety of men.

Dennis Diderot, *D'Alembert's Dream*

Probably everyone has the sexuality he deserves. . . .

Robert Musil, *The Man without Qualities*, III

For the Kaguru of Tanzania, East Africa, initiation of adolescent boys and girls defines and educates them as a unique people. This study is as much about cultural identity and morality as about age and gender; for Kaguru these cannot be separated. I here elaborate on my earlier contention that Kaguru notions about gender and sexuality are at the heart of Kaguru beliefs and values and consequently animate most Kaguru social life (Beidelman 1986: 212). These involve moral imagination.

Given the many years it has taken and continues to take for me to report the Kaguru world, the theoretical orientation underlying my writings changes with each volume. This is true not only for my ethnography of Kaguru culture but also for my study of Christian missionaries (Beidelman 1982) who attempted to change Kaguru life. That study is deeply indebted to the writings of Max Weber. My subsequent study (Beidelman 1986) of Kaguru thought owes much to Georg Simmel, Marcel Mauss, and Émile Durkheim. Readers of this present volume should recognize that it too is influenced by Simmel, Mauss, Durkheim, and van Gennep, but also in a negative way by Jean-Jacques Rousseau.

I mention intellectual influence because I believe it is important to acknowledge such debts and that this facilitates a reader's understanding. Such explanations also allow me to comment on the relations between theory and exegetical ethnography. Some of my theoretical assumptions and values have changed as I have matured. Yet a switch in theoretical position from publication to publication need not reflect disaffection from earlier views and conversion to new ones, as though each theoretical stance were a commitment to an exclusive system of beliefs. No single theoretical system entirely explains any society. A resourceful social anthropologist employs different, even seemingly contrary, analytical means to comprehend any manifold society and culture. Different theoretical approaches are useful in order to grasp different topics and problems.

This present volume is centered on four interrelated topics. First, I am concerned with how gender is defined or imagined by Kaguru, how it is expressed, and what implications such imagery holds for how Kaguru behave. Second, I am concerned with how notions of gender are associated with other key notions, especially those related to sexuality, age, and time, and to power and authority. Much has been written on such issues, especially in the past decade. I see little profit in reviewing material that has already been repeatedly scrutinized. Rehashing these writings, especially those on gender, seems unlikely to provide new insights for my ethnography. Third, I am concerned with how Kaguru initiation and its related themes of age and gender provide moral education to produce proper Kaguru. Fourth, I am concerned with how these preceding factors produce Kaguru ethnic identity and preserve this identity in the face of what Kaguru see as serious threats to its continued existence. In my conclusion I try to relate these issues to older, broader questions regarding moral (social) education, especially as these were voiced by Rousseau, as well as by those who influenced him (Plato and Montaigne) and those who were influenced by him (Nietzsche and Durkheim). The importance of Rousseau for understanding modern views on education is argued by Schwartz (1985), Bloom (1979), and others. Rousseau provides a key to understanding these matters; as the first to articulate such issues in a modern voice, he put forward important arguments in a fresh, provocative manner that still prompts thought. For that reason it has long struck me as odd that Lévi-Strauss is the only important social anthropologist who repeatedly cites Rousseau, even though Rousseau's ideas must be grasped to understand Durkheim, Marx, and other social thinkers (Lévi-Strauss 1974: 315, 390–92). Indeed, Lévi-Strauss sees Rousseau as the precursor of modern social anthropology (Wokler 1978: 107, 123; Lévi-Strauss 1963: 99, 101–2; Horowitz 1987: 48–49).[1] My interest in Rousseau was rekindled by extensive rereading of Lévi-Strauss, where the common threads of French social traditions are particularly striking. Rousseau hovers impressively and seductively behind my own ambivalent views toward society, despite many repellant aspects of his ideas, life, and personality. The present book is a useful place for me to come to terms with Rousseau's intellectual presence by examining some of the profound issues that he raised, even though I do not enumerate these one by one in the course of my discussion. As is my usual mode of approaching theoretical questions, I do so in response to ethnography. I hope what follows will be a useful description of how Kaguru view gender and initiation, what Rousseau and Durkheim would call "moral education," though I hope my conclusions reflect a less doctrinaire, more humane, and more playful view than Rousseau's. Above all, this is about how Kaguru make and remake their identity.

My fieldwork with the Kaguru was carried out for two eighteen-month periods (1957–1958, 1961–1963) and two three-month periods (1975, 1976). In addition, I corresponded with Kaguru informants between 1963 and 1978. During this time I witnessed two circumcisions and attended about a dozen ceremonies and celebrations connected with male initiation. I never was permitted to witness any operations on or instruction of female initiates, but I did visit two villages when these were taking place. I lurked outside the initiation house and recorded what occurred in public. I also later spoke to women about what happened.

I collected material using Chikaguru and Kiswahili but found that much about initiation required help from Kaguru who spoke fluent English. That is because words used at initiations are often ambiguous, allusions complex and often veiled, and archaic and exotic terms sometimes employed. One purpose of Kaguru initiation is to present material that at first appears unclear to un-tutored, naive young Kaguru, so it can then be explained by elders to the young within the heightened moral context of the special and separated arena of the teaching camp or recovery house. This didactic side of initiation facili-tated my collection of this material. Most Kaguru consider it reasonable and desirable for someone to want to learn these traditions, and they were trained to explain them. Even so, readers will find that some arcane terms eluded both me and my informants.

I collected texts related to initiation from both men and women. To specify how many informants I used is difficult. I assembled three or four men or women (rarely the two together) and had them recount such material. Often others passing by joined in for a bit and then left. Some commented on or tried to amend what others had said. This informal method has its drawbacks, but at the time it seemed a useful way to elicit comments. It often generated lively exchanges. Later I queried individuals about particular points when these seemed unclear even after I had mulled over matters. At least a dozen informants were questioned intensively, and perhaps a dozen more con-tributed useful comments. I was struck by the high degree of consistency with which such material was interpreted. Since my aim is to ground notions about initiation within a broader context of everyday Kaguru social life, information was never restricted to inquiries about formal rites and ceremonies. Nearly every day of the forty-two months I spent in the field provided useful infor-mation on men and women that added to a general picture which I under-stood only long after fieldwork. Whenever Kaguru patiently taught me some aspect of etiquette or moral propriety, they were, I realize now, teaching me attitudes essential to appreciate the catechisms of initiation itself.

This is a study primarily about what symbols and rituals mean. Before do-ing fieldwork I entertained unrealistic notions about what rituals would be like in an African rural society. I left the field no longer sure what a ritual or ceremony was and how these could be distinguished from etiquette. My thinking is now clearer, but I still consider such concepts difficult to define. Kaguru initiations of adolescents are ceremonies with many attending and much fuss. These certainly are rituals, yet other activities are less clearly la-beled. Proper ways to eat a meal or enter a house or greet a stranger or neigh-bor are all highly formalized by Kaguru. Are these rituals? I recall mountain-climbing with several Kaguru (my idea and definitely not something that made sense to Kaguru). Atop a peak I was asked for some tobacco. I thought my companions wanted to smoke. I almost missed the requester's subsequent murmured prayer as he invoked the ancestral dead and scattered tobacco on the ground to placate ancestral shades and other spirits thought to inhabit the woods and pools at mountain peaks. Was this brief act a ritual? Even at initiations, marriages, or namings, all clearly rituals, it was often difficult to tell what was part of the ritual. On such occasions there was distracting conduct and disorder as people carried on mundane activities amidst the scene. I found it easier to get Kaguru to describe what a ritual should be like than to observe what was going on during the hullabaloo surrounding some ceremonies. Furthermore, certain rituals, such as rainmaking or purifications for sexual misconduct, were concealed not only from me but from most Kaguru. Rituals were thus not the easily labeled and neat occasions I had naively expected. Yet Kaguru do have many rituals, and if one looks long and carefully, their daily affairs can be seen to be rife with symbols. In general, this study takes a broad view of what symbols and rituals might be and might mean and tries to relate seemingly special ceremonies to more ordinary routines. My own fieldwork experiences helped lead me to this Wittgensteinian approach toward finding meanings.

During fieldwork I also spent time studying the Ngulu, the matrilineal people neighboring Kaguru to the northeast. Discussing gender and initiation with them refined my thinking about Kaguru. I asked Ngulu about differences and similarities in their beliefs and those of Kaguru. I also discussed the Ngulu with Kaguru. This encouraged both Kaguru and Ngulu to speculate about their beliefs and practices. I hope I can eventually publish my Ngulu material for comparative purposes.

Throughout this volume, unless I remark otherwise, the ethnographic present tense refers to the times when I did fieldwork among the Kaguru. While some practices are probably now gone, my ethnography has value in itself by recording what one people did at a particular time, though my analyses seek significance beyond that. Even though Kaguru rituals of initiation are described as a tradition to be valued and preserved, that slice in time that I record represents only a facet of what such practices involved and meant, not an unchanging tradition. I am certain that rituals of initiation were more complex and better known by more Kaguru before they were attacked by Christian missionaries in the 1890s. The present African national government also appears unsympathetic to many traditional activities. For these reasons, rites and beliefs that I describe for the 1950s and 1960s have already probably changed, even though they are still presented by Kaguru as enduring tradition. Recent visitors to Tanzania assure me that Kaguru still initiate, and my main argument, equating initiation with preservation of ethnic identity, leads me to believe that Kaguru will strive to continue such initiation despite outsiders urging them to abandon such practices. While my descriptive ethnography may present practices now altered, the themes and motives behind these practices endure as basic themes underlying Kaguru culture.

This study may appear concerned with Kaguru past traditions, with rituals and oral literature, rather than behavior as it is currently changing with modern education, a cash economy, Christian conversion, and what in totalitarian new-speak is now often termed "nation-building." While modernization has inevitably altered Kaguru tradition, that tradition still resists new values and practices even while absorbing them. Kaguru society, even at its most seemingly conservative, is a product of the very forces of change that it at times appears to reject. Kaguru emphasis on tradition, which they think of as unchanging, is itself a defensive response to forces of modernization. I am concerned with the beliefs and values behind Kaguru rituals of initiation of adolescents because Kaguru pictured such ceremonies as the most important means by which their traditions and thereby their cultural identity were maintained.

A brief remark on citation of authors in this text: Besides citing authorities for ethnographic information, theory, comparative source material, and valuable quotations, I cite authors for ideas or theories that today seem common intellectual property no longer needing citation for support. I do this for two reasons. Sometimes the cited authors provided what were among the first and best arguments for such ideas; when they wrote they were innovative, and it is because of their brilliant writing that such ideas are now common intellectual capital. Sometimes the cited authors are not innovative but provide especially clear accounts of views I advocate, or they suggest fresh applications of older ideas. I am keen to cite works by nonanthropologists because I want to indicate that the issues touched upon here are of wider significance than would be implied if I cited only anthropologists. I prefer authors from the past; this is because we often forget that what appears innovative often is not. Consequently, Plato, Rousseau, Montaigne, Kant, and Wollstonecraft appear alongside contemporary scholars.

In my earlier books I indicated debts to various institutions for supporting my fieldwork with Kaguru. The present writing was supported by grants from the National Endowment for the Humanities and New York University. I owe a special debt to my former chair, Professor Annette Weiner, for granting me release time for this project. I thank Professors Anne Marie Cantwell, Ivan Karp, John Middleton, Fred Myers, Rodney Needham, and Annette Weiner for reading drafts of this text.

Note on Transcription

The Chikaguru texts I present in this book were transcribed by Kaguru who were literate in their own language in addition to Swahili and some English. The texts were collected from a wide range of Kaguru speakers, many of whom knew only Chikaguru and Swahili. As these texts were collected without tape recorders, transcribers took down a text as they heard it repeated to them.

Like many vernaculars, Chikaguru was never standardized, and its written form frequently displays variation in orthography. The variation reflects a number of important social and linguistic factors, including dialect differences, educational level, and interference across languages, which include local varieties of English and Swahili. The variation in these texts therefore must be preserved, as it may reflect local speakers' language competencies, indicate their ideas about their language and how it should be represented, or represent their lack of need to systematize their spelling. The reader should note that code-switching (the use of more than one language) in the texts also contributes to variation. To alter these texts would misrepresent speakers' written text production. For ease of reading, I have added some punctuation and capitalization, which Kaguru do not apply consistently.

CHAPTER I

Introduction
Problems of Ritual, Gender, and Identity

Because of the values we place on sexuality in life, because of the terrible
taboos which surround it, the endless lies, the forlorn wishes, the sad fantasies
we wind around it like gauze about a wound (whether these things are due to
the way we are brought up, or are the result of something graver—an unalter-
able quality in our nature), everyone's likeliest area of psychological weakness
is somewhere in the sexual.
William Gass, On Being Blue

What they call "heart" lies much lower than the fourth waistcoat button.
G. C. Lichtenberg, Aphorisms

Love, the common passion, in which chance and sensation take place of choice
and reason.
Mary Wollstonecraft,
Vindication of the Rights of Women

This is an ethnography; its main purpose is to describe some of the life and
beliefs of an East African society, the Kaguru of east-central Tanzania. It considers such material according to my assumptions about how societies do and
do not work and what approaches seem useful for understanding the difficulties of social life. This work's most enduring value is to record a way of life
that is vanishing but which may help us better appreciate the varied worlds
constituting our common humanity. That task, rather than any broader argument, is my central goal.

The themes of this study are personal and ethnic identity and the transformations necessary to achieve and maintain them. These two forms of identity are inextricably related. For Kaguru, this means identity as adults, as men and women, because Kaguru do not consider children full social persons. My study concerns the creation of Kaguru persons through cultural education. This process begins at birth and involves innumerable everyday activities, but Kaguru believe that certain key rites are especially critical in establishing this sociocultural identity. These are the rituals of birth, initiation of adolescents, marriage, and death that mark out (personalize) the social career of everyone born into Kaguru society. The most important of these, so Kaguru assured me, are the rituals of initiation that transform children into adults, into responsible and knowing social beings. This initiation involves what Durkheim termed moral education, by which humans become aware that they have no meaningful identity outside society. Such initiation transforms "raw" humans into social, cultural persons through the beliefs, values, and customs of the society that envelops them. That society offers a seemingly enduring past and a promising future, which provide persons with significance beyond their own, limited experience.

How people of a society think that they indoctrinate their members lies at the heart of how they define themselves. Thinkers as diverse as Plato, Rousseau, Kant, Freud, and Dewey developed philosophies about humans and their social life out of these issues of education. In considering initiation, Kaguru present their views of what they most value and seek to preserve in their world. In the oral literature imbedded in initiation rituals, Kaguru reflect on how they think of themselves as a people, on their human nature (cf. Redfield 1952: 32).

THE COOL KNIFE

Before examining these complex issues in more detail, I explain the title of this book. "The cool knife" is not a Kaguru expression, yet the phrase suggests how Kaguru characterize social (moral) education (transformation). A knife is one of many Kaguru weapons. It is also a tool used daily in innumerable ways. Special knives are set aside for the initiation of boys and girls, though in appearance they are like any other small knives. These initiation knives can be used for no other purpose, and one used for girls cannot be used for boys and vice versa. In the past knives were also used to shave Kaguru, both to make bodies more attractive, more human and less like animals, and to designate mourning and other times of social transition. (Now razor blades are sometimes used.) For Kaguru, a knife, along with hoes, arrowheads, and spears, is a ubiquitous metal object. All such objects, not just knives, constitute negotiable wealth and epitomize Kaguru cultural artifice. In precolonial times Kaguru were esteemed for their skill and knowledge in smelting and forging iron (see Last 1883; Beidelman 1962b). A metal artifact is produced when raw iron ore has been transmuted through domesticated fire *(moto)*, the Kaguru epitome of culture *(umoto)*; "that which has gone through the ordeal of fire has gained in homogeneity, and hence purity" (Bachelard 1964: 103–4). A knife is an objectification of Kaguru cultural acumen. It is the tool of sacrifice by which the most prized wealth of Kaguru (livestock) is transformed (slain) in order to communicate with the ancestral dead.

In all these associations—grooming, rituals of status change, expression of knowledge and wealth, and sacrifice to ancestors—the Kaguru knife evokes manifold themes brought together in the initiation of adolescents. The knife physically objectifies many powers, intents, and values. It cuts away the feminine foreskins of boys, turning them into true men, and it cuts the labia of girls, softening them and making them supposedly more manageable. In these procedures, cutting has a cooling (stabilizing) effect, even though shedding blood is thought to create heat and the knife itself is fashioned in fire, a force deeply associated with culture (cf. Goudsblom 1992). At initiation a knife expresses profoundly ambiguous or ambivalent powers and possibilities. It hurts and kills in order to heal and perpetuate; it heats (disturbs) in order to cool (stabilize); it separates in order to link; and it transforms in order to facilitate a never-ending cycle that embodies permanence. (Compare Scarry's insights on the ambivalences of tools as weapons [1985: 73–176].) The phrase "the cool knife" catches these complexities at the heart of Kaguru transformational rituals.

Kaguru rituals of initiation are concerned with several broad, interrelated themes. One involves the ways moral beliefs and values are taught to young people in order to prepare them for the difficulties and complexities of adult life. Another involves the ways the social person is defined and constructed, especially as that personhood is formed around ideas of sexuality and gender. Sexuality and gender cannot be separated from notions of age and therefore time. These, in turn, relate to kinship and marriage because these are what knit together and perpetuate Kaguru society. Initiation into a world beyond adolescence constitutes the crucial point in aging, where Kaguru youths are prepared for domestic life and parenthood and are told how these perpetuate Kaguru society and provide means for individuals to fulfill their goals as social persons. Such initiation is a form of education (Precourt 1975).

Education, personhood, gender and sexuality, age, and ethnicity constitute crucial and problematical concepts defined through "the cool knife." These also constitute key concepts in social anthropological thinking. I next briefly consider each of these topics in turn as they relate to rites of passage. I do so to illustrate how I employ these terms and concepts in my elucidation of the Kaguru world. I do so also to indicate the earlier thinkers whose works inform and inspire my analyses. In doing so I hope to show how these Kaguru concerns about moral education lie at the heart of central contemporary concerns of anthropology, sociology, and social philosophy.

EDUCATION, SOCIETY, AND CULTURE: WESTERN SOCIAL THEORY

Rousseau's *Émile* is the first and classic modern account of moral education of youth. It has influenced nearly all subsequent Western thinking on the topic, for better or worse. Kant drew on Rousseau for his influential ideas about the dangers of imagination inflaming desires, about repression feeding passions by thwarting them (Cassirer 1947: 1–2, 20–21; Kant 1983: 51–52, 54), and about how social relations are rooted in drives for power (Kant 1988: 417).

I begin this survey by considering how Rousseau's concepts illuminate my analysis. I hope to show how Rousseau's ideas often resemble those of Kaguru and, equally important, to show how much of our subsequent thinking, as anthropologists, about education and gender remains rooted in Rousseau's thought.

In *Émile* Rousseau recognized that young people become full members of society only at puberty because the passions and fundamental (gender) differences underpinning society are realized only at full sexuality. For such forces to be ordered, education is essential, especially at puberty (Rousseau 1979: 38). This is achieved through combining bodily experiences, social interaction, and the use of things.

For Rousseau, sexual passions underlie and link all feelings and motives (Bloom 1979: 15–16). Sexual difference, a basic categorization of human life, separates and distinguishes, yet it presupposes interdependence. Such differences are the sources of those divisions by which reciprocity and exchange are first established. Yet sociocultural elaboration (imagination) is needed to intensify these differences (ibid.: 16), which are not sufficiently intense, complex, or constant to provide a basis for society. "Imagination thus ensures both that the human drives are open to the moulding influence of culture and that the driven are in a continual process of transformation" (Horowitz 1987: 79). Rousseau thought this necessary to integrate men and women equally into society. Women were a special problem because sexuality is more deeply ingrained in them than in men, presumably because male sexuality begins and ends with arousal and copulation whereas pregnancy and nursing as both possibilities and outcomes bind women to their bodies and feelings more enduringly (ibid.: 361). According to Rousseau, these same qualities, along with women's natural physical weakness as compared to men's, lead them to compensate by developing greater moral powers (ibid.: 37). Rousseau believed this moral influence is more effective than physical force, due to a woman's skills in manipulating feelings. In these exertions of force and sentiment, both men and women are impelled by common passions and needs to seek to control and dominate one another (cf. Freud; see Rieff 1979: 159). Interdependence and reciprocity find unity and cohesion through forms of hierarchy (domination). Sexual differences, drawing men and women toward one another, doom the sexes to frustration because attempts at controlling one another, so as to guarantee satisfaction, never fully succeed. Yet, like Freud, Rousseau thought social inhibitions and repression made sexual passions more inflamed and therefore psychologically powerful (Rousseau 1960: 81–84). Resistance and repression unite self-regard with desire to produce formidable drives (Rousseau 1979: 388).

Rousseau's arguments appear inconsistent and ambivalent when reviewed over the entire course of his writings. In some passages he extols the "natural," culturally uncomplicated individual, while in others he stresses the needs for cultural fashioning of the person. This guarantees proper sociability, making biological beings more dependent upon one another, thereby strengthening social needs and bonds (Rousseau 1968: 84–85; 1979: 40). Despite his professed commitment to freedom, for Rousseau the most compelling arguments often envision the individual being "swallowed by the citizen" (Hampson 1991: 25), the person engulfed by the good society. Yet the civic is linked to the selfish (Bloom 1979: 3), much as the social, for Weber, is linked to domination.

Rousseau's arguments and contradictions frequently concern tensions between culture and nature, a powerful dichotomy characterizing much subsequent French social analysis, from Durkheim to Lévi-Strauss. This assumes a need for culture to improve on nature in order to construct more-enduring, broader social groups. It also assumes a need for hierarchy, domination oscillating first in one direction, then in another, in order to integrate groups whose cohesion derives from elaborated and altering differences expressed through dependence and exchange.

In making these points, Rousseau raised several perennial questions worth considering here since they continue to perplex anthropologists but also characterize Kaguru questioning of their cultural experience.

While Rousseau is sometimes hailed as an advocate of freedom, his works repeatedly stress needs for dependency from which social cohesion stems. According to Rousseau, we need others in order to define ourselves (Shklar 1985: 76). The difference between the sexes creates their mutual attraction (Rousseau 1979: 360), and from mutual needs arise love and happiness (ibid.: 221). To teach the nature of these realities, human beings are best indoctrinated through everyday things (Starobinski 1988: 145–46). Development of physical feelings and sentiments does not guarantee development of moral sentiments; these must be culturally created and sustained (Rousseau 1986: 164). A sense of imagination, of reflection, is developed in such ways, especially at puberty (ibid.: 206). "He who imagines nothing feels only himself; in the midst of mankind he is alone" (ibid.: 261). For Rousseau the cultural imagination lies at the heart of social (moral) life.[1] That morality is imbedded in a sense of community. This led him to be among the first modern writers to analyze education as a primary means for fostering ethnic identity (nationalism) (Vyverberg 1989: 80). This turns out to be a key feature of Kaguru education at initiation. For Rousseau, as for Kaguru, education hinges on imagination. For him, imagination, at its best, is the source of compassion, of humanization or empathization of our physical dependence on others, and ultimately of a welcoming acceptance of the bonds that society imposes (Barber 1978).

Rousseau was one of the first modern writers to stress sexual interdependence as a political relation, providing different advantages to women and men (Schwartz 1985: 39, 143). Yet the very interdependence that fostered such cross-cutting lines of power (see *Émile*) prevents individual autonomy (see *The Second Discourse*) (ibid.: 74). Rousseau emphasized the powers of women that often threaten men (especially the unsureness of paternity), but these are never credited with the moral force of authority. While Rousseau's feminist contemporary Mary Wollstonecraft advocated gender equality, Rousseau argued that inherent differences lead women to prevail by guile and deception, even while appearing to be dominated (ibid.: 85–86; Rousseau 1979: 360).[2] Rousseau saw women's skills in cultural imagination as necessary to arouse male desire. He recognized that women's acknowledged sexual performance (birth) appears more easily achieved than men's potency, which women often have to arouse or even protect through cultural artifice (Schwartz 1985: 34–35). In such remarks Rousseau revealed thinking and biases that uncannily resemble those of traditional Kaguru.[3] Although his work is two centuries old, it resonates with much that Kaguru believe about gender and education. It also presages an extraordinary range of arguments still current for those debating gender and education. In part this is because Rousseau's ideas were taken up by Kant and thereby found their way into much nineteenth-century thinking (see Tuana 1993: 82–87).

Durkheim is the crucial bridge between Rousseau, Kant, and modern anthropological and sociological thinking. Rousseau's ideas suffuse Durkheim's thinking and are most easily discerned in Durkheim's early lectures on education. Like Rousseau, Durkheim appreciated a sense of habitus as a basis for social indoctrination (Durkheim with Buisson 1979: 154). Durkheim's reading of Rousseau stressed the power of things, their amoral or premoral necessity, which implements a child's education, which addresses the imagination and makes things the "instruments of culture" (1979b: 188). Durkheim believed that a society's system of education invariably implies social structure (1956: 94) and creates "the social being" (ibid.: 126, 193). For Durkheim, as for Rousseau, natural sentiments are insufficient bases for society. Durkheim's nephew and disciple Mauss went on to recognize that "there is perhaps no 'natural way' for the adult" (1979b: 102), so everything essential to proper social life, even bodily techniques, must be transmitted by instruction and orchestrated emulation (ibid.: 104). These powerful but hoary ideas have recently been promoted by anthropologists citing Bourdieu as though he had formulated them for the first time.

Above all, for Durkheim "the fundamental element of morality [and hence society] is the spirit of discipline" (1961: 31). Durkheim stressed punishment and repression in teaching (ibid.: 47, 176). He advocated hazing as reinforcing the authoritarian gap between generations (ibid.: 193–94). We shall see that Kaguru education (initiation) also emphasizes hardship of instruction as expiation for past, childish thoughtlessness.

Durkheim believed sexuality presents a unique challenge to moral life and education. The moral anxiety sex creates poses a threat to the social boundaries of personhood. In sexual relations each person is engulfed by the other. Only the social manufacture of moral mystification through customs and rituals eases this jeopardy to the dignity of socially assumed personhood (1979a). To provide coherence and stability for a family, social invention had to improve upon sexual differences. For Durkheim, "what gives to this relationship its peculiar character and what causes its particular energy, is not the resemblance but the difference in the natures which it unifies" (1949: 56). Sexual division of labor and imputed differences rationalizing this provide moral and conjugal solidarity (ibid.: 60–61). Durkheim's views on cementing conjugal solidarity through sociocultural invention are later taken up by Lévi-Strauss (1960).

EDUCATION AS WORD SKILLS: PAIN AND PLAY

The most striking content of education, including Kaguru initiation, involves instruction in the meaning and use of words (Durkheim 1977: 345; see also

Durkheim 1952: 41). Kaguru and Western theorists such as Rousseau, Durkheim, and Nietzsche are all concerned with this. Yet there are different kinds of word knowledge with many different boundaries, so that some of the rites and words one is taught are at first received without the inductee grasping their full meaning (Brandt 1980: 125–29). Sometimes the supposed profundity of teachings is couched in esoteric, archaic language, said to be "purer" and "truer" than current speech. In such instruction, novices undergo a psychological transference toward their mentors, repeating a lifelong struggle with the authority of the aged (Rieff 1979: 170). Thus, ironically, the teachings that supposedly lead to a new freedom of adulthood actually affirm the power and authority of elders and a traditional past. In this sense Durkheim appreciated the impact of violence and suffering to convey a sense of subordination and sociable altruism. Pain, fear, and morality are intimately connected. Nietzsche rhetorically asks: "How does one go about to impress anything on that partly dull, partly flighty human intelligence—that incarnation of forgetfulness—so as to make it stick?" He answers that "there is perhaps nothing more terrible in man's early history than his mnemotechnics. . . . Whenever man has thought it necessary to create a memory for himself, his effort has been attended with torture, blood, sacrifice" (1956b: 192–93). Schilder even argues that sadistic impulses, such as those exhibited by elders who haze and harass initiates, may relate to a desire to overpower and intimidate potential rivals from the rising generation (1950: 120).

While some of what is taught at initiation involves the esoteric, the overwhelming body of such material often, as in the Kaguru case, involves the ordinary. This is necessarily so since the central aim in educating adolescents is to prepare novices for conduct as adults in everyday life.[4] The prevailing theme of French social thought about education emphasizes this illumination and integration of the ordinary, not the revelation of the esoteric (cf. Rousseau 1954: 381). Early on, Rousseau envisioned what Mauss later termed "the habitus" (Mauss 1979b: 101).[5] Compare Wittgenstein's assertions: "And to imagine a language is to imagine a form of life" (1963: 8e); "We don't start from certain words, but from certain occasions or activities" (n.d.: 3).

Kaguru initiation aims at proper grounding and added reflexivity concerning the meanings of words and related rules and behavior—in short, the difficulties and resultant strategies of living together as adults. Gusdorf describes adolescence as a revolt in the usage of language (1965: 40). For Kaguru, initiation is not a revolt but a revelation bestowed by elders "from the past" as to what words and things really mean and their deeper, previously ungrasped sense. This involves acquisition of seemingly new forms of speaking and acting. In fact, this is a rebirth of order out of a ceremonial crisis, perpetuating the world of language first encountered in childhood but then not properly comprehended (ibid.: 73).

The words and ideas examined at initiation are "unpacked," much as in psychoanalysis (Rieff 1979: 79). They are openly but playfully shown to be rooted in the passions that preoccupied Rousseau and later Freud. This playful, reflexive, imaginative aspect of education (playful, but work) is embodied in much of the instruction that takes place at Kaguru initiation and deeply concerns ambiguity. Words, ideas, and behaviors are "unpacked" but never denuded of their multiple meanings and motives.[6] Kaguru education encourages ambiguous expressions rooted in manifold social relations. This underlying ambiguity informs rites of passage that both invite and inhibit independent consciousness (Myerhoff 1982: 115). Complex, playful unpacking of moral expressions is prevalent in Kaguru initiation teachings, which are filled with aphorisms. The term *aphorism* (from the Greek *aphorismos*, "a definition," from *aph*, "from," plus *horizein*, "separate") has associations with ideas of detection of causes and with notions of diagnosis. Aphorisms are powerful tools in a world where systematic knowledge often fails (Ginzburg 1986: 124).

Three aspects of education relevant to Kaguru initiation require further discussion: the ways ambiguities and contradictions are presented and explained; the nature of the secrecy characterizing the indoctrination of adolescent initiation; and, finally, the ways communal festivities provide educative support to the instruction that precedes and follows them. All these have a long history of concern in Western social analyses of education or socialization. In the West, nourishing (and nursing) has a long association with physiological and psychological, even intellectual, feeding and support, of parental images. This is reflected in our term *alma mater* (Jeanneret 1991: 135). Kaguru also mix instruction and care with feasting and feeding as modes of socialization and ways in which nonparents take over such kin-conditioned modes of feeling and dependence.

LEARNING THE LANGUAGE GAME:
OPENNESS, SECRECY, POETRY, AND MEMORY

One sign of adulthood is the acquisition of fuller skill in speech and thought, in knowing what to say or not to say at the right time. This involves both eloquence and taciturnity, which reveal and conceal information to others. Successful education involves the development of language in ways that enhance adroitness in what Wittgenstein terms "the language game" (1969: 28). These skills require the development of moral imagination for constructing and deconstructing different social scenarios as well as the motives and demands that animate them (cf. Beidelman 1986).[7] To deal adroitly with others, to suppose others' reactions to one's own conduct, requires imaginative skill. The complexity of words, the ambiguity and treachery of their meanings, constitutes an important resource.[8] It provides a "density of imagination" (Kundera 1991: 4). Wittgenstein repeatedly stresses this gamelike aspect of understanding (1963: 34; 1964: 81; 1969: 28, 30). Understanding depends on pushing concepts and terms to their limits (Wittgenstein 1984: 72e). The capacity to reflect, to play with the contradictions and ambiguities of language, marks a person's mastery of her or his culture. Long ago Vico observed that a crucial aspect of maturity is the ability to transcend bodily metaphor in favor of fuller, more complex linguistic mastery (1968: 236). Such reflection on the language game is a formidable task. This is because each meaning is so imbedded in its everyday use that its full implication may at first elude us (ibid.: 20). To get clear about the meaning of words one has "to describe ways of living" (Wittgenstein n.d.: 11). Apprehension of such realms of meaning poses challenges, since some involve worlds of experience not readily accessible to another. By *worlds* I mean congeries of meaningful people (Lewis 1990: chapter 9), those involved in "shared structures of the imagination" (Johnson 1991: 85). Education also involves comprehending the other, men trying to fathom women and women men. All societies comprise multiple, overlapping worlds that are accessible to the imagination of others.[9]

Kaguru rites of initiation at adolescence constitute the most sustained, serious time at which Kaguru are made intensely mindful of others and their thoughts through being encouraged, even forced, to reflect on words and meanings, though children's stories began this process more haphazardly much earlier (Beidelman 1986: chapters 10 and 11). Initiation is also a time when a wide range of contrasting feelings are evoked: anxiety, fear, pain, nurturance, guilt, gratitude.[10]

The goal of education is knowledge, and sometimes skills as well. Among Kaguru, this especially involves wit in using language (cf. Lewis 1990: chapter 4). To appreciate these complexities, I review some assumptions about education posed by Socrates (Plato) in the first study written about educating people so that they are fit for a proper society, *The Republic.* I realize this seems to be reaching back far beyond what most anthropologists ordinarily do, but the views of Socrates and Plato on education have a powerful, if often unsuspected, influence on our grasp of education.

Plato's view of education (or should one term it Socrates's?) raises broad and complex issues in social theory. *The Republic* (1968) is the greatest single Western work written on the moral meaning of society, and it criticizes the greatest single poetic work in Western culture, the epics of Homer. *The Republic* is also crucial because of the thinkers it directly or indirectly influenced—for my purposes here, Rousseau, Nietzsche, and, through Nietzsche, Weber. Through this distinguished intellectual genealogy Plato colors our anthropological and sociological perception. Nietzsche saw Plato's critique of poetry and its educative powers as a great negative turning point in human thought (1956a: 76–96). He attacked Socrates and Plato as ushering in an anti-Dionysian, rationalistic perspective that generated both our modern sense of analytical power and an aridly destructive scientism, a seductive intelligence that would lead to the "iron cage" and Weber's deep, brave pessimism.

In *The Republic* Plato attacks poetry for serving the characteristic weaknesses of the many by attaching them to particular actions and emotions (Plato 1968: 394–95). For Plato, Homer fails to reflect on any holistic character of wisdom, providing instead an odd-job, narrative poetry of deeds and feelings (ibid.: 427–36). He sees him as "a servant of convention," not dissecting experience but knowing only what makes people laugh and cry (ibid.: 432–33). Homer's works, along with those of other poets and dramatists, constitute the major educative media of Greek culture. Plato follows Socrates in banning such works from society to prevent their educative influence.

This attack on literature is integral to Plato's educational theory, which is hostile to poetic experience and imagination (Havelock 1963: 4–12). The epics, along with poetic myth and plays, provided the common understandings, the opinion *(doxa)*, that gave ethnic identity and unity to Greeks (ibid.: 235–51). For Plato, these works' ambiguous, morally self-canceling but powerful reality had to be effaced in the name of authoritarian idealism.[11]

As Havelock writes, "The epic therefore is . . . to be considered in the first instance, not as an act of creation but as an act of reminder and recall. Its patron muse is indeed Mnemosune in whom is symbolised not just the memory considered as a mental phenomenon but rather the total act of reminding, recalling, memorialising, and memorising, which is achieved in epic verse" (Havelock 1963: 91). Such poetry not just recalls but also transmits a way of life (ibid.: 94). Greek poetry functioned much as Kaguru oral literature functions, promoting ethnic identity by a "recital of the tribal encyclopedia" (ibid.: 119, 152). Such poetry is empowered by its association with pleasure in its imagery, wit, sound, and rhythm.[12] Poetic metaphor encourages a conservative oral expression in an essentially nonliterate world. (I employ the term *conservative* in both its senses, that of tradition and that of preservation.)

To carry these issues into modern times, I mention Nietzsche, the father of modern philosophy and a great poet, who linked his attack on Christianity

("Platonism for 'the slavish people'") with an attack on Socrates and Plato (Helm 1976) and with a return to the necessity of coupling sexuality and emotion with true understanding (O'Flaherty 1976). Nietzsche praised that side of Homer attached to physical existence, appetites, and desires (Heller 1976: 115; cf. Helm 1976: 22–23). Yet Nietzsche remained fascinated by both Plato and Rousseau, whom he linked together as his perpetual, worthy opponents (Heller 1976: 125).

I see close parallels between the mnemonic, mimetic education that Plato and Nietzsche saw epitomized in poetry and the methods and content of Kaguru education in oral literature, legends, and *rites de passage*. Otic education—learning through recitation and listening, through poetic forms, rather than through seeing or reading—is an enduring mode of learning and is at the core of Kaguru education.[13]

So far I have emphasized the ways in which education encourages richer perspectives in considering social life. I have stressed the ways by which persons may be made more aware of cross-purposes, of changing goals and demands, set by ever-shifting social roles. But young adults should be made aware of the ways in which this kaleidoscope of different meanings and values may yield unity. One way is to employ powerful symbols that extend across different domains of space and time. In the fourth chapter I try to show how Kaguru employ different aspects of space to convey such coherence—the house, the settlement, the clan, and the ethnic domain. These convert space into social place. Another way is through symbols that appear especially ubiquitous yet malleable, spatially pervasive even though seemingly evanescent. In this sense, Bachelard writes: "Fire is thus a privileged phenomenon which can explain anything. . . . Among all phenomena, it is really the only one to which there can be so definitely attributed the opposing values of good and evil. . . . It can contradict itself. . . . It is a phenomenon both monotonous and brilliant, a really total phenomenon" (1964: 7, 147). This inclusive capacity does not derive from any inherent attributes of fire, but from its infinite usefulness and potential for good and harm. Fire is not a "natural symbol" in the silly sense in which that term has been used. Rather, this is because "fire is more a social reality than a natural reality . . . an interaction between the natural and the social in which the social is almost always dominant" (ibid.: 10).[14] Social and ritual uses of fire provide a rich, pervasive, ambiguous, and ambivalent field for Kaguru social imagination, repeatedly featured in their educative work. I have chosen fire to illustrate my point because Kaguru themselves see fire in this inclusive way. This is why the imagery of fire *(moto)* provides Kaguru, via the hearth and cooking, with their concept of culture *(umoto)*.

Play is a second example of how ambiguous imagery educates by driving home a deeper awareness of the moral complexity of social life. Highly stylized, extreme forms of speech—the comic, the ribald, the highfalutin, the rhetorical verging on bombast—all express the manifold complexity of social relations (cf. Bakhtin 1984: 165–66, 248). Even seemingly harmless speech often takes on subversive and ambiguous possibilities, and adept speakers learn to manage this.

There is an inherent ambiguity to the opposites of gender, a theme powerfully emphasized in the Kaguru material. For Bakhtin, the uproarious play of carnival fiercely expresses such ambiguity, reminding people of its force, especially in expressing gender (Bakhtin 1984: 235–40). He draws attention to the powerful relations between celebratory feasting and work that is both bested and celebrated through food (ibid.: 281–85). Many peoples, certainly Kaguru, link feasts to *rites de passage*, where harvest and consumption of crops are tied to the development (cultivation) of the person and framed in group conviviality.

Kaguru initiation is a form of education, but it confers by disclosure as much as it teaches to think and reason. Conferral imparts special worth to those who receive it. Elder Kaguru bestow important secrets on the young, who are made to feel special and deserving of this knowledge on account of the suffering and deprivations they have just endured as the price for this gift. Such secrets are bestowed by elders but come ultimately from the ancestral dead.[15] Many young Kaguru already have a fair idea about much they are told, so it is not the information itself that counts. What is conferred is acknowledgment by the living and dead that a novice now has a right to speak about such matters and be "heard." Conferral also assumes that this right is coupled with a newly acquired skill in expression and subtlety, as well as discretion. These make the novice a responsible person fit to exercise such new knowledge. "In a Symbol there is concealment and yet revelation: here, therefore, by Silence and by Speech acting together, comes a double significance" (Carlyle 1896: 199). After her or his education the initiate may choose to express matters more or less directly or through indirect mystification (see Bellman 1984: 76, 88, 100). At the same time the secrecy of initiation implicitly proclaims that others lack such information. In fact, the opposite sex and the young may know much about initiation, but by consensual agreement between all concerned they pretend not to know (contrast Bellman 1984 with Warren and Laslett 1980). "The existence of secrets thus reinforces the idea of alternate versions of reality" (Bellman 1984: 76; Simmel 1950: 330).

At initiation, acknowledgment of the rights and responsibilities of choices in expression and communication is more important than any fact one actually learns. After all, a great deal of the learning has been going on informally all along. In the Kaguru case, uninitiated children are earlier encouraged to sharpen their wits with riddles (Beidelman 1963d), which they learn from older children and adults. The rich lore of stories fills the evenings of most Kaguru children. These inculcate a sense of questioning, subversion, and moral amplitude invaluable for later social survival, at least to those sharp enough to perceive how they themselves are imbedded in such manifold relations (Beidelman 1979). Yet these childhood Kaguru exercises in imagination touch only fleetingly on sexual matters, never directly confronting the erotic force behind the family and procreation, which are "the green fuse" (to quote Dylan Thomas) propelling such social relations. For Kaguru, then, initiation is not a radical revelation of totally unknown secrets; it completes a process of disclosure that goes on over many years and occurs in many other less formal, quotidian contexts. Kaguru rituals and symbols do not teach Kaguru what they do not already know; what they do is teach Kaguru what they know or, rather, teach them how to organize and think about what they know.

In English the term *secretion* refers to both concealment and production, and what semantically joins these seemingly contrary meanings is a sense of setting something apart or aside.[16] At initiation, these combined processes are evinced by the ways such ceremonies convey what traits differentiate adults from minors. That knowledge prompts deracinating speculation and play over events and motives essential to, yet apart from, social action. Earlier, childhood mini-dramas of witty exchange and storytelling only suggest this, while the segregated instructional camps at initiation epitomize this in a more open manner and at a more intense pitch.

Everyday affairs are part of an experiential continuum along with the notable occasions of *rites de passage*. Likewise, imparting or secreting knowledge manifests a comparable experience of continuity, even while demarcating those who know from those who do not. At initiation, young people leave the mass of those who do not know and join those who do. In this sense Simmel saw the secret as offering the possibility of a second social world, here that of the initiated (1950: 330).

Divulging (secreting) knowledge is essential to its nature as hidden (secreted), as a secret. Secrets must ultimately be disclosed to be considered secrets in the first place (Simmel 1950: 332–34; Bellman 1984: 144), hence the secret's paradox (Bellman 1981). Yet at some deeper level, even the divulged secret may remain unfathomed. Where such knowledge purports to explain gender, birth, and death, telling answers may only deepen the mystery by revealing the inadequacy of any purported solution (Moore 1976: 368). To sustain many close, intense relations there must be some residual unclarity, some ambiguity that provides hope, possibility, and negotiations about perception.

Concealment and disclosure constitute the commerce of everyday life (Simmel 1950: 329; Bok 1982: 18; Beidelman 1993). Secrets hold varied implications for those who hide them and those who find them out. For example, Goffman distinguishes many types (1959: 141–43). There are "entrusted secrets" (Kaguru initiation) and "free secrets" inadvertently discovered and consequently involving no corresponding obligations by the receiver. There are "strategic secrets" involving skills and "inside secrets" separating knowers from outsiders (both characterizing Kaguru initiates). There are also "dark secrets," ones concealed in fact, not simply muted by customary form (Kaguru women's initiation, whose details appear unknown to men, whereas men's initiatory affairs are for the most part familiar to women). Secrecy is a complex concept whose many permutations may all be found among Kaguru.

EDUCATION AS CONSTRUCTING THE SOCIAL PERSON

The self is best imagined through the body (cf. Barkan 1975: 8). The topic of this study is the production or reproduction of social beings (persons), which involves education about the body and its appetites. The body's sexuality is the central aspect of adulthood, and the body's senses are marshaled through language and ritual in order to domesticate the body to social needs. Conversely, individual bodily needs, one's selfish impulses, are defined in social terms. "Our bodies, then, are the fine instruments of both the smaller and the higher society in which we live" (O'Neill 1985: 21). Our body is "our first 'property'" (Simmel 1950: 322), and society makes incessant incursions upon it to tell us what we are. It is through bodily needs that we are bound to others (Bloom 1968: 386).

One of the most important points driven home in any successful system of education or indoctrination (and Kaguru initiation is a successful form of this) is that the person or self is a social construct expressing the community (Mauss 1979c; Durkheim 1960: 122). An individual experiences the self or person through others who objectify this definition by communications to the individual (Goffman 1967: 81–85). Sociocultural construction of the person continues throughout a lifetime. Among Kaguru the key construction of personhood is said to take place at initiation. Only after initiation may Kaguru be held fully responsible for their behavior. Later, through parenthood and death, they become suprapersons, ancestral spirits commemorated through rites to the dead and generationally cyclical naming.

Kaguru education at initiation involves memorizing knowledge that perpetuates collective memory (culture). Links between knowledge and memory are complex and deep.[17] Indirectly memory is linked to terms for mourning and grief in many languages. Ties between knowledge, memory, and the emotions are reflected in the ways rituals of initiation construct personhood through metaphorical imagery and through nurturance (pleasure) and hazing (pain). The capacity to recall and debate concepts, essential to memory, is cultivated through question-and-answer learning (consider Bateson 1958: 229).

Yet we must never assume that ethnic education produces some kind of cultural clone. Lienhardt argues that the communal factor in the construction of personhood in Africa may have been unduly emphasized (1985: 145).[18] If he means that Africans manifest diverse personalities even within one society, then there is little to argue. If he means to underplay the immense value that initiation attaches to community and group, then he is wrong. Language (words, gestures, and the expressive significance of personal possessions) defines the self, and these meanings are grounded in the group. Even so-called selfishness derives from the social. "A doctrine of self-interest requires a language in which the self and its interests can be defined, and this language, like all language, will be social in its origins and in its terms. For it is only in a social universe, cooperatively constructed and maintained, that the motive of self-interest (or any other motive) can be a rational or coherent basis for thought and action. The language that makes ambition possible, by giving it form and object, at the same time imposes limits on it; it commits the individual to the culture that alone can give meaning and reality to his desires" (White 1984: 76; cf. Burke 1962: 607–8; Hallowell 1967: 83–89).

We may usefully envision the complex, contradictory aspects of personhood through Coleridge's characterization of the Christian holy trinity: "In the Trinity there is, 1. Ipseity, 2. Alterity, 3. Community" (1871: 289). This model is consistent with how Kaguru imagine a person in their rites of initiation. Personhood involves individuality (ipseity), difference from others (alterity), and a sense of commonweal between the person and the group (community). The self (person) changes dimensions and foci with different places and occasions. Kaguru initiation teaches these changing dimensions, that "we are boundaries" (Simmel 1971: 353).

Construction of the self is imbedded in things and in feelings that enhance things by being repeatedly connected to them (Collingwood 1958: 65–66, 274). The development of our imagination, through verbal and other skills, allows us to assert ourselves as owners of our feelings in order to try to dominate them, to evoke them and play with them as we need (ibid.: 222–23). These imaginative resources involve manual techniques as well as verbal skills, for manual skills also manifest "self-organization and self-correction," serving as "ontological metaphors" for self-understanding (Harrod 1981: 425–26).

Hence rites of passage incorporate everyday tasks that add regularity and reality to ceremony.

While this is a study of many topics—education, time, ethnicity, and social space—it is above all else a study of the ways in which social identity is attached to age, gender, and sexuality, as conceived by Kaguru. But this is not a study of the immense literature on gender. That would consume this volume. Even so, the ways Kaguru think and speak about gender require brief mention of current debates but also, more important, of our debts and burdens from earlier scholarly thinking.

In a famous passage in her groundbreaking study on the idea of the feminine, Beauvoir describes men and women in a manner that is both eloquent and ethnocentric, contrasting men's supposedly neat, blatant, active sexuality with women's supposedly messy, hidden, passive nature (1974: 431).[19] In contrast, duBois describes how in ancient European times (Greek) favorable attributes of women's sexuality were gradually replaced by less favorable ones similar to those mentioned by Beauvoir, all as part of a scheme by men to subjugate women (1988: 29–34, 109). These contrasting interpretations indicate how difficult it is to find common terms to portray sex and gender free of misleading metaphors, even by those seeking objectivity. The sexual attributes described by Beauvoir reflect notions couched in the subordination of women even though her aim is to make her readers aware of such stereotypes in order to change them. Her continued use of such metaphors reflects the victory of Platonic, Aristotelian, and Pauline thought, attacked by duBois but seemingly ineluctably still with us. The power and utility of ideas about gender and sexuality depend on the emotional and ambiguous qualities with which they are endowed. My task in this volume is not to criticize such Kaguru concepts but to describe and understand them. Yet we ourselves are often not on firm ground in such thinking. We need to see how both women and men make use of these concepts (cf. Sydie 1987: 54–55), not only among Kaguru but also among contemporary analysts.

To understand how Kaguru characterize gender and sex we must approach these concepts with sympathy rather than search for analytical precision.[20] Quotidian Kaguru usage of ideas about sex and gender gains subtlety, connective complexity, and power from verbal imprecision. It is the diverse, negotiable aspect of meanings, especially as these apply to gender, that provides Kaguru symbols with force (Beidelman 1986: 207–10). It is by addressing these ambiguities and complexities, not by trying to rise above them, that we can appreciate how gender and sex work for Kaguru.

Weber and Simmel provide useful leads for analysis of sex and gender, even though they are not usually associated with these issues. Weber rarely considered gender, but one of his few observations on the subject perceptively asserted that the only "natural" tie between persons arising out of sexual relations is the tie between a mother and her child. Weber based his contention on the fact that suckling and maternal care necessarily link the two beings for some time. He situated the authority of a father over his family outside "natural" ties, in his control of a family's economic maintenance (1968: 357). Weber's observation is borne out by the Kaguru, and probably by many other African societies. That view endows maternal ties with profound weight, even in societies professing deep commitment to agnatic values, such as the Maasai and Nuer. In these same seemingly paternalistic societies, women's ties to their children present formidable challenges to male power.

Kaguru generally counteract these powers of women by elaboration of male rights couched in economic and/or ritual terms, requiring economic output of goods and labor for payments, sacrifice, and entertainment. These are negotiated between men, who exclude women from open, public expression of such claims. If Kaguru women try to voice such claims, they are encouraged to do so through their ties to male kin. Kaguru women's demands are rarely given credence in terms of what they may have contributed economically through their labor, though this is often considerable. Instead, women's claims are justified by both women and men in terms of women's fertility and nurturance. The more offspring a woman has borne and suckled, the greater her supposed needs and rights to the wealth required to sustain and advance them. Of course, both husbands and wives share parental interests, but both polygyny and matrilineality powerfully differentiate a father's and mother's interests in such offspring. The Kaguru correspond to Weber's judgment. While the imagery Kaguru conjure up around the sexes is concerned with a wealth of different attributes, including those involving seduction and passion, it is mainly focused on the sexual attributes of parenthood. Sexuality outside conjugality may be fun, but it is distracting, even inimical, to the work of building and holding together Kaguru society through family and kinship. There are many attributes with which gender may be endowed and enhanced, but for Kaguru, those associated with political advantages attach to males. Parenthood for Kaguru men is defined economically (by payment) and not physiologically. In contrast, women's parenthood is associated with procreation and fertility. Kaguru men are pictured as transcending their bodies, quintessentially through circumcision and metaphorically by paying bridewealth. In contrast, women are drawn back to their bodies through emphasis on menstruation and childbirth. These contrasts provide means for expressing male domination but also means by which females elude that domination. Weber's brief theoretical observation animates a good deal of this ethnographic analysis, as well as echoing Rousseau's earlier views on the politics, conflict, and deception of sexuality.

Weber's friend Simmel brings his deep sense of pathos and contradiction to explain the social significance of sexual attributes (1950: 131n.). Simmel emphasized two key issues related to gender: its connection to male domination over women, and the flimsy footing that sexuality itself provides for marriage. "For the man, there is a sense in which sexuality is something he does. For the woman, it is a mode of being" (1984: 107), though Simmel fails to consider how problematical that male performance may be (Strage 1980: 81–82, 124–25). Simmel relates women's reputed unperformative nature to their supposed preoccupation with conception and pregnancy, oddly failing to consider these too as performances. He observes that men regard most social institutions as neutrally gendered, whereas they are actually male-defined. Men forget or deny that many institutions and beliefs they describe as socially general and ungendered are actually simply a reflection of male hegemony and indeed very much gendered. Men deny the maleness of many institutions that they maintain are socially universal while at the same time proclaiming a host of female traits that restrict and subordinate women (Simmel 1984: 103–4). Simmel points out that men may forget this domination but women are never able to do so (ibid.: 102–5). What Simmel fails to do is emphasize how often actual physical violence becomes part of men's domination of women, an oppression well understood by Rousseau (Lange 1981: 367–68). In terms of marriage, Simmel notes that "whatever marriage is, it is always and everywhere more than sexual intercourse. However divergent the directions may be in which marriage transcends sexual intercourse, that fact that it transcends it at all makes marriage what it is" (Simmel 1950: 132n.). Simmel recognizes that such double-talk about gender characterizes "the cultural dilemma of women" (Vromen 1987: 564) but fails to discuss adequately what this entails, much less suggest that this implies cultural dilemmas for men as well.

Besides Weber and Simmel, two other classic thinkers have proven useful to me in considering Kaguru notions about sex and gender: Ortega y Gasset and Montaigne. I briefly consider them and then discuss a number of more contemporary authorities.

Ortega's observations concern hunting. Ortega's insights merit consideration here because they illuminate Kaguru thinking, in which hunting provides a major metaphor for male domination of women. Oddly, Ortega fails to discuss hunting's long and powerful associations with sexuality, with *venery's* double meaning of the sexual and the taking of game.

Ortega contrasts fighting with hunting, the former involving mutual aggression, the latter involving striving for mastery while the victim seeks escape. Hunting is always a relation between unequals (1986: 49). Yet hunting can be dangerous, especially in Africa. Hunting also is imbued with mystery: "The enigma of death is multiplied by the enigma of the animal" (ibid.: 89). For Kaguru, surmounting danger, whether from wild beasts or cantankerous women, validates men's power to dominate as hunters and lovers. Ortega realizes that wily detection is a key of hunting (ibid.: 76). This connects with a possible venatic origin to conjecture, to exploratory thought (Ginzburg 1986: 115–16). Men even appropriate other animals (dogs) to assist them in hunting, and the Kaguru hunter and his dogs are synonymous with a powerful man, a leader or chief. This search for game involves skill and knowledge, an alertness that is the essence of men's claim to moral domination.[21]

It is always useful to consult Montaigne. Without him, we may wrongly assume many current arguments to be modern inventions. Montaigne is in himself an intellectual world. Four hundred years ago Montaigne was keenly aware of men's hegemonic and unjust impositions on women (1965: 649, 685). On marriage he advised restraint, advocating a calculated and discreet voluptuousness that recognizes moral and social complexities taking marriage far beyond sexuality (ibid.: 645).

What most distinguishes Montaigne's thought about sexuality and gender is his abiding sense of their comic, grotesque, undignified, and consternating sides. He is constantly aware of how sexuality betrays culture, even though it is essential for its perpetuation. Few have combined such appreciation of the ridiculous, violent, and vulnerable in sex, though Kafka saw the hilarity (Kundera 1991: 4–5). We should keep the spirit of Montaigne in mind to savor the harsh and mocking thrusts of Kaguru sexual literature (Montaigne 1965: 654, 668). Montaigne is a useful preface for appreciating Kaguru songs for sexual initiation.

In considering later writings, I cite only a handful of authors, relying on a few surveys that sum up what is currently maintained.

A key work marking a watershed of analytical attitudes about gender in contemporary intellectual circles is Beauvoir's famous study of the concepts of "female" and "feminine," *The Second Sex* (1974 [1949]). Hers was the first feminist intellectual voice to attract a truly international audience since the Second World War and was perhaps the most remarkable since Mary Wollstonecraft, 150 years earlier (1985 [1792]). While Beauvoir may now seem wrongheaded or conservative in some respects, she provides a searching scrutiny and solemn eloquence rarely matched in subsequent literature. This remains true even though her work displays a cross-cultural naïveté surprising in one so fearless and adventurous.

My debt to Beauvoir centers around her use of metaphor and bodily imagery to convey a sense of gender. Beauvoir's account resembles those of Montaigne and Rousseau, two thinkers to whom she, like most other French intellectuals, is indebted. Like Montaigne and Rousseau, she questions preconceptions in order to admit new light upon issues whose meanings actually shift over time, although she, like her two predecessors, tends to present these issues as universal and timeless. She envisions the body as a basis from which all ideas and social experiences stem. What sets her work apart from much feminist writing both preceding and following her is a pervasive use of bodily images. Beauvoir grounds her moral imagery in the deterministic modes of human physiology. She describes male sexuality as extensory and transcendent, qualities that supposedly facilitate objectivity, dominance, and sharper definition. In contrast, she dwells on women's passivity and self-containment, their sexual self-conceptions and experiences being more diffuse and vague, and women's lack of self-sufficiency (1974: 54, 83, 414–15, 431, 441–42, 480).[22] Beauvoir describes the supposed externality and uncontrollability of men's sexual arousal as leading them to think of their sexual organs as having lives of their own, and she concludes that this supposedly encourages male objectification of their sexuality (1974: 54, 83). Women's genitals also are described as uncontrolled; here Beauvoir dwells on the nastiness of menstruation and the unpleasantness of other secretions and odors, and on the deep hiddenness of what accounts for conception: The ovum is not visible, but semen is (1974: 431). Yet there seem no reasons why such contrasts might not produce different positive or negative associations for both sexes. That which is hidden and that which smells can be attractive. Later, Beauvoir seems to realize the ethnocentric weakness of her logic (though she never disclaims her concern over the power of metaphors) when she concedes that the outreaching and objectification she describes are actually defined socioculturally and are not universally determined physiologically (1974: 414–15). Elsewhere she concedes that males too are passive in their subordination to bodily urges (1974: 810), so that her contrast between male assertiveness and female passivity loses its clarity. Beauvoir works her way toward a view of gender and sexuality that eventually sees both sexes as potentially distracted from many sociocultural values by their bodies' imperious demands.

What is valuable in Beauvoir's analysis is the poetic intensity and power of bodily imagery that she conjures up as directly as Montaigne. A reader should, however, remember that the valences of her metaphors are imbedded in her class and culture and do not demonstrate any universal connections between physiology and the values and practices associated with gender. It is undeniable that bodily metaphors are at the heart of any powerful, popular rhetoric of gender. This is because the body conveys a sense of necessity and facticity not easily disputed, even though such associations do not stand up well to sustained critical analysis. Such metaphors are in themselves not signs of bias; rather, the bias is in how metaphors are employed. When I present Kaguru sexual imagery in later chapters, many characterizations made by Beauvoir are repeated in this African material. It is unclear whether this is because such thinking is universal (I doubt this) or because it represents a common but not inevitable feature of patriarchal, masculinist societies.[23]

In another sense, too, Beauvoir's observations parallel Kaguru explanations. She, like Rousseau, discusses women's dissimulation as both protection and revenge against domineering males (1974: 684). She maintains that men are deeply concerned in compartmentalizing two aspects of the feminine, the mate and the mother (1974: 169). Oddly, she writes nothing about men's comparable need to separate two aspects of the male, the mate and the son or brother, nor about men's apparent lack of concern at separating mate and father. Certainly no woman, Kaguru or French, would argue against Beauvoir's contention that "in a world in which woman is essentially defined as female, it is as female alone that she can find justification" (1974: 486). Yet for Kaguru at the time I lived among them, this was not a situation to be directly challenged but a fate to be comprehended and then turned to what advantage it might hold.

Such concerns about sexual imagery, about modes of rhetoric detailing attributes of gender, have continued through more recent writings, though rarely with the suggestiveness and pathos evoked by Beauvoir. Those works that have are mainly studies by European or American literati who consider such imagery in texts ungrounded in quotidian life and social structure. Often such work emphasizes features of only one gender, usually women, rather than both sexes. The most elegant and eloquent recent exposition in this literary mode is duBois's study of changing metonymy and metaphor in imagining women and the feminine in classical Greece (1988: 39–166). If I can improve upon duBois, it will be because I consider men as well as women, and because I interrogate a living culture, allowing a more detailed social context.

To conclude this discussion of sexuality and gender I briefly refer to a few examples from the current anthropological literature, which has proliferated, since Beauvoir, to an awesome, even numbing degree. Despite the flood of contemporary writings, surprisingly few resemble my present exposition, which considers detailed sexual and gender imagery of a particular non-

Western society. Instead, much current writing emphasizes general arguments about women outside the contexts of particular groups. For example, a recent, sensible essay by diLeonardo (1991) surveys current work by feminists but provides almost no account of how particular men and women actually picture the attributes of sexuality and gender. She advocates more studies of gender in non-Western societies, presumably such as the one provided here, but then immediately moves on to postmodernist issues (1991: 17). Unfortunately, her account of gender is almost exclusively about women. Similarly, a survey of gender in Africa (Potash 1989) considers only women, with no suggestion that males' sexuality is a social construct central to defining the gender of both sexes. Two linked essays by Collier and Yanagisako (1987a, 1987b) constructively argue for more holistic studies of the attributes of gender (1987a) but provide little helpful advice as to how this may be accomplished and neglect how males figure in this. (They provide no useful comments on how gender and sexuality are imagined. Yanagisako's earlier survey of family and households takes little more notice [1979: 191–93].) Collier and Yanagisako reject biological differences as providing significant bases for construction of gender in societies (1987a: 48–49). This extreme, dubious position is developed into a questionable assertion that men and women have different views of how the social system in which they live works (1987b: 115).[24]

My account of the Kaguru rejects these views of Collier and Yanagisako. Kaguru women and men have different goals as well as different means for attaining them. Yet these strategies require a grasp of what the other gender also sees and wants. Pursuing their strategies, Kaguru women and men recruit members of both groups into wittingly or unknowingly supporting these aims. Kaguru women's goals are sometimes amalgamated with those held by their brothers and sons and at other times opposed to those of their sisters-in-law and even their own mothers. These goals constitute a shifting kaleidoscope of aims, sentiments, rules, and actions, making it difficult to separate out the understandings and actions of Kaguru women and men into some neat gender-based dichotomy. Kaguru women and men express different judgments about men's and women's needs, natures, and claims, and they do so at different times and in ways that continually change with the context. Each appreciates that the opposite sex or even others of their own sex have different social agendas. As Rogers notes (1978: 131), males and females may well share many common cultural values and information, but their means of reaching goals are only sometimes held in common.

Gilmore (1990) provides the only recent anthropological survey of male gender and sexuality. This is unhelpful to my aims, though he makes the valuable point that the construction of male gender is as highly problematic as that of the female. Gilmore promotes a post-Freudian view that young men have a more difficult time than young women in achieving attributes of their gender because they must break from nurturant mothers (1990: 26–27). His view strikes me as culture-bound. Kaguru women as well as men face challenges from their mothers and mothers' kin when trying to assume potential powers in a matrilineal system (Beidelman 1961a).

One of the few assumptions that these different and sometimes antagonistic writings seem to share is Scott's banal discovery that gender and sexuality merit intensive analyses because these deeply inform power relations in all societies (1986), a point probably even older than Rousseau. Such contemporary analyses appear counterproductive when they deconstruct ideas (and presumably related behavior) to the degree that no differences are credited as perduring between men and women, who manifestly are not the same. These differences appear particularly sharp in non-Western, nonmodern societies, where technology has not yet muted, much less overcome, biological constraints. Yet to credit biological differences in no way implies neglecting sociocultural causes behind gender. It is, however, useful to recall how malleable sexual attributes may be and that this tractability lends itself to a remarkable array of possibilities for power and manipulation (Foucault 1980: 103). The family and household are best seen not as sexually restrictive institutions, but as anchors to which sexual thinking and activities are tied and referred (ibid.: 108).

The definition and implications of male gender cannot be separated from those of female gender, and both pose challenges to analytical revision. Today women's gender studies are frequently isolated from men's gender studies, thereby conveying a false sense that only one gender requires radical reanalysis in our analytical thinking.

VAN GENNEP AND RITES OF PASSAGE

I conclude this introductory survey with a brief comment on van Gennep, the source of our concept of rites of passage and still essential reading for anyone considering such issues. Many anthropologists underrate his achievement. They acknowledge van Gennep's great initial insight but add that he merely provided a label and a descriptive, triadic model for analysis but no further useful insights. Gluckman's self-promoting account fits this stereotype (1962); Fried and Fried are even more dismissive (1981: 116), and La Fontaine is not much more enthusiastic (1985: 24–38). In their well-known textbook, Chapple and Coon devote an entire chapter to describing rites of passage (1942: chapter 20) but follow this with a chapter on "rites of intensification," which a number of subsequent writers see as a valuable advance on van Gennep. Chapple and Coon consider the term *rites de passage* as more properly confined to ceremonies addressing changes in the life cycle of a person, whereas their new term, *rites of intensification*, applies to ceremonies such as calendrical rites and celebrations or counteractive ceremonies in response to group success, threat, or anxiety. They contend that van Gennep wrongly grouped all these rites together and therefore muddled our understanding of their significance. They do not appreciate the power and subtlety of van Gennep's views.[25]

Every anthropologist knows that van Gennep coined the term *rite de passage* in 1908 (1960: 10–11). He described *rites de passage* as a triadic process: preliminary rites of separation *(séparation)*, liminal rites of transition *(marge)*, and postliminal rites of incorporation *(agrégation)*. Van Gennep appreciated the importance of classifying social phenomena, but he aimed beyond this. He wanted to discern broader forms rather than contents. He avoided the Frazerian practice of extracting materials from wider sociocultural contexts. For van Gennep, the significance of rites depends on a ceremonial whole, a set of ceremonies in which rites contribute to a process, embracing an entire way of life (ibid.: 191).[26] Van Gennep was one of the first structuralists, aware of powerful relations between belief, society, and the physical environment that produced overarching systems of classification. He presented a structuralist credo of breathtaking grandiosity in the final sentence of his book: "It is indeed a cosmic conception that relates the stages of human existence to those of plant and animal life and, by a sort of pre-scientific divination, joins them to the great rhythms of the universe" (1960: 194). Lévi-Strauss recognized van Gennep's structuralist bent, which connects systems of classification to both social structure and physical environment (Lévi-Strauss 1966: 109, 162–63; cf. Belmont 1979: 137–38; van Gennep 1960: 166; V. Turner 1962a: 145).[27]

Van Gennep grounded his analysis of rites of passage in space and time. He opens and closes his book with references to marking time (1960: 3–4, 178–80). He ends with a reference to space (ibid.: 192). The second chapter of his book is devoted to territoriality. Space and time provide two dimensions for all life and hence all social transitions and transactions. Critics of van Gennep consider him wrongheaded to lump together rites of personal change with rites of calendrical and communal change, with harvests, and with rites of territorial definition. They fail to grasp the grandeur of van Gennep's argument, which comprehends the broadest features of social classification. Van Gennep recognized that these make processual sense in terms of more universalistic features of time and space. Those are the two modes in which changes challenge cultural order. Van Gennep's 1908 volume addresses "rites of passage," but it implicitly advocates a "global" or total phenomenal approach to understanding the structure of society, a view comparable to the best of Mauss and Hocart.

Van Gennep's concern about classification is inextricable from his concern with transition, with persons passing from one status or role to another, and with the movement of goods. It involves problems of boundaries between groups or between a group and the outside. It involves the ways in which boundaries are transcended through exchanges of persons and goods that both define and blur those boundaries (ibid.: 27–31). Van Gennep compares his models of society to houses with many carefully isolated rooms (spheres of identity and activities), in which considerable work is required to negotiate passage from one to another (ibid.: 26). In the societies van Gennep considers, age, gender, and kin groups involve more-resolute and sustained negotiations in order to be bridged than do many comparable positions in modern societies. For van Gennep, societies' categories, such as sex and age, turn out to be essentially sociocultural contrivances. Thus "one cannot conceive of any institution being founded on an element as undeterminable and as irregular as puberty" (van Gennep 1960: 66). Socially assigned meanings contain a wide spectrum of significance and aims, not merely ones that people assert (ibid.: 11–12). These meanings provide powerful potential for change (ibid.: 191–92), a point elaborated by anthropologists such as Turner and Leach.

Van Gennep displays concern for the physical and physiological groundings of social life. In 1932 he concluded that "from the most primitive species up to the most highly evolved man, sexuality is the pole around which all impressions, all feelings, all thoughts entwine" (quoted in Belmont 1979: 142). He asserted that these drives are infinitely plastic and subject to sociocultural modifications. He cautioned readers against approaching such materials with cultural presuppositions, involving sex and gender, that we are apt to assume to be obvious and natural (van Gennep 1960: 72–73).

My analyses in this study owe a great debt to van Gennep. He is a source of insights and tantalizing suggestions. To him I owe my grounding arguments in social space (chapter 4). To him I owe my commitment to a holistic approach linking Kaguru rites of passage to other transitions, including calendrical ceremonies, rites of purification, sacrifices to ancestral dead, and the entire range of Kaguru comings and goings in everyday routine. Such holism leads me to consider women's identities as inextricable from men's. Like Rivers (1926: 49–50), I credit van Gennep with allowing me to see connections among birth, naming, adolescent initiation, marriage, and funerals, and to link these to broader transitions of calendrical time and construction of ethnic identity, social space, social history, and the seeming trivia of quotidian life. Because of van Gennep, I broaden my focus on Kaguru initiation of adolescents into a wider consideration of Kaguru personal and ethnic identity.

KAGURU INITIATION AND THE MEANING OF RITUAL,
SYMBOLISM, AND METAPHOR

Victor Turner has written that "ritual is transformation, ceremony confirmatory" (1967: 95). In fact, ritual is both. "Ritual action is a means by which its
participants discover who they are in the world and 'how it is' in the world"
(Jennings 1982: 113). Ritual creates knowledge peculiar to itself, even as it
transmits tradition (ibid.: 112; cf. Precourt 1975: 231). My account of Kaguru
initiation covers more than ritual, for it necessarily considers a large body of
beliefs and oral literature associated with it. To do this, I reconsider arguments raised in my earlier book on Kaguru moral imagination (1986), where
I discussed ways Kaguru picture their social world.

Symbols and rituals construct a cosmology, beliefs that both mystify and explain the world. In my earlier book (1986) I showed how Kaguru symbols are
rooted in quotidian life and how their evocative power stems from this. The
meanings of these symbols are constantly negotiated by participants in ritual.
Such negotiation engages diverse persons with diverse perspectives within
various arenas of debate and reflection; it also stimulates the imaginative cre-
ativity of members of a society even as it conserves tradition.

The most frequently mentioned aspect of symbols and rituals is how they
contribute to creation and maintenance of an inclusive cosmology, how they
conserve a social system through being repeated. Powerful symbols form "associational clusters" that weld social and natural (physical) realms together
(Burke 1957: 436). Rituals undertake organization of time and space (Scheffler 1981: 436). But we must not overestimate the unifying, global aspects of
rituals.[28] Rituals are imaginary expressions, even syntheses, of selected beliefs,
feelings, and activities within society. They are not global representations of
reality; rather, they are models that enhance understanding of some things at
the price of simplification and limitation of others. Models do not encompass
myriad experiences. That limitation constitutes their strength, in that it provides focus. In this sense, Kaguru employ rituals that reflect themes such as
movements in and out of domestic and public spaces, shedding blood, cooking and consuming food, and demarcating zones of social and wild habitation.
No single Kaguru ritual encompasses all the key organizational principles
characterizing Kaguru society. Different rituals illuminate cultural principles
with different degrees of efficacy. Not even Kaguru themselves (much less I)
would argue that the cultural themes or principles expressed in rituals amount
to all that is most important in Kaguru experience. For example, these hardly
touch upon the give-and-take of economic or political affairs. What these
themes do and what much Kaguru ritual does is represent those aspects of
Kaguru life that Kaguru say are characteristically (uniquely, ethnically) Kaguru.

Aside from their common language and everyday routines, Kaguru lack powerful unitary perspectives. This is probably true of many other small-scale societies. People employ diverse and sometimes even contradictory rituals because different social occasions prompt different responses and because different protagonists have different social motives. If Kaguru experience a sense of holism, it comes from other directions. For example, the regularities of quotidian life inform the motives of ritual and provide nexi between the pervasive and continuous roles of everyday affairs and periods of change and stress. It is out of such pervasive habitus that different ritual protagonists present an "emergent parallelism" (Kratz 1990b: 44) even while involved in a wide range of different materials and activities.

Kaguru adolescent novices are not familiar with all Kaguru rites and ceremonies and hence cannot grasp the broader themes that reoccur in many rites over many years. For novices, initiatory rituals teach limited lessons of understanding and obedience. As initiates grow older and attend more rites, sometimes as novices, sometimes as leaders or assistants, sometimes as audience, they may, after decades, attain a broader, more global view. This will not derive from any one ritual. Instead, it stems from a wide range of occasions, which are further enriched by an aging Kaguru's experiences throughout the life cycle. Kaguru initiation of adolescents is the most elaborate and sustained of Kaguru ceremonies, but until a Kaguru enacts roles as teacher and audience as well as novice, and, perhaps more important, until she or he experiences subsequent ceremonies of marriage, procreation, death, ancestral propitiation, and cleansing, her or his full appreciation of any broader configuration of these activities is limited if not missing. It is only after initiation that some of these rituals, such as funerals and rites of ancestral propitiation, cleansing, and marriage, may be attended.

Finally, the reader should realize that this introductory chapter is more fully explicated by my earlier book, *Moral Imagination in Kaguru Modes of Thought* (1986). There I point out that Kaguru social thought and therefore Kaguru morality are imaginative exercises. There I try to show how the power and attraction of such thought, its imaginativeness, is rooted in the myriad images of everyday experience. I try to show how the richness and seductiveness of Kaguru symbols stem from the pervasive and manifold visions evoked by daily surroundings and routine. I try to show that quotidian affairs unite Kaguru in a common experience even while they provide means that are perpetually contended and negotiated in terms of their details and valences.

My earlier book attempts to chart the scope and character of the Kaguru imaginative world. In this second book I attempt to describe how such imagining is taught. Education itself is an imaginative exercise—imagining how others think, feel, and will act—and it is also a way to develop one's skills in imagining. These skills involve the ways one can develop means of expression through language and actions, but also the ways one can think and reflect about what imagination itself might mean. This second volume, *The Cool Knife*, is therefore a continuation and elaboration of my earlier book. It is also itself an introduction to a third volume not yet written, a book on Kaguru politics in the colonial era. That book will complete what I hope to be a trilogy on Kaguru imagination: the first volume about mapping an imaginative sense and the imagined world it reflects, the second about moral education, and the third and final volume about how that imagination is challenged and altered by modern colonial and nationalist experiences as evinced through Kaguru Native Authority government and courts.

With these useful concepts in mind, drawn from the past, we can now proceed to see how Kaguru initiation of adolescents educates them into being proper social beings aware of what it means to live with other Kaguru and to be themselves identified as Kaguru.

CHAPTER 2

Constructing Ethnicity
Imagining Kaguruland and Kaguru People

All communities larger than primordial villages of face-to-face contact (and perhaps even these) are imagined. Communities are to be distinguished, not by their falsity/genuineness, but by the style in which they are imagined.

Benedict Anderson, *Imagined Communities*

Ethnicity is a product of the social imagination (Anderson 1991: 6) and must be constantly worked at to be achieved. In some respects it resembles gender, which also is constructed through considerable social effort. For Kaguru, gender and ethnicity are thought to be confirmed by the same process, the initiation of young people. When I arrived amongst the Kaguru, they often told me how pleased they were that I was studying them because it was important that their way of life be written down. They thought this would enable outsiders to read about their customs and consequently respect them, and that this would also aid in preserving their culture. Kaguru assured me that the single most important thing I should study and record about them was their initiation of young people because such initiation was the main way Kaguru learn and remember their customs *(umoto)* and thereby understand who they are. I have followed van Gennep's advice to take people's interpretations about themselves very seriously (quoted in Belmont 1979: 101), and consequently I see the study of Kaguru initiation as the study of the construction and perpetuation of their ethnicity. Where I differ from Kaguru is in seeing that identity as more problematic and less ancient than they often maintain. Yet even in this I may perhaps not have strayed far from how Kaguru actually think. After all, it is probably because Kaguru identity is problematic and precarious that they are so concerned to assert and protect it when asked about it.

Kaguru notions of ethnicity resemble Anderson's notions about nationalism (1991: 4). Both are vague in details and in some ways are recent, even though both are subjectively viewed as ancient. Both are products of the imagination, and imagination must work on substance. For the Kaguru, the stuff of that substance especially involves landscape, language, food, and gender. I discuss these in detail in later chapters. Here I consider aspects of landscape, language, and customs as these relate to broader geographical, historical, and cultural features that set the Kaguru within their region and the Tanzanian state. In sketching these outlines of Kaguru ethnicity I provide an introduction to the Kaguru and their country.

THE LANDSCAPE AND KAGURU IDENTITY

Kaguruland (Ukaguru) is today a country of about 3,600 square miles in area lying due west inland from Dar es Salaam. It comprises three sharply differently terrains. Its core is a mountain mass known as Itumba, some peaks reaching 6,000 feet. It is composed of steep peaks and an intricate lacework of valleys. A few mountains remain thickly wooded, but most have long been deforested, cleared for arable land and to provide fuel for a once thriving iron-smelting industry. Itumba represents a third of Kaguruland. Its cool climate and high rainfall (up to 100 inches on the peaks) ensure continuous production of vegetables and allow some rice, plantains, and millet but no maize. During precolonial times of raiding, Kaguru fled to Itumba for safety, but as more peaceful conditions prevailed, many migrated to the warmer, less rainy plateau. Over half of Kaguruland makes up this plateau (varying in height from about 3,000 to 4,500 feet), a land of rambling valleys with rivers fed from the mountains. The valleys are separated by large intervening expanses of scrubland and forest punctuated by scattered peaks and rocky outcrops, some towering to four or five thousand feet. This is a land dependent on the annual rains and, despite its streams, marked by a sharp contrast between dry and wet seasons and periodically subject to famine due to drought. This is a land of millet, sorghum, and, above all, maize, supplemented with tobacco, plantains, and vegetables. While cattle, sheep, and goats are held in all areas, it is here on the plateau that the largest livestock holdings exist. Less easy to defend than Itumba but considered less unhealthily chilly and damp, the plateau saw a massive increase in population once Kaguru no longer had to rely on the mountains for defense. The plateau, rather than Itumba, is now the area where most Kaguru live. The third area, the lowlands, comprises about a fifth of Kaguruland. This is subject to the harshest contrasts of the dry and wet seasons and since colonial times has been the site of vast sisal plantations run by Europeans. The lowlands are the least dependable area for the cultivation of traditional crops and most prone to cattle diseases. Before colonial times the lowlands were the most vulnerable to raiding, and the small population often mixed with outsiders who had settled as part of the caravan trade. More recently vast numbers of outsiders have resided there as workers on the estates. The lowlands have always been a peripheral area to Kaguru identity.

Kaguru speak of Itumba as the heartland of their country, the area where Kaguru are least affected by outside influences and where the supposedly purest customs are followed. It is the area where great rainmakers are said to have gained their powers. Both Itumba and the plateau are marked by dramatic natural features: high peaks, rocky outcrops, and sharply defined valleys, many with well-known names. These are the areas famously associated with different clans, and the legends of those clans' histories repeatedly relate incidents connected to particular events explaining why the clans are as they are. The names of particular clans are often associated with such landmarks. Thus, for Kaguru the sight of their surrounding landscape can repeatedly remind them of their very history and loyalties to different clans and kin groups (Beidelman 1970; 1986: chapter 5). The particular contours of the land provide the tags for Kaguru identity, while the ecological and geographical differences between the three basic regions account for contrasting ways of life, especially between the mountains and plateau, on the one hand, and the lowlands, on the other. The very name *Kaguru* refers to highlands, and it is as highland people that Kaguru identify themselves as contrasted to others. Seen in relation to the stark Maasai Steppe to the north, the dry Gogo Plateau to the west, and the unhealthy Mkata Plain to the east, the Ukaguru highlands do constitute a striking homeland pronouncedly different from the surrounding areas. From a distance of many miles they rise violet and hazy, inviting and yet alien to the flatlands about and below them. Of course, similar highland regions lie to the east (Uluguru), northeast (Ungulu), and southeast (Usagara), and Kaguru recognize that these regions and their peoples closely resemble them. Indeed, all these mountain peoples are matrilineal and pursue very similar cultural ways of life.

THE HISTORY OF KAGURU IDENTITY

Kaguru history is deeply rooted in its geography. Kaguruland is one of a string of mountainous islands extending across Tanzania in an arc. This scattered chain of highlands long stood as refuge to African migrants fleeing drought, disease, and raiders. In this, Ukaguru shares many features with the other highlands in this mountainous arc, though Kaguru never emphasize that they share many such common experiences with other peoples. As a land of possible refuge, Kaguruland has taken in assorted alien peoples. In their legends of their ethnic origins Kaguru explain these differences not as due to inherent culture but as due to various events that led one unified band of migrating people to break off into different groups once they reached Kaguruland. It is therefore the land itself that has imposed its conditions on the identity and differences of the inhabitants. Still, Kaguru admit to absorbing other alien peoples more recently, such as refugees from neighboring lands or strangers who entered Kaguruland, willingly or otherwise, as a result of the caravan and slave trade. For Kaguru, initiation provides a way to make such people part of themselves, however shakily.

During the past century Tanzania experienced a vast and impressive caravan trade inland to the sources of ivory and slaves. Such caravans often numbered several thousand people. Lying directly on the best route between the ports of Dar es Salaam and Bagamoyo and the Great Lakes, Kaguruland was the last good site for caravans to take on supplies and water before crossing the great, dry interior plains, and it was the first good supply and rest point after crossing those plains on the way back to the coast. As such it became an important site for supply stations to Arabs and later Europeans as well as African traders. Many African outsiders ended up at such supply stations and were slowly absorbed into Kaguru ways. The Kaguru managed to retain their political and cultural identity in the face of these caravans and traders, but some leaders made important use of the weapons and supplies these outside contacts afforded. They used these advantages to persuade or force outlying Kaguru into their orbit of rule. Yet the power of these leaders and their usefulness to Arabs and, later, to the first Europeans continued only so long as such leaders could claim a united following of other Kaguru. For over a century Kaguru have had to ponder ways to assert and preserve their ethnic identity as a means to bolster their integrity and power against aliens. Yet that identity was not so much a given of traditional life but rather a reaction to the pressures and needs generated by outside, alien contacts (Beidelman 1962a, 1982c). The very fact that Kaguru in some ways closely resembled some of their neighbors culturally perhaps intensified their cultural assertions about their particularity (compare Southall 1972).

The earliest European accounts of Kaguru often gave them other ethnic names. Sometimes Kaguru were merged with neighbors to the south or west. At other times early European travelers described the mountain and plateau Kaguru as ethnically different from each other. What served to solidify

Kaguru as one people were the claims of ambitious Kaguru leaders, on the one hand, and the expectations of domineering Arabs and Europeans, on the other. In part, a few Kaguru leaders, mainly those at Mamboya at the main caravan trading station in central Kaguruland, claimed that they could deliver services and law and order to passing traders in return for recognition and the munitions, trade goods, and cash that went with it. Such opportunists also claimed to their Kaguru supporters that they could maintain an alliance with the Arabs and their African helpers (Nyamwezi and Swahili). Consequently, they could protect local Kaguru against these dangerous, armed outsiders, who were demanding supplies and labor and clearly were ready to kill or enslave any local Africans who offended them. More important, both the Arabs and, later, the Germans and British assumed that all Africans should have leaders and form coherent, orderly ethnic units. They sought such leaders and groups, and a few imaginative and ambitious Kaguru filled these colonialists' expectations, creating conditions to fit such stereotypes even where they had not earlier existed. The pseudo-tradition of a Kaguru paramount chief and clan, with a legend to support it, had its roots in such needs and aims (Beidelman 1978).

During the early colonial period, before World War I, Kaguru ethnic identity was expressed as an interplay between responses to the German colonial administration and responses to the British Church Missionary Society (CMS) workers who had settled in the area. The Germans had treated the Kaguru harshly, burning villages, publicly hanging some Kaguru dissidents, and confiscating livestock and firearms. The Germans considered the Kaguru unreliable and to them this was proved by the initial resistance of some Kaguru leaders. Unlike the Arabs, who had recognized Kaguru leaders and worked with them (even though such leaders were opportunistic upstarts), the Germans sought to rule through coastal Swahili *akidas* (political agents) who did not know the local language or customs. This still gave some unofficial power to those Kaguru who met and talked with *akidas*, but the proper ethos and language of local African rule were seen by the Germans as Swahili. In this period, when very few Kaguru knew Swahili, they considered Swahili as even more colonialistic and alienly intrusive than now. For one thing, they associated it with Islam and consequently with the Arabs and the slave trade. In contrast, the local Christian missionaries, who had arrived in the area from Britain long before the Germans and who constituted the only permanent European residents in Kaguruland, took Kaguru ethnic identity far more seriously than the Germans. They continued to recognize the Kaguru chief first promoted by the Arabs and went to work trying to understand who and what Kaguru actually were. They sought, unsuccessfully, to convert the Kaguru putative chief and other leaders. They began their work by trying to learn the Kaguru language (Chikaguru), though, of course, they hoped eventually to work in Swahili. In part this was due to the missionaries' economic and political problems with their own image. By being able to present the Kaguru as a coherent, meaningful ethnic group to mission supporters back in Britain, local missionaries were better able to encourage support for their work in Kaguruland. Few would have been interested in supporting mission work amongst people who did not seem to have a goodly population and a clear-cut identity, so as to make concerted efforts and donations worthwhile.

The Church Missionary Society workers wrote the first ethnographic accounts of the Kaguru and published the first grammar and dictionary in the Kaguru language (Last 1886) as well as the first actual text (the Book of Matthew [Matthew 1894]). Up until the First World War, some CMS missionaries remained committed to learning Chikaguru as well as Swahili, whereas colonial government administrators and merchants were not. Later, the only extensive ethnography of the Kaguru, however faulty, ever prepared prior to my own work was an unpublished tract by an African (Ngulu) CMS archdeacon who deposited his study with the British District Administration (Muhando n.d.). Other educated, Christian Africans, especially schoolteachers, prepared their own, briefer accounts of local history, though these were never deposited with any mission or administrative officials and were fashioned mainly to provide the authors with advantages for formulating debates in local clan politics (one such account may be found in Beidelman 1970). One could therefore argue that in many respects Christian missionaries carried on and intensified the Arabs' implicit message that the Kaguru must be an integral people meriting recognition and therefore presumably some investigation. They fostered a European belief in Kaguru ethnic identity that would not again be taken up by colonialist administrators until British rule.

Yet the Church Missionary Society also promoted many policies that severely attacked Kaguru ethnic identity and culture (Beidelman 1982b: 127–52). The mission condemned a wide range of Kaguru customs, some because they conflicted with Christian teaching but a great many more simply because the missionaries found anything that contradicted their ethnocentric, prudish, and dour views of society to be wrong. (They had condemned a great deal of contemporary European culture as well.) Of course, the missionaries attacked polygyny, ancestral propitiation, and the use of rainstones and other magical medicines. They considered Kaguru adherence to matrilineal descent and inheritance to be a sign of evolutionary backwardness. They also condemned alcohol consumption, dancing, native jewelry and dress, native hairstyles, ear piercing, red ochre as a cosmetic, Kaguru music and songs, and many forms of Kaguru etiquette. Had the missionaries been successful, they would have effaced most of Kaguru culture and identity. Yet the missionaries found it particularly difficult to condemn outright what Kaguru themselves regarded as their quintessential custom, the initiation of adolescents. The mission, of course, tried to ban all dancing or drinking associated with initiation and forbade all the sexual songs and rituals that were part of it, even though Kaguru considered all these essential. The missionaries could not, however, forbid all initiation outright since the Scriptures related that Christ had been circumcised; that, presumably, was a form of initiation. The mission attempted unsuccessfully to Christianize circumcision of boys, putting it in the hands of African evangelists and male nurses. The mission also tried to segregate Christian initiates from their pagan fellows, but that failed. They were especially unhappy with girls' initiation but did concede that some instruction about growing up was needed for girls as well as boys. The missionaries violently opposed any physical operations on girls but found no easy way to prevent it since such operations were not performed in public, as were those for boys. Kaguru continued to perform such operations in seclusion, as they had in the past, simply not calling them to outsiders' attention. Despite these conflicts, the Church Missionary Society did much to promote a sense of Kaguru identity by showing an interest in Kaguru customs and, more important, by encouraging Kaguru to write down their beliefs and practices. Above all, the missionaries did not discourage the Kaguru language. While the missionaries attempted to suppress many traditional aspects of Kaguru life, they proved to be remarkably unsuccessful, mainly because the European missionaries increasingly confined themselves to being supervisors at their residential stations and relied upon local Africans to tour the villages, enforce morality, and teach. These Africans, nearly all local Kaguru, were far more eager to accommodate Christian beliefs to traditional Kaguru thought and behavior. Kaguru evangelists saw nothing wrong with initiation or the sexual instructions that were integral to it. For them, these were inseparable from the legends that explained who Kaguru are.

Shortly before the outbreak of World War I, the Germans completed the railway linking the coast to the inland lakes. Since this ran just south of the borders of Kaguruland, it was seen as heralding new and important changes in the area, including a new influx of outsiders to the estates and towns to the south, if not to Kaguruland itself. Consequently, the British who took over from the Germans at the close of the war saw an urgent need for more-efficient colonial administration. This was to be done as cheaply as possible (by using Africans, not Europeans) since the government was poor due to the postwar economic depression. For these and other reasons, the British dismissed the resented, alien *akidas* and in their place sought to establish a form of Indirect Rule modeled after that advocated by Lord Lugard for Uganda and Nigeria. This had two important effects on Kaguruland. First, Kaguru local administration was drastically reordered into new, supposedly tradition-based units, creating new stakes for competition amongst local Kaguru. Second, the new territories into which Kaguruland was incorporated brought Kaguru into more prolonged and potentially unsettling confrontation with ethnic outsiders with whom they now vied, as ethnic blocs, for attention and respect from British colonial officials. Both these changes, in different ways, heightened a Kaguru sense of ethnic identity—or at least a sense that such an identity should be better-defined and more strongly asserted.

In this reordering of German East Africa into the British-mandated territory of Tanganyika, Kaguruland was divided administratively. The eastern two thirds of Kaguruland was placed in Kilosa District and the western third in Mpwapwa District. This represented a considerable division since these two districts were located in two different provinces, Kilosa in Eastern Province and Mpwapwa in Central. Ironically, then, while the British saw their new policies as ones that built positively upon African ethnic solidarities and pride, in the Kaguru case they undermined that identity by splitting the land and people in ways that persist even today, for Kaguruland remains administratively divided even though the present African national government of Tanzania reformulated some colonial administrative boundaries after 1961.

At the time I did fieldwork (1957–1966) the Kaguru numbered over 80,000 people. Two thirds lived in Kilosa District (over 50,000) and a third in Mpwapwa (30,000). In Kilosa District, the Kaguru were the largest single ethnic group, but they still represented only 33 percent of the total African population. In Mpwapwa District, the Gogo far outnumbered Kaguru (the Gogo's main center of population adjoined Mpwapwa District to the west), who represented 21 percent of the population. What is more significant, however, is that Kaguru did dominate within their traditional homelands in both districts. In both districts Kaguruland was assigned its own administrative unit, or Native Authority, with chiefs, headmen, courts, schools, and powers of taxation. In Mpwapwa District the Kaguru area represented only a relatively small administrative unit of about 20,000 people and an area of about 1,200 sq. mi. centered around the settlement of Mlali (the remaining 10,000 Mpwapwa Kaguru lived outside the government-recognized Kaguru chiefdom). There, Kaguru dominated, with over 75 percent of the population. In Kilosa District, where I did my fieldwork, the Kaguru area formed the single largest (2,400 sq. mi.), most important native administrative unit in the district and was dominated by Kaguru. There were, however, two other native administrative units in the district. Since Kaguruland in Kilosa District is the unit considered in this volume, I provide more detailed data and analysis for it than for Mpwapwa. In many ways, however, both Kaguru Native Authorities faced similar problems with other Africans, British colonial administrators, and the Church Missionary Society regarding the ways they could assert and maintain their ethnic identity.

These colonial governmental policies encouraged Kaguru to think seriously not only about ethnic identity but also about local traditions and clan affiliations. Inspired by the theory of Indirect Rule, viz., making use of traditional institutions in order to set up local native governments, the British administrators in Kilosa District visited Kaguruland and held meetings to ask Kaguru elders about who Kaguru's rightful, traditional rulers might be. This prompted a spate of reports about Kaguru legends and histories of clan origins and ownership of lands. The British finally decided to set up a Kaguru Native Authority with a paramount chiefship located at the old caravan station at Mamboya in the central plateau of Kaguruland and then to divide the land further into four additional subchiefdoms, two more (Geiro and Idibo) in the plateau, one in Itumba (Nong'we), and one in the lowlands (Msowero). Each of these five areas would have its own court and tax records, with the four subchiefly courts appellate to the one at Mamboya. In addition, forty-four headmen were recognized: nineteen in Mamboya, eleven in Idibo, six in Geiro, eight in Nong'we, and ten in Msowero. Chief, subchiefs, and headmen were all selected on the basis of membership in certain matrilineages that claimed ownership of the particular lands in question. Final judgments about such ownership and appointments were in the hands of the local district British administration. Since this policy selectively recognized some Kaguru clans as owners and ignored others, this led to lasting resentment amongst some Kaguru. It gave Kaguru new meanings to clan (and hence ethnic) membership and legends since it equated offices in the local Native Authority with clan affiliation and supposed ethnic history.

KAGURU ETHNICITY IN THE 1950S AND 1960S

In Kilosa District, at the time of my fieldwork, the Kaguru Native Authority covered the northern third of the administrative area. It had a population of 67,000, 44 percent of the district's total population.[1] Over 48,000 of these were Kaguru, 72 percent of the chiefdom's population. But these figures are deceiving. Most of the ethnic outsiders resided in the lowlands, workers connected to the sisal estates or other foreign enterprises in the region. If one

considers the chiefdom's population in terms of its three ecological zones—
the central Itumba Mountains, the surrounding plateau, and the outlying lowlands—a far different picture emerges. Over 98 percent of the people inhab-
iting Itumba are Kaguru, as are over 85 percent of those in the plateau, but
only 35 percent of those in the lowlands are Kaguru. Furthermore, over 90
percent of all Kaguru in the entire chiefdom live in the plateau (where I did
my fieldwork). One can readily see that the lowlands remain, as always, peripheral to Kaguru identity; while officially they are within the chiefdom's
boundaries, they rarely figure in any discussions by Itumba and plateau
Kaguru. It is the Itumba and plateau that characterize Kaguruland for most
Kaguru, and in those areas Kaguru predominate. While there are ethnic mi-
norities in this core area, mainly in the plateau, these constitute a different
kind of outsider from those in the lowlands. In Itumba outsiders are negligi-
ble (less than 100), but in the plateau they constitute socially important
groups: Baraguyu (1,384), Ngulu (1,917), and Kamba (1,684). Their importance far exceeds their actual numbers. The Baraguyu, a Maasai-like people,
possess relatively large herds of livestock (six times more per capita than
Kaguru). This wealth plus Baraguyu language and cultural differences from
Kaguru are sources of complex hostilities but also economic interdependences
(Beidelman 1961c). The Ngulu reside mainly in the northeastern plateau, near
the Kaguru border to Ngululand, and stand out as local traders and artisans
more prosperous and skilled than many Kaguru. Their presence is in part explained by their ability to provide skills and services that Kaguru cannot perform as well. The Kamba also are large livestock holders, and although they
have lived in Kaguruland for over a century (Beidelman 1961e), they retain
their own customs and language. Their influence is considerable since they
reside almost entirely within one subchiefdom (Idibo), where they constitute
11 percent of the total population. Unlike the lowlands, where ethnic outsiders are often transient and where few such people were born, in the Kaguru
Itumba and plateau the ethnic outsiders were mostly born in Kaguruland, and
many descend from people who have resided there for several generations.

Although the Baraguyu, Ngulu, and Kamba are important ethnic minori-
ties in central Kaguruland, they have no formally recognized representation
in local government. They are officially subject to Kaguru courts and tax col-
lectors, but Baraguyu and Kamba appear before Kaguru officials only when
forced, when they have broken Kaguru laws or disputed with Kaguru over
debts. They settle all difficulties amongst themselves outside Kaguru courts.
Baraguyu reside in cattle camps in the forest and scrub far from any Kaguru
settlements. The agricultural Kamba live near Kaguru in separate villages. In
contrast, the matrilineal Ngulu, whose customs closely resemble those of the

Kaguru, have settled and intermarry amongst them and consequently litigate along with Kaguru.

Plateau Kaguru have important economic relations with Baraguyu, Kamba, and Ngulu, and these relations are viewed as part of the social status quo of local plateau life. But the greater wealth of all these groups, especially the cattle-rich and traditionally aggressive and proud Baraguyu, has at times led to bloodshed and ill will. Kaguru are determined to exert domain in what they consider their own homeland, in which these ethnic outsiders are only tolerated as useful, long-term aliens. The main way Kaguru have exerted dominance is through their monopoly of local Native Authority affairs, especially the courts, which ultimately may call in police to enforce their judgments (something never actually done during my stay). Kaguru courts invariably judge in ways favoring Kaguru against all outsiders (Beidelman 1966c, 1967b). During the colonial era, Kaguru maintained their local domination by having convinced the colonial administration that they alone had the right to rule Kaguruland and that their numerical dominance made their rule the most feasible (easiest and cheapest) way available by which their European masters could control the district.

When I did fieldwork in Kaguruland during the colonial period, Kaguru repeatedly raised questions about how they might better define their ethnicity so as to control their land, both for themselves and against outsiders. In 1957–58 these anxieties produced two local Kaguru organizations aimed at promoting these goals (Beidelman 1961c). These epitomized two contrasting modes of Kaguru concern about identity: an older, tradition-bound definition of ethnicity, and a more modern view accommodating ethnicity to literacy, capitalism, and social change. The first of these, Umwano, was promoted by Kaguru chiefs and elders and by less-educated Kaguru distrustful of the new changes taking place about them. The second, USA (Ukaguru Students' Association), was promoted by young, educated Kaguru who felt shut out from official opportunities for running local affairs.

Umwano is a Kaguru term meaning "war cry." This was a vigilante-type group begun in the Idibo subchiefdom but soon taken up by Kaguru throughout the plateau, mainly under the encouragement of Kaguru elders. As its popularity grew, the paramount chief himself joined, his main motive apparently being to prevent other elders, especially the Idibo subchief, from using the organization to circumvent the paramount chief's influence. The reason given for founding Umwano was the need for stronger means to counteract Baraguyu violence against Kaguru. At this time a number of Kaguru had lost livestock and claimed this was due to rustling by Baraguyu. Other Kaguru claimed their crops had been trampled by Baraguyu herds, which perhaps had

Figure 1. Kaguru men garbed in the old, traditional manner no longer acceptable to more modernized Kaguru in eastern areas such as Berega, Iyogwe, and Idibo. They are from Geiro and are visiting the Chakwale cattle market. Photograph taken at Chakwale in 1958.

been deliberately driven through Kaguru gardens. Some Kaguru had been beaten and speared during these thefts and trespasses. Kaguru noted that there were no government police stationed in the chiefdom and that they themselves were not authorized to enforce the law with weapons. They argued that they had no way to protect themselves other than to be vigilantes. What else were they to do when Baraguyu elders often traveled about the countryside with staves and knives, and Baraguyu warriors went about with clubs, spears, and swords? At the Umwano meetings Kaguru brought their traditional weapons, bows and arrows and spears, and a few brought shotguns.

Kaguru elders recited their traditions of bravery, noting that they had maintained their land against Baraguyu and other outsiders by fighting back. These Umwano assemblies were dominated by elders who orated in traditional fashion; the younger men, even those in their thirties, for the most part sat acquiescently with their weapons and confined themselves to supplying cheers that acknowledged agreement with their elders' speeches. These were old-fashioned meetings, ones where elders (often Native Authority officials) monopolized decisions. Such armed meetings were illegal according to colonial law, and so Umwano met in the bush far away from any settlement. Women and young people were not admitted.

While Kaguru at these meetings spoke as though they would have liked to drive the Baraguyu out of their land, this was hardly so. Baraguyu provided one of the major sources of ready cash (exchanged for beer and tobacco), which Kaguru often found hard to come by during the lean times before harvest. Baraguyu poll taxes and cattle-sales taxes provided an important part of the revenues for the Kaguru Native Authority. Kaguru and Baraguyu both frequently recounted their long history of mutual animosity, but I daily encountered Baraguyu buying beer in Kaguru villages and found Kaguru and Ngulu engaged in selling many craft goods to Baraguyu during the monthly local cattle market. Even though Baraguyu claimed to be like traditional Maasai, existing on a diet of meat and milk, many Baraguyu had to purchase grain from Kaguru to supplement their diet, especially during the dry season, when milk grew less plentiful. In truth, Baraguyu and their host Kaguru needed each other economically even though this was a relationship laced with occasional animosity, made worse by the fact that Baraguyu often were drunk and misbehaved in Kaguru villages where they bought beer. When I attended Baraguyu celebrations of marriage and initiation, where large supplies of beer and meat were consumed, Kaguru, Ngulu, and Kamba were always also guests, though, of course, quarreling and violence sometimes did break out. These Baraguyu and Kaguru relations were clearly long-term interdependences and animosities, not new underlying causes of the call for Umwano.

Umwano represented a glibly articulated, opportunistic rallying cry for Kaguru solidarity along traditional lines, referring to past warlike times that evoked the authority and power of Kaguru elders. In the precolonial past, what solidarity Kaguru had maintained was principally due to their need for cooperation in the face of outside threats by raiders from other ethnic groups. According to such traditional thinking, younger Kaguru men (warriors) would be assembled by their elders, who would make the decisions about what was to be done; then the younger men would obediently implement these judgments. Of course, the ostensible reason for these meetings was the loss of livestock, and livestock was mainly held by Kaguru elders, who meted such animals out to young kinsmen in order to pay bridewealth. In this sense, even the supposed livestock crisis making Umwano necessary was implicitly expressed as a threat to the power of elders over their young dependents. At such meetings the talk was mainly about Kaguru bravery, the rightfulness of Kaguruland for Kaguru, and the manliness of Kaguru young men, a manliness learned through initiation, especially circumcision. Above all, talk was about the land, which was repeatedly described as belonging both mystically and legally to Kaguru. It was Kaguru identity with the land that gave them the right to use any means possible to defend it against abuse by alien outsiders. It was Kaguru identity with the land that provided rationalization for the Kaguru Native Authority. That identity with the landscape is a fundamental reality of Kaguru initiation, anchoring both gender and ethnicity to Kaguru everyday life and welfare.

In contrast, USA (Ukaguru Students' Association) was led by a group of young, educated Kaguru men who were unable to secure jobs in the Native Authority and who had dropped out of government or mission employment. The chief founder was a maternal nephew to the paramount chief and therefore a person with a legitimate claim to rule. These young men held their meetings on grounds near the Kaguru Middle School, for Kaguru the seat of their highest education. The area near the school, along with the nearby shops, was the nearest thing Kaguru had to a rendezvous spot for intellectuals and would-be sophisticates. In contrast to the hidden character of the Umwano gatherings, the USA meetings were public and attended by many people of all ages. This was seen as a strikingly modern gesture, for in the past such formal gatherings for deliberations were the realm of older men. While only men spoke, women and children were spectators, whereas at the Umwano meetings the only outsiders were myself and my Ngulu assistant.

The leaders of USA argued that the older leaders were uneducated (true for the most part; indeed, the paramount chief was illiterate). They rightly noted that the British colonial administration actually liked having uneducated Kaguru leaders in the Native Authority, since these posed no threat to reforms and progress. The leaders of USA called for a new form of Kaguru identity, a form that would blend the best of past traditions with literacy and economic progress. They called for a newspaper to be published in Chikaguru, and they were able to put out several issues of *Sauti ya Ukaguru* (Voice of Ukaguru), which they mimeographed on mission-owned appliances at the school. They even argued that Ngulu (but not Kamba or Baraguyu) should be admitted to this Kaguru organization. It should be remembered that the Ngulu are the matrilineal people bordering the Kaguru to the northeast and that they are linguistically and culturally extremely similar to Kaguru. The main reasons for admitting Ngulu were that perhaps a quarter of the teachers and staff at the school and mission were Ngulu, and Ngulu were needed to constitute a meaningful bloc of educated locals. Many of these Ngulu had married Kaguru and were permanently settled in the area. Baraguyu and Kamba were not admitted, both because they were patrilineal people with customs far different from those of Kaguru and because they were mainly illiterate and viewed as epitomizing all of the backwardness that USA was attacking.

After I learned more about Kaguru initiation, I was struck by how many themes developed by USA derived from initiation. USA emphasized the Kaguru language and called for its reemphasis in popular expression (just as initiation emphasizes refinement and development of the novices' appreciation of Chikaguru as a tool of sociability). It was to foster the language that USA's leaders proposed to provide a newspaper in Chikaguru; in fact, the three or four issues that appeared contained only a smattering of Chikaguru and were mostly in Swahili. This was inevitable and actually proved USA's own arguments. The USA leadership lamented that at present most younger Kaguru had only an imperfect knowledge of Chikaguru since nearly all of their schooling had been in Swahili and English. USA argued that Chikaguru should be fostered as well as English and Swahili and that by doing so they could raise Kaguru's sense of ethnic pride and identity. The leader of USA spoke beautiful Chikaguru and attempted to use it whenever possible but was forced to revert to Swahili or even English (which he also spoke very well) to make his points clear to his youthful audiences. USA held a number of rallies where speeches were given in a mixture of Chikaguru, Swahili, and English. The aim here was not only to emphasize Kaguru ethnic roots but also to make it clear that a commitment to such roots was by choice and not because one could not speak Swahili or even English if one chose to do so. It was important to the USA leadership to present Kaguru culture and Chikaguru as being as worthwhile as Swahili or English ways. At the rallies USA members performed skits and dances and sang songs with responses, all teaching practices deeply ingrained in Kaguru tradition through initiation. The USA leaders repeatedly compared new forms of education to Kaguru initiation. They pointed out that both were essential to social survival. People who failed to take advantage of initiation did not grow up, and people who failed to learn new ways in government, in education, and in means to earn cash were also still children. To demonstrate that USA was a truly Kaguru organization, its leaders maintained that, like initiation, the values of USA had been passed down from generation to generation. Here they were comparing the educated leadership of USA to the wise or educated elders who conducted and taught initiation. Just as elders transmitted their traditional wisdom through initiation, so too the USA leadership would transmit their learning and insights to those who would follow. Like all proper traditions, USA would be blessed by the Kaguru ancestral dead, who clearly approved of it. In this too, USA leaders were speaking the rhetoric of initiation as well as that of ethnicity. The USA leaders claimed that the ancestral dead had caused some of Kaguru's current difficulties because they were unhappy with the divisiveness and shortsightedness of today's Kaguru. The unity of USA would bring benefits to all, not only because cooperation would enable Kaguru to achieve more and better things together but also because the dead would then bless the land on account of the Kaguru's return to solidarity. In this, the message was rather simplistic when compared to initiation, which provides manifold resources and inspiration for Kaguru as contending individuals as well as assertions of holistic ethnic integrity. But then, the overriding view expressed by both the new leaders of USA and traditional Kaguru initiators was that one can realize oneself, be a proper person, only by means of the language, customs, and styles of Kaguru life. In this deeper sense, the leaders of USA were remaining true to the ethnic meanings evinced by initiation.

The deeper basis for the dissatisfaction of USA's leaders derived from their frustrations as educated young men with no ready means to realize their ideals and ambitions. But the immediate causes for their complaints, and the reasons that USA was popularly supported, were the current abuses by the Kaguru Native Authority. While local Kaguru officials had long taken bribes and used their positions to further their own kin and supporters, at this time the Native Authority had seemingly stepped beyond such expected, tolerated, minor abuse. The Kaguru officials had been forced by the colonial administration into supporting a land resettlement scheme that displaced some Kaguru from their homes and fields in order to create a government forestry project. To provide labor to construct a mountain road to service this project, Kaguru officials were ordered to seize local Kaguru to perform forced labor. This led to numerous meetings of protest, attacks against local Kaguru officials, and a widespread questioning of the fitness of some Kaguru leaders to rule. British colonial officials were forced to visit Kaguruland and to threaten to bring in police to keep order. Kaguru wrote petitions to unseat the chief, and I was drawn into the dispute and consequently for a time was denied all government cooperation (though not deported from the area). Things got ugly. Dissident Kaguru were chained and beaten by Native Messengers, protesting onlookers beaten and insulted, and political opponents of local officials harassed by being selectively chosen for forced labor and fines. Feelings often ran high

Figure 2. Kaguru schoolteacher. Photograph taken at Iyogwe in 1958.

against the present system. USA leaders exhorted people to resist this confusion *(kuhasa)* of British colonial interests with what was good for Kaguru. USA saw the forestry project as benefiting the British and in no way helping Kaguru. Local leaders had tried to use labor levies as opportunities for consolidating their positions by persecuting longtime local opponents. Such all-out Kaguru condemnation of a project supposedly meant to prevent erosion and provide future income for the area may have been unfair—at least it seemed so to the British—but USA's use of the term *kuhasa* is significant. The term refers to any kind of confusion or mixture of practices or things that should be respected and kept apart. Clearly Kaguru officials, in order to keep their jobs, were following British orders either because they were lackeys or because they found this a convenient way to get back at their own local enemies. In either case, this was in contradiction to their proper roles as leaders *(wadewa,* "herders," "shepherds") of their people. One of the major functions of initiation is to teach Kaguru how to respect social relations, how to make responsible judgments that will bring success and ancestral blessings by taking note of how things should not be muddled *(kuhasa),* should not be contradictory. The underlying message in USA's use of the term *kuhasa* is that Kaguru were suffering in a world where people were behaving as though they had not understood the moral distinctions taught at initiation.

At this time, the ethnic and political unrest in Kaguruland was expressed entirely in terms of local groups espousing Kaguru ethnicity. During the 1950s and 1960s, even the most disgruntled Kaguru remained unresponsive to overtures of African nationalist politicians. Visiting party and labor union organizers were either ignored or mistreated by local Kaguru. This does not mean that Kaguru were blind to the need for political and economic reform; rather, at this time these were almost entirely visualized in terms of local ethnic identity and needs, even by those younger, educated Kaguru who might be expected to support a national political movement. It was USA, not the nationalist political party, the Tanganyika African National Union (TANU), that appealed to and rallied local sensibilities against abuse and injustice. USA failed to unseat any local officials, but the unrest and letters that USA generated against the forestry scheme did lead to that project being canceled. USA did succeed in organizing a cooperative, mainly subsidized by schoolteachers and mission employees, who purchased a truck and tried to market Kaguru crops in town. Eventually the cooperative failed due to theft of funds and failure to maintain the truck properly, but it did represent one of the first attempts by Kaguru to organize themselves in order to enter the cash economy in a bigger way than as small-scale farmers. That such organization was begun at all was because such appeals were made in terms of Kaguru ethnic pride and Kaguru solidarity. In contrast, Umwano leaders (who were often Native Authority officials and therefore guilty of the offense of *kuhasa* in terms of mixing spheres of interest) did fine local Baraguyu for cattle theft and assault, using their authority as local officials but pocketing the fines for themselves as leaders of Umwano. They were eventually reprimanded by the British district administration and Umwano was disbanded, but such leaders continued to persecute Baraguyu through the courts whenever possible.

CONCLUSION

Erikson writes that each new newborn human is received into a way of life prepared by tradition, but that very tradition may threaten to destroy that way of life and even that person (1958: 254). Traditions give us our identities, but they may rigidify and destroy a society and those in it if they are too demanding and unchanging. Kaguru ethnicity and its ways are perpetuated by initiation, and they inform Kaguru of their being and meaning. Such an ethnic tradition has changed strikingly even in those times when its proponents were proclaiming its fixity. But then tradition itself is something of a contradiction. Part of its strength lies in its claims to continuity and endurance, while another lies in its capacity to provide multiple and changing meanings and purposes. The account of Kaguru initiation that follows underscores that these powerful, constructive ambiguities have long been the essence of Kaguru initiation and hence ethnicity.

Kaguru repeatedly told me that rites of initiation, and all comparable rites of passage, work to maintain Kaguru unchanging tradition (custom, *umoto*) and hence Kaguru ethnicity. These traditions, while seemingly enduring, are in fact assertions of transmutable beliefs and practices that are precarious constructs maintained in the face of undermining time. Such traditions may not even be as uniform or as ethnically unique as Kaguru describe them. (Certainly much that I encountered amongst Kaguru resembled traditions I found or read about amongst neighboring matrilineal peoples.) The Kaguru ethnic identity I encountered during my fieldwork was itself the result of a local sense of particularity and regionality that had coalesced and grown. During the colonial era, the British colonial administrators and missionaries encouraged the congeries of people in present-day Kaguruland to think of themselves as one people in contrast to their neighbors.

Kaguru were gratified by the prospect of my writing a book about them because it affirmed their distinction from other Tanzanians and their ethnic and regional identity, an identity that Kaguru have seen as politically useful and providing a sense of popular pride. Local allegiance and identity continue to be attractive goals to Kaguru since these represent powerful grounds for meaningful and respectable cohesion at a geographic level. Where people believe that they share common local economic and political experiences and needs that are different from those experienced by peoples around them, popular, symbolic modes of local identity are embraced and enhanced. This trend is further encouraged by a kind of cultural schizmogenesis (to borrow a term from Gregory Bateson [1985: 171-97]) whereby Kaguru have intensified their own identity in their response to encountering growing assertions of ethnic identity by neighbors such as the Maasai, Luguru, Hehe, and Gogo.

Kaguru have practiced various rites of passage, including initiation of adolescents, as long as they can remember. Yet it was only as they began to experience a wider colonial scene (and later a national political one) that these customs and beliefs took on added, poignant value and significance in reassuring Kaguru that such practices may serve to identify them as special and particular people. It is ironic and paradoxical that just as pressures have grown for many East Africans to think in broader, transethnic terms, their contemporary exposure to other, new outside pressures, threats, and conflicting interests lends these age-old beliefs and customs added, precious value as rallying points of cherished local tradition.[2] Kaguru realize that what benefits them and their region is not necessarily what benefits their neighbors and other Tanzanians.

Kaguru are keen for their children to learn reading, writing, and other modern skills. They admire persons who are fluent in Swahili and English. Yet, increasingly, younger Kaguru share with their elders a deep esteem for what is essentially Kaguru: the Chikaguru language and some of the customs of the past. Even where some customs are now rejected by many, such as ancestral propitiation, many Kaguru now believe that the young should know what earlier practices were and meant. It is significant that in the Swahili magazines published in Tanzania since independence, the only article I could find dealing with Kaguru describes their unique ethnic character and in doing so devotes particular attention to adolescent initiation (Mtey 1968).

Kaguru want to believe in their ethnic identity and unity and take pride in them. These are consequently social facts important to study. Given more years of fieldwork in more locales of Kaguruland, perhaps I could demonstrate striking local differences in Kaguru life. Yet what I propose to do in this study is to emphasize the coherence and uniformity of Kaguru belief as a growing phenomenon throughout the past century. After over three years of fieldwork in several Kaguru areas, I found that these similarities, rather than differences, were what mattered. This is what Kaguru themselves seemed to

want to convey to me, and this study thereby conspires with Kaguru in promoting that aspiration, even though events since I left East Africa may be
eroding this cultural and social coherence.

Kaguru initiation is paideutic. It teaches youth about gender, about right
and wrong adult conduct, about what it signifies to be a proper Kaguru, about
what should not be contradicted or muddled. It is a means by which Kaguru
replicate and confirm their social world and reveal why it is rich and rewarding.[3] In current anthropological jargon, one would term this the Kaguru's
means toward cultural reproduction. To do this Kaguru draw upon items
from their storehouse of traditions to construct a medley redolent of the remembered and imagined past yet strong in the heady sensations of the pal-
pable moments of daily experience. Kaguru initiation and ethnicity are as
much confrontations with a changing present as they are recollections of a
past that Kaguru would like to think of as reassuringly linked to and anchoring the present. The quotidian rote of daily affairs pervades ethnic, initiation
imagery, and this enshrines a way of life, a view of "human nature" (Redfield
1952: 20). As Calvino remarks in an epigraph to chapter 4, each generation's
identity derives equally from its resemblance to its predecessor's experiences
and from the very fact that those experiences inevitably involve an unexperi-
enced future imbued with the impulses of procreation (the deeper meaning of
generation), which lead to parenthood, maturation, replacement, and death.
In the long run, these generations are as much linked as they are divided by
temporal differences that in the short term briefly put them into opposition.
Yet the land and everyday life provide an illusion of constancy.

Education and initiation involve a painful dilemma for modern Kaguru. To
gain a valued sense of personal being and self, Kaguru engage in practices that
assert ethnic or tribal beliefs in ways that may make them seem backward
when compared to some others in their new nation. Yet how better to construct a social self, a self built on particular, substantial experience, than in
terms of the everyday experiences of local life? That "self is the axis of world
view" (Redfield 1952: 30).

Clinging to ethnic traditions over the years united Kaguru in the face of divisive modern influences (for a review of social uses of tradition, see Kratz
1993). Regardless of being pagan, Christian, or Muslim, educated or illiterate,
rich or poor, almost all Kaguru embrace traditional initiation as an educative
process (albeit sometimes modified) that must be followed if Kaguru identity
is to be preserved. This identity constitutes a singular priority in constructing
a Kaguru self. This is the most strikingly enduring aspect of Kaguru social
life. Yet to carry out circumcision in the bush rather than in a clinic or hospital, to employ traditional cutters rather than doctors or nurses, and to instruct

at camps or in mud and thatch houses rather than in tidy government or mission classrooms seems backward to non-Kaguru, whether these be government officials, Christian missionaries, or simply progressive outsiders.

It is naive to be confident that even such a valued institution as Kaguru initiation can withstand modern forces of change, especially if these changes have a modern national government behind them. Consequently, one cannot be confident that Kaguru ethnic identity can survive. That identity is rooted in particular notions about age and gender, and about the fact that persons are inextricably imbedded within complex but small-scale social relations of the family, lineage, and local community where age and gender are of paramount importance. In these terms, the Kaguru person remains defined within a restricted and parochially embracing world. Traditional Kaguru identity is gained at the expense of broader, more universalizing values and points of reference that transcend ethnicity. It is gained by curtailing some degree of individualism, however illusory that may sometimes appear.

Kaguru identity, as all identities, remains imbedded in a particular local culture and society. Yet the degree to which this allows deviation and self-realization, personal autonomy, is problematic, even though initiation does teach skills of guile, manipulation, and self-survival. I do not assume that traditional Kaguru life is truly homogeneous (which it is not). Nor do I assume that modern societies necessarily provide wide avenues for personal autonomy and expressivity. Modern life may provide means to enforce conformity and control of others. Kaguru initiation is counterproductive to the interests of a national state but serves as well as any alternative system as a means to create a sense of self and worth for maturing persons. If it is considered superannuated, that is because it is out of phase with the contemporary nationalist agenda that denigrates ethnic particularities even as it contradictorily trumpets African identity. Yet that same nationalist agenda provides no immediate safeguards or anchorage for setting the personal self into any meaningful social group, other than a flatulently proclaimed litany of nation-building and a hypocritical call for social altruism and sharing by an already impoverished and struggling rural population.

This study draws the contours of Kaguru identity and fills out the details of Kaguru style, moods, and ways of expression that produce that identity. It does so by considering the ways that space, diet, gender, sexuality, and speech create Kaguru life. That is a way of life that the elders of Umwano, the leaders of USA, and many others consider worth preserving as much as possible. For Kaguru, initiation appears to be the primary means for achieving this.

CHAPTER 3

Kaguru Personal Strategies of
Kinship and the Family

As the ends of such a partnership [society] cannot be obtained in many generations, it becomes a partnership not only between those who are living, but between those who are living, those who are dead, and those who are yet to be
born. Each contract of each particular state is but a clause in the great primeval
contract of eternal society, linking the lower with the higher natures, connect-
ing the visible and the invisible world, according to a fixed compact sanctioned
by the inviolable oath which holds all physical and all moral natures, each in
their appointed place.

> Edmund Burke, *Reflections on the Revolution in France*

One realizes that even in harmonious families there is this double life: the
group life, which is the one we can observe in our neighbour's household, and
underneath, another—secret and passionate and intense—which is the real life
that stamps the faces and gives character to the voices of our friends. Always in
his mind each member of these social units is escaping, running away, trying to
break the net which circumstances and his own affections have woven about
him. One realizes that human relationships are the tragic necessity of human
life; that they can never be wholly satisfactory, that every ego is half the time
pulling away from them. In those simple relationships of loving husband and
wife, affectionate sisters, children and grandmother, there are innumerable
shades of sweetness and anguish which make up the pattern of our lives day
to day. . . .

> Willa Cather, *Not under Forty*

The identity of Kaguru persons and their wider identity as Kaguru people are inextricably linked to each other and to attributes of gender, age, and membership in kin groups and settlements.[1] It makes little sense to consider Kaguru as members of an ethnic group without also considering their particular matrilineal clan *(ikungugo)* or where they live in Kaguruland. A Kaguru may tell an outsider that he or she is a Kaguru and explain no further, but all identification in Kaguruland itself ordinarily includes mention of one's own and father's matriclans and the neighborhood where one dwells. Kaguru explain themselves as a people with reference to matriclans and neighborhoods because Kaguru legendary accounts of their origins and history are formulated in terms of clans and the various lands with historical and mystical ties to them (Beidelman 1970; 1971a; 1978; 1986, chapter 5).

Clans and lands are common themes uniting all Kaguru, yet these also divide Kaguru into competing groups. Kaguru contend for claims to historical and mystical domination of lands. Settlers on such land are traditionally described as politically and ritually dependent on the goodwill of the owner clan for their rights and welfare. Members of different clans dispute the ownership of lands and the histories that validate such ownership. Within any settlement Kaguru negotiate ties to the land, rights to perform ritual, and the transmission and distribution of bridewealth, fines, and inheritance in terms of membership in kin groups. Kin allegiances are reckoned through ties of birth and marriage. Kaguru identity is refracted personally in local terms figured by kinship, marriage, and residence. Such refraction shifts personal identities into ever-changing roles as kin and neighbors. These determine a Kaguru's goals and strategies in social relations. Success or failure in achieving these ends remains crucial throughout a Kaguru's life in determining and maintaining her or his personhood or identity. The common give-and-take of everyday life provides the bases for such activities. Kaguru personhood is constructed out of the stuff of that life, as are the symbols and beliefs that underlie and give meaning to that personhood and those activities. Initiation and the less dramatic cues of everyday affairs are aimed at teaching the young to master these manifold and changing roles of kinship and village neighborliness. Consequently, a brief portrayal of Kaguru economy and politics, social organization, and domestic life is essential for understanding the substance of Kaguru initiation rites and oral traditions and the personal and ethnic identity these express.

KAGURU ECONOMY AND POLITICS

The central, formative factor behind Kaguru economic and political life relates to their need to establish and maintain broad yet diverse ties between people. For Kaguru, the number and range of people whom one can enlist for support remains the major traditional resource leading to personal prosperity and security. Unlike some other East African areas, Kaguruland is endowed with more rainfall than surrounding regions. The mountains once held workable iron deposits, and coveted tobacco was widely grown. Unfortunately, access to Kaguruland by outsiders has never posed a serious problem. Consequently, while Kaguru have had more natural resources than some of their neighbors, they were vulnerable to raids by these poorer folk during times of need. What Kaguru sometimes lacked was an adequate supply of people to work the land, defend its produce, and guard themselves against outsiders seeking goods and captives. Politically and economically, people rather than land were the scarcest, most sought-after resource.

Kaguruland is mountainous and hilly, which provided retreat and defense against more warlike peoples to the north, south, and west. Those areas were subject to more food shortages and armed conflict than Kaguruland itself. These difficulties led to periodic forays by neighboring peoples into Kaguruland, which they rightly saw as much more likely to provide essential resources than these less favored, neighboring areas. In the 1800s Kaguruland lay astride one of the major east-west caravan routes in East Africa. For over a century, it was the last stop for water and supplies before caravans crossed the more arid and hostile central plateau en route to the great lakes to the west, and the place for caravans to replenish supplies and recover after re-crossing the plateau on the trek back to the coast. This location afforded Kaguru opportunities to trade, first with their less prosperous neighbors, then later with huge passing caravans of strangers. Kaguru goods could and would be seized by force rather than traded if Kaguru themselves did not present a semblance of unity and strength. Kaguruland's environmental advantages meant that Kaguru needed large, stockaded villages defensible against outsiders. After raiding and marauding ended as a result of the peace brought about by German and later British rule in the early 1900s, Kaguru settlements decreased in size and spread more evenly over the countryside.

Kaguru needed people to keep order within their own society. Traditionally there were no firmly established chiefships or political hierarchies. Instead, big men (wakula) or leaders (wandewa, "herdsmen") sporadically arose as they built up neworks of kin, affines, and blood-friendships. It was through the number and range of these ties that Kaguru secured their claims to safety, retrieved stolen goods, and regained abducted or runaway kin. With the influx of arms and trade goods through caravans in the mid-1900s, some Kaguru leaders became particularly powerful and tried to claim special rank and privileges.

Assemblies of people were also important for Kaguru agricultural production. While good land was readily available, it required intensive labor to be cleared, planted, weeded, and harvested. Strong men were needed to clear new land, and men, women, and children all labored at cultivation. Boys were needed to herd livestock and guard against human and animal predators. Labor during key times in the agricultural cycle was particularly demanding and critical since work had to be synchronized with the progress of the annual rains. The size of holdings was limited by the number of workers available at these crucial times. Europeans, seeing a more leisurely pace of work outside these peak periods of planting and harvesting, have sometimes found this labor shortage hard to appreciate.

While I have described Kaguruland as environmentally more favored than neighboring countries to the north, west, and south, readers should not assume that it is a land of plenty. Prosperity is a highly relative concept. Much depends upon the rains, which fluctuate greatly from year to year and from place to place. Surpluses are never large enough to carry over much beyond the year and, in any case, long-term storage of foodstuffs is risky if not impossible. This means that every third or fourth year some Kaguru can expect lean times. Every seven or eight years some expect even harder conditions. This means that a person's diverse range of social ties is crucial, since sharing of resources is essential for getting through periodic difficulties. Because harvests and droughts vary from one locale to another and from year to year, Kaguru seek ties in other areas of Kaguruland where further support can be found. This might involve more than sharing harvests; it might involve borrowing livestock or gaining permission to resettle temporarily (or even permanently) in other, more flourishing areas where one has kin, affines, or friends. For survival in their changing environment, wise Kaguru have to maintain as wide a range of social ties as possible. Kaguru are forever caught in a precarious balance between trying to meet their own needs and having to meet the demands of others who sooner or later might in turn come to their rescue. No Kaguru can afford to let any one category of kin or neighborly ties outbalance any others, though matrilineal and patrilateral kin ties constitute the central modes of social reckoning. Advantages of building up cohesive local kin groups have to be balanced against possible emergencies, when further-ranging ties become essential because local conditions are bad.

KAGURU SOCIAL ORGANIZATION

Being a Kaguru means being organized around two basic principles that complement and oppose each other: matrilineal descent and familial domesticity.

The first principle is embodied in matriclans and their constituent matrilineages, which provide the most inclusive means by which Kaguru associate with one another. The second principle is embodied in the myriad individual households that provide the immediate surroundings from which Kaguru construct most of their everyday life. Both these modes of organization have profound implications for the roles and goals of Kaguru men and women. I first consider Kaguru social organization from a broader perspective, both structural and holistic, in terms of the ways these two types of groups, matrilineages and households, characterize contrasting values and beliefs. I then consider Kaguru social organization from the narrower, more immediate perspectives of particular persons, noting the strategies different women and men follow to succeed and survive, and the kinds of social dilemmas such strategies pose.

Kaguru society comprises about one hundred exogamous, matrilineal clans (*makungugo*). Each clan is mystically associated with one or more tracts of land that it claims to own. As owners, clan members organize rituals to purify and revivify the land annually. Traditionally elders of an owner-clan had to give permission before outsiders could settle on their land. While members of an owner-clan tended to be more numerous than those of any single other clan in the area, total membership of all outsiders outnumbered these owners. Despite seeming traditions, actual ownership of clan areas was negotiable and contested, especially as demographic and political realities changed. Whatever actual changes took place over many generations, local Kaguru politics and rituals were cast in terms of legends and mystical beliefs supporting one matriclan to which other groups were linked through intermarriage and exchange of goods and services. Members of Kaguru matriclans are scattered throughout Kaguruland but exert dominant positions of putative ownership in only a few or no particular areas.

While Kaguru speak of matriliny in terms of clans, most having thousands of members, their essential matrilineal relations are determined by descent reckoned from named, known persons. Such relations may be traced through six or seven generations in some cases. This is where political or ritual powers are claimed, as with those seeking ties to the former paramount chief and who can write up genealogies. Most Kaguru rarely reckon kinship beyond great-grandparents. Even so, reckoning may involve considerable kin.

Kaguru see a person related primarily to two matrilineages, one's own (one's mother's) and one's father's. These two matrilineages are viewed as complementary and competing. Both entail obligations of economic, political, and ritual support toward fellow members. Conversely, each group's claims are repeatedly seen competing with those of the other, given the Kaguru world of limited resources. These two matrilineal groups are both constituted by the same type of recruitment. Yet from any single Kaguru's perspective, her or his connection to one group is maternal and to the other paternal, so that notions of one's parents' gender suffuse such thinking.

A Kaguru's deepest, most integral identity, flesh and blood, derives from her or his mother and links a Kaguru physiologically and mystically to the other members of the matrilineage (and, less intensively, to all members of the matriclan). Blood is the body's most potent element, and its disturbance, defilement, or compromise through physical injury, incest, homicide, ill will, or disrespect may cause bodily illness and ancestral wrath to the kin concerned, not just the offender or offended. Ties of blood reinforce lineal allegiance and solidarity, though loyalty is buttressed by common interest against inroads by other, comparable groups.

Every Kaguru is also thought to be physiologically related to her or his father. Paternal bone and cartilage provide identity and form, discriminating or separating out, just as maternal blood connects and blurs. In these terms, different fatherhoods potentially distinguish component groups amongst those with common blood flowing within a matrilineage. Jurally recognized paternal ties provide one's most readily assumed public name and one's natal household identity. Paternal kin provide a countervoice against a chorus of merged matrilineal kin at crises such as deaths, illnesses, divorces, and various disputes. Yet mystical and physiological ties of paternity, even the threat of the fatherly curse, are not as powerful as maternal ties or their rejection.[2] Furthermore, while maternal ties are conveyed automatically at birth, jural ties toward paternal kin are established only after payments.

One's own matrilineage imbeds a Kaguru within a long social strand in time and place. It provides one's deepest extended social ties; one is a member of a matriclan as fully as is any other person in it. In contrast, one is not a member of a comparably imbedding patrilateral group, yet that group's members are deeply concerned with one's personal well-being. One is a child of that clan, while those within it are full members. One's father's matrilineage is tangential to one's own matrilineage in both place and time. It marks one's particular identity off from many other persons within one's own matrilineage (except, of course, for one's own paternal siblings, though with polygynous fathers siblings are not always in one's patrilateral matrilineage). Rules of exogamy, forbidding multiple marriages of close maternal kin to members of another matriclan, ensure this pointillistic social effect of many different matrilineages attaching patrilaterally upon one matriclan.[3] Women forge the links of common matrilineal identity, whereas in-marrying men lend lineage members divisive and particularistic identities and loyalties. For Kaguru, these paternal ties, however deeply important, remain external or tangential to deeper

Figure 3. Kaguru girl, who, while smiling, has assumed a pose traditionally associated with mourning. Photograph taken at Berega in 1957.

matrilineal membership and loyalties. Paternal parenthood produces a child-like attachment. (Even one's cousins in that clan [FZC] may call one "child.")

This externality of one's patrilateral matrilineage (one's *welekwa*, "those born into") is reflected in the priority of loyalties toward one's own matrilineage *(ikungugo)*, which traditionally (though not always today) makes major claims for bridewealth, bloodwealth, fines, and the inheritance of office and ritual powers. Yet even traditionally, a paternal matrilineage *(welekwa)* occasionally confers office on "a child of the matriclan." In more recent times, with the new importance of individual households, claims by or through a father, though not usually expressed in terms of a father's matrilineage but rather in terms of household resources and loyalties, have undermined matrilineal priorities. Both Christianity and Islam have fostered growing paternal values to the loss of influence of matrilineal kin. During the colonial period and beyond, paternal claims often outweighed matrilineal ones in courts, despite protests by Kaguru traditionalists. Courts were dominated by elder Kaguru men who, due to the declining political and economic importance of lineages, are now beginning to think of themselves more as fathers than as mother's brothers or women's brothers.

Traditionally one's paternal matrilineage embodies a public or external aspect of the person, whereas matrilineal identity is considered so inherent and profound to one's social being that it requires no everyday expression (compare Bourdieu's notion of centrifugal [male] and centripetal [female] [1977: 92]). Undue, open mention of a Kaguru's matrilineal affiliations can sometimes be in bad taste. Names and consequent social identities conveyed by paternal kin are what Kaguru most readily voice. Matrilineal names and identities are less freely cited. It is said this is because these are too important to bandy about, not because they are secondary. Members of one's paternal matrilineage are essential at public inquests and disputes that might become occasions for conflict when a person might be ganged up on by the other members of his or her matrilineage. At such times, paternal kin are expected to take one's side wholeheartedly, since they would be interested only in one's particular welfare, not the good of one's matrilineage as a whole. They are concerned only about what is good for their child. Paternal kin constitute a fail-safe against one's matrilineage. Maternal and paternal kin are repeatedly played off against each other.

So far, I have presented Kaguru society primarily in terms of two matrilineages conjoined through marriage and the subsequent birth of children who are considered members of one matrilineage (the mother's) and children of another (the father's). Less reliable ties can be constituted through one's mother's father's matrilineage, one's father's father's matrilineage, and so on. Marriage, if the ancestors bless it with children, transmutes affinity into manifold matrilineal and paternal ties. Each union between two matrilineages results in a household, ordinarily headed by a male (husband). Most Kaguru men have one wife at a time, though divorce and remarriage have always been frequent and easy. Elder, prosperous men often have several wives, usually all residing in the same settlement, though sometimes they remain in separate villages and the husband travels from one to another.

At the turn of the century, Kaguru stayed in larger, palisaded settlements in which sufficient men dwelt to resist outsiders raiding for livestock, grain, metal goods, or captives. In such settlements women were never free from constant male scrutiny. With colonial rule, settlements became smaller, and many women now live without being directly overseen by either husbands or male kin. Some of these women are divorced, some widowed, and a few have never been married at all. Where women reside without a man in the house, they often have a grown son, brother, or other kinsman near. Even today, Kaguru find it difficult to picture women, even old ones, making legal cases or paying fines without advice or help from men. Courts and government officials often give women a hard time when they speak out unaccompanied by men. In any case, no Kaguru, man or woman, is so rich and powerful that sooner or later kin or neighbors are not needed to help out in inevitable hard times, so women are often reluctant to buck the prevailing views of many kin and neighbors.

Women may face many checks against their attempts to give public voice to their complaints, esecially in the face of men's control of most public ceremonies. Men monopolize all rituals promoting the benevolence of the ancestral dead and the fertility and well-being of land, kin, and livestock. Yet flour and beer, as essential to sacrifice and celebrations as are livestock and poultry, are provided exclusively by women, and both men and women serve as reservoirs of knowledge about the names, histories, and genealogies of the dead and the living. Women are actually as essential to ritual as men, but only during very unusual emergencies have women publicly performed some rituals in lieu of men.

Women provide the essential means by which matrilineages reproduce themselves. While men are necessary for procreation, mere siring of a child provides men with no rights to control offspring. Such rights inhere in the matrilineage. They are conveyed by blood through women but manipulated by male lineage elders, these women's brothers and maternal uncles. In this sense, marriage is a subsidiary rite, negotiated by men and conveying secondary rights in women's children and labor.[4]

Socially, parenthood is more difficult for Kaguru men than women, for men must command social resources, property, labor, and/or kin to provide payment in order to father children, whereas women may become parents even while ignoring or defying social conventions. Furthermore, women's kin accept fatherless children readily since these are social assets, doubly so because no husbands claim a share. Yet in another, biological sense parenthood is more difficult for women than men. A woman's marriage in no way guarantees that she will bear children, and no form of adopting children is recognized. Women may become mothers only through the mysterious, combined workings of their own bodies and the imponderable beneficence of the ancestral dead. In contrast, a married man is almost certain to become a father, especially in the past before Christianity banned divorce and polygyny. A man could divorce a barren woman or could take further wives if he was rich. Even a sterile or impotent man could father children socially, either with his own connivance or unknown to him through deceit by his frustrated wife. Payment of bridewealth guarantees a man paternity to all his wife's subsequent offspring if he wishes to claim them. Any children she bore prior to this would belong exclusively to her matrilineage unless a man paid for rights in one or more of them. This difference between the prospects of men and women is reflected in the kinds of social abuse leveled at each. A man may be rebuked by being told he is unmarried or acts as though he is uncircumcised. While this is an insult, it denigrates him in ways that could be amended. In contrast, a woman may be rebuked for having no children. This is a graver insult since there is no ready solution. It implies a flaw in the woman's person, deterring the dead from yielding life to her.

Men pay for marital benefits with wealth and labor (bridewealth and brideservice), yet the overwhelming, residual control of women and their children remains inalienably within their matrilineage. In some cases poorer, in-marrying men gain only a few rights in exchange for moving into women's villages. This often involves cross-cousin marriage. In contrast, wealthy and powerful men secure broader control of women and take them to their own settlements far away from the women's homes. Terms of residence and proximity to a woman's natal home indicate the degree to which a lineage (or sometimes a paternal household head) holds on to women. In no case (except pawning and enslavement, in the precolonial past) is a woman lost to her kin.

Given traditional matrilineality and rules of clan exogamy, sisters and brothers figure prominently in Kaguru thinking about the difficulties of negotiating kinship relations. Sisters marry outside the matrilineage but produce lineage heirs. Such women usually move out of that group's settlement but in later life they and/or their offspring are urged to return or at least maintain close ties. Kaguru men remark that they must never openly mention their sisters' sexuality (only an incestuous witch would do so), yet they are deeply concerned with it since it provides them with heirs and adherents. The matrilineal sibling relation is reproductive but asexual (Schlegel 1990: 35). Bridewealth received for a sister often enables her brother to marry. The goodwill, loyalty, and fertility of sisters therefore constitute a problem since these can be compromised by the man to whom a sister is married (cf. van Baal 1975: 77). Her consent to be married off and not run away secures her a debt from her brother. Yet in later life brothers may encourage their sisters to leave their husbands. Ideally, a Kaguru sister is given away but not lost. She is inalienable to her brother and matrilineage (cf. A. Weiner 1992). A brother hopes to make claims on the loyalty and labor of a sister's sons and the bridewealth from her daughters. He also hopes for his sister's blessings toward his own children, who are in competition with hers for his favors. He does not, however, benefit from his sister's labor after she is married. He can hope for her continued interest only so long as he seems likely to promise help to her sons, his matrilineal heirs. Kaguru men are members of matrilineages and husbands and fathers to children of other lineages. Men are committed to two contrasting paths to power and authority. As elders within their own matrilineages, they must retain the loyalty of the women of these matrilineages, their mothers, sisters, and sisters' daughters, and control these women's offspring. The weaker the marital ties between such women and their husbands, the better chance matrikinsmen have to retain or retrieve the women. These same matrikinsmen are also keen to control their own wives and children, who constitute the corresponding social future of the outsider matrilineages into which these men themselves have married. All the weaknesses a man encourages to undermine his own kinswomen's marriages are the very ones he hopes to avert in his own. Wealthy, forceful men manage contradictory postures in this struggle, but many men do not. Kaguru men are committed to inconsistent moral positions to augment their ambitions. Men encourage marital instability and disloyalty amongst their own sisters and nieces. At the same time they urge marital stability and paternal allegiance within their own households.

Kaguru women confront matriliny and domesticity with a very different perspective from that of men. Kaguru women face no such double standards over children. A woman's children are the persons within her own lineage who provide her with influence and power. She does not balance ties to nieces and nephews against ties to her children. A woman's parenthood does not generate deep, conflicting interests on her part.[5] Of course, a Kaguru woman has an interest in the possible fragility of her brothers' marriages. She hopes her brothers will favor matrilineal nieces and nephews in providing support, even at the cost of helping the brothers' own children. Women see whatever help their brothers provide to their own offspring as undermining what support is available to these brothers' own matrilineal kin. Women see the resources their brothers garner within their own households as resources withheld from matrilineal nieces and nephews living outside. Of course, these same women would take an opposite stance toward their own husbands, urging them to keep wealth for their children and not to give it out to other households (to their husbands' matrikin). This competition for loyalty and support is heightened by the fact that resources are not abundant in Kaguruland, so some protagonists must suffer. Yet even if available resources were greater, there would still probably not be enough to satisfy demanding kin.

Kaguru repeatedly claimed that matrilineal ties were more powerful in the past than when I did fieldwork. With colonial times settlements became smaller, the population became more scattered, alien missionaries and government officials promoted patriarchal values, and households rather than lineages became the major productive and protective units. While Kaguru still describe themselves as traditionally matrilineal, most adult everyday experiences are acted out in households where a wife and children are dominated by a father/husband and familial household integrity is stressed. Matrilineal ties, except for those claiming political offices under colonial rule, are increasingly seen as alternate ties that supplement those reinforcing the solidarity of parent and children. In this sense, Kaguru women rather than men are more likely to find matrilineality consistent with the modern emphasis on households and parenting, since women's roles as mothers are consistent with both household and lineal values; it is as matrilineal sisters and aunts that women's roles seem to be undermined. Matriliny is consistent with women's primacy as mothers but not with men's primacy as fathers of children not of their own matrilineage. Men and women as brothers and sisters were always at odds with domestic stability and remain so. In any case, loyalties of uterine siblings hinge most on ties emphasized by mothers and not so much by fathers. Patriarchal household integrity yields to matrilineal ties most frequently where cross-cousin marriage has been arranged. In such cases, elders manipulate bridewealth, brideservice, and residence in ways to allow them to dominate younger men through the wives they have provided.[6]

To a Kaguru woman, her husband's loyalties to his matrilineage threaten the welfare of herself and her children. To her, the chief threat to his support and loyalties are the women of her husband's matrilineage, especially her husband's mother and sisters. Touchy relations toward father's sisters and some grandparents stem from this. Yet whatever a woman herself might think of her affines, to her children they remain kin. A woman's fears and annoyances cannot efface the fact that these people are loved by her husband, who presents them to her children as valued kin. The ambiguity and ambivalence characterizing these relations are reflected by the fact that such persons are viewed as possible sexual partners. Of course, one does not sleep with one's actual grandparents or father's sisters, but those more distantly related in these kin categories are potential mates. Sexual joking and familiarity may sometimes occur with grandparents and father's sisters. Kaguru say one jokes with and may marry "enemies," and these are amongst one's potentially inimical kin who compete over inherited resources.[7]

Finally, the problem of divorce raises important questions about the contrasts between matrilineal and household values and ties, as well as contrasts between the roles of women and men. The longer a couple is married and the more children they have, the more likely they are to develop common values and sentiments on account of their offspring. Even if a couple's union ends with death or divorce, so long as their children live, the two matrilineages they link will repeatedly interact and compete at rites of passage and other crises. Ironically, the more children a couple has, the more advantage the wife's kin find in divorce. If she is divorced, her matrilineage withholds a portion of the refunded bridewealth for every child born, even if these died. Furthermore, the proceeds of the husband's brideservice are never refunded. If a woman has borne five or six children, none of the bridewealth goes back. Yet if such a divorced woman remarries, her kin could again secure bridewealth and brideservice for her. Or they could encourage her to return to live with them, preferably bringing her children with her, and bearing subsequent children out of wedlock. Divorce always poses an economic threat to a husband unless his wife is barren or considered so unpleasant that the community supports his refund. No divorced man wants to remain alone for long. He will struggle to secure wealth for another mate. Mature men cannot manage easily without a wife to cook and fetch water and wood, whereas women manage rather well now that raiding is not a problem. For these reasons, divorce is rarely favored by men, even when a wife is difficult, whereas many women press for divorce or use it as a threat (cf. Brain 1969).

Kaguru parenthood poses profound conflicts for Kaguru men, who pursue power through pressing equally both matrilineal and paternal (domestic) ties. In contrast, Kaguru women face no such conflict regarding parental interests. Matriliny is buttressed by maternal links and loyalties. "Women are mothers or preparing themselves to be mothers, and motherhood conditions their behavior and gives shape to their ways of life and their outlook. It is only the blessed myopy caused by their vanity which prevents men from perceiving that women are always mothers, also in their relations with men" (van Baal 1975: 78).[8] Of course, Kaguru women are also sisters, but it is because sisters are daughters of mothers and potential mothers themselves that they are important.

For Kaguru women, their domestic priorities are consistent with ties to their children. Resident men are not essential to their economic livelihood. Women's husbands remain secondary in women's loyalties. For Kaguru men and women alike, the foremost social tie of affection and mutual interest is between a mother and her children. Ties between uterine sisters and brothers are derivative and secondary to those between them and their mothers. Indeed, on the death of mothers, sibling ties begin to lose strength. Ties to fathers and spouses occupy a lesser place in Kaguru values.

KAGURU PERSONAL STRATEGIES

The most important role that a Kaguru woman may hold is that of mother. For this she need not even be married, though she should be initiated. Whether or not she is married in no way affects a woman's claims toward her children. When I questioned Kaguru women about this, some said that there are advantages to being married: A husband is expected to provide clothing, tools, and other goods, and he should take his wife's part against others in disputes, though as it turns out, the persons with whom his wife is most apt to quarrel—his kin—are those persons a husband is unlikely to criticize. From a woman's viewpoint the best reason to marry is that she gets a man to oppose her own father and mother's brothers. During disputes a clever woman repeatedly reminds her natal kin of her loyalties to her husband and his kin, and vice versa when she quarrels with her husband. A woman thus seeks maximum attention and concern from each vying group. Marriage provides a woman's children with two blocs of kin for support instead of one. This is important to a woman since she envisions her long-term loyalties as identical to those of her children. Kaguru women are excellent examples of the *tertius gaudens* (the third party who enjoys) so dear to Simmel in his analysis of social triads. A woman's freedom derives from the matching, canceling strengths of her husband's natal kin and her own (Simmel 1950: 154–62; cf. Rustin 1971: 181–83). Triadic tensions contribute to the ongoing struggles for influence within a domestic group (see Rustin 1971: 196–97). Both affinal and natal kin must be readily accessible (ibid.: 185). This relates to what Richards long ago called "the matrilineal puzzle" (1950: 246). Matrilineal systems may not pose more problems than patrilineal or cognatic ones and, in that sense, Watson-Franke may be right to dub the phrase ethnocentric (1992: 476). Yet Kaguru themselves spoke of such conflicts as a problem, and some complained to me that their patrilineal Maasai (Baraguyu) and Gogo neighbors had easier kinship.

Unlike a father, who is also concerned with his sisters' children as heirs, a Kaguru mother focuses nearly all her hopes and plans for her future security upon the welfare and loyalties of her children. Kaguru point out that one's mother is the person most likely to provide sure and heartfelt advice and support on account of her own needs for security being so wrapped up with those of her children. Whatever value a Kaguru woman holds for her brothers and husband stems from her importance as a mother to children. Men also depend upon children, but unlike women they convert the value of children into advantages to their own ends, which may be different from what is good for the children. Sons and daughters are laborers. Daughters bring in bridewealth. Such resources may be converted into livestock, metal goods, medicines, political and ritual offices, and, above all, more wives. In contrast, mothers are more interested in their children themselves becoming powerful persons.

The affection and loyalty that a mother commands draw her offspring's attentions toward kin favored by the mother and deflect these children's allegiance away from those she dislikes. A wise woman encourages her children to love and respect both their father and their maternal uncles. Rousseau's observation about the role of a mother is apt here: "She serves as the link between them and their father; she alone makes him love them and gives him the confidence to call them his own" (1979: 361). A mother withholds or bestows love and approval as she pleases and can undermine the loyalty and respect her children hold for others. Her most powerful advantage is her children's confidence in her love and indulgence. These favors are crucial in polygynous unions. A mother's influence is enforced by the prolonged, intense nurturing ties Kaguru women develop with their children. Over time, women serve as many kinds of nurturers: as mothers, as wives who feed and tend their husbands, sometimes as sisters who help their brothers, and often as indulgent grannies and aunts. Women compete amongst themselves as nurturers (van Baal 1975: 109), especially as sisters who compete against one another for a brother's interest and as maternal aunts whose blessings express their tolerance of their brother's wife's fertility.

Maternal affect is rooted in the fact that one's own self-interest is nearly identical with one's mother's most of the time and certainly always far closer than one's interests are to one's father's. After all, he has competing matrilineal loyalties different from one's own and would be committed to other households if he were polygynous (cf. Solanas's denunciation of fathers [1968: 39]).

A woman's support is vital to men for securing children's loyalty. Most Kaguru mothers work hard at cultivating need and trust from their children. Such deflecting of loyalties, first one way and then another, pits a woman's husband against her brothers and leads her brothers to compete for her favor.

When a woman grows older, her focus upon her children increases. As her daughters and sons become marriageable and their children in turn mature, she becomes an ever more important link between them. A man seeking to control his sister's grown children needs her loyalty and support. If she is widowed, her influence may increase since her offspring now have no father to interfere. Matrilineages cohere so long as the women linking offspring remain alive, but they begin to split up after these women die (Beidelman 1961a).

A woman's absorption with her children becomes intense if she is part of a polygynous arrangement. She is keenly competitive against her husband's own wider domestic interests and those of his kin but also against her cowives. Her position vis-à-vis her competitors depends upon the number of children she has borne in contrast to his other wives.

A childless woman can have none of these aims. Her greatest concern is finding kin likely to care for her after she becomes old and her barrenness confirmed. Brewing, prostitution, and midwifery become her likely means for added income. Help during illness and want becomes undependable as she ages. Her lot is hard. All Kaguru women desire as many children as possible whether in or out of marriage. Barrenness, not an illegitimate child, is a Kaguru woman's greatest disgrace and catastrophe.

CONCLUSION

A Kaguru man's most important roles are as a husband and brother. Unlike a woman, he has two avenues toward influence: his wives and children and his matrilineage. He may be unlucky and have few wives and children; he may even have no actual sisters or have many brothers with whom he competes. If a man has wealth, he acquires many wives and attracts kinswomen seeking help and protection for themselves and their children. The usual means by which a man secures wealth is his kin ties. Regardless of whether or not a man has sisters whose marriages provide bridewealth, he tries to marry as soon as possible. To secure respect he must become head of a household where he sleeps and eats apart from his parents. Only by marrying does he ordinarily gain paternal rights to children. A woman's main problems stem from her biological ability or failure to procreate, not marry. All Kaguru women who want to marry do so. In contrast, a man's problems spring from his economic difficulties in securing rights in the labor and sexuality of women. Need for wealth means that men marry considerably later than women. Consequently women are more likely to outlive their husbands. A Kaguru man seeks to satisfy his wife and children but would like to please his sisters as well. Unfortunately, he may have too many offspring to please everyone. While men are interested in fertile sisters, women, whether they openly admit it or not, gain by their brothers' infertility (or that of their brothers' wives). Women are not even necessarily pleased by their sisters' fertility. This explains the concern Kaguru have to secure a father's sister's blessing for their children, since such women's hopes for their own children clash with one's own ambitions.

A man's relations toward his sisters are his most problematic and complex social ties. He is interested in his sisters' affairs, especially their sexual lives, though he must never openly speak of such matters. Only an incestuous witch

Figure 4. Young Kaguru householder and father. Photograph taken at Berega in 1957.

would do that. A Kaguru man hopes his sisters' sexual affairs are successful so that they produce many offspring, yet ideally he would like such relations to be flawed so that a sister's loyalty to him, her nonsexual partner, surpasses her loyalty to her actual sexual partner, her husband or lover. Kaguru oral literature, etiquette, and jokes reveal troubled ambiguities and anxieties in this sibling tie, an emotional loading found in no other Kaguru social relation. Neither brothers nor sisters have a long-term commitment to the marital stability of siblings of either sex. All are concerned to maintain affection and loyalties between them, though brothers are more likely to fall out with brothers, and sisters with sisters, than are brothers and sisters with each other.

The most important ties for women are with their mother and with their own children, and the force of such ties is couched in affectual, not jural, terms. Women's ties toward siblings, fathers, and husbands are more ambivalent. Except for their bonds with their mothers, men's ties, even with children and heirs, exhibit affectual conflict and ambiguity due to competing jural obligations and affectual attachments, which undermine wholehearted commitment in any direction. Brothers compete for the favor of sisters and sisters for that of brothers. This is in jural and affectual terms on account of lineal loyalties conflicting with marital ones. Aged mothers try to overreach separate households to hold together crosscutting sets of sibling ties and feelings. The domestic arena becomes a source of strength (the affections of nurturant maternity) and conflict (the demands of spousehood) regarding matrilineal allegiances. This is not to say that mothers may not be demanding or that spouses do not inspire affection. Yet customary Kaguru modes of speaking about these contrasting sets of domestic relations are contrasted with each other: unmitigated maternal affection, spouses' varying and unreliable erotic passion, and more-qualified affectual and jural obligations and demands toward others.

Lineal and domestic themes permeate Kaguru life. Conflicts and ambiguities, contrasts between feelings and actions, between women and men, color etiquette, ritual, and oral literature. These animate Kaguru social interaction and sentiments. Such crosscutting forces provide an oscillating, restless quality to Kaguru social relationships, making them appear as dangerous and adventuresome as they are reassuring and supportive. At this sociocultural center are feelings and thoughts lived out but never fully understood and solved by Kaguru.

Kaguru matriliny and domesticity contrast with yet complement each other. They deeply affect Kaguru roles of gender and the attributes assigned to them. Women are integral and interior to matrilineal relations yet are at the centers of contrastingly divisive domestic households as well.[9] Men are more exterior to such relations, manipulating and contending amongst themselves to control lineages and households through jural and ritual negotiations.

Women's powers rest primarily on their capacities to bear and nurture children and only secondarily upon their contributions of labor. Men's powers rest primarily upon their control of jural affairs, manipulation of public functions, ritual, ceremony, and the allocation and production of wealth. Men justify this on account of their greater physical strength and supposedly greater sagacity (cf. van Baal 1975: 82), but their strategies rest on domestic and matrilineal loyalties, which are centered on women. As Watson-Franke remarks (1992: 478), "matrilineal men are women-defined men" (this is also true for patrilineal societies). As in so many societies, we "should look at socially structured alternatives not as coherent sets of normative expectations but as clusters of norms and counternorms which codetermine action" (Levine 1985: 10). The broadest structures of Kaguru society are repeatedly cast in dualistic imagery (Beidelman 1973); this is how Kaguru express their norms and values, and I repeat such thinking here even though it may be out of analytical favor. Yet mention of dualism may wrongly suggest an overemphasis upon coherence in Kaguru society (cf. Levine 1985: 11). Instead, Kaguru society, whose members struggle through complex, ever-changing, and varied strategies, exemplifies "a pronounced openness for experiential ambiguities [which] may be functional for and reinforced in specific kinds of social contexts" (ibid.: 13). This means not that Kaguru are not rational in their choices but rather that choices and the freedom to make them are circumscribed by shared sentiments and mutual understandings.

In this survey of strategies employed by Kaguru men and women in terms of matrilineal and patrilateral kin and domestic household relations, I have stressed these broader kin affiliations and narrower familial allegiances because these are at the heart of traditional Kaguru social organization, which is framed in kinship. Gender with its modifications through age provides the mode of defining and contrasting Kaguru kin ties. Examining such ties reveals that women provide an enduring matrilineal core of allegiances, imbued with maternal and nurturant affect, around which Kaguru men struggle to negotiate controls and allegiances. A mode of female gender permeates the language of Kaguru matrilineal thinking, though men possess jural authority in such groups. These lineal rights and obligations are modified by men in terms of formal payments, services, and ancestral propitiation, negotiated and debated at public meetings. At the same time the core of women, forming a common element linking Kaguru households and lineages, divides men from one another according to conflicting claims men make on their own households and on others linked to them through women.

In contrast to matrilineages, Kaguru households reflect more equally divided, complementary relations between supervising, protective males and nurturant females. Yet women's nurturant roles as wives and mothers outdistance men's roles as husbands and fathers in terms of providing a foundation for domestic life. Unlike men, Kaguru women have few divided loyalties according to the two primary Kaguru modes of reckoning allegiances: membership in matrilineages and membership in households (families). The divided loyalties of men account for their aggressive, legalistic, outreaching claims toward descendants (offspring and nieces and nephews). Women's claims on their children and siblings are more focused, affectual, constant. The Kaguru role of sibling embodies divided loyalties toward lineages and spouses. Claims between siblings refer to natal households and the mother who focuses (*focus*, Latin for "hearth") these claims in terms of powerful nurturant affect. Kaguru sibling bonds are consequently steeped in feminine metaphors. Unfortunately, siblings' parenthood eventually undermines their mother's struggle for solidarity. Jurally fractious men and affectually insinuating women contrast sharply with each other. Formalistic and publicly debating men contrast with women committed to steadier, less debatable claims made behind the formal arenas of public debate. These strategies and motives produce evaluative readings far more complex than those expressed by Kaguru when they are asked about the attributes of women and men. Characterizations of gender are learned and repeated through a lifetime of rites of passage and quotidian etiquette. The metaphorical explication of gender and personhood is linked with the full panoply of everyday activities and experiences, with things and space, with feelings and senses. The rich vocabulary of Kaguru terms for gender and sexuality, the main subject of this book, anchors Kaguru social (moral) life in perceived reality. To understand Kaguru thinking about gender, sexuality, and age is to understand how Kaguru construct their world and their ethnic identity.

Three linked attributes form Kaguru personhood: gender, age, and the sexuality they modify. In Kaguru society most everyday activities are orchestrated in terms of kinship, where one rarely encounters others who cannot be fitted into some category of kin. Attributes of age, gender, and sexuality provide approaches (for both Kaguru and ourselves) for determining how Kaguru behave. They do not provide fixed modes of conduct. They are polyvalent attributes related to many possibilities, some advantageous, some not. For example, aging begins as a growing advantage enhancing a person's motives, needs, and capacities. In youth these qualities become highly ambivalent. Young people are at a threshold of autonomy as householders and parents in their own right. Yet they are also pawns in the negotiations between elders over bridewealth, brideservice, and residence. Interference by older kin is never more onerous. Coming of age consequently liberates yet further constrains the young. With subsequent aging, Kaguru acquire new powers, especially in the case of women with grown children. Finally, as old people nearer the dead, elders exert growing moral authority, though this is increasingly undermined by physical and mental weakness and by the very bases of their powers as elders—the more descendants available to control, the more difficult the task because those beneath resent and subvert that authority. Similarly ambiguous and ambivalent attributes characterize gender and the changing implications of sexuality. These involve conjugal and matrilineal fertility, adultery, lust, deception, and competing allegiances to sisters, brothers, spouses, children, nieces, and nephews. The rich and varied traditional songs and riddles of initiation recount these problems. What Kaguru learn about age, gender, and sexuality at initiation is not that these are easy and clear, but that these generate a world of play, manipulation, machinations, and struggle, the essence of Kaguru social life. To learn how to deal with these is to grow up, to become a proper Kaguru. That is what initiation is about.

Initiation is also about the assertion of Kaguru matriliny. In part, this is axiomatic with asserting Kaguruness, since Kaguru are traditionally a matrilineal people. But matriliny appears to be in decline amongst the Kaguru. Christian missionaries, Muslim traders, and outsider officials have all denigrated matriliny and advocated strengthening patriarchy and the nuclear family at the expense of uterine sibling loyalties and the solidarity of the matrilineage. In more recent times, African officials have also denigrated all extensive kin ties beyond the family, especially where these represent loyalties competing with the state for local political and economic allegiances. None of these critics of tradition, however, has dared to downgrade motherhood. Today, many Kaguru, conservative and uneducated traditionalists and also ethnic advocates with Western education, have reemphasized Kaguru culture, especially as it differentiates Kaguru and their land from their neighbors and as it separates Kaguru from the interference of unknowledgeable outsiders, missionaries, merchants, and government officials. Some of the exhortations for Kaguruness proclaimed at USA and Umwano meetings (discussed in the preceding chapter) referred to matriclans, mother's brothers, and ancestors. To some extent, the idiom of Kaguru matriliny and the social relations imbedded in it have gained new value beyond that of organizing local Kaguru kin groups. Today, for Kaguru, matriliny and its associated values and practices provide means by which Kaguru may distinguish themselves from ethnic outsiders, including some of their encroaching African neighbors—the patrilineal Gogo, Maasai, Baraguyu, and Kamba, and Swahilicized Africans. Ties beyond a household are still often important from time to time for Kaguru but have weakened drastically with the absence of raiding and the availability of cash from sources outside local land and livestock controlled by elders. In the colonial and postcolonial eras, Kaguru matriliny has assumed new and intense value as a badge of ethnic identity, even while actual allegiances between siblings and toward mother's brothers often suffered against the claims of paternal heads of households. These traditional ties have unquestionably provided more advantages to Kaguru women than have narrower values prompted by new concerns for the patriarchal family, though, of course, some men as well as women see maintaining Kaguru matrilineal customs as advantageous and important. In promoting traditional Kaguru beliefs and values, especially matriliny, Kaguru initiation represents many motives, and (perhaps surprisingly) draws some interests of Kaguru women, conservative traditionalists, and ethnic radicals and antinationalists onto common, if at times uncomfortable, ground.

CHAPTER 4

Space and Memory
Ritual, Ethnicity, and Personhood

The real distance between two generations is created by the elements they
have in common, which require the same experiences, as in the biologically
inherited behavior of animal species.
Italo Calvino, *Mr. Palomar*

Man for the field, and woman for the hearth. . . .
Alfred, Lord Tennyson, *The Princess*

Geography is the wife of history, as space is the wife of time.
Guy Davenport, *The Geography of the Imagination*

"Aha!" said my host, reading in my eyes one of those sparkling desires so art-
lessly expressed at my age, "you scent a pretty woman as a dog scents game."
Honoré de Balzac, *The Lily of the Valley*

This book is concerned with the construction of several identities: the identity of an ethnic group, the Kaguru, and the identities of persons who make up
that group.[1] In all these cases, identity is constantly challenged and eroded by
two factors. One is the sheer variety of people and experiences that a society
must somehow knit together. The other is the onslaught of time, which constantly alters people and even many of the things that people possess. Means
must be found to give a sense of containment to changing time itself. Kaguru,
like all people, have developed ways to bring order and hence identity to these
rich but unruly characteristics of human experience. Kaguru say their most

important means for doing this is through initiation of adolescents. Yet for this to work, such initiation must be grounded in deeper, more widespread processes that influence the divisive effects of multifariousness and time. These synthetic, constructive processes relate to Kaguru habits of speech, etiquette, and routine—in sum, to the rote of Kaguru everyday behavior. Yet even rote behavior is varied; what gives such multifarious activities a semblance of commonality is space—the space of Kaguru country, of clan lands, of settlements and neighborhoods, of homesteads. In this chapter I consider various Kaguru notions of space as means by which Kaguru hold together and sort out their manifold experiences. It is space, for Kaguru and probably for all people, that constitutes a concept that facilitates an ordering both of diversity in people and things and also of time itself.

By examining Kaguru notions of space I hope to do two things: to outline this unifying factor holding together Kaguru concepts of difference and time, and also, in the course of presenting this outline, to provide the reader with a coherent, introductory picture of Kaguru cosmology.[2] This cosmology informs the Kaguru way of life and hence their identity in general. This cosmology also gives detailed significance to rituals of initiation, which, Kaguru say, perpetuate that life.

The identity of the Kaguru people and culture, and hence of Kaguru as persons, is grounded in space, but it is, as I have noted, also challenged by time. Kaguru are fond of observing that their way of life, their ethnicity, continues for generations, beyond the lifetimes of individuals. Yet Kaguru, like sociologists, recognize that society is composed of individuals whose lifetimes are limited. Kaguru beliefs, values, and practices must be taught anew to each generation in order to reproduce and perpetuate Kaguru society. Furthermore, as with all societies, individuals who make up Kaguru society are themselves constantly changing. It is not simply a problem of individuals entering society by being born and leaving it by dying. Even while they live, they mature, marry, procreate, and take on many roles and tasks. These changes too must be incorporated into a sense of continuity and wholeness for Kaguru and not allowed to create a sense of dissolution and division.

Kaguru rites of passage create and sustain such changing personhoods through time while also affirming a more encompassing Kaguru identity. These rituals and the myriad, changing activities of Kaguru everyday affairs that underpin rituals all achieve their goals by endless, varied repetition enacted within well-defined and ordered social spaces. Rootedness in place, that is, in socialized space, anchors rituals to a seemingly enduring world. Contrary and quicksilver experiential time is thus subdued; time holds no fixed, workable meaning outside spatial grounding.

Kaguru repeatedly emphasize the central importance of the initiation of adolescents in constructing ethnic identity, yet we should appreciate initiation rituals within a more encompassing repertoire of rites. Initiation rituals may be the high point of a Kaguru's ritual experience, but this is because they are imbedded in a much wider matrix of experience. At the most mundane level, all Kaguru habits endorse and reinforce Kaguruness: speech, etiquette, bodily comportment, work, layouts of houses and villages, alimentation, grooming, apparel. These myriad, seemingly trivial experiences accumulate to create an enveloping cultural reality. At the ritual level as well, rites preceding and following initiation provide a broader symbolic and experiential matrix that gives initiation fuller meaning. Thus, rituals of birth and naming precede initiation, and those of marriage, parenthood, and death follow it. Rituals of ancestral propitiation, rituals of cleansing, and other rites of crisis also repeatedly interweave with other experiences marking a Kaguru person's career. Whenever any rites are performed, some persons recall past rituals or anticipate those yet to come. No Kaguru ritual exists outside an awareness of many comparable, related practices.

This chapter sketches out Kaguru notions about space, and in doing this I also describe Kaguru cosmology, thereby orienting the reader to rites, symbols, and ideas that follow. Yet I have a further purpose. I hope to use the theme of Kaguru social space to tie together the various rituals and everyday practices that constitute Kaguru symbolic behavior. In most previous accounts of initiation of adolescents in Africa, only rites of initiation are discussed. Such a narrow approach has vitiated our understanding of initiation. I here use my account of Kaguru space to sketch out a fuller range of rites and symbols that a Kaguru experiences in her or his lifetime. This should support my argument that Kaguru rites of initiation, though singled out by Kaguru, make proper sense only when seen as underpinned by far wider and longer ethnic experiences.

This chapter presents a "topoanalysis" (Bachelard 1969: 8) of a "topocosm" (Frye 1963: 64), a world founded upon space. Space is a "privileged phenomenon" (Bachelard 1964: 7), pervasive and instrumental in explaining myriad experiences.[3] An account of Kaguru cosmology, centering around space, indicates how inextricably self, gender, time, ethnicity, and space are interconnected for many people, including Kaguru. "Who one is in a domesticated society is largely a function of where one is" (Wilson 1988: 70).

Traditional Kaguru notions of both self and ethnic identity are imbedded in space. "The *personnage* is a member of a bounded tribal society" (Allen 1985: 31). This concerns "constructed space, which depends on the power of the mind to extrapolate far beyond the sense data" in order to construct a "geometric personality" (Tuan 1977: 17). It concerns how Kaguru traditionally saw their surroundings as a physical reality informing and supporting a seemingly enduring ethnic group, even though historical evidence suggests that some ideas that Kaguru held of their identity during colonial and postcolonial times were fairly recent constructs.[4]

Kaguru see changes intrinsic to life—birth, initiation (maturation), marriage, parenthood, and death—as imbedded in fields of moral space that confirm and echo a seemingly changing but broadly enduring moral (social) universe. Society and the persons comprising it are subject to "deceptive time" constructed from myriad divergences and convergences of social phenomena (Gurvitch 1964: 27). Halbwachs argues that "resemblances are paramount" (1980: 85) in creating the illusion that change is encapsulated within a broader frame of constancy. This "collective memory" is achieved by impressing people with common life-cycle experiences. Kaguru achieve this because experiences and memories from earlier fragments of a life cycle are repeated at later phases, thereby endowing each phase in the cycle with a sense of both the past and what is to come. The ways space is endowed with moral valences, with "the accretion of sentiments" (Tuan 1977: 33), and the ways appropriate actions and persons are associated with places facilitate this symbolic orchestration to "immobilize time" (Halbwachs 1980: 126).[5]

Space perpetuates a sense of the timeless (Halbwachs 1980: 129–31). "Hence each group cuts up space in order to compose, either definitively or in accordance with a set method, a fixed framework within which to enclose and retrieve its resemblances" (ibid.: 156–57); "it is the spatial image alone that, by means of its stability, gives us an illusion of not having changed through time and of retrieving the past in the present. But that's how memory is defined. Space alone is stable enough to endure without growing old or losing any of its parts" (ibid.: 157; cf. Hutton 1988).[6]

When I lived amongst the Kaguru, they rarely discussed changes in their physical environment, even though I often asked about these. For Kaguru, the broad uses of space appeared relatively constant over decades. To be sure, individual dwellings were abandoned and new ones built; old fields were overgrown or left fallow and new ones cleared. But configurations of settlements and bush remained generally the same, except that a few Kaguru lamented that past villages had been larger and more prosperous. No one seemed interested when I asked about the profound changes in social space that must have resulted when masses of Kaguru moved down from the mountains at the onset of colonial times, when raiding ceased (Beidelman 1962a). For Kaguru, the great and significant changes in social space were not in recent, historical time but during distant, legendary time when matriclans first arrived to claim their

respective lands. Then each clan found its place. The colonial and administrative system threatened this thinking when it established courts and offices
favoring certain matriclans, but to most Kaguru such concerns seemed less
important than the broader themes of ancient clan domains. Kaguru emphasized the enduring continuity of their surroundings.

I am not suggesting that Kaguru denied more recent social changes with
their new sociopolitical and economic uses of space, but during my fieldwork
they appeared only dimly aware of the environmental changes gradually over-
taking them and which now, with greater governmental interference, may en-
gulf them.[7] For Kaguru, valences of different spaces, stemming from their different everyday and ceremonial uses, convey the essence of ethnic identity.
Space contains actions even as these actions entail movement and hence
change. This capacity of space to form a stage or arena embracing self and
others, actors and spectators, movement and constancy, makes it crucial for
traditional Kaguru who are acting out and replicating their society over time.
Such "a recurrent pattern or schema of containment" is essential for rites of
initiation to present a sense of stability conducive to social (moral) order
(Johnson 1991: 77).

KAGURU SPACE AND HUMANITY

The broadest moral space with which the Kaguru are concerned is Ukaguru
(Kaguruland), the place where the Kaguru language (Chikaguru) and customs
prevail and which consequently contains and defines their ethnicity. Kaguru
acknowledge that other ethnic groups are human, but they frame their accounts of what true humanity involves in terms of Kaguru beliefs and customs. They consider those outside Ukaguru as lacking proper culture and at
worst as savages unfit for full respect.

Kaguru define true humanity in terms of social conventions that differentiate themselves from other ethnic groups and also from animals. These conventions fall into three categories: proper language (Chikaguru), proper alimentation, and proper restraints and rules regarding sexual behavior. These
constitute culture (umoto, "hearth"). Kaguruland is the space occupied by people who believe these modes of behavior are the only fit ways to behave. Yet
examination of these ideas and practices indicates ambiguity and contradiction as these occur in varied places. This reveals inevitable tensions between
village and domestic affairs, between open and concealed social life, and ultimately between society and the individuals comprising it. Moral space in Ukaguru is more complex and heterogeneous than Kaguru generally maintain.

Space, Speech, and Gender

Judging speech morally, Kaguru sort it into three broad categories determined by ethnicity, age, and gender.

First of all, Kaguru argue that sharing a natal language, Chikaguru, assumes commitment to a fair exchange of information. In contrast, outsiders are said to be false or shameless in speech and merit little consideration or respect as to how Kaguru speak to them. Some Kaguru describe ethnic outsiders as uncircumcised and consequently unlikely to know how to speak or otherwise conduct themselves properly.[8] (By mentioning circumcision, Kaguru are saying that outsiders have not been transformed by proper movements through space: out of settlements and into the initiation camps in the bush, and then returning to settlements.) In any case, speech is always constituted spatially (J. Weiner 1991: 64).

Second, only with maturation (initiation) do true (jural) responsibilities adhere to what Kaguru say. Kaguru adults, especially initiated males, are responsible for their speech. In contrast, women were never traditionally conceded full jural adulthood and remained jurally subordinated to the men responsible for them. That, of course, is slowly changing with modern laws and customs.

Both male and female novices emerge from initiation with a new sense of responsibility, although only with further age and experience are social skills in speech perfected. Younger adult men rely upon elder kinsmen to speak for them. Only recently have Kaguru women felt free to plead legal cases without support from men. A man who never attains skills in public speaking is "like a child" or "like a woman" (uncircumcised). Kaguru say that mature men should speak in measured ways reflecting careful thought. To speak wisely is to speak slowly, since this indicates deliberation and consideration of what others will think. Kaguru often say that women would feel uncomfortable speaking in public before many men.

Verbal abuse and slander are serious jural offenses for adult Kaguru of either gender. Since only men speak openly at meetings and ceremonies, it is what men speak that is publicly disputed. Still, adult women are accountable for what they say, and older women, especially mothers of adult men, exert considerable moral force in their comments. The main negative sanctions against improper speech by both Kaguru women and men is not litigation but the everyday give-and-take of household and village communications. In contrast, children's speech is not seriously accountable.

Third, gender governs how and also where speech is judged. Kaguru distinguish between spaces in which it is appropriate for men to hold forth verbally and those where women may appropriately do so. Kaguru agree that men traditionally should conduct public ritual invocations and supplications, plead and judge legal cases, and negotiate exchange of bridewealth and payments for damages. Yet everyone knows that such speeches, as everywhere, are often tedious in their sanctimonious compliance with public decorum, in their smooth attempts to kowtow to important people. Formal speeches often accounted as the exclusive domain of men are therefore also those most prone to criticism by both men and women as being full of hot air, humbug, and hypocrisy. The very decorum accounting for men's supposedly deliberate public speech also may lead some to criticize that speech as artificial, as lacking spontaneity and candor.[9] Kaguru men also engage in secret speech where they convey knowledge about divination, curing, and lore hidden from others, especially the young. Kaguru men engage in important forms of both public and covert speech, though it is the former that is most mentioned as distinguishing men from women and children.

Kaguru say women should not speak freely in formal, large assemblies but instead depend upon male kin to speak for them. This is because women should feel shame or fear at speaking before people in a public square. Some men say that women often speak too quickly because they do not always take care in what they say or because they get rattled. Yet many Kaguru (and I myself) recall memorable occasions when Kaguru women spoke out vigorously and well to make points that men missed. Yet for women to do so implies either that they have no confidence in their men or that their men are henpecked. Kaguru women and men commented on the weakness of men who allowed their wives to dominate them verbally in public. For a woman to criticize her husband before an assembly of other Kaguru might signify her intention to break with him, especially if she alludes to domestic sexual matters, which should on no account be mentioned outside household space.

While Kaguru men agree that "nice" women do not ordinarily speak at public gatherings, both men and women often mention the verbal skills of women. Such speech by women is best undertaken in private, most often within a house. All agree that it is the woman of a household who is most committed to the welfare of those within it, especially if the husband is polygynous and has other households or if the husband has wider political ambitions conflicting with his household loyalties. Because of a woman's supposedly deeper and narrower commitment to household solidarity, it is said that her children in particular should trust and rely on her advice and motives. She is said to be more heartfelt and sincere than a man. Women's speech therefore is likely to reign morally supreme inside a house.

Both men's and women's speech may be valued or criticized by other men and women, depending upon a person's social aims and needs. Virtues and flaws in men's and women's speech appear simply as two ways of evaluating similar attributes, with considerable overlap in how such evaluations are made. To the degree that men speak secretly or privately amongst themselves, especially regarding magical activities or political plotting, their words resemble the allegedly veiled speech of women. And to the degree that irate women risk speaking out in public, their speech takes on an open aggressiveness more ordinarily associated with men. If men's speech is stereotyped as wise because it recognizes public, political realities, others may condemn this for these same reasons, describing it as hypocritical and scheming. If women's speech is more discreet, more committed to affectual loyalties toward those nearest in kinship and residence, critics may condemn these qualities as signaling overemotionalism and being sneaky and shortsighted. The supposedly striking differences in men's and women's speech appear to be varyingly reflected in how different male and female protagonists judge particular situations and how they evaluate the open or closed milieux where speech occurs. The very qualities described as good sides to women's and men's speech can be twisted into being flaws, but also vice versa, as when a man holds his tongue to keep peace or when a woman speaks out to try to right a wrong.

So far I have considered only speaking, but not speaking is also a powerful means of expression. Kaguru consider silence, especially when associated with anger and resentment, to be more dangerous than open criticism and cursing. This is because one cannot be sure what the silent person feels and thinks, and the unknown may be more dangerous than the known. For Kaguru, withholding phatic speech, the conventional greetings and small talk that one should exchange when encountering another Kaguru on a path, at a market, at a watering point, could indicate hostility and danger. For Kaguru, an uncommunicative person is acting like a witch or zombie; all persons interacting in a commonly shared, public space should speak to one another often.[10]

Alimentation and Space

Kaguru believe their diet distinguishes them from neighbors, even though this is often not actually so. More important, Kaguru maintain that it is through diet and related etiquette that they, as social beings, are set apart from wild creatures of the bush. When Kaguru criticize someone's manner of eating, they compare her or him to an outsider or beast. Proper eating involves three interlinked acts: cooking, sharing, and restraint. Cooking food implies a household hearth and hence a proper home. For Kaguru, such an enclosed fire is almost exclusively the domain of women, as is processing that food, especially conversion of maize or millet into flour. For Kaguru a meal

Figure 5. Kaguru wife dressed in her best clothes for the photographer. Photograph taken at Berega in 1957.

expresses an integrated domestic unit: a woman has prepared it at a hearth (her domain), which in its turn is sheltered by an overarching roof and supporting beam (associated with a man). The processing and consuming of food move spatially in and out of Kaguru domestic space. Food is stored in the deepest recess of a house, accessible only to a householder, usually the wife. Consequently, a householder's actual food supply is secret and thus unsociably concealed from outside kin and neighbors. For that reason Kaguru speak of these same food stores as havens for witches' familiars, presumably expressing libidinous, more properly concealed tendencies toward individual aggrandizement.

While food is stored in a private, covert manner, it should be consumed openly, preferably with others. Yet ordinarily men do not eat publicly with women. To do so would display intimacy, permissible between women and children but signifying blatant, shameless sexuality between men and women. Therefore, men and women of the same matriclan should never eat from the same bowl. Commensality involves restraint. The presence of others should ensure that one shares and observes inhibiting etiquette demonstrating that one is a sociable, considerate person rather than a greedy and uninhibited beast. Restricting food consumption to public space expresses Kaguru concern that neighbors and kin be prepared to share and monitor resources.

For Kaguru, inversion of such alimentary behavior defines wild as contrasted to cultural behavior. It also signals immoral attitudes. For example, uncontrolled consumption of improper food in the bush, often gluttonously, indicates witchcraft. In such covens, commensality links humans and beasts sharing one feast of human flesh.

Yet lack of public alimentary restraint, while beastlike in many circumstances, is encouraged at village feasts celebrating the most important rites of passage, such as completion of the initiation of adolescent girls and boys into adulthood, the completion of marriage arrangements, and the end of mourning and the settlement of a deceased's estate. Then Kaguru try to outdo one another in unrestrained consumption. Meat and beer are preferred unstintingly, and anyone who holds back in providing or consuming is considered mean and witchlike (bestial).[11] These ceremonies mark the conclusion of powerful ritual work.[12]

Sexuality and Space

For Kaguru, sexual restraint also defines humanity. Proper humans do not couple randomly, as animals are thought to do. Rules of exogamy should be observed, and bridewealth and brideservice socialize (domesticate) sexual relations. Households cannot perpetuate themselves but rely upon other households and indeed upon other matrilineages and settlements to reproduce themselves. Such restraint is made visible socially at public exchanges validating marriage. Unions are recognized only after public receipt of wealth ratifying the match but also displaying information about the resources of the two groups involved. In contrast to public exchanges of bridewealth, the sexual act itself, like cooking, is appropriate only in the marital space at the very heart of any Kaguru house, a spot as secret and secluded as the food storage loft. This is a space deep within the house, near the hearth (feminine) and center pole (masculine), sectors epitomizing the wife and husband but also what Bachelard regards as the two key features of any dwelling, its "centrality" and "verticality" (1969: 17).[13]

Kaguru remark that sexual relations often produce a sense of shame and dirtiness, which requires them to be hidden from view. Even alluding to such matters indirectly in front of one's spouse while others are present is a serious breach of propriety. More than the consumption of food, sexual relations evoke profound ambiguity. Alimentation and sexuality force disparate groups to cooperate, exchange, and share. While domesticity conjoins groups through a married couple, it generates ties of loyalty and passions that divide that couple from the natal groups from which they come. For example, ties between adult siblings or between parents and adult children suffer in competition with intense relations between spouses. Self-interest, embodied in resources (readily externalized), may merge with domestic relations, but such seemingly rational factors may be overridden by hidden passion and sentiments sometimes generated in marriage. No formal (external) rules cover these private, intense possibilities. In contrast, immoral sexual relations are said usually to occur in the bush, often by day (potentially open and unsequestered and thus shameless). The most immoral acts of all, the incestuous fornications of witches, are thought to occur in the bush "as amongst wild animals," though often at night.

Most of the preceding observations pertain to space occupied by a married Kaguru couple sharing one dwelling. In this, "the house image would appear to have become the topography of our intimate being" (Bachelard 1969: xxxii). It is a haven of "intimate geometry" (ibid.: 218). Yet Kaguru homesteads often necessarily involve several dwellings. If a man is polygynous, each wife must have her own hearth, bed, and storage loft. Furthermore, once a couple's offspring reach puberty and are initiated, they cannot dwell in the same space as their parents. Boys must occupy a house (*isepo*) for single men and girls a house (*ibweti*) for unmarried women. The reasons for spatial segregation stem from previously mentioned notions about alimentation and sexuality. No adult of either gender may reside with a domestic couple. No unmarried man should have intimate access to a hearth. While a house may have some fire within it, especially for warmth and dryness during the cool, rainy season, only sexually mature women should use such a fire as a hearth for cooking. In the past nearly all hearths were controlled by married women or widows; today many divorced and single women keep their own homes and hearths. In any case, men do not ordinarily cook or brew beer, and they all depend upon women for meals, usually a wife or mother, occasionally a sister. For Kaguru men, initiation separates them from ready access to a woman's hearth, for they may no longer reside at their mother's. Only by marriage can men regain culinary access. Other than spouses or lovers, the only adults who might share a hearth would be adult women living together, such as a mother and daughter or two sisters, though this would be uncommon. Consequently, Kaguru settlements contain constellations of houses, some autonomous with their own hearths, others linked by their dependence on the hearths of others. Sexuality may integrate a simple homestead, but alimentation links many homesteads together in some settlements.

Village houses constitute physical manifestations of joint local labor, since most villagers help build each dwelling. While some Kaguru men specialize in laying out the frame and plan for a house, others help out by collecting wood, fiber, and thatch, carrying water, and digging and mixing earth for plaster. While a house is a private dwelling of a couple, it also exemplifies a joint investment in communal time and labor, which endows it with neighborly values.

SOCIETY AND THE BUSH

A broader aspect of Kaguru notions of space involves graduated contrasts between houses, settlements, and the bush (*kunyika* or *kumbago*). Just as a Kaguru house embodies a variety of moral spaces, ranging from the innermost interior through the doorway to the semipublic verandah, so too a settlement as a constellation of houses presents a graduated range of moral spaces. Houses are clustered around a plaza that comprises all the frontal spaces (*lugha*) lying before various house entries.[14]

Entryways to houses tend to face one another around a central village space.[15] Each frontal space is swept daily by the wife of the house and constitutes an area where residents sit during the day. These swept and ordered spaces externally represent the order of the households. Kaguru utilize such areas as stages where they present themselves for daily inspection by neighbors. Only seriously ailing Kaguru (or possibly witches) remain indoors for prolonged periods rather than sit outside.[16] Conversely, Kaguru settlements are encircled by disorder. Behind the cleared space of any house lies a trash heap, often thrown into a pit dug in order to secure earth for plastering the house. Farther from the house are areas where Kaguru urinate and defecate. ("The bush" *[kumbago]* is a Kaguru euphemism for "latrine.") A Kaguru settlement faces inward with its metaphorical backside toward the bush and strangers. At its farthest reach is the crossroads *(njila mkanda)*, where paths radiating from different villages intersect. That spot is a spatial void. It is not wilderness since it is cleared, yet it cannot be unequivocally assigned to any settlement from which the paths that constitute it stem. Such an equivocal space is the site where one discards polluting substances to be excluded from both social (settlement) and wild space (bush).

While a hearth, a bed, and a food storage loft constitute the core of a house, the plaza is the heart of a settlement. There a village presents itself to outsiders, much as those within a house present themselves to other villagers at the *lugha* before each entryway. Such a village square is truly public space, associated not with any particular household but with the village as a whole. It is in the central plaza that villagers entertain outsiders at weddings, initiations, and funerals. It is there that ceremonies marking rites of passage publicly acknowledge persons' new identities. This is achieved via formal speech, alimentation, and allusive sexuality (dance), the three modes by which Kaguru envision society and culture. In the central space of the village Kaguru greet visitors and discuss important events (those involving more than one settlement) with others. Such events are marked by feasting and drinking, essential for acknowledging social changes. Above all, such changes must be "danced," a group activity that Kaguru compare to sexual relations (cf. Evans-Pritchard 1965: 176–78). While actual sexual congress is a thing of shame and privacy, dancing—sexuality by artifice—is a desirable, sociable ceremony. Kaguru dancing involves regulated beats, postures, and movements followed within a public space; it never involves casual pairing of couples or bodily contact. Kaguru dancing sets men and women in complementary opposition to each other in ways that Kaguru find erotic (cf. Spencer 1985: 32–33). Women form circles, beating drums and singing. Men enter the enclosed space formed by such a group, a kind of "dance plaza," where they perform singly or in twos and threes, in competition with one another and vying for women's attention and approval. Men are central, exhibitionistic dancers, while women encircle men, set the beat, and impart inspiration. Of course, men sometimes stand and drum, and women sometimes dance vigorous solos, but a general contrast prevails between the more active, soloist males and the more stationary, grouped, encircling, observing women. Yet the most important feature of

Figure 6. Kaguru men and women dancing at a girls' initiation. Kaguru women would wear such beaded headdresses only at initiation or marriage dances. Photograph taken at Berega in 1957.

Kaguru dancing at ceremonies is more than sexual; it conveys a sense of validation to some communal event, an "intelligence of feeling" (Blacking 1985: 72).[17] The spatial presentation of self and groups is paramount at such Kaguru affairs. These observations and my earlier remarks pertain to Kaguru festive dancing that celebrates the rites of passage that affect everyone. In contrast, modern romantic dancing, where bodies touch to the beat of a guitar and a tapped bottle or to a band on a radio, would not be allowed in the public space of a settlement. This might occur in a bar or at a government market. When a few young Kaguru in a village where I stayed wanted to dance to music from a radio, they had to dance out in the bush at night where "no one" could see or hear them.

Speech, alimentation, and sexual relations represent personalized modes of sociability, but for Kaguru these are also means for expressing transcendence into society (cf. Bakhtin 1984: 256). Rites of passage evoke all three of these expressive modes, which represent a total, socialized human state, a submergence into the group. The festive gatherings staged within a settlement present eating, drinking, and dancing amongst men and women in an open, publicly monitored manner. This divests such activities of their otherwise intensely personal and dangerously charged egoistic implications. Informal eating and drinking or extensive physical expressivity between adults of the opposite sex should not occur in small, open, casual gatherings, where they would signify actual sexual relations. Such dances are the only occasions when men and women openly flaunt their grooming so as to appeal seductive to each other. Some Kaguru do use ceremonial feasting, drinking, and dancing in order to flirt or make assignations. In contrast to such public, valued festivities, the secret night dancing of witches in the wilderness is said to end in incest and other defilements.

Kaguru are keenly aware that public festivities are permissive and consequently potentially dangerous to domestic and village order, even though on the surface they epitomize the very opposite, village and neighborly solidarity and joy. Kaguru speak of such valued gatherings as being particularly vulnerable to the hidden powers of witches and the magic of sorcerers. The contradictory feelings of excitement and release that Kaguru say they experience at such celebrations undoubtedly derive from the opportunities these occasions afford to express what is ordinarily repressed or constrained. Just as it is proper etiquette to show restraint in daily public speech, mealtime etiquette, and avoidance of sexually suggestive behavior, so too it is proof of one's festive spirit and good nature that one is willing "to let one's hair down" at public celebrations. To act in a cool manner at such public affairs might suggest that one had something to hide, such as ill will. To be reserved at celebrations is as inappropriate as it is to act in an abandoned manner when not celebrating. Falassi's phrase "time out of time" (1987: 4) seems most apt for such occasions, but then so would "space beyond space."

While plaza and household spaces alternate as sectors of expression and repression at celebratory and everyday occasions, extrasettlement space may be deployed in an equally complex, ambiguous manner. The bush is space where both highly social (moral, public) and highly individualistic (amoral or immoral, private) acts occur. These apparent inconsistencies confirm the moral order of settlements: "Sometimes, it is in being outside itself that being tests consistencies" (Bachelard 1969: 215). The wilderness helps define what we think we are not, though the wild is never truly alien because it often represents our libidinous desires (White 1972: 5–7).

Kaguru commit adultery, are said to practice witchcraft orgies, and secure powerful sorcery, medicinal, magical, and rainmaking substances in and from the bush. When doing so they are said to speak magical words, often while alone, in contrast to proper speech, which must be exchanged with a fellow listener. Such substances reach full power only with the help of words uttered to oneself in the wilderness. Unlike public lore, that of the bush and the words that make its magic are secretly held and never revealed or passed on in any openly acknowledged, regulated manner.

The bush evokes a morally blurred set of forces to which the dead correspond in their obscure and sometimes capricious nature. The Kaguru dead are buried in the bush, and consequently Kaguru repeatedly assemble there in order to invoke the dead to provide fertility, well-being, and protection. Yet the dead are often sources of illness and misfortune if they are forgotten or crossed. At ancestral invocations, spatial order is reversed and the wilderness is treated like settlement space. These are the only occasions when people properly assemble in the bush. (In contrast, witch covens are said to assemble there secretly at night.) The burial space is swept clean and clear, like settlements (sometimes even a miniature fence and roofed shelter are temporarily erected and graves marked by stones similar to hearthstones), domestic animals are slaughtered, beer and flour are aspersed, and ritual meals consumed (see Briggs 1918: 17). These activities (except slaughtering) are ordinarily conducted in settlement clearings. At gatherings for the dead, public, formal oration occurs in the bush, quite improper under other circumstances. (The only other public gathering I ever attended in the bush where oration occurred was an illegal vigilante meeting.) The most sacred, social act of communion with the ancestral dead thus occurs in wild space, which for a passing time is demarcated and reclaimed by and for ordered society. Yet the dead's association with the bush has a dangerous side similar to witchcraft. The disgruntled dead not only cause misfortune but also may trespass quite literally into the nonbush. Kaguru believe that the angry dead may assume forms of wild animals that destroy crops, such as bush pigs and baboons. Boundaries between the space of the dead (wilderness) and the living (settlement) may thus be positively broken at ceremonies of invocation by the living but negatively broken when the dead return on their own, uninvoked. Death itself is sometimes described as a wild beast of the bush, an elephant or a person-eater that has entered a village.

Both the private sorties of magicians and witches and the open pilgrimages of ancestral propitiators take Kaguru into the bush because they recognize that the disorder of the wilderness is a kind of wholeness constituting potency, both constructive and dangerous. The order of settlements and of sociable living precludes such unbounded force. Yet for society to tap indiscriminate powers, people must leave domesticated space temporarily for the bush. The hidden, individualistic powers of Kaguru diviners, herbalists, curers, magicians, and sorcerers (not to mention morally dissolute witches and adulterers) arise from these people's capacity to confound spatial separations. They bring powers of the wilderness into settlements. The hidden powers of the wilderness tapped by such Kaguru resemble the hidden sexual and alimentary resources nested in the interiors of Kaguru dwellings. Both doctors and wrongdoers evince problematic space beyond ordinary control. The space that is most interior (within the house) and that which is most exterior (beyond settlements) are equally libidinous and privatized. Both the walls of a house and the undergrowth of the bush conceal much that outsiders want to learn in order to gain power.

Kaguru repeatedly describe the Itumba Mountains as the moral heart of their country and the part that is least inhabited, least socialized; mountaintop forests, pools, and burial sites are rarely visited, even avoided, yet they are imbued with supernatural powers.[18]

Finally, there is the most problematic space of all for Kaguru: sites of abandoned settlements. Such places are assumed to have seen some misfortune—death, disease, witchcraft. Why else would people flee a spot they had settled? Kaguru believe that witches meet in such places. Such sites are problematic because they are morally unclaimed and no longer properly owned, yet they are not engulfed by the bush. Kaguru abhor the unclaimed; for example, they fear taking presumably lost goods found on a path or at a marketplace. Unclaimed property is dangerous in its unknown identity (owner). (The bush is not owned by anyone unless perhaps by the dead or God.) An abandoned village, like lost goods, is problematic because, as a social artifact, it should have, but lacks, an identifying owner.

SPACE, TIME, AND AGRICULTURE

Kaguru notions of space cannot be separated from those of time; space is "compressed time" (Bachelard 1969: 8). That time in turn is linked to a round of rituals redolent of the symbols and space of initiation.

Kaguru mark the onset of each new calendrical year with rituals to the ancestral dead. These precede clearing of the land for the annual agricultural cycle. In the past, these rites involved the extinguishing of all hearths and their subsequent rekindling with fire made in the bush (making fire with firesticks is a symbolic sexual act). After the hearths are rekindled, fire is used to clear the fields and encourage new grass.[19] Ritual acts involving orations and alimentation (sacrifice) and symbolizing sexuality (fire making) are conducted in the wilderness but ultimately enrich social, domestic space (Beidelman 1986: chapter 3).

The annual cycle of rainy and dry seasons imposes a systole and diastole of social density upon Kaguru social space. During the rains members of individual households work intensively in fields outside their villages with little concern for sociability between households. Even the rules against cooking food outside the household and against men and women openly eating together are relaxed, at least when some Kaguru spend prolonged periods outdoors cultivating away from settlements. Work parties of men, women, and children catch a snack together whenever they can while working long hours in the fields.

During the dry season after harvest Kaguru find more leisure, and households of different villages visit. Food resources are at their height and sustain group rituals and sociability. Food may and should be openly consumed and shared as the tangible "triumph through work" (cf. Bakhtin 1984: 281-82). Kaguru regularly change their spatial focus with the two seasons, turning inward socially with the rains (though spending more time outside their villages) and turning outward socially with the dry season and harvest (though now spending more time in villages [cf. Mauss 1979b]).[20]

RITES OF PASSAGE

In contrast to the changes of the seasons, Kaguru rites of passage, the rituals of birth, initiation, marriage, and death, mark and celebrate societal time as it relates to personal time. They domesticate or enculturate the biologically rooted processes by which we as individuals become aware of socially unruly time. They socialize individual careers into comparable, repeated units. Such rites stage actions at an accelerated pace and within a restricted social space. This staging provides a sense of mastering the challenge of change. The least complicated of these rituals are associated with birth; the most complicated are associated with initiation of young people into womanhood and manhood. We should consider these rites not only set by set but also as a single system. What is important for Kaguru (and consequently for us as analysts) is that these rites represent different facets of a unitary, cyclical developmental process. Kaguru see each of these ritual occasions as redolent of what lies ahead and what has already passed. Kaguru remark on the similarity of all these processes and associated rites. They infuse these with the common cultural themes of constrained or elaborated speech, alimentation, sexuality, and, above all, play with space. Rites of passage confront bodily change but embroider upon it, "cooking" and "garnishing" its rawness with cultural conventions. The social mannerisms of cuisine, dress, language, and conventionalized gestures enshroud and yet also reveal such bodily flux, just as the order of garb both conceals and reveals the body by enhancing it.[21] Similarly, by managing movement within regulated, morally valenced spaces, change is further orchestrated and controlled. The ceremonious acts performed at each such rite evoke and echo those at others. Consequently, those involved—the attendants and officiants even more than the actual subjects of the ritual attention—are repeatedly made aware of how this series of rites of passage, spanning an entire lifetime, reflects a single, integrated whole.

KAGURU RITES AT BIRTH

Giving birth is dangerous to women; the Kaguru, like Medea, compare this to the battles of men. Women sometimes die in childbirth and always shed blood, a polluting substance. Children enter this world from the land of the dead *(kusimu)*. Birth *(cheleko)* is secluded because it places both mother and child in a profoundly vulnerable position: they are in contact with death, they are hot because of shed blood and broken body surfaces, and in their physically weakened state they are open to the malevolent forces of witches and sorcerers.

A Kaguru mother and child remain deep within a house for the first four days after birth. Usually only female kin go within a house where a woman is delivering. Certainly no men are allowed. During and immediately after birth the infant is considered poised precariously between the land of ancestral dead *(kusimu)*, whence it came, and that of the living.

On the child's fourth day of life the umbilical cord *(chikufa)* should be sufficiently dry either to drop off or to be cut. It is then secretly buried by the midwife. Now the ceremony of *kakula*, "it has grown," may be held and the infant brought out through the entryway of the house in order to meet the social world. The child is placed upon a winnowing tray *(iselo)*, which is later waved over it *(kuhunga)*. The tray, used by women to separate edible grain (social) from chaff (wild) in ordinary household chores, here facilitates a separation of the infant from the other world, epitomized by a bateleur eagle *(ikungu)*, which is believed to be warded off by this action. The eagle is a Kaguru convention for the dead, who yearn to have the newborn infant back amongst themselves and who sometimes take the form of raptors in order to seize it (Beidelman 1964a; 1974b: 187). At this coming-out rite neighbors and kin assemble about the doorway to greet the child. It is especially good to have the father's sister present, the father's kin being complementary to one's own matrilineage. (As I noted earlier, a man and his sister have especially profound moral and emotional ties with each other.) It is father's kin who provide one's most public name (Beidelman 1975), as contrasted to terms referring to one's own matriclan, which are too personal or private to be freely mentioned. It is also father's kin who will, presumably many years ahead, occupy a prominent ritual place in conducting one's inquest and funeral, that rite mirroring birth. Finally, it is a father's sister whose own children will constitute some of one's keenest rivals for inheritance and who therefore may resent one's birth.

In this simple rite of *kakula* a Kaguru enters social space, separated from the dead. The infant moves from the innermost, secret sector of a dwelling to the *lugha* facing the village square. There it is greeted by kin who have journeyed from other villages and who stand affinally to the woman in whose arms the infant is now proferred. Death and sexuality are problematic attributes of the deepest recesses of a dwelling, generative yet dangerous and powerful. The infant's social emergence from this private core of the house into the outer verge involves a spatial acknowledgment that it has now embarked on a passage away from these concealed, inner forces (including the dead) toward more stable social relations beyond its mother. Ideally, this ceremony constitutes the first of what will be many social occasions in which maternal and paternal kin, household and collateral kin, will interact. (We shall later see that this social emergence from the mother's sphere is echoed at boys' initiation.)

Infants continue to undergo further, comparable rites as they grow and become ever more separated from the space of the ancestral dead. I here cite only one more of these rites, *kugeta* (shaving). I briefly mention this because the shaving of hair figures prominently in initiation, in mourning, and in sexual imagery in general. First- and second-born children are likely to receive their first significant names (public identities) at such a ceremony. (Subsequent children may not always receive such treatment.) The firstborn's hair is cut by maternal kin, the second-born's by paternal. These two sets of kin thereby acknowledge that they are now linked for many years, at least so long as these offspring, and subsequent ones, survive, even if the parents' marriage itself dissolves. This rite also is thought of as a kind of spatial emergence, figuratively and literally, from a house (which Bachelard aptly likens to a cradle [1969: 7]).

Infants, at least for a year or two, nurse at their mother's breast. This is thought to make a child especially close to its mother, both physiologically and emotionally. A good mother should put nursing ahead of enjoying a return to sexual relations. Sexual intercourse during nursing is thought to turn a woman's milk hot (*moto*) and consequently dangerous to the child.[22] Many argue that only selfish parents would resume sexual relations so early as to hinder an infant's growth. Some women resist husbands' urgings to resume sexual relations by pointing this out. If a Kaguru woman has difficulty nursing, her husband or kin might hold a small dance and beer party to encourage the ancestral dead to bring her milk.

INITIATION OF ADOLESCENTS

Kaguru girls undergo most of their initiation into womanhood deep within a house, removed from the view of men but still within the heart of some man's settlement. A girl comes into prolonged association with that kind of space with which she will be later constantly associated as mistress of a hearth inside a home. Some related rites may be performed in public view outside, but these do not involve the novice herself, who remains concealed within. On some days, women gather indoors with the initiate to sing and even dance, the only time in Kaguru life when anyone dances indoors. It always struck me as one of the most powerful occasions at Kaguru women's initiation when those waiting and watching outside hear singing, drumming, and commotion as part of women's concealed, house-enclosed festivities, which are said to bring destructive creatures of the bush, such as bush pigs, into a settlement. At times women leave the house and appear in the village plaza to enact fragments of this scenario.

During a girl's confinement she is thought to undergo a gradual change produced by intensive care from the women attending her. They feed and nurture the childlike novice (*mwali*), making her more fit to become a wife and mother. A well-initiated girl should emerge fat, pale, soft, and well schooled in sexual and household matters. At the end of this period, the girl is brought out from the initiation house and into the village square to be recognized as a newly constituted woman, ready to be wed and bear children.

In contrast, at a boy's initiation into adolescence he is taken into the bush far from any settlement. He is circumcised and then remains there in the bush until he has recovered. He is said to have died (to his childhood, viz., to his maternal ties) with the shedding of his blood and foreskin. He is now considered reborn as an adult. Instead of being protected, nurtured, and concealed, a boy is exposed to the elements, hazed by older males, and disciplined. As part of this ritual death, the boy is threatened by the destructive beasts of the bush, which, his initiators warn, may devour him. He should emerge strong, tough, lean, and hardened from his ordeal as well as properly informed about sexuality and manly behavior. No such dramatic and abrupt transformation is thought to occur for girls. Kaguru describe changes in girls as gradual and less strikingly reflected in subsequent comportment. Unlike boys, girls remain in a familiar social environment, doing the same household chores (albeit in con-finement). They remain jural minors with continued and unbroken access to a domestic hearth, though no longer that of their mother unless the mother is widowed or divorced and living apart from any man.

Unlike a boy, a girl bleeds "naturally" at the onset of adolescence (men-struation) and then again when she undergoes an operation comparable to boys' circumcision, labiadectomy. Neither the girl's "natural" bleeding nor her socially inflicted wound is thought to change her radically in the way cir-cumcision is believed to alter boys. Yet it is girls whose lives most rapidly change after initiation on account of early marriage, whereas boys rarely marry until much later. Kaguru remark about the greater drama of boys' ini-tiation; this stems from the fact that Kaguru believe that boy initiates undergo a kind of death, whereas they reject such a dramatic view of the changes un-dergone by girls. Initiated boys die to society by being engulfed (or ingested) by the wilderness before being reborn or disgorged as jurally adult males, no longer so bound to their mothers. Kaguru sometimes speak of actual death it-self as an ingestion by a beast *(dikoko)* of the wilderness and of a corpse as a wild elephant *(nhembo)*. Kaguru girls undergo no such spatial uprooting until initiation is past.

At initiation Kaguru males become keenly aware that their adult identities derive from forces outside a household and are bestowed by other males. Male transformation occurs in a wild space open to the scrutiny of any adult males who care to look but removed from the ready sight of all women and children. It is the only place where Kaguru males ever eat and sleep for much time out-side both house and village. Yet even after all this is acknowledged, it remains that the deepest level of men's identities derives through mothers and sisters, the matriline. This, however, is so basic that it is rarely even spoken about.

SPACE AND MARRIAGE

Kaguru marriages, while important, hardly compare to either initiations or funerals in their significance for constructing personhood. One may marry several times, late or early, with ease or with difficulty. In contrast, birth, ini-tiation, and death each occurs only once and inevitably. Marriage requires the sponsorship of kin; attempted against their auspices, it requires considerable individual persistence and resources. Marriage remains a rite of passage sub-ject to social manipulation and strategies; birth, adolescence, and death brook little such particularized tinkering.

To marry *(kutola* or, more traditionally, *kukwela)* marks true and successful adulthood for a man. This is because proper fatherhood exists only within marriage. Parenthood is profoundly important for both Kaguru women and men, but while both sexes usually marry, men are acknowledged as parents only through some publicly witnessed payments (such as bridewealth) even if they might have fathered a child.

This problematic importance of marriage payments (or brideservice and associated arrangements), collectively termed *lusona*, accounts for the emphasis on the open enactment of all transactional ceremonies. Marriage arrangements should be conducted in open village space. They should be readily visible to everyone involved and preferably to outsiders as well because they may then serve as future witnesses in case these matters are later contended. Marital negotiations involve formal assembly of both the bride's and groom's kin at the village of the bride's parents. There the bride's and groom's relatives confront each other, occupying separate, oppositional spaces, and each is in turn further separated into matrilineal and paternal kin. Protracted speeches and slow deliberation of nuptial exchanges (even when the terms are more or less already settled) all contribute to a sense of gravity and open, contested ceremony. Such discussions consume time regardless of whether or not they were quickly settled privately because these should publicly demonstrate the concern and importance of the groups involved.

Once arrangements are settled, their conclusion is often marked by the public anointing of kin, a ceremony also associated with both naming and the end of initiation. After marriage, a wife may be addressed as an extension of her new spouse, for example, "wife of Chilongole." Similarly, birth ceremonies implicitly involve new names, not only for the infant but also for parents, who may now assume teknonyms. Actual consummation of a marriage is staged spatially in ways that recall both birth and death, emergence into a new social status, and end of an old one. It also suggests births of children that should follow. New couples are secluded within a house, usually at the bride's village. These are days of confinement *(majuwa mifungata)*. The couple remains indoors, presumably engaged in sexual intercourse. There is no working hearth in their dwelling because they are fed (like children) by elder women from other households and consume food together indoors (very sexy), not separately and outside like proper married people. The bride and groom are termed novices *(wali)* just as if they were newly shaven and anointed initiates. Secluded, dependent persons, oriented both inwardly within the closed house and externally through their dependence for sustenance upon others, they remain confined for the traditional four to seven days. In the past some couples did not use cooking hearths (and were therefore not fully autonomous spatially) until after their first harvest or until delivery of a first child. The couple's social autonomy was not spatially and alimentarily confirmed until the union appeared productive, either through offspring or at least through the harvest of crops, demonstrating successful cooperative labor.

Public confirmation of a couple's full marital status is made by the rite of entering *(kwingisa)*. The new husband enters the household of his father-in-law and eats with his new male affines. Correspondingly, the new wife resumes eating with other women, usually her new affines. About this time, the emerging couple is given examples of various Kaguru utensils associated with adult men and women, weapons for men and food-processing utensils for women. They are shown how to use these as though they were children learning skills for the first time. The couple emerges technologically, not just spatially and commensally, from private domestic space into open, cooperative household space. Marriage is sealed by a negative spatial reorientation. From now on, the husband should sedulously avoid open association with his wife's mother and other senior women of her matrilineage. This recognizes the sexuality that he and his wife enjoy. Open association with such affines would suggest that he did not respect his marriage but rather wrongly assumed sexual rights over all women of his wife's lineage, thereby making such women sexual competitors. Marriage thus involves spatial transitions, enacted first through inward retreat into libidinous seclusion within intimate household areas and then followed by gradual reemergence into the restrictive open space of the local settlement.

SPACE AND DEATH

Two very different spatially staged sequences are enacted to observe death: one involving burial, the other, mourning and funerals. Burial involves transference of a dangerous and polluting corpse from the open, orderly space of the settlement into the bush and under the ground. Funerals and mourning involve movements and transformations of the living survivors within a settlement as these move from inverted use of open and secluded space back to their ordinary employment. Observed properly, these two sequences should effect a transference of the deceased's spirit into the land of the dead.

At death, a corpse is given immediately to joking partners *(watani)*, who wash, shave, and enshroud the body, preferably in an even number of cloths, sometimes compared to an enfolding womb. They then transport it out of the house to the burial site in the bush. The dead are so dangerous that their own kin may not safely come into contact with them. The dead are especially dangerous to children, who may be lured back into the land of their ancestors. Burial is undertaken by joking partners because they stand spatially apart in an ambiguous, pivotal social category. Joking partners epitomize spatial peripheries, traditionally coming from areas beyond a settlement. They relate to settlement owners as settlements stand to adjacent areas in clan-defined space (Beidelman 1966a). These *watani* bury the corpse out in the bush yet near enough to a settlement for the grave to be readily reached for future propitiation. There in the bush joking partners perform the first such ancestral sacrifices, after clearing the burial area and making a small cairn of rocks. Such rites will be repeated over the years as Kaguru periodically leave their settlements to seek help from the dead who, though now in the wild, continue to influence the settled living. Contact with and propitiation of these dead are facilitated through clearing, sweeping, and marking of their burial sites, invoking their names, and sacrificing goods, all of which temporarily impose a precarious social order onto undomesticated, wild space. Death, burial, and associated sacrifice constitute another form of initiation. Kaguru say that death is a birth into the land of the dead, for it produces a new ancestral spirit *(musimu)*.

Back at the settlement of the bereaved, the hearth fire at the deceased's house is extinguished. During mourning no food may be prepared within the house. The deceased's female kin must remain deep within the house, continuously crying so that those outside who cannot see them know that those within are grieving. Outside, male kin of the deceased assemble to greet visiting mourners and there relate the events associated with the death. During mourning, men and women comport themselves inversely from ordinary life in that women remain indoors but are heard wailing by the public outside; conversely, men remain outside but their speech and comportment now resemble those of women in being quiet and subdued. Mourning men sit around a fire, the alternate to the extinguished hearth within. This is one of the very few times that fire is appropriate within a Kaguru settlement plaza outside the confines of a hearth.

Mourning continues for four to seven days, about the same length of time observed for ritual preparations associated with marriage and birth. Mourners should shave their bodies and heads and refrain from work. At the end of mourning, they are said to be reborn and may resume their ordinary activities. The degree to which these restrictions are observed depends upon how closely one is related to the deceased. Close kin are often presented with basic Kaguru utensils and shown how to use them, much as is done for Kaguru newlyweds. At this time, too, key personal possessions of the deceased are brought out from the privacy of the house and transmitted to some heir.

Figure 7. Newly dug and covered Kaguru graves. The cut banana stems and leaves on top mark them as new. The stones mark them more permanently so that they may be located and cleared of undergrowth at times of sacrifice and propitiation of the dead. Photograph taken at Berega in 1957.

These objects are closely associated with gender, such as a man's weapons, a woman's cooking utensils and her cosmetic-oil gourd. A wife's main cooking pot is shattered, signifying the end of a particular hearth.[23] The culmination of these mourning ceremonies, sometimes held long after the bereaved have actually emerged from their mourning restrictions, involves a feast at which the deceased's estate is publicly settled (*madango*, "cutting into pieces") and various claimants are given their due. Kaguru say that the main subjects involved at such occasions are marriage and birth since the bulk of such wealth stems from rights and payments connected with bridewealth associated with the deceased, the deceased's spouse, and the deceased's descendants. Kaguru link funerals, marriages, and births in this way, saying that they are all occasions for eating (*kudia*), referring to the devouring of wealth but also to sexuality, which is associated with appetites and sustenance.

My discussion of death and mourning applies only to adults. Traditionally Kaguru could not openly mourn the uninitiated, who were never considered full social beings. The uninitiated could only be mourned covertly and were not buried with the ancestral dead. They were deposited near settlements and, according to some Kaguru, occasionally even in the grounds of the settlement itself, especially if they were infants. Executed witches and those dying of polluting diseases were left in the bush, but unlike other dead they were unburied and unmarked. They became not ancestors but instead malicious spirits.

The mourners' movements in and out of domestic (private) and settlement (public) space ritually reflect a repeated interplay between a household, their kin, and neighbors. The public side of burial rites is dominated by joking relations (with neighbors and affines) situated at the margins of a household's social loyalties and social space relations. Household mourning is contrastingly manifested by female mourners confined within the house and male kin confined to the place outside. Combined, these three contrasted modes of mourning reassert a sense of social and spatial order in the disturbed household and neighborhood.

Funeral deliberations further express this interplay of insiders and outsiders. Paternal kin take charge of the final accounting of those social issues on everyone's mind, the reallocation of resources and the question of possible blame regarding the circumstances behind the death. Such paternal kin both complement and oppose the centripetal tendencies of the household and matrilineage. It is the "outsider" paternal kin who speak out and express all that need be spoken, while "insider" maternal kin and household members remain silent. Kaguru themselves are keenly aware that these same paternal kin perform crucial activities at birth and naming ceremonies. Matrilineal, paternal, and affinal ties interplay, each taking center stage for a time, at these various rites and ceremonies. Each in turn enacts the varying dimensions of a Kaguru's individualized career. In this, Kaguru funerals and mourning reveal the attributes that Falassi reports necessary to define a festival: "reversal, intensification, trespassing and abstinence" (1987: 3), though nothing here is festive.

So far I have considered the relation between Kaguru notions of space and Kaguru social life in terms of both everyday and ceremonial orientation, in terms of both quotidian life and dramatic rites of passage. I next want to consider the motifs I have previously discussed in terms of broader, deeper patterns. I now consider how Kaguru notions of space relate to Kaguru historical and legendary times (the cult of the ancestors) and, finally, to the broadest aspects of Kaguru thinking and social organization, to Kaguru social structure. In doing this I hope to show how Kaguru spatial references in quotidian and ritual experience are consistent and supportive of a coherent and integral Kaguru world picture.

SPACE AND LEGENDARY TIME

Novel manipulation of space facilitates imagining a distant, legendary past. It does so in two ways: through incorporating familiar bodily sets and processes into alien frames of space, and through incorporating the landscape into broader, cosmic levels. These two poles, the human and the cosmic, are combined in Kaguru legends of the origins of their society (see Beidelman 1970; 1986, chapter 5). As Tuan notes, "The intention to go to a place creates historical time" (1977: 130). According to such legends, the Kaguru's ancestors came from the west, trekking with men to the right (south) and women to the left (north). They marched out of the wilderness and into what is now home, where they settled, clan by clan. For Kaguru, movement from east to west, like the sun, epitomizes normal process. The movement portrayed in this legend represents a reversal of this, leading to the extraordinary, the birth of society and culture as Kaguru understand them. Through this trek the Kaguru as a people came into public being; they came to light; they took on historical visibility. It is a process comparable to human birth itself, which is an emergence from the unfathomable sphere of the dead (west). It is also similar to initiation (*mlao*, "emergence"). In contrast, ordinary or daily transformations are marked by movement from east to west, as with the rising and setting sun. (Certain negative magical processes should, however, proceed from west to east.)

The various Kaguru clan origin legends all stress the difficulties of the trek. Effort and struggle help construct notions of great distance in time and space. Such pain and effort parallel birth and initiation and are consistent with Kaguru ideas about sacrifice and struggle being needed to create and reap rewards (cf. Tuan 1977: 129). In telling such legends Kaguru recite a catalogue of place names linked to clan histories and their present surroundings; place names become "iconographic incapsulations of a human history" (J. Weiner 1991: 50).

The Kaguru origin legends relate how the first settler for each clan was an adult woman who claimed clan land through kindling fire (hearth), clearing and cultivating land, and settling upon it in a cave. She began the process of imposing order upon wild space. Yet she did not establish full social order, for she had no proper mate or house. That she inhabited a cave rather than a house implies that she needed men to construct full social space, a domestic place, a home.

Eventually this primal Kaguru woman encountered an immature youth who was hunting in the wilderness, a pursuit associated with men and suggesting male sexual potency and aggression. (Kaguru associate hunting with the cultural subjection of wild space and sometimes with political leadership.) The befriended (mothered) young man was eventually circumcised and, no longer a child, married the woman and established a proper household. To do so he first had to vanish from the area and return after his sexual transformation. The woman, first described as dwelling in a cave (a feminine recess in the bush), is now situated in a house with male (center pole) and female (hearth) attributes. A female cultivator and a male hunter are now paired and settled, establishing society in miniature. The legend portrays the creation of society by establishing ordered activities in ordered space (place). It portrays that society's fundamental attributes in terms of gender, property (land and house), and the associated activities of kindling fire, cooking, clearing land, and hunting, motifs repeated in most Kaguru rites. It conveys a sense of place (differentiated clan space as contrasted to general space) through a litany of place names that conjure up images of streams, drifts, valleys, and rock formations, the physiognomies of ancestral lands.[24]

These origin legends are repeatedly recited at Kaguru ceremonies, especially at adolescent girls' and boys' initiations. This teaches how the birth of Kaguru society and culture parallels the birth of an adult person. Kaguru society emerges from an ethnic and cultural wilderness to be established in ordered, settled space; Kaguru adolescents emerge from childhood and irresponsibility (and infantility) through initiation, a cutting held for males in the bush, in order to enter established, ordered, productive households.

ANCESTRAL RITES AND SPACE

Kaguru repeatedly conduct sacrifice *(nhambiko)* to propitiate the ancestral dead (see Beidelman 1986: chapter 7). Contact with the dead ensures life, for the dead are the ultimate sources of fertility in humans, livestock, and land. The dead are also a source of misfortune, largely because they feel annoyed at being neglected by the living or because of the living's misdeeds. Kaguru ambivalence toward the dead is consistent with the dead's profound power. For Kaguru, power (as contrasted with authority) is invariably ambiguous, bearing the capacity to harm as well as to help (see Beidelman 1980; 1986: chapter 11). The dead's space, the bush, reflects this. The bush is a realm of dangerous disorder but is also a source of enormous, potentially useful force. Rainmakers, diviners, and doctors, as well as sorcerers and witches, good as well as evil, all draw power from the wilderness. Kaguru repeatedly enter the bush in order to sustain their lives back in their settlements. During such forays they temporarily tame a small portion of that wild space. Sometimes they appropriate bits of the bush—certain leaves or roots, rainmaking stones, parts of wild animals—in order to make medicines that they take back into social space. More often, at ancestral rites elders convert a portion of the bush into a domesticated space through clearing or sweeping *(kushagila)* it of undergrowth, remarking a grave with stones evocative of the stones of a hearth, and sacrificing domestic animals, beer, flour, and tobacco. Some of this is consumed by the dead as it is scattered *(kunyaga)* on the cleared earth and stones, but much is also consumed as a feast by the living assembled there in communion with the dead. At other times, the character of the wilderness is thought to enter a settlement, causing misfortune and sterility, usually due to the ire of the dead but sometimes simply because the balance between the spheres of bush and settlement mysteriously falls out of joint. The settlement retaliates by temporarily entering ever further into the wilderness in order to reestablish order between the two spheres. Villagers do this by sacrifice.

While the members of a Kaguru clan (and its constituent matrilineages) bear responsibility for ancestral rituals, at the most important of these rituals, joking partners and not matrikin are in charge. Employment of such peripheral relatives for ritual parallels the spatial incorporation of the wilderness. A *mutani* stands on the side of the ancestral dead *(yekwima lwe musimu)* and speaks for and with them. For Kaguru, then, there is core and peripheral space and corresponding core and peripheral (supplementary) social groups. These are repeatedly confounded when confronting the dead, who are themselves a confounding of social and spatial attributes. The dead are manipulated by elders in ways that would be difficult to manage toward living people. Yet, conversely, the dead possess powers that influence the living in ways beyond any influence by those alive. The dead are a reservoir of moral judgment and punishment transcending the powers and justice of living elders; yet, at times, the dead appear perplexingly quirky and inexplicable in their wrath. The dead are sources of life yet sources of death and illness as well.

These ambiguous and ambivalent notions about both the wilderness and the dead are exemplified in Kaguru notions about wild animals. Here it is useful to digress briefly on Kaguru notions about animal life and about some human officiants at rituals as well, especially since animals and their lives in the bush figure prominently in Kaguru initiation rites and songs.

A great, admired, and envied hunter is a man who dominates the bush and all that dwells in it. A hunter invades the bush and triumphs over that space. Yet for a Kaguru to have very close relations with wild animals signifies not only domination but also possibly witchcraft. Witches share goods with beasts at the expense of fellow humans, whom they exploit. Sorcerers and magicians also dominate other humans. Like witches, sorcerers hunt fellow humans and not animals. Kaguru also believe that inauspiciously born infants (*figego*, which includes twins, breech deliveries, and those teething improperly) should be slain because they sap strength from kin and neighbors; *figego* have uncanny skill as hunters because they are born like animals. *Figego* resemble witches, antipathic to humans but in touch with beasts (Beidelman 1963c).

Human invasions of the wilderness bring power for good or ill. Conversely, for wild animals to invade social space such as cultivated fields signifies moral disorder; often the incursions are by angered ancestral spirits who take the forms of animal pests or predators. For creatures of the wilderness to enter a settlement itself, or worse, a plaza or house, means utter disaster (Beidelman 1963c, 1964a). Yet a few wild animals, such as porcupines and pangolins, provide hunting or fertility magic for some doctors, and these are slain and brought home to villages.

Joking partners *(watani)* bear comparison to wild animals in their ambiguous and pivotal peripheral positions in both society and space. They epitomize both the danger and power of conflated spheres (see Beidelman 1966a). Such ambiguously categorized people assume dangerous ritual tasks for a clan, such as burials, executions, purifications from incest, and ancestral propitiation, tasks that must be performed in the bush and which are too dangerous for direct exposure to immediate kin. In such rituals, joking partners introduce obscene, disruptive public behavior into settlements. They visit their partners and threaten to expropriate their property. They freely make accusations that few neighbors would dare make. Such acts bring disorder into a settlement. For these reasons joking partners are sometimes sarcastically compared to witches, to bush people. Such topsy-turvy behavior is consistent with joking partners' position as border people. They belong to clans whose lands traditionally border lands of people they abuse but also ritually serve in dangerous and polluting ceremonies. It is said that such border people are often one's affines (one marries enemies). In terms of group membership and attributes, joking partners invade or transcend space that is ordinarily respected and guarded against incursion. They are less than natal kin but more than strangers, less than members of a settlement but more than unconnected aliens. Actual affines (even spouses) or cross-cousins may in emergencies substitute for joking partners in carrying out rituals. This underscores the wide scope of these ambivalent social features since those kin are also considered highly problematic in their loyalties. Joking partners move spatially across boundaries because they belong to groups that straddle social loyalties as well as social space. Since most Kaguru ritual, and indeed ritual everywhere, involves movement across boundaries, Kaguru joking partners are ritual practitioners par excellence.

CONCLUSION

In the preceding pages I considered Kaguru rituals and daily activities in terms of the spaces, the social stages, in which they are enacted. This may appear obvious since, after all, human beings necessarily occupy space and must negotiate it to live. Space fits Bachelard's category of a "privileged phenomenon" (1964: 7) in that its universality allows its association with nearly anything. Pervading all situations, space provides a powerful means for integrating thinking and conduct over myriad situations. (I here refer both to how Kaguru themselves integrate their thoughts and actions and to how outsider analysts such as myself may best bring together their observations.) Space's integral relation to time means that it figures prominently in any portrayal of process or change. In such portrayals, encompassing space often lends a sense of seeming constancy to movement and individual change, as manifest in rites of passage. Such continuity and pervasiveness are essential for developing any sense of moral responsibility (cf. Hallowell 1967: 92–100).

Space is endowed with intense personal immediacy because of its association with the body. Kaguru spatial imagery bears this out. Moral attributes assigned to space repeatedly derive from bodily orientation, the senses, and physiological processes (cf. Mauss 1979a). The most powerful and striking example amongst Kaguru is the house, a bodily haven. It "constitutes a body of images that give mankind proofs or illusions of stability" (Bachelard 1969: 17). "The house thrusts aside contingencies; its councils of continuity are unceasing. Without it, man would be a dispersed being" (ibid.: 7). It invokes memories "as an invitation to repeat the practice of the past" (Hutton 1988: 322). The spatial imagery of the house, of domesticity, as expressed through regulated sexuality and alimentation provides the core of Kaguru notions about being social persons, about being properly human. For Kaguru the space of the house with "its countless alveoli . . . contains compressed time" (Bachelard 1969: 8). Kaguru notions of space extend out from this central, nesting model to include settlements. This presents a contrast between varied forms of socialized space and the outlying wilderness. Space, then, is integral to how Kaguru build up conceptions of the social self or person but also of more individualistic, divisive aspects of the self (Mauss 1979c). It provides the different stages on which these scenarios of selfhood are enacted. Centripetal and centrifugal social relations separating and linking houses, settlements, and neighbors have associations with gender for Kaguru.[25]

Kaguru notions of space are indissoluble from their notions of time. This is inherent to the problem of how humans can represent change in the first place. Consequently, the powerful moral valences that Kaguru attach to both space and the body are crucial to how Kaguru represent social change in the body and person. For Kaguru, and indeed for all people, ideas of bodily change are essentially appetitive. Our most powerful realizations of bodily change relate to the rise and ebb of hunger and sexual capacities. Our keenest realizations of other beings' existence lie in our dependence on others for nurturance and sexual fulfillment and the sexual reproduction of those who will replace or displace us. Even sustenance (alimentation) is redolent of sexuality, being associated with conjugality and parenthood. For Kaguru, time and hence space assume sexual associations related to growth and domination but also to dependence and death. These are prominent in rites of passage, particularly initiation, where full sexuality bestows full social personhood and hence recognized entry into the human cycle generated by sex itself.

In the preceding pages I indicated how space and time appear central to gender and rites of passage, and I refer to such rites in the broadest terms to include not only the creating of personhood but even the emergence of an entire society. This allows several conclusions.

First, space, time, and sexuality are inextricably linked for Kaguru. Readers will appreciate the connection between time and space and between time (age) and sex. Perhaps not so many will appreciate the profound sexual dimensions of space for Kaguru. The integral relation between all three should be obvious once we recognize that in traditional Kaguru society social personhood is almost entirely imbedded in family and kinship, which in turn are enacted in households, villages, and neighborhoods.

Second, concerns about proper speech, proper alimentation, and proper sexuality permeate every Kaguru social situation. How these attributes of culture and sociability are variously utilized, emphasized, downplayed, and twisted constitutes a main concern of this study. This is because initiation, and indeed all social education, rests on defining humanity, and for Kaguru (as perhaps for all societies) that is in how one masters these vital processes. The is tricky to learn because rules change with different social spaces.

Third, by organizing this chapter around one theme—space—rather than around a single ritual or set of rituals, I have shown how various themes or symbols crop up repeatedly in many different Kaguru rituals and ceremonies. The evocative power of these Kaguru symbols depends on their constant reappearance in different guises, contexts, and emphases. Any single Kaguru ritual evokes others, sometimes merely as a kind of ironic echo or hint of another occasion. Kaguru themselves see this déjà vu effect as one of the most compelling aspects of their ritual and etiquette. Each occasion is redolent of a wider and unending circle in space and time.[26]

While we can discern a series of powerful and repeated motifs in Kaguru thought and action, the meanings to be read into any single theme constantly change in tone and implications. This is because different Kaguru hold different interpretations of them. Furthermore, some things themselves have a particular density, an opacity, a particularly rich potential for embodying many different, even seemingly contrary meanings. Space is only one such thing. Sexuality is another. As people scrutinize and dissect matters over time and in different situations, these assume myriad significances. Bachelard is aware of this house-of-mirrors effect when he remarks on considering the seemingly rudimentary contrast between the inside of a house and outdoors: "Intimate space loses its clarity, while exterior space loses its void, void being the raw material of possibility of being" (1969: 218). While Kaguru assort persons, things, and acts into categories, these groupings continually dissolve, resume, and again lose focus as they are subjected to continued pondering and analyses. For Kaguru such speculations and judgments are invariably made with reference to the space in which such acts take place and where persons are observed. Space, like our bodies, is subject to flux and contested definitions over time, to various modes of the imagination. It is for this reason, surely, that in his classic study of rites of passage van Gennep anchored his analysis in a powerful introductory chapter on space (1960: 15–25). Time and person remain profoundly imbedded in territory. To take off from William James, there is not space but spaces, and they must be studied in detail.[27]

Finally, I should mention the Kaguru landscape itself as a space conducive to fostering a sense of ethnic identity. The lowlands, valleys, and plateau that comprise Kaguruland extend out from the Itumba Mountains, which rise to the south-central part of the country. Kaguru refer to the Itumba as the heart of their country even though today it is not well populated; these mountains dominate one's sense of space wherever one is in Kaguru country. Yet all of Ukaguru is topographically remarkable. To the west, north, and east of Itumba, plateau and valleys are marked by dramatic outcrops of rocks forming solitary mountains, many of fantastic and striking shape. These provide unforgettable markers rich with references to clan histories, stories, and the sagas of individuals and their families. Kaguru point to these striking features and relate them to the memory of both their ethnic and individual identities. I know that all land, however plain, provides scope for social memory, but I am tempted to argue that the dramatic vistas of Kaguruland provide an especially powerful basis for what Tuan terms "topophilia," the enduring affectual ties people feel toward their physical environment, which encodes experiences, memories, and history (1990: 93). The beauty of Kaguruland was an important factor in my choosing to work there, and few days pass in which I still do not think of it. It seems a physical space particularly rich in possibilities for attachment.

In the coming chapters I shall focus more narrowly upon initiation of adolescents, upon only one sector of Kaguru rituals, and the ideas and values attached to them. Yet this closer focus will not restrict the complex, global significance of the symbols and rituals involved. Kaguru themselves repeatedly reminded me that comprehending the full dimensions of initiation required an understanding of all Kaguru rituals. They asserted that understanding initiation would lead to my understanding in an encapsulated form what really counts most in all Kaguru life and society.

CHAPTER 5

First Encounters with Sexuality

> For there is a society of men and a society of women.
> Marcel Mauss, *Body Techniques*

> Possession which is not reciprocal is nothing. It is at most possession of the
> sexual organs, not the individual.
> Jean-Jacques Rousseau, *Émile*

> O! men with sisters dear,
> O! men with mothers and wives!
> Thomas Hood, *The Song of the Shirt*

> Diguise our bondage as we will,
> 'Tis woman, woman, rules us still.
> Thomas Moore, *Sovereign Woman*

Kaguru say that growing up and becoming proper Kaguru requires initiation
because only such rites teach young people what sexuality and gender fully
mean. Yet Kaguru young people already know a good deal about both sexuality and gender long before initiation. They would have to, considering how
quickly the knowledge of initiation is learned. Kaguru first approach teaching
about sexuality and gender through stories to children. Furthermore, the
everyday talk of adults provides plenty of allusions to sexuality and what
women and men do (see Beidelman 1972–73). Initiation may be the most

dramatic step in making Kaguru into ethnic adults, but the process begins much earlier.

Kaguru are not initiated until they reach puberty, but while they are still children they are aware of what lies ahead.[1] This is made clear through stories such as the two I recount below. Since these stories are told to children long before they are eligible for initiation, such accounts both reveal yet conceal understanding of these rites. Children learn enough to anticipate the changes to come but are also made to realize that they are still ignorant of much they need to know to be adult. As with all secrets, children are made aware that information from initiation is hidden and hard to come by but will one day be revealed if they are obedient and good (Bellman 1984: 144; Beidelman 1993).

Before discussing storytelling and other ways that Kaguru children first learn about sexuality, it is important to understand how Kaguru think of children.

For Kaguru, children are morally limited beings, and as such are excluded from full social, moral affairs. Because children are not yet aware of the full implications of moral choices (because they are uninitiated), they cannot be held entirely responsible for their behavior. Of course, children are punished for misbehavior, sometimes by harsh and shaming words, sometimes by beatings, sometimes by being deprived of food, but they are thought incapable of serious wrongs. They cannot be witches. If children do things that harm persons outside their own kin group, then the children's elders, not the children, are held jurally responsible for the damage.

Serious wrongs are committed only by truly adult, sexual beings. Only sexual beings can commit incest and adultery. More important, other serious offenses such as homicide, assault, and theft are the result of selfish motives rooted in sexuality and desires for property and control of others that children cannot entertain realistically. It is also such selfishness and greed that prompt witchcraft. This is because power and success are realized through kinship, which is synonymous with procreation. Thus only sexual, jural adults have serious grounds for conflict and envy. Only as adults can Kaguru provide and withhold resources to or from kin and neighbors. Finally, only adults have ritual access to the ancestral dead whereby they can indirectly praise or condemn the behavior of others. All of these powers are held only by sexually adult Kaguru, especially men in the case of conducting ancestral ritual and dispersing rights to land, and by both women and men regarding the production and control of resources and the bestowal or withholding of sexual pleasure and loyalty.

Kaguru do not, as do many Europeans, describe children as innocent; rather, they describe them as incomplete social beings.[2] Children are passively tied to the dead. The dead can afflict children or even draw them back to re-join the ancestors. Infants are born as a result of the dead yielding life's essence to the living. The dead often do this grudgingly and may at any time snatch children back. As children grow, they become ever more anchored into the realm of the living and ever less prone to the dead's influence. Yet it is only with initiation at adolescence that children are formally demarcated from the dead. Before initiation, children who die may not be mourned and cannot be-come ancestors; since they have not yet truly lived as adults, they have no full social identity. This incompleteness in children implicitly involves an inca-pacity to harm others, a dangerous possibility in adults. Ironically, then, for Kaguru the initiation of young people into adulthood conveys not only ad-mittance to social responsibility and the moral order but also a new capacity to do harm, to betray, to disrupt, to go against this very social order that the initiate has entered. In this sense, initiation, while establishing new and clear social (moral) distinctions, also necessarily emphasizes the problematic nature of adult social motives and actions. With their new adulthood Kaguru must ponder the complexities involved in discerning and establishing social propri-ety and justice as these converge with and diverge from one's own interests and sentiments and those of others. Initiation effaces the incompleteness of children (who are not full social beings, not fully alive, not fully sexual) and establishes the moral ambiguity of adulthood, in which judgments and actions involve danger and power.

KAGURU STORYTELLING

Stories told by elders to children gathered around a hearth or on a verandah at night are amongst the fondest recollections that many Kaguru hold of their childhood. Stories constitute some of the most important ways by which young Kaguru begin to learn how to think about many social issues (see Bei-delman 1979; 1986: 160-82). The two stories provided below are amongst the first direct accounts that children hear about the initiation rituals that will later make them adults.

Such accounts of initiation represent only one amongst many kinds of knowledge that old people's storytelling reveals to children. A story or legend (*lusimo*) represents an informal exercise in learning that will be repeated far more intensely and formally during initiation itself. These contrasting cases of indoctrination—informal storytelling around a hearth and rigorous in-struction during the seclusion at initiation—share several features. First of all, the young are assembled in a restricted space removed from the ordinary sphere of everyday affairs. In storytelling, information is conveyed within the intimacy of the home and not in a public part of a village; at initiation, information is provided in a cleared piece of bush outside any settlement (for boys) or in the innermost confines of a woman's house (for girls). Second, in both cases elders work at revealing some of the adult knowledge *(usungu)* or cleverness that is ordinarily concealed *(kufisa)* from the young. Growing up *(kukula)*, becoming an adult *(mukulu)*, being a proper Kaguru, involves learning information and moral distinctions that constitute the stuff of responsible social life. Storytelling is casually educative; initiation is unremittingly so. Yet such learning continues throughout one's life and does not end with childhood or even with initiation. In gerontocratic Kaguru society, elders hold much of their power because they know and the young do not. Unfortunately, the most powerful knowledge of all, that hidden in the bush and held by the ancestral dead, is never fully accessible and remains morally problematic and consequently always dangerous, even to the elders, who, being nearest to the dead, have most access to it. As Middleton observes, the divine secret of life and death lies at the heart of all African cosmological systems, and what access is afforded to it provides final authority (1987: 41–42).

For Kaguru, a direct approach to understanding does not usually constitute the surest means of grasping deeper realities. Stories, riddles, and songs play major parts not only in everyday education but also in the special indoctrination of initiates. These methods all require that the listeners themselves work hard at puzzling out the full dimensions of what such accounts signify. We shall see in the two stories soon to be related that certain moral conclusions are explicitly drawn, but the deeper meanings and moral colorings surrounding such tales require further cogitation and analysis in order to come to light. One could even argue that some of these meanings remain debatable and forever problematic. For Kaguru, knowledge and understanding are never gained by crude, direct intellectual assault. Rather, one approaches such prizes indirectly; one sneaks up on them. One works for them. One earns knowledge. In a way, this conforms to some Western insights about learning. We believe one learns and remembers better when creatively contributing something of oneself to the endeavor. From the analyses that I provide after the two initiation stories that follow, it ought to be clear that Kaguru should and do find more in these accounts than what the storyteller explicitly tells the listener.

The information presented in these Kaguru stories involves more topics than sexuality, though it is mainly sexuality that is our concern here. Sexuality truly is the single most important factor lying behind most Kaguru stories. This is because sex and gender are the pivotal factors for Kaguru in determining how many social decisions are made and how persons are judged to have made such choices. True adults, that is, fully responsible, moral persons, are sexually mature and their toughest choices stem from their domestic and parental relations rooted in that sexuality. This is hardly surprising in a society organized around kin and household groups. Such sexually colored experiences are ultimately beyond the full grasp of children, yet such thinking and feelings must begin to make some inroads on children as soon as possible or else social reproduction would not succeed. There is a teasing, sexually provocative aspect to Kaguru children's stories that could be termed precocious. While Kaguru insist that such stories are appropriately told only to children and not to adults, it is only adults who can probably fully grasp all their dimensions. But then, despite adults' protestations to the contrary, I have little doubt that elders thoroughly enjoyed the storytelling sessions that I witnessed.

This teasing or precocious aspect of Kaguru stories may be seen in how they frequently play on sexual matters, in how they allude to such problems but never fill them out in detail. Stories portray many situations concerning sexual attraction and the dilemmas of family life, including the relations between spouses, but the feelings, passions, and physiological processes that these relations involve are rarely if ever explicated. Such stories educate but only partly reveal. Initiation provides the final revelation by which questions about such matters are at last supposedly answered for children—or, at least, made as clear as they will ever be.

What, then, do Kaguru children know about sexuality? Certainly small Kaguru early on know that older youths are initiated. They know about this because initiations are celebrated at dances and feasts at which children are amongst the crowds of celebrants. Furthermore, no resident of any Kaguru village could fail to notice the rowdy singing and merriment that go on within the houses where girls are being confined at initiation. In contrast, the initiation of boys remains far more mysterious since no uninitiated person is allowed near a boys' circumcision camp in the bush.

It is unlikely that an immature Kaguru has a truly vivid picture of just what initiatory operations actually mean or what physiological maturation explicitly involves. Given the rules of Kaguru etiquette, no immature Kaguru ever would have been able to scrutinize an entirely unclothed adult of either sex. Certainly traditionally Kaguru were quite prudish about any kind of public nudity.

Traditionally, little boys were accustomed to go about naked, but shortly after they could toddle, little girls were provided with a small string or beaded cover *(igala* or *iguni)* over their genitals. Traditionally, initiated Kaguru men wore the kind of togalike garments now associated with Maasai and Gogo. The entire body might be intermittently visible in an active male, but the genitals are almost always somewhat difficult to see clearly or for long. Today Kaguru men take great care not to appear naked. Even when they bathe around others, men take pains to keep their genitals between their legs so that other men will not see them. Traditionally, Kaguru women always wore a skirt. Consequently, small Kaguru are unlikely ever to see adults unclothed, and indeed the only adult people whom other adult Kaguru are ever likely to see fully unclothed are their own spouses or lovers. For these reasons, much of the information that young Kaguru secure about genitals and sexuality at initiation is more striking to them than it would be to us as sexually jaded Americans.

Given the rules of Kaguru etiquette, all sexual allusions are strictly forbidden between Kaguru of adjacent generations. Even easy converse between siblings considerably different in age is inhibited, and certainly no sexual allusions whatsoever are possible between brothers and sisters or even by a third person in their presence. People should feel shame *(chinyala)* about such things. Kaguru society is certainly not one that would readily understand a heart-to-heart talk between a parent and a child about sexual matters (or even between a big brother and a little brother or between younger and older sisters). For Kaguru, such talk would appear somewhat shameless and perverse. Instead, it is grandparents or grandchildren, cross-cousins, or unrelated peers of the same age who are expected to be free to mention such matters. It is such persons who are likely to break the ice in talking about sexuality, where an informed older person provides knowledge. Indeed, sometimes members of alternate generations or cross-cousins, like joking partners, are apt to engage in obscene joking and sexual horseplay. It is very likely that young Kaguru first hear stories such as the two recounted here from a grandparent, the typical Kaguru storyteller and confidant to the young.

Westerners are sometimes apt to think of African farmers and herders as living closer to biological realities than we. Certainly it is true that Kaguru children are likely to have seen copulating and pregnant livestock and to know the general facts of sexual life. Small children often sleep in the same room where their parents have sexual relations, though often even before initiation some older children are transferred to a neighboring dwelling for unmarried males or females. Even where children sleep near parents, their elders' sexuality is carefully shielded from them. A Kaguru child may not even touch a bed of a parent. In any case, Kaguru etiquette inhibits spontaneous discussion of sexual topics between most older and younger kin. What is striking for adolescent Kaguru is that it is only at initiation that such questions and infor-

Figure 8. Kaguru girls getting ready for a dance. Photograph taken at Berega in 1957.

mation can at last be freely mentioned and, indeed, are a constant and required topic of instruction. In this, at least, a Kaguru initiation at puberty truly does mark a dramatic alteration in a young person's view of sex, one of the most important sides of life. Yet until that dramatic point is reached, it is storytelling that constitutes one of the very few formally acknowledged social situations in which sexuality is openly alluded to in front of children.

The first of the two stories that I present relates the origin of circumcision amongst the Kaguru.[3] After presenting this text I indicate how it exhibits many of the educative features that I have mentioned above.

The Origin of Circumcision

Long ago, more years than we can remember, people were not going to circumcision (*kulusona*, also a term for "marriage payment"). One day a woman set out with a very small male child (*mwana*), still an infant (*cheli*) carried on the back. She went to the forest to fetch firewood. When fetching the wood, she had no ax but was breaking it up into small sticks with her hands. While she was breaking up the wood, a splinter wounded the child's genitals (*mwasi*). The mother saw the child bleeding with splinters in him so she brought the child home to her husband to treat the wound. When the husband saw this, he took a small knife and removed the child's foreskin (*kunja*, "that which enfolds") and the splinters in the wound at the tip of the child's private parts (*mwasi*). Then they put medicine (*miti*, a Swahili word referring to trees and their parts) on the wound. After a month the child recovered. When he had recovered, both were pleased by the private parts of their child. The husband and wife were no longer troubled with periodically washing off the lower part (*kusika*), as everyone is accustomed to do. The woman told her husband, "My husband, see how you'd be if you got to be like this child. I see that getting hurt has benefited this child." The husband replied, "I am also pleased and would like to be made to be like that, but who will make me that way, since the people do not know how to do it?" Then the wife told him that if he would like that, he should ask her and she would do it to him because when she had nursed the child, she had seen that treating the wound was not much work. The husband agreed. So the next day the woman took the same small knife that had been used on the child and she removed her husband's foreskin (*kunja*). He bled so very heavily that the people were summoned. When the people arrived, they were shocked to see a man injured by having his genitals (*kusika*) cut. They asked the woman, "Who has hurt him or what was he doing to have cut himself like that?"

The wife concealed what had happened and did not tell them. She said that she had found him like that and that she did not know how it had happened. The people made medicine (*mabiki*, a Chikaguru word for trees and their parts) with which they stanched the flow of blood. When the blood was stopped, they told the wife to make porridge. As they gave this to him, they saw that he was recovering his strength. So some of the people stayed to look after him until he recovered. They nursed him until he got well. When he had recovered, they were pleased with how their comrade looked, but they were afraid of being cut in the way that he had been. So they made beer and the people came, and then he told them all about what had happened to the child and the firewood and then later to himself. The people drank the beer, but they were afraid when they recalled what they had encountered when they had met him and his wife. Their own wives told them outright *(muchieti)* that they would like them to be circumcised *(wagatoligwe,* "be brought forth," "exposed"). When the wives had finished the beer, they all said, "When we get home, our husbands will be treated *(wetendigwe)* the way our comrade is." So when they had decided that, they told their husbands, who agreed with their spouses. Then they summoned their comrade so that he would have them circumcised *(yawagtoligwa)*. From then until today, initiation *(kumbi,* "uncovering") has become the custom *(umoto)* of the Kaguru, but it commenced with that child and then was demanded by the women.

Even today, when boys reach the age of wanting to sleep with their counterparts, these young girls refuse them, saying that they have foreskins *(masubu)*, which are dirty *(mwafu)*. When boys are told that, they want to be circumcised *(kugotolwa)*, and if you keep such matters quiet and yet they learn that others are to be cut, they will still run off to where it is taking place. The circumciser is *mung'hunga,* "one who exposes" or "one who lays bare" the penis or knowledge; he is also called *mwanabakwa*. In lands where there is no mission, other initiators *(wang'hunga)* do women. All possess their custom of initiation *(dikumbi)*.

Discussion

The most striking message in this story is that males must submit to initiation on account of women. Not only was the practice of circumcision first inadvertently hit upon by women, but it was their public insistence *(muchieti)* on it that drove all men to continue it. It is implied that men would have been ashamed to back off from this challenge addressed to them when all the people were assembled. For Kaguru, circumcision is here a matter of aesthetics. The foreskin is considered dirty *(mwafu)*. This is not merely because smegma may inevitably gather beneath it, though reference to the inconvenience of periodic washing suggests this. Rather, the uncircumcised, moist penis makes a male unclean because this makes boys resemble women, whose moist genitals, especially during menstruation, are sources of pollution. Circumcision is also a matter of both pleasing women and showing women and others that one is not afraid and will face dangers in public. Similarly, male genitals are referred to as *kusika* (the lower parts), a Kaguru term that also alludes to moist or rainy areas. It is said that Kaguru women would reject intercourse with uncircumcised men. As Wittgenstein observes, "Ethics and aesthetics are one and the same" (1981: 183).[4]

While women are said to demand circumcision of men, today it is only men and not women who properly perform the operation. The story neatly separates these features. A woman was responsible for the first two circumcisions.[5] The first was due to female carelessness (actually a splinter from a wild tree) and required a man to complete it successfully with a knife (a product of cultural artifice, for only men may smelt iron); however, unlike this tale, in actual practice a father could never cut his own child. Later, when the father himself is circumcised by the woman at his behest, this appears to have been botched and would have ended in death were it not for the elder men who provide medicines (from the bush) and care for him during his recovery. Thus, while it is women who demand circumcision, only elder men are portrayed as having the knowledge and skill to perform it properly. Women have sexual wants and needs, but this Kaguru story maintains that only men have the cultural as well as biological abilities to satisfy them in a safe and constructive manner.

The first circumcision takes place in the bush. The woman has gone there for firewood, a daily wifely chore associated with her responsibilities of maintaining a hearth and pleasing her husband by cooking and heating bath water. Therefore when she cuts the boy, she is in the right place (the bush) for the right reasons, but it is done by the wrong kind of person, the wrong way, and for the wrong reasons (no reason at all, but by accident).

The second circumcision occurs in the wrong place (a settlement) and involves the wrong gender (a woman operates with a man's knife). Only when men exclusively take over with their mastery of the bush, as evinced in their use of medicine (*miti*, a Swahili word for trees and their components, and *mabiki*, a Chikaguru word for the same) does the initiate recover. Men's mastery over the medicines of the bush parallels their mastery in hunting animals there. It is this double aspect of male ascendance over the bush (*nyika*) that accounts for the Kaguru euphemism *kunyika* (in the bush) for the genitals.

Circumcision is thought to please women because it makes males even more different from females than they already are, and the sexes are attracted to true opposites of each other.[6] (Later, we shall see that cutting women has different purposes.) Yet men and not women have the exclusive power to make this transformation of themselves, and it is older men's mastery over knowledge about the wild bush that confirms this power. What we have is a complex shifting of blame and responsibility for suffering. Women want men to be circumcised but cannot do it properly. Only older men have the knowledge and skills to accomplish this dangerous deed. Therefore, older men subject younger men to a very painful and dangerous experience that involves not only cutting but also hazing in many forms, all in order to please women by strengthening males. Younger men should be grateful to and even awed by older men who circumcise them, for without this they could never leave their mothers and secure (master) wives. Indeed, they would supposedly not even aesthetically appeal to women. For circumcision to take place, older men temporarily take on the nurturant role of stern mothers, and the hearth of the settlement is replaced by the campfire of the bush circumcision camp. Watson-Franke maintains that matrilineal peoples always emphasize the role of fathers as nurturers, presumably so children can secure added resources from men (1992: 481–82). Certainly both parents in many societies are nurturant, though often in different ways. Kaguru emphasize mothers' nurturance in providing breast milk and cooked food, but fathers are also repeatedly described as providers of food as well as protection. At male initiation men do take over cooking and feeding, which are ordinarily monopolized by women. Men's semen is also described as a kind of milk that feeds others, contributing to a young woman's nubility and later feeding a pregnancy. In this sense, men do usurp some feminine attributes at male initiation, but they continue to do so even later on. While at first glance circumcision appears to enable maturing males to learn to control their own physical destinies, it is actually also a practice that enables older men to control and intimidate younger ones, as is common in many other societies. Initiation enables older men to impress younger ones about the need for conformity to traditional values and beliefs, and about the supposed superior knowledge and authority of elder males. Furthermore, it is only older men who provide young men with social (jural) access to women. Kaguru circumcision ritual is a cultural cosmetic that expresses the socioeconomic reality of power rooted in elders' abilities to monopolize both sociocultural information and socioeconomic access to women and property. (Much ethnographic material from eastern and other parts of Africa and elsewhere is similar.) This is accomplished through physiological and psychological assault, which induces pain, fear, and anxiety. Schilder suggests that the pain that men inflict on young boys may relate to a desire to overpower and intimidate their future young sexual rivals from the next generation (1950: 120). This may even apply to the pain that women inflict on girl initiates. Yet nothing ever told to me by Kaguru would support this argument. When we consider and contrast male and female initiations more carefully in the chapters to follow, we shall find that women's initiation appears different from men's in terms of these issues of power and domination and their integration with physiological processes.

Given the Kaguru assumptions stressed here—that circumcision makes youths more sexually attractive and acceptable in marriage—I should mention briefly how marriage itself is repeatedly implied by the very terms employed in the story. The first mention of male initiation involves the word *lusona,* a term that I earlier indicated usually refers to the arrangements surrounding bridewealth. Kaguru are fond of employing euphemisms for initiation and do not ordinarily mention any actual physical operation such as cutting *(kudumula).* The use of *lusona* at the start of the story already gives a forward impetus to the narrative, suggesting how initiation inevitably leads to marriage itself. Initiation is therefore just the first of many necessary social arrangements linking elders and young and different kin groups together. Also implied in the term *lusona* is a notion of reciprocity with corresponding implications of debt. The obligations toward elders generated by their contribution of resources of money, food and beer, knowledge, and time must be repaid with respect and obedience. In this, initiation is like marriage, where one's advance toward greater maturity is also secured by debts to elders for bridewealth and skill in negotiating an alliance with other Kaguru. Throughout the text, the terms employed for initiation derive from the root *kutola.* I first heard Kaguru use *kutola* to mean "to marry," but I eventually heard it and related forms used for "to initiate," "to divorce," "to join," and "to separate," as well as for "to remove the foreskin." This seeming confusion relates to common themes of presenting and taking away, conjunction and disjunction; these are all tied to changes of social and bodily state associated with initiation, marriage, and divorce.

THE SECOND TEXT

The second of the two stories purports to account for the origin of baboons.[7] At first it appears to be a mere cautionary tale meant to inculcate obedience to custom. In the discussion following the text I hope to show that in fact it also invokes many complex symbols at the core of Kaguru values.

The Origin of Baboons

Long ago, ever since people got the custom *(umoto)* of going to initiation camp *(kwilago)* and of women being confined *(kwikigwa)* indoors *(kugati)* when they are novices *(wali)* to be initiated *(kufinigwa,* "to be danced"), there were prohibitions *(minyiko)* that are still observed to this day regarding newly circumcised boys *(waluko)* and girl novices *(wali wa chanachike)*. If these are delayed in recovering so that they have yet to return home even by the time the rains are threatening *(ifula ididime,* "rain penetrating"), it is still better to return them even if they are not yet fully recovered. If not, these girls and boys will turn into baboons.

One year people initiated *(wagotola)* boys *(waluko)* and also girls *(wali we chanachike)* and then celebrated them *(ng'oma sakufina,* "danced a celebration"). Every day the people enjoyed beer and dancing without pause. Because they enjoyed the pleasure of celebration, they forgot about how the time of the novices *(wali)* was passing day by day. Then as one by one the days went by, they did not realize that the rains were about to threaten. Since there was not a single baboon in existence then, no one had any real reason to be afraid about someone turning into one. The people had yet to see a baboon.

Then one day as the people were dancing and drinking in all the villages, they suddenly saw the rain clouds gathering. Suddenly it began thundering and pouring rain. By the time that it was raining hard and heavy, they had forgotten the prohibition *(mwiko)* regarding the boys and girls. The people who had initiates inside suddenly found their girls inside running out. When the girls got out, they ran into the trees in the forest. All had got hair *(bahila)* and had grown tails *(mikila)*. The boys also were running into the trees and they also were hairy and had tails. The people had lost everything. The children had turned into baboons and the celebration was over. They tried every way, even divination, but they were told that the children had already changed and could not turn back into human beings. So when those baboons got together *(fogakihasa)*, they produced offspring and still more offspring until they formed many groups of baboons. Those are now the baboons, which we see even today. That is why baboons have hands, legs, faces, fingers, and nails just like those of people, because in an earlier time they were humans. That is also why prohibitions are observed. If you are told something is prohibited, keep it truly prohibited. If that past prohibition had been kept properly, there would be no baboons.

Discussion

The most obvious message in this story is that rules must be observed. Rules are what make humans different from animals, and Kaguru rules *(umoto,* "custom," but also "hearth," literally "place of the fire") make Kaguru more properly human and therefore more reasonable and more attractive than others. As I noted in the preceding chapter, such rules essentially involve restraint, sometimes in observing polite and decorous speech, sometimes in observing proper diet and alimentary etiquette, and sometimes in being restrained sexually by observing customs of bridewealth and ritual associated with marriage and prohibitions against incest. For Kaguru, then, prohibiting *(umwiko)* or restraining desires and appetites constitute the sine qua non of culture. What one does not do is as important as, perhaps more important than, what one does. Without observing such rules, then, one would be a beast (baboon). It is appropriate that one of the Kaguru euphemisms for the genitals is *mumwiko* (prohibited place). Kaguru are intrigued by our kindred primates. These appear as grotesque mirror images of ourselves. Kaguru play with the similarities and differences between monkeys and people. Kaguru believe that the monkeys that most closely resemble humans are baboons, both on account of their size and on account of the fact that baboons travel and feed on the ground as well as in trees and gather in sociable troops. Yet if baboons resemble humans in their shape, features, gestures, and sociability, they also are sharply different. As beasts, baboons are shameless in that they are thought to be sexually promiscuous. The story itself suggests this by the term used to describe the baboons mating, *kuhasa* (to couple in a mixed manner). The same verb is also applied to forms of Kaguru sexual relations that are prohibited (though amenable to purificatory rituals), questionable, or, at the least, risky and undesirable from some perspective.[8]

Furthermore, baboons are greedy, that is, they show no restraint in their appetites, and it is a similar unrestrained appetite that led greedy Kaguru to feast overtime, thereby producing the first baboons. Baboons' insatiability means that the food resources within their own proper sphere in the bush are not enough. Instead, baboons steal food from out of people's gardens, transgressing the boundaries between the bush and socialized space. They devour food immediately and uncooked rather than showing restraint by waiting until it is properly prepared. It is, of course, true that other wild beasts also eat food raw and stolen from gardens, but these creatures do not resemble humans. Furthermore, baboons' appetitive features are demonstrated by their having tails. These tails are repulsive not only because they are blatantly bestial attributes fixed on a humanoid form but also because the Kaguru associate the tail with sexuality. The term *mukila* (tail) is a slang word for penis. (This parallels our English term, derived from the Latin *penis,* "tail.") The red bottoms of baboons, especially those of females in estrus, are also considered particularly gross.

Above all, baboons are morally problematic because, although humanoid, they are uncouthly hirsute. Full understanding of this requires a brief discourse on Kaguru ideas about hair. Puberty (Latin *pubes,* "pubic hair") is one of the major signs of sexual maturation everywhere. For Kaguru, and probably for many other societies, hair itself is an attribute of vitality and power. In the past, young Kaguru women and men carefully braided their head hair *(idosi)* into plaits, men often imitating neighboring Baraguyu, Maasai, and Gogo warriors, who pride themselves on their long, red-ochered locks.[9] These were signs of sexual vitality and beauty, or power seductively enhanced by the color red. The red locks were cut when young people settled down as householders. When I did fieldwork amongst the Kaguru, some Kaguru men and women in isolated regions still braided and ochered their hair. Kaguru women still often braid their hair into patterns drawn close to the scalp, though usually only for special occasions. In contrast, old people always keep their hair cut plain so as not to suggest any sexuality. A few Kaguru, such as the mad or those claiming magical powers, sometimes let their hair grow unkempt. For example, the only Kaguru I ever met who publicly boasted about being a witch wore her hair long and unkempt, even though she was an elderly woman. Women who were following special magical procedures to enhance their fertility in order to become pregnant also sometimes let their hair grow untended. In the early 1960s, a few young Kaguru men who attempted to form the USA political movement let their hair grow long, something like modified Rastifarian dreadlocks (see Beidelman 1961c). Head hair is shaved at initiation and also during mourning, under the assumption that shaving signals a temporary abatement of sexual interest and availability.

Unlike head hair, Kaguru body hair *(ujoya)*, especially pubic hair, was often shaved or plucked. Kaguru no longer usually do so, but the assumption underlying such practices was that such hair signaled undisciplined sexuality and desire. Chest hair on men, however, is sometimes jokingly seen as sexy, as a sign of potency and successful acquisitiveness. (When I did fieldwork in Ukaguru, a woman tribal outsider working in the area was unusually hirsute, with hair visible on her bosom. Kaguru were convinced that she was sexually promiscuous. They were consequently thrilled when she was rumored to be having an affair with a European colonial administrator.) It is therefore not surprising that Kaguru contrast humans, with their relatively little body hair, with hirsute monkeys, whose appetites run along similar lines to those of humans but who appear greedy, undisciplined, and shameless.

Given these notions about hair, the adolescent onset of body hair signals a new and potentially challenging alteration in the forces of bodily desire, a new danger. Sexual adults (Latin *adultus*, past tense of *adolescere*, "to grow") embody new desires that must be brought into line through bodily grooming and etiquette so as to prevent greed and selfishness from undermining society. Pubescent Kaguru are now more dangerously animalistic in their wants and desires than they were as glabrous children. Therefore stringent instructions are vital in order to keep these appetites in check. Grooming, etiquette, and rules about bridewealth and brideservice all work along similar, complementary lines to channel animalistic, sexual appetites into socially productive paths. Considering all these facts, the hairiness of baboons is unquestionably the most strikingly nonsocial of their attributes.

Kaguru ideas about human and animal hair are reflected in the fact that they employ one term for animal hairiness *(ubahila)*, such as that of baboons, and employ other terms for human hairiness. To be covered all over with hair is to be visibly unruly and dangerously sexy. Kaguru themselves sometimes compare body hair to the undergrowth that must be cleared for cultivation. Yet, of course, Kaguru know that densely vegetated bush may be potentially the most fertile areas for future cultivation. Similarly, hairy people are considered sexy, though not necessarily in ways pleasing to Kaguru.

These contrasts are particularly striking in the story since at the time of initiation the novices themselves were hairless, presumably having been shaved before being cut. One may even safely assume that initiation itself may be spoken of as a means of dealing with hairiness. Before puberty, a child was hairless and consequently did not require special controls. The hair of puberty requires repeated shaving, and even head hair now requires extra grooming to conform to adult decorum. On no account should such young people let hair go messily unattended. The attentions that initiates are taught to administer to their bodies are but the cosmetic aspects of the wider set of observations that they are taught to observe in order to keep their sexuality socially restrained and in order.

Not only are baboons represented as moral disorder incarnate, but their very existence is thought due to such tendencies toward incontinence in humans. The initiates became baboons because the elders disregarded the prohibitions against such rites being prolonged into the rainy season.[10] The elders had broken these rules on account of their own baboonlike, undisciplined appetites. Unable to control their lusts for food, alcohol, and sexuality (dancing), they destroyed the proper social process by which children (not fully social beings) were to be transformed into truly social persons. Instead, these children regressed into being even more uncultured beings, baboons. This failure to observe such rules in turn is tied into a failure to separate the sociocultural spheres of time. This is reflected in respecting divisions of behavioral forms proper to the dry and rainy seasons (Beidelman 1986: 88–90). Hence, improper mixing *(kuhasa)* of spheres of time led to improper conflation *(kuhasa)* of species (humans/beasts becoming baboons, humanoid beasts) and blurring *(kuhasa)* proper divisions of moral space (bush and human clearings whose boundaries baboons repeatedly transgress).

BASIC SEXUAL TERMS AND NOTIONS

Having indicated how these Kaguru tales can inform children about sexuality and initiation, I want to present the general terms and ideas that young Kaguru are likely to pick up from everyday speech, for adults cannot be verbally circumspect about sexuality at every moment. For the most part, I do not elaborate on these terms except in the most rudimentary manner. The point made here is that no one enters initiation ceremonies utterly ignorant of all such matters. For that reason, we ourselves should grasp these rudiments before considering initiation itself.

Kaguru recognize that sexual intercourse produces pregnancy, and they believe that physiologically offspring are equally but differently related to both parents. A child is related to its mother through the softer portions of its body, its blood and flesh, and to its father through the harder portions, its bone, cartilage, and teeth. This is reflected at conception, which occurs when a man's sperm *(udoko)* combines with the blood *(sakame)* of a woman in her belly *(tumbo)* or womb *(inda,* but compare to *sanda,* a carrying cloth or a winding-sheet or shroud). Blood, unlike bone, however, has an infinite capacity to link, joining together entire matriclans through endless generations. In this sense, its ductile and formless nature relates to its infinite transmissibility. In contrast, while bone provides definition and particularity, these very attributes prevent its extension over space and time (Beidelman 1963b; 1986: 33–34).

For Kaguru, blood is the most problematic of bodily substances. It is the basis of the closest social bond (matrilineality) and a source of life. Yet it is also a sign of enormous danger. Any spilling of blood requires payments to cleanse the area and/or the persons violated. The blood of menstruation *(kutumuka,* "to be involved," "to be taken up with") is so dangerous that menstruating women may not sleep in their husbands' beds, and, while menstruating, women should avoid entering cultivated fields, attending ritual gatherings, brewing beer, going to court, and many other situations. They should wear dark or unattractive clothing and should not try to appear seductive to men. Yet menstruation is valued, for it is a sign of fertility. It is thought to mark a plenitude of blood that signifies a readiness to bear children. Buckley and Gottlieb wonder whether in societies that see menstruation as overflow this is viewed as a sign of a missed opportunity for conception. They argue that this

Figure 9. Kaguru boys with staffs used in herding goats and sheep. Photograph taken at Berega in 1957.

negative association may be reflected in the development of theories of menstrual pollution (1988: 39). I could find nothing in the Kaguru data to bear this out. The cessation of menstruation at menopause is said to signify having one's womb cut away (*samba idumuka*, "cut up one's carrying cloth"). A woman who never does menstruate may be termed *masilatungula* (one who never becomes formed, one who is disintegrated). In this sense, the commonest words for menstruation are negative: *nhama* (sickness) or *na hasi* (being down or being under). Given the great variability in food resources in traditional Kaguru society, there is reason to suppose that onset of both menstruation and menopause was less easily predicted and more variable than today (see Delaney, Lupton, and Loth 1988: 49, 64). Kaguru recognize that menstruation is a repeated phenomenon somehow resembling the waxing and waning of the moon, just as we do in our use of the term *menstruation* (Latin *mensis*, "month"). I was told that menstruation was rarely explained to Kaguru girls before it happened, so its onset often shocked and upset many girls. Even so, this seems a poor reason to argue, as Buckley and Gottlieb do, that some sense of mystery accounts for belief in the dangerous potency of menstrual blood (1988: 45). For Kaguru, all spilled human blood, menstrual and otherwise, is considered very dangerous and polluting.

Kaguru have a series of names for the male and female genitals and for sexual relations. The "proper" terms for these are not at all evocative, whereas the various euphemisms and slang employed provide metaphoric insight into some of the ways Kaguru think and feel about sexuality and gender.

The formal Kaguru term for penis is *mbolo;* for the foreskin it is *usubu,* or sometimes *kunja* (that which is enfolded). Because the foreskin keeps the glans moist, like a woman's genitals are thought always to be, it is said to have feminine attributes. This is one of the reasons given for why it should be removed at initiation, to make boys more masculine. The glans is *ng'helekenge* (not removed), and the testicles *mapumba* (lumps). (As a Swahili-speaking reader would suspect, it may be that some of these terms are modified borrowings from that language.) The vagina is *ng'huma,* the clitoris *ligi,* its tip *ibumba* (a large packet), and the labia *malemba* (wrappers). None of these terms seems to suggest any humor or zest, and during joking, seduction, or ordinary casual conversation other terms would be more appropriate, just as we ourselves rarely use such "proper" terms when telling jokes, making love, or playfully chatting. These appropriate terms tell us little about how Kaguru feel or think about such sexual matters. The terms for sexual relations are also varied, though I am not sure just what their derivations may be.[11] I was told by Kaguru that the most unequivocal terms for sexual relations were *kusola, kugoloka,* and *kwingilila* (to enter in, to empty in) and *kufita* (to stick?). These verbs were not ones I heard people regularly using.

Kaguru euphemisms were far more frequently employed and more evocative. The penis may be called *mutwango* (pestle), *isago* (grinding stone), *mume* or *mulume* (husband or male [active] firestick). The penis may also be compared to a spear *(mugoha)* or a stick *(fimbo),* or even a tail *(mukila).*[12] For Kaguru, a vagina may be an *ituli* (mortar), *luwala* (the bottom stone for grinding flour), or *muke* (wife or female [passive] firestick). It can also be insultingly referred to as *kufala* (to fart) from the noise it is said to make during sexual intercourse, or *ifula* (rain) on account of the dampness it produces. More likely, genitals will be mentioned without any distinction of gender, as in *mumwiko* (prohibited), *kunyika* (in the bush), *mwasi* (exposed), or *kusika* (lower parts). Kaguru also regard the buttocks *(madaka)* as sexually attractive in both sexes and mention them to refer to sexuality.[13]

Kaguru euphemisms for sexual relations are varied: *kufina* (to dance), *kudia* (to eat), *kubwalisa* (to lie down), *kugona* (to sleep), *kutwanga* (to pound flour), *kusanjila* (to grind flour), *kuhegesa* (to make fire with firesticks), or *kukola* (to seize). Many such expressions, including Kaguru association of sexuality with hunting (venery), involve an association of phallic aggression with potency (compare Vanggaard 1974: chapter 8). To reach orgasm is, not surprisingly, *kweja* (to come), a term also used for urination. Kaguru sometimes refer to male ejaculation as *musindo* (gunshot). I got no comments regarding masturbation *(kudinha)* other than the observation that boys whose initiations were postponed might do it frequently. Kaguru believe that sexual relations are desirable not only because they produce children, which everyone values, but also because they actually hasten the maturation of women. I was told that adolescent girls would benefit physically, growing larger breasts and buttocks, if they were regularly filled with semen.

While it is wrong to mention anything sexual when both parents and children are present, Kaguru do not seem otherwise to mind discussing some aspects of sexuality so long as it does not get personal. Sexual joking is quite frequent at dances, at beer-drinking parties, and sometimes where men congregate alone. Presumably women also get together and talk and joke about such matters. Certainly any Kaguru, including children, may sometimes inadvertently hear sexual references from time to time, especially where people get careless as they drink and mingle in large numbers at celebrations at rites of passage. What is, however, never likely is for children to hear such words spoken directly to them by their parents, elder siblings, or affines. Some Kaguru did tell me that sexual openness was always bad *(fiha)*, but presumably they meant intruding messy sexual matters into places or activities where formal, neat social relations were involved. No one can do much about what is said and sung at drunken beer parties or when hundreds have gathered at celebratory feasts and dances.

Certainly sexual relations are thought invariably to produce heat *(moto)*. While this is acceptable, even desirable, as part of generation, much as the comparable creative acts of cooking and brewing require heat, this can be out of place and therefore disruptive. Sexual relations should never be mixed *(kuhaswa)* with other important activities such as preparing food, brewing beer, propitiating the dead, divining, or undertaking formal negotiations with others. Sexual relations are said to be hot because they are potentially disruptive, especially if they befuddle or distract from these other doings. Sex is so powerful because it obscures other activities. Like fire or pain, it prevails over a multitude of cultural fabrications. After copulation the actors must be cooled *(kuhoswa)* through washing. In the case of prohibited sexual acts, this cooling also involves cleansing rituals. The tenor of ordinary, quotidian existence is antipathetic to blatant sexual behavior, for the proper order of everyday life is repeatedly described as cool *(mheho)*. All this reference to sexuality as hot is consistent with Bachelard's observation that "fire suggests the desire to change, to speed up the passage of time," that "it magnifies human destiny" (1964: 16). Indeed, Bachelard speculates that "the love act is the first scientific hypothesis about the objective reproduction of fire" (ibid.: 23–24). Kaguru ritual, etiquette, and even slang all bear him out. We shall see that many Kaguru clan legends and rites of passage involve a meditation on fire and its products, again a perspective consistent with Bachelard's views about any *pyromenon* (product of fire) (ibid.: 58).

Finally, what young Kaguru are unlikely ever to find discussed is pregnancy, either by or about someone actually pregnant. Pregnancy is never announced or celebrated, as it often is in our society, and it is bad manners for Kaguru to mention it openly. This was one of the first matters of propriety that I was taught. Kaguru women conceal their pregnancies as long as possible. While pregnancy is a blessing from the dead confirming one's moral worth, it is also grounds for envy and ill will from others who have failed to conceive or who have lost children. Kaguru women harbor this blessing to themselves and are expected to guard and hide it from harmful outside influences until its fulfillment. Consequently, young Kaguru are never encouraged to consider pregnancy as an everyday event subject to free enquiry and discussion, even though it is one aspect of sexuality that may at times be quite difficult to ignore.

CONCLUSION

Sexual and gender awareness figures constantly in Kaguru everyday life, in determining proper conduct of speech, meals, bodily comportment, and etiquette. Even the most basic deployment of space and utensils involves recognition of their sexual references. Yet only Kaguru who have been initiated have been made truly self-conscious about all that these actions express and involve, because only initiated Kaguru are given to understand that they are to be held seriously responsible for their conduct in such matters. Long before initiation, young Kaguru commence their slow indoctrination into such awareness. From their first obscure bits of information about sexuality, young

Kaguru are made keenly aware that this involves dangerous, difficult, and tricky matters. Yet at some times sexuality also evokes humor, wit, and fun. After all, while sexual affairs may often be serious, sometimes even painful business, they may also be amusing and ridiculous. Initiation songs and stories evoke laughter as well as fear, humor as well as solemnity.

To be a Kaguru is to comprehend a cultural code whose fundamental contours are greatly determined by sexuality, in terms of gender and in terms of the aging and reproductive processes associated with it. Kaguru children are repeatedly told that only after initiation will these matters be clear. This is true in a sense, yet at many levels these sexual modes, so rooted in everyday affairs, are already deeply part of quotidian life and therefore touch Kaguru from their earliest years. Why Kaguru adolescents themselves clamor to become initiated, even while dreading it, is because they have been promised that what they already half comprehend will become fully revealed, so that they may perhaps begin to let some of these notions work for them rather than simply find those notions working upon them. Many Kaguru probably already know a great deal sexually before initiation, but those rituals provide such precocious Kaguru with the right to have this awareness acknowledged. Initiation is therefore not simply learning lore but also earning the right to be recognized as knowing what only an adult should know. At initiation all previous reflection and analysis implicit in storytelling and in learning language and etiquette will finally come into its own, will be openly discussed, indeed will become the central theme of all talk and actions. Only after initiation will the young start along the road toward some sense of autonomy, because they have gained a sense of being able to choose what to express and what to hide in their deepest feelings and concerns, those about gender and sexuality and the power and authority related to them. Yet this very process toward some sense of choice is still replete with domination by elders. To approach adulthood, maturing Kaguru must temporarily regress to a condition of childish dependence and subordination, enforced in the initiation camps and houses of confinement. In this treatment, Kaguru elders, especially men, utilize initiation to intimidate and repress youths. This is a form of control reinforced by a youth's subsequent subordination regarding bridewealth. In contrast, women's initiation appears to stress sororal solidarity of women far more than intimidation or repression.

In the cases of both women and men the initiates are impressed with the fact that knowledge and understanding are not simply individually acquired skills but social gifts whose meaning and the right to employ them are always subject to social play and control.

CHAPTER 6

Ceremonies of Men's and Women's Initiation

Those who know that their members are naturally obedient, let them take care only to counteract the tricks of their fancies. People are right to notice the unruly liberty of this member, obtruding so importunely when we have no use for it, and failing so importunely when we have the most use of it, and struggling for mastery so imperiously with our will, refusing with so much pride and obstinacy our solicitations, both mental and manual.

> Michel Eyquem de Montaigne, "Power of the Imagination," *Essays*

It sometimes has intelligence of its own and although the will of men desires to stimulate it, it remains obstinate and unresponsive. Sometimes it starts to move without permission of the man, whether he is sleeping or waking. Often the man is asleep. Frequently the man wishes it to act and it does not desire to do so; many times it wishes to act and the man is compelled to forbid. It seems therefore that this creature has a life and intelligence separate from man. Man is therefore wrong in being ashamed to give it a name or to exhibit it, seeking constantly to conceal what he ought to adorn and display with ceremony as a ministrant.

> Leonardo da Vinci, *Notebooks*

Why, ever, would a gal trade her atomic bomb for some guy's cannon?

> Kit Schwartz, *The Female Member*

The male is, nonetheless, obsessed with screwing; he'll swim a river of snot, wade nostril-deep through a mile of vomit, if he thinks there'll be a friendly pussy awaiting him. He'll screw a woman he despises, any snaggle-toothed hag, and, furthermore, pay for the opportunity. Why?
Valerie Solanas, *S.C.U.M. Manifesto*

The first evening I spent in Ukaguru I heard constant drumming from beyond the hilltop Christian mission station where I first resided. As it grew darker I could see fires like blinking yellow eyes in the night landscape. I saw a missionary returning from her work at the local clinic and asked her what the drums meant. She explained, "It's a blinkin' orgy, that's what it is." My newly hired African assistant appeared, and when I asked him, he said it was probably some local Kaguru "dancing" the initiation of some boy or girl. The drumming, silhouettes of clusters of Kaguru houses against the violet night sky, fires, and faint sounds of singing and shouting combined into an exotic stereotype that beckoned a novice anthropologist. I and my field assistant hiked out through the outlying valley to the nearest lights and pulsing sounds, about two miles away. There we found about a hundred Kaguru drinking, dancing, and singing around fires stoked in the center of a settlement. We were offered beer, and I was even allowed to try my hand at drumming and dancing, which I did rather poorly, to the amusement of the Kaguru assembled. I stayed many hours, even after my assistant had left for bed, and I was invited to return the next day. I was assured that there would be more beer and dancing and that a goat would be slain and roasted. I did return, and so I got to know my first Kaguru friends and informants.

I had begun fieldwork during the dry season, when Ukaguru was most accessible, so I could easily bring in supplies. (I then had no auto, only a bicycle.) I did not know that I would be arriving at the peak of the season for the initiation of boys and at the time of the year preferred for celebrating the coming of age of girls. All three of my other stays with the Kaguru included times for initiation, and my recollections of my very last days in Kaguruland (again in the dry season) are inextricably associated with the nighttime drumming and dancing of initiations. To this day, most remembrances I have of Kaguru conjure up memories of initiation.

It is appropriate that my first introduction to Kaguru tradition involved a celebration of a boy's initiation. Kaguru told me that this was fit and proper because I was thereby first encountering them at their most traditional, their most truly Kaguru. Certainly no other occasions find so many Kaguru assembled and pleasurably singing and speaking so much Chikaguru unmixed with any Swahili. Initiation is the most solidary of Kaguru public occasions. No other *rite de passage* brings so many Kaguru together undivided by counterdemands from competing kin groups (such as the contentions inevitable at weddings and funerals, where people dispute over property). Throughout my years in their land, Kaguru repeatedly urged me to learn all I could about such ceremonies and encouraged me to attend boys' initiations. Kaguru even acknowledged that as a stranger wanting to fathom Kaguru customs and ways, I should even inquire about girls' initiation, though everyone agreed that as a male I could not actually attend all those proceedings. For all these reasons, it was clear to me, and repeatedly underscored by Kaguru themselves, that ceremonies of initiation of adolescents were crucial to understanding what Kaguru most valued about themselves as an ethnic group, about what they thought made them Kaguru.

In this chapter I describe the ceremonies by which Kaguru initiate boys and girls into adulthood.[1] I first present what I saw and learned about how boys are initiated and then what I know about girls' ceremonies. I conclude by contrasting these two initiations. Their similarities and differences reveal many Kaguru ideas about the two sexes. Yet these ceremonies are not just about conferring full femininity or masculinity upon adolescents, about confirming what we today term gender. They are, at a deeper level, about confirming Kaguruness. They evoke recollections of places, practices, and ways of thinking that create a sense of being and belonging to a land and to a shared cultural life. They form an encyclopedia of Kaguru ethnic identity.

In the conclusion to this chapter I point out ways in which Kaguru ceremonies of initiation resemble Western notions of history and autobiography. They work toward establishing a sense of a people's ethnic identity, continuity, and entitlement to place, and also a person's sense of identity, not just as a member of a clan and ethnic group (what colonialists termed "tribe") but also as a woman or man, elder or junior, kin or affine, neighbor or outsider, whose identity and roles alter over a lifetime. They comprise what G. H. Mead termed the "social structure" of the self (1956: 217).

BOYS' INITIATION

For Kaguru and indeed for most societies, manhood is more a social achievement than a biological one. Yet, ironically, Kaguru manhood's most crucial social sign is physical, a cut penis. No matter how old he is, a Kaguru male cannot become a man (jural adult) without undergoing circumcision. Emergence of pubic hair, change of voice and musculature, and physical growth do not suffice. While social changes through initiation usually run in tandem with the physiological changes of adolescence, they need not. A few Kaguru may undergo initiation before the onset of actual physical puberty. In some cases youths' initiation may be delayed past physical puberty.[2] Furthermore, males of other ethnic or religious groups known to Kaguru confound traditional Kaguru expectations about circumcision and age. For example, adult Hehe and Nyamwesi men, who sometimes enter Kaguruland, are uncircumcised. Kaguru also have long encountered Arabs and Africans converted to Islam, especially neighboring Ngulu and Zigula, so they know that Muslim males are usually circumcised a few days after birth, and thus they are aware that the operation need not have any relation to moral instruction.

For Kaguru, manhood is attained through a combination of four interrelated factors: physical maturation, circumcision, extensive hazing and instruction conducted at a circumcision camp established in the bush and directed by knowledgeable elders, and public witness to the successful accomplishment of initiation through having its completion "danced" by kin and neighbors. (Many Kaguru, however, argue that full manhood is not attained until a man becomes an actual householder after marriage.)

Initiation links moral and aesthetic qualities with biological ones. For Kaguru proper, physical circumcision produces an aesthetically attractive male by achieving a more masculine penis, since the feminine foreskin and resultant moisture are thus eliminated.[3] The pain and consequent psychic vulnerability generated by this operation should be utilized as a means for transmitting information and teaching discipline to the initiate. None of this would succeed if the initiate were not sufficiently old enough to be impressed; it would be lost on a true infant, such as one cut according to Muslim custom. Kaguru Christians acknowledge that the Bible endorses circumcision (Christ was circumcised) but go on to point out that Jews circumcise mere infants, which defeats the Kaguru purpose of cutting. The pain of initiation must be remembered, and this should be associated with complicated teachings and the memorization of songs and sayings. Proper initiation refers to an expansion of mental as well as physical capacities that can be accomplished only by a nearly adult person.

The wide range of Kaguru terms for male initiation emphasizes the manifold social implications of the process. It is more than just talk of "cutting." The two traditional terms most often employed are *kufina* (to dance) or, just as often, *kufinwa* (to be danced), and *kugotola* (to separate) or *kugotolwa* (to be separated). *Kufina* underlines that initiation for males and females is more than a surgical process; rather, it requires public validation epitomized by dancing, itself a socialized form of moderated sexuality. Kaguru have a term, *ifunga* (shut in), for someone who has undergone circumcision camp but whose change in status has not yet been acknowledged (*kufinwa*, danced). To keep a novice in his place, elder Kaguru may remind an *ifunge* that they have not yet drunk his relatives' beer, which is paid to them for their dancing to recognize the initiate's readmission into society. The term *kugotola* (to separate) can refer to the actual cutting, but it more appropriately refers to the initiate's separation from everyday village life while at the initiation camp. Both these terms, *kufina* and *kugotola*, are far more often employed than *kudumila* (to cut) or *kalama* ("to mark," as in marking livestock with cuts in the ears or marks on the hide), which explicitly refer to the operation involved. Kaguru also speak of initiation as *kwingila* (entering), because initiates enter into a process that transforms them into adults. They also sometimes refer to boys' initiation as *kubwila* (catching), implying that the boys are seized and taken off against their will, even though many older youths are actually eager to be initiated. *Kubwila* suggests the harassing side of boys' rites. A far less common term for boys' initiation is *luwango*, referring to the visits (*luwango*) made to the initiates' camp in order to bestow congratulations, sympathy, food, and gifts. This term suggests the isolation and passive vulnerability of the initiates and also the nurturant role of the community during this transition. In more sophisticated parlance, educated Kaguru may use the Swahili verb *tahiri* to refer to initiation; this is more aptly applied to Muslim initiation and has associations of ceremonial cleansing (e.g., Mtey 1968: 8).

I now describe how a Kaguru youth passes through male initiation. I divide this description into four sections: preparations prior to the boy's removal to the initiation camp, actual circumcision, treatment while the boy is recovering from the operation, and his reentry into the social life of the community.

Preparing the Initiate

As they approach their teens, Kaguru boys *(wanika)* are made increasingly aware that they must face initiation sooner or later. Early on they witness village dances and feasts celebrating the initiation of older boys and girls. Elders sometimes tell stories mentioning initiation. Most striking of all is the teasing of younger boys by older boys who were recently initiated or who are about to be. The older youths warn the younger ones of how horrible initiation will be but also mock them for still being uncircumcised children. Initiation is an ordeal that boys both anticipate and dread. It should eventually lead to more respect and responsibilities, yet they know it is painful and possibly dangerous. Many youths dread anything not known. Whatever their attitude, most Kaguru boys undergo initiation sometime between the ages of about twelve and fifteen, though a few undergo it at a much younger or older age.

Very young initiates have usually been pushed into this in order for them to assume responsibilities. For example, in the past a young Kaguru likely to inherit livestock or office prematurely due to the death or illness of an elder might be initiated somewhat earlier so that he could take on an adult jural status. Such early initiation would be encouraged by a boy's mother, since she would fear that without attaining jural recognition her boy might lose his wealth to elder male collateral kin who would push themselves forward as caretakers. Of course, the boy's own mother might well serve as the actual caretaker once he was initiated and until he was more mature. More often, young Kaguru would find their initiation postponed until they themselves clamored to be cut. This was because so long as a young Kaguru remained uninitiated, he was held back in his timetable to demand wealth to secure a wife and establish a household, which would make him more independent of his elders. Instead, he would be kept doing household chores such as herding livestock, guarding fields against pests, or running errands for older persons, signs of childhood that he would increasingly resent with age. If a household was short of such help, a boy's initiation was sure to be postponed. In the past, initiation and the securing of bridewealth were more firmly controlled by Kaguru elders, who orchestrated arrangements in order to foster and prolong control of junior men. Today, elders might push for earlier initiation in order to foster obedience in the case of schoolboys who reside away from home. The argument would be that boys who have been initiated are likely to be more sober and more responsible than those who have not. Since advanced schoolboys already reside not with their elders but in boarding school dormitories, they are already utilizing space away from home in a manner consistent with youth who have been initiated. Today, too, many boys pester to be initiated simply because peers at school have been cut.

Possibilities to control younger men (through control of both bridewealth and access to land) are slimmer today with a cash and wage economy and constant government and missionary interference. (The promise to provide money for schooling, however, is a new power for some adults.) Many elders no longer care one way or the other when their juniors are initiated, so long as it is properly done. Some do say that today boys are being initiated at a much earlier age than in the past. The one change in boys' initiation that most Kaguru frown upon is that both Christian missionaries and outsider African officials try to discourage traditional circumcision in the bush and instead advocate cutting supervised by personnel trained in Western medicine. While some Kaguru have been cut in local mission and government hospitals, these are few, and often they are made fun of by other Kaguru if this is discovered.

When a boy's father decides his son is ready to be initiated, the man visits other senior relatives about this.[4] He particularly seeks assurance that an elder in the boy's own matrilineage (a mother's brother) concurs. Ideally, a wide range of kin should support the decision and should demonstrate this by visiting the boy at his initiation. Given that the boy is of a reasonably appropriate age, there remain two factors affecting the decision. First, it is necessary to secure the approval of the ancestral dead through consulting divination. Second, wealth for food, beer, and fees for the circumciser must be amassed. Further wealth is also needed to entertain the many people attending the boy during his recovery as well as the many others participating in the dances and feasts essential to validate his recovery and readmission to society. Whatever an elder's actual motives, he is unlikely openly to oppose initiation on the grounds of lacking wealth or on account of needing the boy's steady services at home, since both would reflect his lack of power. Most likely, those who may oppose initiation will hope that various divinations *(masalu)* will turn up some grounds for postponement. Unfortunately, such consultations themselves also cost wealth, and their results are never binding and their interpretation is open to contestation. In most cases, when a father decides that a boy is ready, at least some of the boy's kin will agree to assist the plan. While the amounts of wealth involved may seem small by our standards, they can run up to several months' income in beer, flour, chickens, goats, and cash, not to mention labor and time. Fortunately, boys' initiation is allowed only in the dry season, after harvests are in, when there is less farm work and people usually have more food supplies and cash.

In the past, the boy's father was expected to secure the permission of the elders of the owner clan in whose area the cutting would be held. This most often required payment of a pot of beer, though chickens or other meat could be provided instead. The payment is termed *lubafu* (ribs), after the cuts of meat provided when animals were slain at a feast where such an owner was invited along with others. As so often with Kaguru, the term expresses an optimistic overestimation of the contribution likely to be actually involved.

The boy's father (or one of his kinsmen) is also responsible for selecting a circumciser *(ibakwa,* from *baka,* "to anoint"; or *muganga,* "doctor"; or *muhunga,* from *ng'hunga,* "circumcision blood," "circumcision wound," or "that which is laid bare"; and very rarely *ngaliba).* He is usually a local Kaguru who specializes in this. Such skills are not inherited, and today men with previous experience as medical orderlies or dressers sometimes claim such abilities. Traditionally, the circumciser's reputation was as much on account of his command of powerful medicines as any skill in cutting. These medicines involve substances to aid the healing of wounds and to ward off witchcraft and sorcery.[5]

Kaguru say that in the past larger groups of boys were cut at one time than are today. When I attended circumcisions and related ceremonies, these involved as few as one boy and no more than five, though I was told that some gatherings I did not visit had as many as a dozen initiates. Kaguru say it is desirable to have as many boys initiated at one time as possible. This ensures the largest possible display at the least cost for each household, since all the initiates' kin share in the payment to the circumciser and in providing beer and food to those attending the boys. Above all, the more people involved, the larger the celebration (ng'oma) danced (kufinwa) both at the cutting and at the time of recovery. The size of celebrations is important for the prestige of those who stage them. The more persons celebrating, the more an initiation effectively confirms manhood for the initiates.

By the time the actual day for initiation has come, many relatives of the initiate have spent considerable time visiting one another to announce the time of the ritual and to secure promises of beer, food, cash, and labor for celebrations. The initiate's kinswomen have worked for days preparing beer. The initiate's kinsmen and neighbors have selected a piece of bush (kumbago) that is near a settlement but not within ready hearing or view. This should be both secluded and shady. The initiate and those who attend will remain there for at least a month. Shade is important because both literally and figuratively the wounds are considered hot and recovery is seen as a cooling (kuhosa) operation. Some Kaguru say it is a good sign when it is overcast on initiation day. The entire atmosphere at cutting is hot because any shedding of blood is both dangerous and polluting and therefore heated. Yet in another sense, the cutting commences a cooling operation because it imposes potential order on hot sexuality.

The initiates' kin and neighbors take machetes and hoes to the initiation site. The fathers of the initiates donate beer for the workers (ibiga dya sengakumbi, "pot for building the camp"). A space is cleared in the bush (luga lulimigwe kumbage) to provide a camp (ilago or ikumbi, Swahili term). This space (lugha) forms a sector of temporary social order in what is ordinarily a bit of wild bush. A shelter (chibanda) is erected, usually a rectangular frame of poles with a thatched roof. Often brush or straw matting is piled on one or two sides for added shade and protection. This shelter usually will accommodate half a dozen people, initiates and attendants, its size depending upon how many boys are to be cut. Sometimes men purchase medicines to make this area safe from witches. The shelter itself is often "doctored" with amulets or horns full of medicines (see photograph, Beidelman 1971b: 102). One may find branches of euphorbia (magole) lying on paths leading to the clearing.

Magole secretes a milky fluid that causes blindness and is thought magically to blind witches entering the clearing.

By the time the first initiates arrive on the day of cutting, a number of men have congregated at the camp, some with stools and mats. A few have brought pots of beer and supplies of tobacco as well in order to pass the time. Some have also brought kudu horns *(migunda* or *mahemba)* that will be sounded repeatedly during the height of the activities. The entire clearing is often demarcated by a series of stakes *(lusimbi)*, which have been doctored with medicines. The initiated novices are prohibited from stepping over and beyond these markers.

For the attendants of the initiates themselves, this camp constitutes a striking departure from their everyday affairs. Of course, all the attendants have themselves been initiated, and many have already assisted at several previous initiations. Some attendants will spend many days at a time in the bush, yet here they will neither hunt nor clear land, the two customary occupations of men once they are in the bush. Instead, they mainly sit around speaking to the initiates and their visitors and put the initiates through their daily regimen. In a kind of inversion, sociable activities are temporarily imported from the regular settlement routine into the bush camp.

Zerubavel emphasizes how rites of separation provide spatial and temporal gaps that define change for initiates (1991: 23). What is sometimes forgotten is that these disruptions deeply affect the adults who serve in such camps and who endure privation as well. Not only will some of the elderly attendants endure the discomfort and cold of sleeping in the bush, something people would not normally do, but some may even have to fetch water or seek firewood. Some may even help cook food, for kinswomen may not always bring all the cooked food that is needed, or even if they do, it may need to be rewarmed. These are all properly women's chores and not men's. Of course, even in this deviant situation no male would pound or grind grain to make flour, which is the main reason why women must keep bringing staple foods to the edge of the camp. All of these activities show that even these elderly instructors, not just the initiates, are undergoing a difficult and unusual period. True, the elders are in control and know all that will be done, so they suffer none of the anxiety and confusion promoted amongst the initiates. Still, these activities recall the instructors' own initiation, and consequently the camp can be emotionally moving and important for them as well as for the initiates. These changes also affect those left behind in the villages, who worry and miss those who are away.

On the day of circumcision, the initiates are offered only a bit of gruel *(uji)*, though most are too anxious to eat at all. The elders tending the initiates are given meat *(nyama)*, termed *ng'hunga* (blood from the wound). Each initiate is shaved *(kugeta)* from head to toe by a kinsman. In part this is because the initiate's lower body should be clean for the operation, but since this also involves shaving the head and armpits, it obviously relates to the boy's transitional state rather than to any more practical, hygienic advantages cited by modern Kaguru who attempt to rationalize such practices to the anthropologist.

Early on the morning of circumcision, the initiates are gathered in the *isepo* (unmarried males' house) along with an elder who has been designated as the one to care for them *(yakwadima,* "he tends children" [or a field, or a herd]). They are all silent *(wanyamala)*. An elder or circumcised youth is sent from the camp to fetch the boys. Usually the women of the village begin to ululate *(ng'henje)* and accompany the boys part of the way along the path out of the village. For Kaguru, women's ululation marks festive and joyous occasions, such as weddings and births. The boys should take courage from this sound.

The Cutting

When the initiates *(wali)* arrive, they are told to sit on the ground in one corner of the camp. Many men and youths are already gathered there, kin *(wandugu)*, neighbors from one's village *(wakaya)*, and outsiders *(wageni)*. The circumciser orders people about. He stands out from the crowd because he holds a special fly whisk *(muse)* with a white-beaded handle, with which he directs others (see photograph, Beidelman 1971b: 105). He wears a beaded headband *(ikuchi* or *chigalama)* with strands of beads hanging down over his eyes like a veil. The headband is multicolored, though white predominates. He also wears various amulets around his neck and on his wrists. Even if he is dressed in Western garb, such beads and amulets set him apart from every other elder present, especially in recent times, when few Kaguru men wear beads. The circumciser has assembled his equipment *(ifinhu,* "things") in the center of the space where the cutting will take place. He has a small pot *(chijungu chidodogi)* of water for cooling his tools and washing away blood. He has a few small knives *(fimage)*, ordinarily stored in chicken or livestock fat, and a whetstone *(chinolo)*. Such equipment must never be used for any purpose other than circumcision. Most Kaguru advocate a small knife *(chimage)*, but a few prefer scissors; razors are said to be too sharp, but I have seen them used. The circumciser carries small pouches said to contain medicines for healing and protection against witchcraft and sorcery. Many of the objects are decorated with white beads, and strands of white beads are strewn into the water pot. White *(-jelu)* is the color of cooling in both the physical and moral senses.

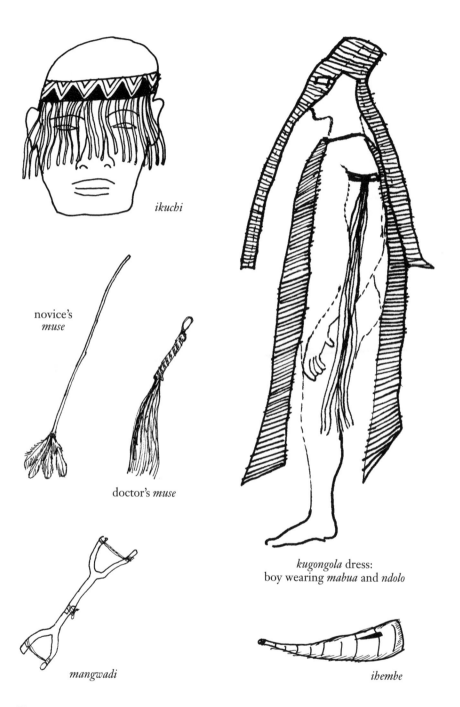

ikuchi

novice's
muse

doctor's *muse*

kugongola dress:
boy wearing *mabua* and *ndolo*

mangwadi

ihembe

Figure 10. Items worn during Kaguru rituals and celebrations.

The circumciser has brought his own special stool (*igoda*). Around it are gathered various skins of goats or cattle, one for each boy to be cut. The circumciser summons the boys to be cut, one by one. The boys arrived at the clearing wearing cloaks or shorts, but they took these off when they entered the camp; as each boy is called by the circumciser, he comes forward naked. He is attended by at least one kinsman and sometimes several other people as well. He sits down on the hide. His kinsman, seated behind him, draws him back while other men and youths hover over him, offering encouragement. It is said that a boy needs to have men around him, especially kinsmen, to provide sympathy or understanding (*usungu*). I was told that while it was good for a boy to be silent and brave while he was being cut, it was not a moral disaster if he cried out. (Maasai and Baraguyu were scandalized when I told them that Kaguru boys would sometimes cry out at cutting.) While the boy is being cut, the circumciser sings and the crowd responds. Repeatedly, he sings "*Matang'ana!*" (said to be an archaic term for initiation). The crowd responds with "*Simba yaluma ng'ombe* [the lion bites the cow]!"[6] At the same time, others blow the horns (*migunda*). This continues until each cutting is completed. After each initiate has been cut, he receives a fly whisk (*muse*) made out of a long, slender stick to which chicken feathers have been attached. (The chickens were newly slain for food for the gathering.) The initiate is supposed to use his fly whisk to ward off insects from his wound. As near as I could tell, there is no distinction attached to the order in which boys are cut. Men do sometimes get named from this, the first person cut being named Chilongola (first) and the very last one cut Musiwanda (last).

Once all the initiates have been cut, they are moved into the initiation hut (*chibanda*), where they will spend the next weeks recovering. Each will be fitted with *mangwadi*. These are leg separators made by two forked sticks tied together so as to keep the initiate's legs from chafing the wound. Initiates often also wear hemp collars to which short cords are attached leading to wristlets, thus holding their hands up and away from their genitals. These are worn at night, when the initiates' caretakers may be asleep and consequently unable to prevent the boys from accidentally injuring themselves. Sometimes a millet stalk is cut to form a kind of half hoop that lifts the penis from the body to prevent the fresh wound from chafing; this is termed *chingowe*. Each initiate sits and sleeps in his own space demarcated from others by small logs or banana stalks. The initiate (*mwali*) is now termed *mwaluko* (he whose circumcision wounds have not yet healed.)

The circumciser should now dispose of the polluting waste from the operations. He must bury the hides, which by now are soaked with the initiates' blood (*ng'hunga*). Even any earth soaked with blood should be scooped up and removed. The circumciser should also bury the foreskins (*amakunja*, "the torn-off"). He should do this secretly since such materials could be used by witches to harm the boys' future sexuality. Some circumcisers might even give these to the boys' fathers, making them assume the responsibility for their safe disposal.

Once all the initiates are situated in the initiation hut, they may be visited. An initiate's close kin should all come to call (*wekwija kuluwango*) (see photograph, Beidelman 1971b: 105). Such visits continue during all of the initiate's confinement, but these are most frequent during the first days after cutting. Each person making a circumcision visit (*luwango*) must bring a gift. Those who are close may bring beer, chickens, or even a goat or sheep, but most bring only a few coins. Close older kinswomen try to make a single visit to the camp on the day of the cutting. When I witnessed this for the first time, it was a very formal visit with none of the nonchalance that men showed. This involved the initiate's mother, grandmother, or father's sister and was said to assure such women that the initiate was safe. Kaguru informants were not helpful to me in resolving my questions about why women were allowed to make such visits. This had perplexed me because I had been told earlier by many Kaguru that women must always avoid an initiation camp. To be sure, I saw women making such visits right after the circumcision itself, yet I never saw women enter the actual camp center after that time. For that matter, I even saw uninitiated boys loitering around the edge of camps, though they were never allowed within. My own guess as to why such elderly women should visit is that they thereby formally accede to and bless a rite that they might be expected to resent since it does separate youths from them forever. No comparable visiting is performed by male relatives for female initiates.

All of these visits are made so that kin and neighbors can bless (*kuhunga*) and kiss (*kuwangonela*) the initiates, which they do by bending over them and putting the initiates' hands to their lips.

The camp (*ilago*) is well marked off from the surrounding bush. A steady stream of visitors passes across the boundaries between the bush and the camp, visiting and bringing supplies to the initiates and attendants, who are camped there for many weeks. Often these visitors are women who have prepared food back in their villages for the campers. Such women never enter the camp itself but hover just on the edge of the clearing until someone comes to collect the supplies. This demarcation of the camp is underscored by the fact that everyone who approaches must announce her or his entry by singing. The entrant may sing "*Sanghola* [delayed]" repeatedly. This is offered as a kind of apology for not coming sooner. Those within the camp, especially the initiates, reply with one of several phrases, such as "*Ng'hunga, ng'hulamusa*

Figure 11. Kaguru circumciser being greeted by elder women kin of newly circumcised boys. The women will be allowed to view the boys briefly but will not be permitted to enter the initiates' enclosure. The circumciser wears a beaded cap *(ikuchi)* and holds a fly whisk *(muse)* with a beaded handle. These signify his role both as circumciser and as the person in charge of all the arrangements at the initiation camp. He wears these red and white beads to signify danger and order, both in the sense of the initiation's bringing order out of a dangerous operation and in the sense that he himself has medicines and knowledge that master danger and allow order to be maintained. Photograph taken at Berega in 1957.

wana [circumcision blood, greeting the children]" or "*Usungu watama* [I feel sympathy for them]." Others might reply: "*Wagomba nakoma* [you say I've killed them]" or "*Namwigala kuwusnga digoya* [I sent him to good makers (cutters)]" A very simple sequence would be the call "*Mutema* [cut you]" and the response "*Temelelaga kuli wana wetu* [you ask about us children]," followed by the response "*Ndege sumila wana ng'hanya* [the bird feeds its young]." Others may call out "*Wana, ng'hulamusa munyamalila* [children, I greet you who are keeping quiet]" and receive the answer "*Chambala uchiwa* [we are worried about poverty]," the exchange initially expressing the visitors' concern about the boys, whose pain is implied by their silence. The boys in turn confirm their suffering by expressing their fear that they may remain debilitated, that is, impotent. Or the boys' attendants may sing either to women visiting at the camp's outskirts or even to the boys themselves as they await their kinswomen's visits: "*Wang'ina gali galikulila meso mung'hodingo mang'ina nenu* [your mothers are crying out and their eyes are weeping, your mothers]" or, less sympathetically, "*Go mai, gowandigage, gowandigage wije ulange dikwangwa sale* [you, Mother, who was scolding me, scolding me, come see my painful wound]." As can be seen, the general tone of the entry calls expresses worry and concern and a sense of pathos regarding the frightened and suffering initiates, but there is also an undercurrent of hostility and resentment. The replies generally are upbeat and meant to cheer the initiates who sing them as much as to cheer their visitors. Exchanges of songs at initiation express a "working up" of feelings that keys up and encourages the participants. In an essay on female initiation amongst the Okiek of Kenya, Kratz describes such songs as giving courage to initiates before their ordeal (1990b: 46–51). For Kaguru, such exchanges occur during recovery and both reassure the sufferers and, as with the Okiek, imply future rewards for their bravery. Thus the stage on which initiation is played out is expanded to include an audience larger than the initiates and their instructors. Home is temporarily banished from the camp, but initiates are never allowed to forget those left behind or the life they represent.

While such initial visiting may be going on, others have gone back to the initiates' settlements to report that the actual cutting has been completed. Some of these men wrap leather thongs or strips of cloth around their legs. To these are attached many small, round bells (*mangala*) that jingle as the men walk. The men have cut staves, which they may also twine with bells. They dance back to the settlement in a rhythmic parade, striking their staves on the earth and stamping their jingling feet. When they reach the initiates' villages, the residents come out to the edge of the settlements to greet them. Most of the initiates' female kin and younger male relatives are in the crowd. They all dance what is termed *ibabwaja*. Again and again they sing, "*Wamutema na mage hoo! Sabe! Ah! Woiye* [they have cut him with a knife! Oh! Sabe (a boy's name)! Ah! Alas]!" Dancing continues far into the night, and the celebrants drink much beer. If a village is prosperous, there may be feasting as well. People may sing of a male dancer, "*Mangala yandeta kwikumbi* [he brought dance bells to the initiation camp]." Such a song may be meant to commend a man for celebrating the occasion, but it can also imply that he came in order to have an excuse to dance and celebrate, not out of any concern for the boys. Kaguru made a point of letting me know that a double-edged meaning was intended in many of these songs. Similarly, the refrain "*Sina mwana gwe* [I have no child]" is often added to such songs. This can mean that the celebrant is there to honor the initiates even though he has no kinship with the boys, or it can imply that a person is not kin and therefore has no good reason for being there but only wants the free food and beer available or the chance to seduce women at the dance. Motives are often kept ambiguous and ambivalent in Kaguru oral play.

All of the songs sung just after circumcision are a mixture of celebration and anxiety. Other songs are:

Mwanangu kaluta! Mwanangu kaluta!
My child has gone! My child has gone!

Ng'hanga solila so luseluse nee! Nyo luse! Nyo luse!
Guinea fowl will cry out, "Luse! Oh, luse! Oh, luse!"

   This refers to the boy being cut and the pain he feels.

Dina diwangala Misungo! Dibwa dyetu hee! Eyo dibwa dyetu!
It has a bell, Misungo [a dog's name]! Our dog, ah! Ah, our dog!

   The bell is said to refer to the glans of the penis, which circumcision exposes.

Ani ngamba mhela kumbe musala hee! Eyo kumbe musala!
I thought it was a rhinoceros, but it is only the leaves of the wild palm, oh! Only the leaves of the wild palm!

   Initiation did not turn out to be as terrible as feared.

Iwandamilia lukolongo lugugu haa! Eyo lugugu!
It has gone down the drainage channel, oh! Oh, the drainage channel!

The blood (impurity) has flown away with circumcision.

Chimile mugongo wa nhembo? Chisonya hee! Eyo chisonya![7]
What is standing on the elephant's back? A sparrow, oh! Oh, a sparrow!

There is a fear of initiation, but it is unfounded, just as the huge elephant is feared yet a sparrow can safely stand on its back.

Nija, nija, gwe na mugeni, nija! Nilonda dilamusa, na mugeni nija.
I come, I come, you stranger, I come! I come, I bring greetings and I, a stranger, come.

The stranger is the circumciser or one of the instructors at the camp.

Ani na mugeni! Nalonda dilalmusa iya!
I, the stranger! I come for greeting, oh!

This has the same meaning as the previous song.

Dida ditulikila usungu ni mweleka mwana.
Guts have pain and I bore a child.

There is pain but also reward at the birth of a child, and so too it is the case with the moral rebirth of initiation.

Go chibunga! Awana katagahi? Awana weja weja mulembula.
You maize cob! Where have you lost the children? The children went to a good thing.

This refers to going to circumcision. The kin, especially the mothers, are likened to maize cobs that have lost their kernels. The children seem lost, but they have gone for a good and proper reason, just as the kernels fall or are plucked from the cob for a good cause, such as making food or planting more maize.

Nhunga dya ng'anja! Ni nhunga dya ng'anja!
Chinengemale mwana lumbudyangu!
Ng'hole chikuku! Ng'ende ng'hamulole!
Woyi! Iyi! Iye! Iye! Ng'ende ng'hamulole!
Dilole go iye iye iye ng'ende ng'hamulole!

Bead string for tradition (initiation wound)! Bead string for tradition
(initiation wound)!
Injured child of my sibling of the opposite sex!
I'll catch a hen! I'll go greet him!
Oh, I'll go greet him!
Oh, I'll go greet him!

These are obviously simply variations on the sentiments evinced in the
previously presented songs. These songs evoke the worry about young
kin who have seemingly disappeared into the initiation camp but who will
survive their ordeal. The worried kin will be allowed to come greet the
initiates after they have been cut. They may bring them food to console
them and please those who tend them. The songs also refer to the ultimate good and cultural continuity achieved by initiation, which may at
first seem a threatening process. Here, a man or woman goes to greet a
nephew. This most likely involves a mother's brother singing about his
sister's child. The mention of the bead string refers to the continuity of
these rites practiced with successive generations within a lineage, like
beads forming a series on a string. Others besides kin will sing parts of
this or other songs, but some may add the phrase "*Sina mwana yee* [with-
out a child, oh!]" to indicate that they are not kin. One meaning of the
beads mentioned in the song involves the beads the circumciser uses to
protect the initiates from excessive bleeding or other harm. The reference
to a bead string here also may refer to the single strand of beads many
adults wear around the waist. That string is seen or felt only in sexual
play and has erotic associations that emerge only after a person is an
adult. The beads, strung in a line, thus imply protection, sexuality, and
continuity.

Recovering from Circumcision

Once the shock of the actual circumcision has worn off, the initiates and their
mentors settle down to spend a month or more in the initiation camp until the
boys' wounds heal *(kuhona)*. This is the time when the ideas surrounding initiation are explained to the boys. The initial operation is essential, of course,
but initiation would not differ greatly from such cutting by the Kaguru's
neighbors were it not followed by the particular Kaguru lore taught to the
boys during their recovery. This information is drilled into initiates by con-

stant repetition of songs *(sinyimbo)* and puzzles *(miseigo)* and other traditions such as stories about the origins of the different Kaguru clans. This is the time for explaining *(kubula)*. It is the first time for these young Kaguru that sexual matters and other knowledge are freely and extensively discussed between the old and young. I do not, however, discuss these matters further here since this oral literature is the subject of chapter 7.

It is important to remember that the Kaguru boys' initiation camp represents the most difficult experience so far faced by any Kaguru young man. It is most unlikely that he has ever before experienced so much physical pain and been in such an alarming situation, surrounded each nightfall by the threatening sounds of nocturnal animal life that childhood stories associate with witches and other dangerous beings. It is probably the first time a boy has ever spent many nights out in the bush, away from his settlement and his family. He probably will never again do so, except to assist as an elder at initiations for others. In precolonial times no Kaguru youth ever spent a night far from some hearth prior to initiation.[8] At such hearths his mother or some other solicitous female relative would have cooked for him and worried about his needs. Now no women are about to care for or coddle him. In modern times, of course, a few Kaguru might go away to boarding school, but that is hardly a very frightening environment, and it is not at all likely to prepare a youth for fearful nights out in the darkened bush.

The boys clearly find their first days in the bush to be unsettling, especially the nights. It is considered especially vital that the elders carefully tend a perpetual fire (sometimes termed *lusimbi*, the same word used for the stalks separating the boys from one another) at this time. This fire, of course, separates the clearing from the darkened bush. During their first days in camp, the initiates present a dejecting, pitiful sight. They usually are clad in plain white cloth and seem to feel as vulnerable and insufficiently garbed as many of us do when wearing hospital-issued gowns. The boys are forbidden to bathe and are repeatedly dusted in white ashes from the fire. They are reminded of this by being encouraged to sing repeatedly, "*Awana we nhembo! Ahe walikoga lulonga* [children of the elephant! They have bathed in mud]." Kaguru believe that when an elephant gives birth, the tiny calf is first daubed by its mother with mud, which protects it until it is stable. So too the "newly born" initiates are covered in ashes to help them emerge into adulthood. We know that elephants cover themselves with dust or mud in what appear to be attempts to get more comfortable. For Kaguru, the ashes are thought to keep the initiates "cool" and "dry." Although Kaguru refused to comment on my queries, I was struck by the fact that the only other people thought to be ashen are witches. When I asked for the reason, Kaguru said that witches cover themselves with ashes in order not to be recognized. My own assumption is that the ashes reflect the peripheral state of both initiates and witches.

During this period of healing, it is especially important that no nubile women be seen by the novices. It is said that were this to happen, a novice might have an erection and that this would cause his wound to bleed. For this reason, old women or young girls are the most likely to be sent to deliver food to the outskirts of camps. During this initial healing period, the attendants employ the various restraining devices mentioned earlier to keep the initiates from touching themselves. They keep a small pot of water by each initiate with which to wash away the blood (inconsistent with the rule that the boys must not bathe). This pot also contains strings of beads, usually all white but occasionally with a very few red or yellow beads mixed in. These beads (and sometimes added roots, herbs, or other medicines) add to the water's power to cool the wound and consequently make it heal. When the initiate has fully recovered and emerges from his seclusion, this pot is presented to his mother. It is said that if the initiate should die during initiation (I never heard of any Kaguru doing so), the death would never be spoken about, but at the conclusion of the confinement of that cohort of boys, the dead youth's mother would receive his pot, broken, as a tacit indication of her loss.

During these weeks, the boys are kept from being bored by the constant drill of learning songs, stories, riddles, clan histories, and other lore. It is probably the single longest period during which any Kaguru male will ever experience so little physical activity. It is also the only traditionally sanctioned time when Kaguru are asked to exercise their powers of memory and analysis in such a prolonged and intensive way. The boys (and girls as well) are given the corpus of Kaguru culture. This is said to be transmitted in unchanging form according to age-old traditions, even though clan histories (see Beidelman 1970, 1971a, 1978) and, as we shall see, songs are sometimes modified and modernized to fit changing conditions. Writing of the European Renaissance's preoccupation with imitating ancient texts, Greene could be referring to the Kaguru: "The version of history implied by this imitative strategy might be called *reproductive* or *sacramental*; it celebrates an enshrined primary text by rehearsing it liturgically, as though no other form of elaboration could be worth its dignity" (1982: 38).[9]

During their confinement, the initiates are encouraged to eat as much as possible. This is said to be a time for fatness (*ugini*) and strength (*ludole*), which the initiates gain through consuming a great deal of meat (*nyama*). I found that this was more an ideal than a reality. Kaguru simply do not have vast supplies of livestock and fowl. Certainly initiation constitutes a time when youths eat more protein than they have ever previously enjoyed, but they must still supplement their diet with considerable starch *(ugali)*. Still, vegetables *(mboga)* are thought not to be good for their recovery, and eggs *(matagi)* must be avoided completely because they are thought to cause wounds to bleed. Eggs also are thought to promote the growth of body hair, an attribute potentially opposed to social order. When the boys are somewhat recovered, they are allowed to wander some distance from camp, where they can trap and hunt wild animals. These are manly endeavors, though considering the hunted-out state of much of Kaguruland today, few initiates are likely to get more than an occasional wood rat, guinea fowl, francolin, or hare for their efforts.

The boys should have no difficulty recovering *(kuhona)* from the operation. Indeed, much of the daily routine at the camp seems designed to make the recovery period more arduous and prolonged than it need be. Yet relatives, especially the boys' mothers, often worry. Some believe that giving up sexual relations during this time will facilitate the boys' recovery. Conversely, in western Kaguruland some believe that should the boys' recovery appear jeopardized, people might perform *sakalakala*, a kind of saturnalia held at night in the bush during which people speak and act obscenely and sometimes have sexual intercourse in a promiscuous manner, unmindful of proscriptions based on birth or affinity. I could find no reliable account that this ever actually did occur. Yet the fact that some Kaguru believe that such activities might take place and promote recovery reveals a side of their thinking about order and disorder and the processes of moral and physical development.

As the initiates regain strength, the elder instructors encourage them to leave the camp and wander as a group in order to visit nearby settlements to beg for food and gifts. Shepherded by one or more of their instructors, the initiates sing songs of walking about *(sinyimbo sa kutalamukila)*. They serenade all the villages near the camp, from daytime into the night. They cannot actually enter the settlements, but they can go up to the outskirts, where the inhabitants can come out to greet them. They receive coins, small quantities of grain, chickens, tobacco, or arrows as thanks. The villagers are said to appreciate the boys' having shown them what they have learned at initiation. The boys' songs and skillful dancing are thought sure to please people. The gifts that villagers give them as thanks are thought to console the boys for the cold *(ukinga mbeho)* they feel from being outside and not in a settlement. Some boys are said to make as much as thirty or forty shillings by the end of their initiation.

On these tours the initiates wear ceremonial coverings of plaited millet straw *(mabua)* that conceal their faces and much of their chests and backs. These are often decorated with chicken or guinea fowl feathers. The boys wear armlets *(ndolo)* trimmed with very long strands of sisal fibers. They sing and dance in unison, single file, whirling their bodies and twirling the long sisal strands hanging from their arms. Some boys have whistles, which they blow to keep time or to call dance signals. These youths are covered with gray ashes and are not easily recognizable. The elders and circumcised youths who accompany the initiates frequently blow kudu horns. Sometimes one elder carries a tall pole with a pennant in order to attract attention. The food and other presents gathered are either consumed back in the camp or sometimes sent by the boys back home to their mothers, who then cook the food and return it to camp.

Both these wanderings and the songs sung during them are termed *kugongola*, "proceeding ahead."[10] At such times the initiates sing, "*Awana we nhembe, aho walikogoa lulenge* [children of the elephant, they bathe in mud]." This is the same song that they were taught earlier to sing within the camp itself. They sing many other songs as well, for example:

Eee mugona, kulamucha!
Wenya kaya mugona, kalamucha!
Go munjengile dikinga, kulamucha!
Mundendawala wadode, kulamucha!
Eee mugona, kulamucha!
Eee, you who are sleeping, it is dawn!
Owners of the village who are sleeping, it is dawn!
You who built the settlement fence, it is dawn!
You who are sleeping, it is dawn!

This is sung at night to stir people up so that they will fetch food for the initiates. It is, of course, not dawn at all, but the serenaders want the people to arise just as though it were daybreak.

Nime mulugongo!
Nhegelese chilonga munya kaya!
Twanga wela uwo aya ahee! Twanga uwo aye ahee ho!
Nyanga uye hoo!
Ase chuile mukaya!
Nhegelese chilonga munya kaya!
Ichikuku kuletele, kuletele, kuletele!
[variant: *Ichikuku mwana ng'wiya!*]
Nhegelelse chilonga munya kaya!
Idipesa mwana njele!
Nhegelese chilonga munya kaya!

I stand on the hill!
Listening for what the village owner says to us!
Pound maize ready, oh! Pound maize, oh oh!
Repay, oh!
We who are in the village!
Listening for what the village owner says to us!
Chicken bring, bring, bring!
[variant: Chicken for child's crying!]
Listening for what the village owner says to us!
Money for child's making noise!
Listening for what the village owner says to us!

   This clearly refers to the rewards of chickens, maize, and money
expected from the villagers. There may be a sly allusion to sexuality as
well, since *kutwanga* (to pound maize) may also mean "to copulate."

Kaila, Kaila, toa dikenje, toa dikenje, iye yi hee!
Toa dikenje cheli wako yi hee
Toa dikenje cheli wako yi hee
Chiwana chali wako!
Chiwana chali wako!
Kaila, Kaila, toa dikenje, toa dikenje, iye yi hee!
Go mai, go mai, genda mhola
Go mai, go mai, genda mhola
Genda mhola, genda mhola iye yi hee!
Genda mhola, genda mhola iye yi hee!
Munjila, munjila muli ng'hwale!
Munjila, munjila muli ng'hwale!
Kaila, Kaila, toa dikenje, toa dikenje, iye yi hee!
Kaila [a woman's name], Kaila, ululate, ululate, eh oh ah!
Ululate for your young ones, ah eh!
Ululate for your young ones, ah eh!
Your young ones!
Your young ones!
Kaila, Kaila, ululate, ululate, eh oh ah!
You, Mother, you, Mother, to one whom you spurn!
You, Mother, you, Mother, to one whom you spurn!
Chicks, chicks, let us eat!
Chicks, chicks, let us eat!

Kaila, Kaila, ululate, ululate, eh oh ah!
You mother, you mother, go carefully!
You mother, you mother, go carefully!
Go carefully, go carefully!
Go carefully, go carefully!
The way, the way is rough!
The way, the way is rough!
Kaila, Kaila, ululate, ululate, eh oh ah!

This alludes to mothers who have allowed their children to go to the camps to be initiated. Now the mothers must make the difficult trek to bring food to them in camp.

Go mai, nagwe ng'hwina sungu na wana!
Go mai, nagwe ng'hwina sungu na wana!
Ng'hona nakuliga udodo wanhuma!
Ng'hwina sungu na wana!
You, Mother, don't pity the children!
You, Mother, don't pity the children!
If I was insolent toward you, it was on account of my childishness!
You don't pity the children!

This is yet another song alluding to the fears of psychological and emotional separation between sons and mothers. Again, the implications are that the suffering son pines for his absent mother and hopes that it is not any bad feelings on her part that keep her from visiting him and bringing food and sympathy.

E waye towa chigenda! Kaluli, muwaga ng'ombe!
E waye towa chigenda! Kaluli, muwaga ng'ombe!
Muwaga ng'ombe, waya! Towa chigenda!
Kaluli, muwaga ng'ombe!
Oh, beating let us go! Kaluli [a man's name], driver of cattle!
Oh, beating let us go! Kaluli [a man's name], driver of cattle!
Driver of cattle, oh! Beating let us go!
Kaluli, driver of cattle!

The herdsman, Kaluli, drives a herd of cattle along by beating them with a stick. The initiates compare themselves to such a herd being driven about the countryside by their initiation instructors.

Eyo dikaya no dyetu! Chogende mulwambe!
Eyo chogende mulwambe!
Oh, the village is ours! We are coming outside it!
Oh, we are coming outside it!

The boys march about, even to the outskirts of their own village, but they cannot actually enter until they are fully recovered and the initiation completed. They march just to the village's edge, where they plead for food and gifts.

Eyo duswa! Eyo duswa! Dya musanga njelele!
Eyo duswa! Eyo duswa! Dya musanga njelele!
Kunyuma duswa! Kumwana duswa! Dya musanga njelele!
Kunyuma duswa! Kumwana duswa! Dya musanga njelele!
Kwa buba duswa! Kwa mai dyswa! Dya musanga njelele!
Kwa baba duswa! Kwa mai dyswa! Dya musanga njelele!
Oh, sunset! Oh, sunset! It is sinking in the sand!
Oh, sunset! Oh, sunset! It is sinking in the sand!
Behind sunset! Ahead sunset! It is sinking in the sand!
Behind sunset! Ahead sunset! It is sinking in the sand!
Father sunset! Mother sunset! It is sinking in the sand!
Father sunset! Mother sunset! It is sinking in the sand!

The villagers are reminded that it is late and they surely do not want to make the boys wait so that they would have to journey back to their camp in the deep night.

When the instructor wants the boys to stop repeating a particular song and commence a new one, he will shout: "*Wanyamalusi* [those who whistle]!" Then the initiates will blow on their whistles all at once and stop that song. In this way, the singers proceed through all the above songs, all dwelling on the theme of striking pity in the villagers.

Dijala, dijala dikonila!
Dijala, dijala dikonila!
Dikonila iye ba!
Dikonila iye ba!
Dijala, dijala!
Dikonile, dikonile, iya abee!

Hunger, hunger is killing me!
Hunger, hunger is killing me!
Killing me, ah, oh!
Killing me, ah, oh!
Hunger, hunger!
Killing me, killing me, ah, oh!

Chiwana, chiwana chiliwenu iye hee!
Chiwana, chiwana chiliwenu iye hee!
Chiliwenu, chiliwenu iye hee!
Chiwana, chiwana!
Chiliwenu, chiliwenu iya ahee!
We children, we children, we are yours!
We children, we children, we are yours!
We are yours, we are yours, ah, oh!
We children, we children!
We are yours, we are yours, ah, oh!

In general, for Kaguru, parents are repeatedly pictured as both obliged and emotionally impelled to feed their children. The settlement is repeatedly pictured as a nurturing locale.

Kudia, kudia, chidiage!
Kudia, kudia, chidiage!
Chidiage iyo hee!
Chidiage iyo hee!
Kudia, kudia!
Chidiage iya ahee!
Eat, eat, let us eat!
Eat, eat, let us eat!
Let us eat, oh, ah!
Let us eat, oh, ah!
Eat, eat!
Let us eat, oh, ah!

Go ngole! Go ngole!
Sinaona chidala chikwangale mulele!
Eyo go ngole! Eyo go ngole!

Mo wana! Go ngole! Go ngole!
Sinaona chidala chikwangale mulele!
Praise! Praise!
I never saw an old woman clean the food paddle!
Oh, praise! Oh, praise!
You children! Praise! Praise!
I never saw an old woman clean the food paddle!

Kaguru were not at all helpful in explaining this song to me. As far as I can tell, this refers to the fact that food has yet to be served and therefore the food paddle has yet to be cleaned. An obscene sexual allusion may also be intended because old women are often associated with loose sexuality and the food paddle appears to be a phallic symbol.

Mo wana, mulawahi nye?
Chilawa kumikungugu kune njoka ina maganja!
Eyo kwetu Malindi woiye! Eyo kwetu Malindi woiye!
You children, where have you come from?
We came from the *mikungugu* tree, where a snake has hands!
Our home is Malindi, eh! Our home is Malindi, eh!

The children came from circumcision camp, which is alluded to as Malindi (a distant and dreaded place on the coast, associated with slaving and witchcraft) where there is a *mikungugu* tree (a tall tree, possibly also an allusion to the matriclan, *ikungugo*). The reference to a snake with hands may refer to a penis, which sometimes is compared to a snake. The hands may well refer to the fact that the circumcised penis is now socialized.

Emergence from Initiation

The initiates go out serenading for several weeks. Then one day the elders supervising the boys hold a secret meeting *(chibumba)* away from the camp. There they make plans to disband the encampment. The next day the boys are told to go out serenading as usual or they are sent out to hunt. While the boys are away, the elders efface most traces of the camp in which they and the initiates have stayed out in the bush. They tear down the sheltering hut and burn it. They dig holes and bury the ashes and other debris. When the initiates return to the camp at dusk, they find some of the elders waiting there for them, but little is left of the camp except the clearing itself.

The boys are questioned about how many days they have spent in the bush. They are asked to repeat some of the songs or sayings they have learned in order to prove that they are ready to leave. They are asked whether they harbor any resentment against their mentors for having been disciplined. While this questioning is going on, the sun is sinking. As it gets dark, some of the attendants hide themselves in the nearby bush and make threatening sounds. They howl like wild animals. They snap and rustle branches. The initiates are told that these noises come from dangerous wild beasts, from man-eaters, out in the bush and that they must now all take special care to protect themselves. The elders lament that they cannot protect the boys with a fire because the wild beasts have swallowed everything *(wamesa fyose)*, including the firewood. All night the boys must huddle there in the darkened, destroyed camp, harassed by threatening sounds made worse by the elders' unreassuring comments and warnings. The boys are not told that it is some of the elders themselves who are hiding in the bush making these horrible sounds.

After being kept awake all night, the boys are sent out at dawn to fetch red earth with which they are told to smear their bodies. Covered in red earth and ashes, the boys are sent off to serenade their home settlements. Now, if anything remaining of the camp was overlooked by the elders, it is effaced.

Before being sent off, the boys are taught a song that warns them against divulging what happened at initiation. (Presumably the initiates should tell none of their experiences either to uninitiated boys or to women, though most women I met seemed to have a good idea of what happens at male ceremonies.)

Wadodo, mwija longa!
Iyao! Yae! Chijakana! Iyae! Yae!
Wadodo, mukudanhai! Iyae! Yae!
Chijakana! Iyae! Yae!
Wadododo, kilaheni! Iyae! Yae!
Kumbi lusimbi! Iyae! Yae!
Wadodo, kilaheni! Iyae! Yae!
Kumbi lusimbi! Iyae! Yae
Aseye chigenda! Chikohigwa na sigi!
Wekugamba mukila wa ng'holo. Wedasi na mimage!
Wadodo mukalonge! Wadodo kilaheni!
Little ones, you are going to tell!
No! No! We shall deny it! No! No!
Little ones, you are lying! No! No!

We shall deny it! No! No!
Little ones, swear! No! No!
Camp gear! No! No!
Little ones, swear! No! No!
Camp gear! No! No!
We're going! We're tied with ropes!
They told us that it would be the tail of a sheep! The liars of the knife!
Little ones, you are going to tell! You are liars!

This song, which is repeated again and again, is meant to remind the initiates that they should deceive anyone who asks them about what really took place at the initiation camp. Earlier, they themselves had been deceived. For example, the camp gear *(kumbi lusimbi)* was actually got rid of by the elders and not taken by the beasts of the bush, as the elders said. Before the boys went to be circumcised, they had been told that they were going to the bush in order to enjoy a feast of delicacies such as the fat tail of a sheep. Instead, they were cut with the circumcision knife. It was not the sheep's tail that was to be cut off but a human foreskin. The initiates were even, as the song mentions, subjected to the indignity of being constrained by ropes, like animals tethered before sacrifice, in order to ensure that they did not touch their wounds.

Now the boys are ordered to march out of the clearing and head for home without looking back at the spot where the camp had previously stood. To look back would cost the boys the understanding and learning for which they had suffered so much.

By now the people back in the boys' villages know that this is the day ending the youths' time as *waluko* (recovering initiates). People turn out to greet the returning boys. The village women fill the air with ululation. The initiates carry staves festively trimmed with *mtobwe* shrub *(Strophanthus courmonti)*. The circumciser and the elder attendants have gathered to see the initiates off, and some accompany the boys to their homes.

The elder initiators sing:

Wadodo mwilawa nase chilawa doo!
Little ones, you have departed, and we too have departed, eh!

The initiates reply:

Mwilawa inyika yetu hee! O inyika yetu hee!
You have departed from our bush, eh! Our bush, eh!

The elder initiators sing:

Wayetu, mwilawa hase, chilawa nye!
Comrades, you have gone out! And we have gone out!

The initiates sing:

Chilawa inyika yetu hee! O nyika nyetu hee!
Chilawa nanye mwilawa!
We have departed from our bush, eh! Our bush, eh!
We have departed, and you have departed!

The boys and some of the people from the village walk to a nearby stream, singing together. There the boys separate from the crowd in order to bathe and remove the red earth and ashes. They now know that this is *dijua dyo ka-tula chifu* (the day of removing the ashes). While the boys are bathing, some initiation attendants hide in the nearby bushes and make the sounds of wild beasts, much as they had done the night before. This time, however, the elders come out and admit that it was they all along who had been making the threatening animal noises. Now the boys are clean, their skins bright and glistening, and they are given new clothes by the people. (Their old clothes from the camp are given as presents to the attendants.) The boys are ready to return to their home villages as new people (literally, as *wageni*, "strangers") who have conquered *(wasuma)* everything in the bush *(gose ga kumbago)*.

The youths arrive home, where they are greeted by as many kin and neighbors as can be assembled. There is beer *(ugimbi wa kulawa,* "beer of emerging"), food, and much drumming. This is a day when the initiates' new status is marked by a *ng'oma* (celebration) that is danced *(kufinwa)*. It is important to have as much beer as possible since this constitutes the payment that celebrants receive for their dancing. At a good *ng'oma* the dancing and singing are likely to go on until nearly dawn. Such dancing is the same as that held when the youths were circumcised, but it is now termed *musasi*.

On the second day, the day after the initiate has returned home, the boy's kin give him his new names. His matrilineal and patrilateral kin gather around him. The male and female representatives of his *welekwa* (father's matrilineage) and his own *ikungugo* or *lukolo* (matrilineage) anoint him. First a senior and respected member of the *welekwa* anoints him. The youth is seated on a stool, and a patrilateral relative pours castor oil onto the top of the boy's head. The relative spreads the oil by using his own chin, rubbing it downward to the right side of the neck, right shoulder, and arm to the fingers. Adding more oil from time to time, the relative smears oil down the right side of the back, buttocks, and leg to the foot and toes. When that relative is finished, a few other patrilateral kin may follow, though this is not required. Both men and women may do this. Just how many take part is not important so long as at least one senior and respected representative of both of the two kin groups has done so. Then a representative of the matrilineage begins the same procedure on the initiate's left side. During this anointing, relatives will speak names that they wish to bestow upon the initiate. These are names of deceased kin that people want to see perpetuated. It is not necessary that the initiate actually use any or all of the names given. Beer has been brewed for this ceremony (*ugimbi wa masina*, "beer of naming"), and this is drunk during the naming. If the novice accepts a new name, he swallows some beer. If he dislikes a name, he spits beer out. As Hallowell points out (1967: 90), personal names provide the most powerful means by which gender is asserted. In the Kaguru case, such formally bestowed names link persons into a perpetual web of ancestral kin, preserving a memory of personal identity for the relatives. When the women bless the initiate, they sometimes lick up (*kulambita*) some of the oil on his body. Such licking by women is viewed by Kaguru as an intensely affectionate and intimate act, very moving and done only by those who love one most, such as one's mother and grandmothers.

These ceremonies conclude a boy's emergence (*mlao*) from initiation. He now must sleep in the unmarried males' house (*isepo*), though he probably did so even before. He now begins to think more about girls and about what it might be like to be married and have his own household. Most important for his own immediate, everyday experience, he must now be treated with more deference by village boys who are still uncircumcised. To merit such respect, he in turn must now comport himself more soberly and circumspectly and can expect to be sharply criticized or shamed when he does not. He is not, however, free from constant interference by his elders. Until he has his own household, his meals depend upon his mother or some other woman whose own concerns and priorities stem from her husband and young children and not from him. He should constantly try to keep on the good side of his elder kinsmen since there is little chance that he will ever establish his own household without their support in raising bridewealth. Circumcision has therefore not given him as much freedom as he probably expected. Quite the contrary—his goals are now beginning to change, and he is now more than ever made keenly aware of how deeply he depends on the respect and support of elders to reach any of his new aims. Indeed, he must now demonstrate a new awareness of his responsibilities. He can no longer expect ready forgiveness of any lapses on account of his being an irresponsible child, for his newly achieved moral training carries new potential for expectations and blame.

Ottenberg (1989: chapter 8) has observed that anthropologists have paid little attention to this postinitiatory period. It is clear that new initiates do not emerge as full adults. They are no longer children, but they remain deeply dependent upon and vulnerable to control by elders.

I postpone drawing broader social conclusions regarding this account of initiation of Kaguru boys until I describe the initiation of Kaguru girls. This is because these two initiatory processes make sense only when considered and compared together.

GIRLS' INITIATION

Kaguru most frequently refer to the initiation of girls as *ng'hola mukono* (taking by the hand). Kaguru also describe a girl being "danced" *(kufinwa)* or even use the Swahili term for initiation *(kumbi)*. *Ng'hola mukono* is a most appropriate term since it conveys a sense of supporting care and instruction seemingly involving far less trauma, harassment, or public exposure than what is experienced by boys. Occasionally Kaguru refer to women's initiation as *inguluwe* (wild pig), which conjures up associations of the uncontrollable and destructive.[11] I suspect that this allusion is made to alarm or tease men, such animals being a common threat to social order since they spoil many cultivated fields. Wild pigs are also associated with the dead, who are the major conveyers of human fertility (Beidelman 1964a).

Kaguru girls are subjected to initiation as soon as they first menstruate *(wekulawa sakame mwesi kwa kwesi*, "blood issues out from month to month"). As soon as a girl has her first period, she informs her older kinswomen, her mother or grandmother or an aunt, who put her in a house apart from other women. Actually, she probably has already been staying with other unmarried girls in such a house *(ibweti)* if she lives in a larger settlement. Now, however, she cannot stay with her mother or other married or sexually active women, even if she had been earlier.

Unlike Kaguru boys, Kaguru girls begin their initiation according to a particular, physiologically determined event. There is no room for any compromise in setting a convenient date. Consequently, a Kaguru girl may commence her initiation at any season of the year. She may begin menstruating during the rainy season at the height of cultivation, when everyone is too busy to take much time off. No matter, she must still abandon her work and go into confinement, even if this means the loss of a valuable cultivator for her family's fields. Furthermore, it is likely that she will undergo this experience as a lone initiate.[12] In the past, when settlements were larger, it was sometimes possible that two or more girls might undergo confinement at about the same time, but today this is no longer at all likely.[13] Still, Kaguru agree that it is always preferable to have several girls confined together if possible. Then the girls can keep one another company and their kin can pool resources for their subsequent celebrations when their initiation is completed and "danced."

Because it is determined by the onset of menstruation, which can occur at any time, a Kaguru girl's initial confinement cannot be predicted nor consequently be always well organized. People must make do with whatever is feasible at the moment. That does not, however, mean that a girl's initiation cannot involve complicated organization and expenditures. What it means is that the process may often be protracted over a great many months so that the final celebrations can take place in the dry season when resources and time are available for the most prestigious form of ceremony. The "dancing" of a girl's initiation, like a boy's, requires beer and food for entertainment and gifts to a cutter and others who tend the novice. This could amount to two or three months' income for a householder, even when supplies are available in the postharvest season.

Kaguru initiation of girls aims to educate them in proper sexual and domestic behavior, in terms similar to those taught to Kaguru boys. Girls are taught about sexual relations, about proper sexual etiquette and comportment, but also about the special care that women must take regarding menstruation and pregnancy. Yet the main purpose most often mentioned by Kaguru is the last of these. They say that the central feature of girls' initiation is "cooling" (*imhosa*), that is, subduing and controlling their new sexuality. Menstruation itself is considered a hot (*moto*), disturbing activity, a source of pollution and potential disorder. To menstruate is to be sick (*nhamu*), to be "under" (*na hasi*), as we might express being "under the weather." The heated state brought on by menstruation requires immediate care, not only at its first appearance but for all future occurrences. Kaguru recognize that its appearance signals a girl's capacity to bear children and that its cessation at menopause (*sanda idumuka*, "cut off the womb") terminates this power. In this sense, menstruation is a sign of female fertility and therefore welcome. Yet despite its welcome as a sign of fertility, menstrual blood (*nhume*) is considered very destructive if allowed to touch men, fields, or tools (though not other women). Anything that it does touch that may later be inadvertently handled by men should be buried. This blood is even potentially dangerous to the menstruating woman herself because it represents a part of her self over which she may lose control once it leaves her body. It could therefore be taken by a sorcerer or witch and used against her. A girl's first confinement marks the commencement of careful monitoring of her bodily processes, which must continue for decades until menopause. True, such loss of bodily elements also involves cut hair, nail parings, and even the umbilical cord, but it is only menstruation that presents a situation of no control as to exactly when and where such loss will appear. To be sure, menstruation follows a monthly cycle, but control of menstruation requires great social contrivance because menstruation's exact time and place of occurrence are not entirely predictable. Given the many food shortages that Kaguru probably faced in the past, it seems likely that menstruation was then even more irregular and unpredictable than it is now.

Confinement

A girl (*chigali*) knows that she is no longer a child (*mwana*) but an initiate (*wali*) as soon as some older, experienced kinswomen (*wadala*) confirm that she is menstruating. This and not any change in height, growth of body hair, or budding breasts proclaims the true onset of her new condition as a mature woman. Other people—outsiders, nonkin—know that she has changed because she has been confined inside a house. She is likely to remain inside for several weeks. It is said that in the past this could have stretched on for many months. The girl is allowed to leave only to urinate and defecate. It is said that traditionally she could leave only by crawling backward, belly up, in and out, although I never witnessed this. What is significant is that most of these proscriptions fall under the term *igubi*. When I first heard this term, it referred to a dance held to celebrate a girl's menstruation, but I later learned that this term actually applies more broadly. *Igubi* and *igubika* refer to "what is concealed," and indeed concealment and confinement characterize most sides of girls' initiation, far more than for boys'.

The girl initiate's confinement is actually organized by her mother and her father's sister or, if these are unavailable, other close kinswomen on both her maternal (*kumoso*, left) and paternal (*kulume*, right) sides. (By maternal kin I here mean mainly members of one's matrilineage, but this can also include the spouses of members of a matrilineage and even one's mother's father's matrilineage. By paternal kin I mean mainly members of one's father's matrilineage, but this also include the spouses of members of that matrilineage and even one's father's father's matrilineage.) Of course, the girl's father and her mother's brother are notified and are said to have authorized such ceremonies, but this is merely a polite convention, for there would be no legitimate way for them to prevent such activities, which must be undertaken once a girl menstruates. These men's main function is to inform various kin that they are expected to contribute food or cash for the ensuing celebrations. Cash is secured primarily from the sale of agricultural produce, beer, or livestock. Close kin are expected to provide beer, food, and labor, but more-distant relatives would donate only a few shillings, not enough to account for any substantial supplies of food or payment for labor needed for a large gathering with several days' entertainment.

The initiate is secluded within a house in her parents' village. She is kept busy with household chores. Many local women bring their grain to the girl to grind or pound into flour or bring other foods such as vegetables to be cleaned and processed. It is said that sometimes girls even paint some of the house walls with designs in white chalk and/or red ocher. It is only girl initiates (never boys) who practice everyday tasks during their confinement.[14]

The various visiting women use their visits to the initiate to coach her on the various songs *(sinyimbo)* and sayings *(misimu)* that she must learn in order to take part in some of the subsequent ceremonies and in order to learn (memorize) useful information about sexual conduct. During these days the initiate must not bathe but instead is frequently dusted with chaff *(imphumba)* from the grain that she is processing. This is sometimes mixed with water to produce a white paintlike paste. This whiteness is thought to cool or regularize the girl, who is otherwise heated by her new sexuality. The initiate is encouraged to eat as much as she can, especially meat and meat broth, which are thought to strengthen her. (Meat is not everyday fare for most Kaguru, and when it is available, older men are given the largest share. Consequently, the initiate's diet of meat and broth is considered to be pampering.) She is forbidden eggs since these are thought to cause excessive bleeding, both at menstruation and at the forthcoming cutting. These also cause hairiness. The length of time that the girl is confined varies, but in the past this lasted many months until the girl had become fat *(kugina)* and got pale *(kwifala)*, both considered signs of feminine beauty.

Beauvoir argues that fattening women is a means of reducing their capacity to transcend their bodies (1974: 178). Certainly Kaguru women emerge with a preoccupation about their diverse bodily processes, about their corporeality, menstruation, pregnancy, parturition, lactation, and menopause. There seems to be more special bodily instruction given to girl initiates than to boys, whose instruction seems to emphasize how to copulate and seduce. Boys appear to receive messages about males' powers to manipulate others through ritual, violence, words, and wealth.

Toward the end of a girl's confinement, the number of women coming to the initiate's quarters increases steadily. The girl's maternal kin predominate in these visits, both in number and in deciding how activities will be carried out. Kaguru say that the mother's side, the left side *(kumoso)*, characterizes most aspects of girls' initiation, far more than for boys'.

A girl's confinement for many days or weeks inside a house affords an excuse for women to travel and visit her, even during a heavy work season, spending time seeing kin and neighbors in other settlements. This contrasts with the visiting of boy initiates. In the case of boys, out in camps in the bush and tended only by men, prolonged visiting is almost entirely by men, who encounter only other males. Women only visit the periphery of a boy's camp in order to deliver food and inquire about the initiate's well-being and then depart. In contrast, the girls, secluded within settlements, are visited by women who can spend time with kin and friends of both sexes. Both male and female initiations provide grounds for reviewing and strengthening ties with kin and neighbors between many settlements, but such opportunities seem more diverse and flexible for women.

Toward the end of this confinement, the number of women coming to the girl's quarters increases steadily. The girl's maternal kin predominate in these activities, both in number and in their influence in deciding how these activities will be carried out. Kaguru say that the mother's side precedes (*yekulo-ngola*) that of the father, which follows (*yekulafa*). The house is crowded with women and filled with the sounds of drumming, singing, whistles, and laughing, which continue throughout the day and often long into the night. These celebrations confirm that the initiate has learned her teachings. This is *ng'oma ya misimu* (celebration of initiation lore). The songs and sayings are sung to the girl indoors, while outside many others, both women and men, have gathered to drink, eat, and dance. No men are allowed inside, and if any male approaches the entry, he may be jostled and abused. When I asked why this was so, I was told that the women inside were often unclothed and that they sometimes simulated sexual relations with one another in order to teach the inexperienced girl about sexual conduct. Everyone agreed that the women inside enjoyed singing obscene (*maligo-ligo*) songs and that the men should not hear them. Certainly one heard the many women inside the initiation house laughing and apparently joking uproariously. Still, I did not find the Kaguru's explanations entirely convincing. What bothered me was the fact that when I had asked why women were not readily allowed near initiated boys, I was told it was because the women would sexually excite the boys and thus disturb their wounds, that women might be menstruating and would therefore endanger the boys' recovery, or simply that such places were inappropriate for women because custom dictated so. In contrast, women and men both explained the exclusion of men from the sphere of women's initiation entirely in terms of preserving women's sense of privacy and modesty. No essentially negative attributes of men were conjured up as part of any rationalization of this separation. The contrast in the two sets of explanations seemed sharp and simplistic. Furthermore, while Kaguru women and men repeatedly told me that the obscenity of women's ritual greatly accounted for women's seclusion, this could hardly be so, since the words of many songs could be heard ringing out clearly from a woman's seclusion house. Gales of laughter and raucous remarks were heard by men and women alike who were standing outside. I believe that the laughter of women asserted their power, even their disdain of men. It seemed a form of playful castration.[15] I believe that men were banned simply because the women, just like the men, wanted this occasion of isolated solidarity to confirm their interpretations of the attributes and meanings of gender against any counterclaims and different interpretations made by the opposite sex.

The singing and dancing indoors continue all night. At dawn, the initiate's patrilateral cross-cousins carry her outdoors to face the dawn. There the sponsors sing a few final songs and then return the initiate indoors to rest. By noon, food and beer have accumulated from a steady stream of visitors who are preparing for this final period of celebration. Indoors a large pot of porridge is surrounded by some of the initiate's kinswomen. The matrilineal kin and the patrilateral kin assemble at opposing sides of the pot, referring to themselves as the left *(kumoso)* and the right *(kulume)* respectively. Then some of these kin, representatives of each of the two groups, remove some of the porridge with a wooden stirrer *(difiga)*, add meat, and take the clumps of food outside. These women dance about the house, eating this food while circling the initiate's quarters seven times. Some women stand at the house's entry repeatedly singing "*Imhosa* [cooling]," and those circling the dwelling respond with the same word. This ceremony of *difiga dye mhosa* (stirrer of cooling) is said to *kutala imhosa* (to mark cooling). After this is done, the dancers return indoors, and everyone gets food from the pot as the initiate's father's sister and mother's sister (actual or someone of that group and generation) supervise the distribution. When women come to take a token bit of this food, they sing: "*Nani yondila digalidyangu* [who will clean my burned residue]?" They keep repeating this until all of the residue at the sides and bottom of the pot is scraped away and eaten. Then they scour out the pot. When it is clean, the singers take hold of the pot and sing: "*Dimwewe, ng'ho nyama, nyama ng'ho* [grow, take the meat, take the meat]." Then the girl is taken outside to be cut *(kwambigwa,* "is caught"), her wound is washed, and she is brought back inside to sleep. Today many girls are apparently either not cut at all or are merely lightly nicked. Yet some Kaguru told me that in the past some people actually did cut rather extensively on the labia. Kaguru never removed any part of the clitoris, as is done by the neighboring Maasai and Baraguyu. Unfortunately, it was very difficult for me to get Kaguru to discuss this matter in any detail or with reference to any particular girl. All that I could learn was that a razor *(lumo)* or small knife *(chimage)* was used and that the girl was cut as she was held down seated on a hide. The cutting took place in the bush *(kumbago)* near the initiation house, either at dawn or more often at dusk, the coolest times of the day. The cutter was invariably an old woman *(mudala)*, who was actually termed *muhunga*, the same term as that used for a male circumciser. The girl rests and sleeps through the night, and in the morning (assuming her operation was slight) she is dressed in new clothing and masses of beads, which she has received as gifts from both her maternal and paternal kinswomen. That day, to the sound of much ululation and drumming, she is reintroduced to society as an initiate *(wali)*, but she is also now a *mungele* (an attractive woman).

Much of the dancing that takes place when the girl is being taught and later when she is cut, if she is cut, is sometimes simply termed *igubi* (covered, concealed). Both men and women drink and dance, some with bells strung to their legs. The settlement of the girl is often decorated with many boughs of *mihumba* (East African laburnum, *Calpurnia subdecandra*), which is sometimes in yellow flower. Often women tie bunches of laburnum leaves to form aprons, which they flip up and down sexily as they dance. These are called *masombwe* (what is shaken). Men and women dance facing one another, stamping with bells on their legs in a dance termed *mhang'hala*. Sometimes men do *kaiyamba*, a dance in which they revolve their shoulders as they keep time with whistles and flattened tins filled with pebbles while women beat drums. The dances held to celebrate initiations are undoubtedly the most culturally conservative public occasions remaining in missionized Kaguruland. It is then that young Kaguru girls would wear great quantities of beads and their best purchased clothes. Many would have oiled their faces, legs, and arms so that they would glisten alluringly as they danced. This is one of the few times left when young girls sometimes dance displaying their breasts.

The timing of these concluding celebrations varies. For example, the time between the girl's cutting and her emergence *(mlao)* depends upon the degree to which she was cut, if she was cut at all.

The celebration of a girl's emergence as a marriageable woman could vary in its importance. Sometimes a girl had been engaged long before she ever menstruated, so her emergence celebration coincided with the initial celebration of her forthcoming marriage. At other times, now more and more often, a girl's emergence merely indicates that she is now available to suitors. The length of time between a girl's cooling at her first menstruation and her emergence as a marriageable woman could vary from a week to several months, depending upon whether she was given a major cutting or merely a token one, whether her cooling ceremony took place during the cultivation season (when

Figure 12. Kaguru drinking and dancing to celebrate girls' initiation. The women hold drums between their legs and wear their best clothing and jewelry. One of the men holds a flattened tin containing pebbles, which he uses to beat time. He also blows a whistle to mark rhythm and signal dance movements. The two small boys have been given sips of beer and are encouraged to imitate their elders in dancing and singing. It is through such occasions that children begin to learn about initiation and start to look forward to being initiated themselves. Photograph taken at Idibo in 1958.

people lacked time and resources for proper celebration), or whether she might even be pregnant. Kaguru observed that it was possible for a girl to become pregnant even though she had never apparently menstruated. Many problems could arise in such a case, leading to divergence from the normal schedule that I outlined above. It could even happen that a girl might become an *ifunge*, an initiate for whom a final emergence celebration was never held at all and for whom no one had danced or enjoyed beer. This would be disgraceful, but Kaguru assured me that such a thing could and did occur, though no one would tell me about any such actual case.

INITIATES' GROOMING

Emergence from initiation marks young Kaguru women and men in one striking, external way. It determines how they should subsequently appear, how they dress and groom themselves.

In bygone days throughout Ukaguru, during the time of German colonialism and earlier, initiation marked important changes in the dress and grooming of girls and boys. Even during the period of my research such traditional changes could still be seen in some of the remoter parts of western and mountain Ukaguru.

Before initiation boys dress plainly, have little or no jewelry, and wear their hair very short or shaved. In the past, boys may have pierced their earlobes but wore nothing in them except sometimes simple wires, threads, or slivers of wood. In the past, after initiation Kaguru youths began to assume styles similar to those of the Gogo to the west and the Maasai to the north. Boys allowed their hair to grow long, extended it with fibers, and drew it into braids. They also often painted their hair, skin, and clothes with red or brown ocher. Many plucked their eyebrows and shaved. Youths put beads or metal weights in their ears, donned necklaces, armlets, wristlets, and anklets, and often wore sandals. Some carried short spears, clubs, staves, or swords rather than the more customary Kaguru bow, quiver, and arrows. Judging from the young western Kaguru I saw in the 1950s and 1960s and from photographs and drawings made by travelers at the turn of the century, these styles were never as elaborate as those assumed by Maasai and Baraguyu even today. Of course, later, after such youths were married, they were expected to reduce their finery, no longer ordinarily bearing weapons and never painting themselves or wearing long hair. Consequently, until the First World War most Kaguru boys underwent the most abrupt and dramatic change in their appearance after they emerged from initiation camps. Suddenly they would appear more el-

egant, virile, and warlike than most other men except their immediately initiated predecessors. In the past this would mark a much praised period of war-
riorhood, adventure, and even some roving. This would in turn be gradually
toned down until the youths married and settled down in a household. By the
time of my fieldwork such transformations in self-image no longer defined the
inevitable experience of most Kaguru boys growing up. Today, for most boys
their garb and grooming remain pretty much the same after they come out
from initiation; indeed, initiation is often marked by no change at all in
grooming but is simply a dry-season event between terms in school, where
youths continue to wear the same uniforms (see Beidelman 1980b).

Kaguru girls also undergo changes in grooming and dress after initiation.
Before initiation girls wear some jewelry and often braid their hair into patterns tight on their scalps, but after initiation far more care is taken in grooming, and clothes are more brightly colored. In the past, masses of brass or fiber
bracelets were frequently worn around the ankles and wrists. Even today, bead
and metal necklaces and chains may be worn in large quantities. This was, of
course, more common during earlier times than today and now prevails more
in the west and mountain areas than in the areas where mission influence is
strong. At dances masses of strands of brightly colored beads are still often
worn to accent movements. On such occasions girls are often oiled and even
ochered. Once girls are married, however, they are expected to curb the
amount of jewelry they wear and the brightness of their decorations and
clothes since they should no longer be seeking to attract men, though even
married women, until late in life, might make special efforts at grooming and
dressing for dances. In general, one could say that for girls their one big
chance to indulge freely in adornment and frivolously seductive apparel is just
after they emerge from initiation.

By the time I did fieldwork in the 1950s and 1960s, only mountain and
western Kaguru women sported large earplugs or heavy armlets, anklets, and
wristlets. Only a few younger, newly initiated girls wore a great deal of beads
at dances. Once girls were married—and this usually occurred quite soon after initiation—they lost their big chance for display and soon resembled their
mothers in more supposedly modest appearance. As a result, youthful, post-
initiation attire is significant for a far briefer period for girls than for boys. As
with the boys, in recent times many Kaguru girls simply resume going to
school and therefore wear uniforms or plain dark clothes much of the time,
even after initiation.

Certainly the constraints on everyday etiquette more appreciably affect
girls after initiation than they do boys. Of course, both boys and girls are expected to chatter far less and to begin to appear more dignified and measured

in speech. But girls are now also expected to take greater care to avoid direct eye contact with others, especially with their elders and with young men, and to keep their heads covered with cloth at many formal occasions (possibly a mannerism copied from Christians and Muslims). Girls' entire repertoire of body movements is now far more slow-paced and constrained than what is expected for boys of comparable age.

These changes in gender etiquette are particularly noticeable in eating groups, which reflect different experiences for Kaguru girls and boys. Throughout their lives, Kaguru females eat together, usually at the back of a house or near the hearth, assembled in informal groups. In contrast, Kaguru males know that they are recognized as growing up when they no longer are expected to eat with women but are expected to join grown men, who eat together at the front of the house facing the settlement square, where they are served by females and young boys. The etiquette in these two contrasting groups, at least regarding deference to elders and guests, is more formal amongst males than it is in women's groups. After initiation, no male Kaguru would ever think of again eating publicly with women.

INITIATION AND PARENTS

The initiation of Kaguru girls and boys occurs ordinarily during a late stage in the cycle of development of a young person's family. If the initiate's parents are still married to each other, they are likely to bear few if any more children after their first child is initiated. This is always the case for women, but if a father has married polygynously, his junior wives may still be bearing children.[16] Indeed, it sometimes happens (presumably more often in the past, when polygyny was more common) that a father's junior wife might be about the same age as some of his daughters. With the initiation of their first child, a married couple will embark on new concerns, increasingly paying attention to neighbors as potential spouses for their offspring and showing concern with their own kin's obligations and demands regarding bridewealth collection and distribution.[17] Initiation spells important changes for a young initiate but also means a new widening of social concerns for a maturing couple. From now on, depending upon the number of their maturing children, a couple necessarily becomes increasingly drawn toward kin beyond their household and village. Initiation is a social emergence for parents as well as for the young person coming into adulthood; it reemphasizes extended kin and affinal ties for Kaguru couples, much as marriage itself did earlier. It draws them ever further

Figure 13. Kaguru girl drumming for men to dance at a celebration of girls' initiation. Photograph taken at Idibo in 1958.

into the web of kinship relations, especially more distant ones, that signify social importance and influence toward a wider community.

Given the fact that women nurse infants for two to three years after birth, and given that women can reasonably insist on not having sexual relations while they are nursing, the birth of Kaguru children traditionally occurred about three to four years apart, even under the most favorable health conditions. Consequently, we can readily see that by the initiation of her first child at the age of about fourteen, a woman is inevitably approaching the end of her own childbearing years and now commences to focus on the advantages of being a mother-in-law and grandmother.

Men's and women's views about the implications of the initiation of junior kin are necessarily different. Women view both their sons' and daughters' initiations as turning points that will herald a new phase of influence through the birth of grandchildren within their own matrilineage. In contrast, men view their daughters' initiations as means to secure bridewealth that may be converted into further marriages, either for themselves or for their sons and nephews. Men view the initiation of their sisters' children as marking a point when they can begin to exert influence over these offspring of other men through the claims of matrilineal ties. In this sense, a father's sister is the one category of senior kin least likely to be wholeheartedly supportive of initiated boys since such youths are in competition with her own sons for benefits. With initiation, men's sons (and nephews) begin to make claims for bridewealth against fathers and uncles and enter the rough-and-tumble sphere of claims and counterclaims for help and allegiance between natal and lineal groups. It appears that at initiation mothers confront their children with less mixed motives and feelings than do fathers. Now, too, is the time when father's sisters and mother's brothers sometimes tend to align themselves with their siblings and against their own spouses. This phase in the domestic cycle reemphasizes the important ties between maturing brothers and sisters caught in a web of conflicting and competing claims for their children. With this, these siblings' mother, the grandmother of the new initiates, assumes new power in arbitrating and smoothing over these claims.

CONCLUSIONS

Male and female initiations amongst the Kaguru sharply contrast in five ways. First, the particular time when girls commence initiation is determined biologically and not socially. While social adjustments may be made to modify subsequent rituals and ceremonies, all girls must commence the preliminary stage of their initiation as soon as they begin to menstruate. This reflects what Kaguru consider a veiled and uncontrollable aspect of female sexuality, placing it outside the full control of social arrangements. It is, as Eliade observed, linked to blood (1965: 44). In contrast, boys may be circumcised when it is convenient, and the entire transformational process may be arbitrarily undertaken prematurely or belatedly in order to meet the social aims of those concerned. Male maturation is more amenable to cultural tinkering. Signs of adult male gender are socially imposed. The incontrovertible mark of sexual maturity (circumcision) is clear-cut and reflects prearranged strategies. Once a boy is circumcised, he is a jural adult, though admittedly often still treated as subservient; this is a social contrivance, not a fact of nature. For a girl, true womanhood remains less clearly defined. It is not entirely attained with menstruation or with the cutting she may receive, though I am told that in any case it is not always easy to discern when the latter has been performed. For a girl to attain full, socially recognized womanhood, she must bear a child. This is independent of initiation and even marriage. Of course, barren women have adult jural rights, and girls might become pregnant before initiation (though this can be covered up). The key features by which females attain adulthood are for Kaguru integrally tied to seemingly mysterious biological processes. In contrast, male adulthood is more a product of social manipulation and ceremonial assertion.

Second, male and female initiations contrast sharply in the degree of violence and prolonged antagonisms employed. Boys must undergo circumcision, which involves considerable shock, pain, and loss of blood, and a prolonged period of recovery. Recuperation is accompanied by considerable physical discomfort because the initiates are kept outdoors in the bush. Along with this, boys undergo periodic psychological and physical harassment by their elders. In contrast, the physical operation on girls is said to be slight or even not to be required at all. It is reported by some that a girl can comfortably emerge publicly the day after being cut. Initiation of women never involves serious concern about medical treatment or recovery. Furthermore, the entire period of a girl's initiation involves constant support and encouragement and no sense of harassment whatsoever. Males are thought to gain strength or character through suffering and discipline. In contrast, females do not. As a result, the women involved with initiation are characterized as solicitous and never as harsh or mean to novices. Male initiation produces a temporary hot situation (shedding of blood) so as to produce a permanent future of a cooler (orderly) nature (circumcised). In contrast, females will become hot periodically with every menstrual period. Initiation for them cannot prevent this. What the initiation of girls does is create a deeper understanding that can control and deal with this supposedly problematic situation. Initiation is said to soften women by making them more adaptable to the challenges of menstruation and childbirth. Consequently, female initiation's overall emphasis is on order unpunctuated by the violence that characterizes the male rituals. It has been argued that the harsher an initiation, the more attractive the group and its lore may appear once these ordeals are surmounted. It is further argued that the secrecy and mystification of indoctrinating ritual undercut initiates' capacity for criticism (Bok 1982: 52; Aronson and Mills 1959). If

Figure 14. Two Kaguru men with whistles and flattened tins containing pebbles dancing before young women at a girls' initiation. Photograph taken at Berega in 1957.

this is so, one would expect Kaguru men to be more doctrinaire in their commitment to stereotypes of gender and sexuality than are Kaguru women. My impressions sustain this, but I have no ready way of proving it.

Third, male initiation stresses a profound ambivalence between the initiates and their home villages, whereas female initiation evinces none of this tension. Girls' initiations are conducted within the heart of the village (except for the few minutes of cutting, if indeed it even occurs). Most of the elements take place within a house, so the girls' surroundings remain almost exclusively the same as during their regular home life. If a girl spends much time in confinement, it is still with the kind of women she would usually see anyway, and she would still spend most of her time involved in the household chores she would perform. In contrast, boys are taken completely out of their customary village surroundings. They spend a long time removed from regular, socialized activities. They perform none of the tasks they usually do (cultivation and herding). Girl novices remain within structures that are integral to ongoing village life; boy initiates are taken into makeshift camps far from stable settlements, and at the end of initiation the recovered novices see these camps destroyed.[18] Boys are torn from the hearth. Girls remain within the milieu of their parents' settlement, domiciled around a regular hearth, while boys suffer out in the bush. Boys are repeatedly reminded of their loss of access to their mothers' hearths. Boys and their instructors repeatedly sing songs dwelling on supposed maternal rejection and on the boys' fears about not being properly nourished by their mothers. At initiation Kaguru girls face no new challenge regarding their key ties with their mothers or with domestic life. In contrast, boys are repeatedly made aware that the central poignancy of their initiation is a profound alteration in their relations with both their mothers and their mothers' hearths (compare with Ottenberg 1989: 309). What little nurturance boys find during initiation must come from men, ordinarily an unusual situation for Kaguru. Boys' experiences force them to confront some of the quandaries posed to maturing males, who in the Kaguru case must try to reconcile group loyalties to a matrilineage (originally instilled in them as children through the image of their mother's hearth) with more personal ambitions within a future paternalistic domicile (to be organized around another hearth, that of a future wife from an outside matrilineage).[19]

Fourth, the approach by the initiators of boys and girls as well as the content of the various songs and sayings the initiates learn (see chapter 7) all suggest two strongly contrasting views of the sexuality of the bodies of men and women. Kaguru boys undergo ceremonies that expose and assault the body, that explicate its nature and possibilities. Circumcision itself is such an act, since it exposes something vital that was previously undisclosed: the immediate and specific locus of erotic pleasure in the male body, the glans. What Kaguru boys experience is a clarification and irreversible exposure of their sexual potential, which they are to consider and, in their future as adult males, control. In contrast, Kaguru girls are introduced to a sexuality that should not be exposed and that ultimately cannot be clearly revealed. The central locus of their sexual pleasure, the clitoris, is not altered. It remains an element that intrudes into and retreats from sight, while their fertility, their wombs, remain mysterious and never guaranteed to yield pregnancies. Finally, menstrual blood, the alarming and polluting sexual sign triggering the whole proceedings of initiation, is described as something to be concealed and separated from all other people, even one's future lover or husband. A great part of girls' instruction concern these strategies of concealment, avoidance, and puzzlement.

It is said that sexual relations are not only discussed but also actually mimed by initiating women. Kaguru women elicit a direct concern about sexual satisfaction and technique never shown by males in their initiation instruction. If this is so, and I believe that it is, then this is probably due to the fact that women have good reason to expect that attainment of sexual satisfaction requires more skill and care than is needed for men. Most significant of all, Kaguru female initiation cannot provide any clear explication of what Kaguru consider to be the central feature of women's sexuality. No instruction or techniques can guarantee the successful production of a child, and it is this, not sexual gratification or coital performance, that remains the crucial focus of Kaguru women's sexual concerns. Women's bodies remain as opaquely undisclosed to women themselves as they are to men. Kaguru women's initiation and associated sexual lore accept and embrace this undisclosed, mysterious element, linked to the unfathomable benevolence of the ancestral dead. They present this as the unifying theme of women's gender. Women's greatest sexual concern, their fertility, remains an unexplicated and uncontrolled factor. At best, it is "contained" and pondered but little more. Kaguru women even seem to elaborate upon this *igubi* or hidden factor and make no effort to diminish it. The overwhelming impression of the sexuality of Kaguru women as revealed by initiation ceremonies is one of an imponderable but vital capacity for procreation, nourished and encouraged but never interfered with even by women themselves, who guard this by protectively closing ranks.

The Kaguru data bear out Beauvoir's contention that girls more easily gain access to their mothers' worlds than boys do to the worlds of their fathers. Male hierarchy, hostility, and divisive struggles over power and domination become particularly keen as aging initiates clamor for more autonomy (seeking bridewealth for marriage) after initiation.

Fifth, both girls' and boys' initiations are filled with expressions of nurturance, as important as the instruction, the songs, the pain of cutting, and the hazing of boys. This nurturant theme is related to notions similar to those behind our own term *adolescence* (Latin *adolescere*, "to grow") with its ultimate roots in the Latin *alere* (to nourish). That young people have attained full growth is the result of years of nurturance by their elders, and young people's growing "ripeness," embodied in their new sexual potency, marks them as ready to embark on a change from being the nurtured to being nurturers. Young men will soon be expected to provide for their new families, and young women will be expected to nurse and tend new offspring and to process and serve food at the hearths over which they will soon preside. Men will nurture their wives' bodies, for semen is thought to enlarge women's breasts and buttocks and to enrich and increase the fetuses that men have supposedly implanted in women's bellies.[20] Alimentation develops in tandem with sexuality as a theme encompassing adult sexual consciousness and responsibility. Nurturant imagery dominates Kaguru ritual markings of life's course. It is an image of historic continuity. It does, however, take different forms for women and men. For women, nurturance has figured throughout their lives; but for men, nurturance becomes expressively prominent only with initiation. Reik observes that there are profoundly ambivalent feelings between men and boys, but men attempt to bridge and ameliorate these feelings and to separate boys from their mothers at adolescence and to bind youths to older men (1946: 151–52). Kaguru male bonding is partly expressed through images of male nurturance.

Although I contrast the violence and hazing of male initiation with the more solicitous and supportive ceremonies for girls, both girls and boys undergo pain, for boys especially at cutting and the first days of recovery and for girls sometimes because of menstrual pain and fear. Pain is central to such ritual transformations (see Morinis 1985). As Scarry observes, the infliction of pain is a powerful means of verifying an invisible reality (1985: 202), in the Kaguru case, the moral order of society and the elder generation who convey it. "To have pain is to have certainty" (ibid.: 11); "the physical pain is so incontestably real that it seems to confer its quality of 'incontestable reality' on that power that has brought it into being" (ibid.: 27). For Kaguru, infliction of pain (the genital operation) is never performed within a settlement, and therefore it is never associated with the quotidian continuity of life. Recovery from that pain is associated with groups; the bush camps of boys and men and the closed initiation houses of girls and their women teachers. It is inextricably related to the creation of social boundaries (see Morinis 1985: 155). Recovery and easing of pain are repeatedly linked to instruction across the generations.

Pain is related to imagination. The instructing elders wield pain and the easing of it as tools to cultivate social (moral) imagination in their young charges. "Pain and imagining are the 'framing events' within whose boundaries all other perceptual, somatic, and emotional events occur; thus, between the two extremes can be mapped the whole terrain of the human psyche" (ibid.: 165). At initiation, an objectiveless pain shatters words (ibid.: 172) but is followed by a succession of recovery states associated with ever-diminishing discomfort and a corresponding construction through words and songs of an imagined world of objects, along with ideas as to how to control them.

Submission to pain is a sacrifice toward a greater good (ibid.: 161–62), and that sacrifice is rewarded with gifts of imagination, knowledge, and admittance into adult ranks.

A final theme characterizes Kaguru initiations for both men and women, and this comprises all the material in the next chapter. This involves instruction on sexual conduct, on flirting and seduction, and on copulation, as well as on sexual etiquette. As a child prostitute is said to observe in an account by Norman Douglas (surely his imaginary construction): "The copulatory act has to be learnt, like every other one, unless we want to remain on the level of the beast" (1967: 32).

Kaguru initiation provides a body of experience and lore that both elders and initiates acknowledge as unique to Kaguru (whether this is actually so is another matter). These are the only occasions when most Kaguru, however influenced they now are by Swahili or even English, make a sustained effort to speak and sing in "pure" Chikaguru as much as they can, repeatedly maintaining that they are trying to teach the riddles, songs, and stories just as their own elders taught them. It is the time, too, when Kaguru are made particularly aware of the moral associations of their landscape. Contrasts between the powers and character of the settlement and those of the bush permeate the imagery and ceremonies of initiation. The stories of clan origins and their relations to the land are often told to initiates as part of their indoctrination during their days of confinement. These features of initiation all contribute to a sense of ethnic solidarity and difference from Kaguru's neighbors. Yet ethnic identity is further strengthened by here being coupled with personal identity as expressed in gaining new meanings as adults, as women and men, with the understanding that this eventually will make these novices into parents, elders, and ultimately ancestors. Procreation, for Kaguru the central feature of gender and adulthood, links all Kaguru with the dead and therefore with an unending tradition of names, propitiation, and mystical rewards and punishments. It is the ancestral dead, buried in the land and providing its fertility and the fertility of those who dwell upon it, who have taught Kaguru these initiation traditions that provide their personal and ethnic meanings. It is the dead who configure Kaguru history and whom the living venerate by preserving these rites, which will provide descendants to carry on their naming and veneration.

CHAPTER 7

Learning Adulthood
Initiation Songs

Et je jouis et je décharge
Dans ce vrai cauchemar de viande
À la fois friande et gourmande
Et tour à tour étroite et large.

Et qui remonte et redescend
Et rebondit sur mes roustons
En sauts où mon vit à tâtons
Pris d'un vertige incandescent

Parmi des foutres et des mouilles
Meurt, puis revit, puis meurt encore.
Revit, remeurt, revit encore
Par tout ce foutre et que de mouilles!

          Paul Verlaine, "Gamineries," *Femmes*

C'est un plus petit coeur
Avec la pointe en l'air;
Symbole doux et fier,
C'est un plus tendre coeur.

Il verse ah! que de pleurs
Corrosifs plus que feu,
Prolongés mieux qu'adieu,
Blancs comme blanches fleurs!

          Paul Verlaine, "Balanide," *Hombres*

Kaguru initiation of boys and girls involves more than cutting genitals and physical isolation. For Kaguru the transformation of children into adults requires the inculcation of basic beliefs and values. Whenever I questioned Kaguru about their remembrance of initiation, they invariably wanted to recite some songs and riddles. For Kaguru the ability to spin off such traditional lore is considered ready proof that they have successfully graduated from initiation. At the close of their sequestration novices recite memorized lore in order to demonstrate to their elders that they have graduated to adulthood. The songs, riddles, and clan legends learned during the many days they were segregated away from ordinary life are as important to initiation as the operation. The content of this lore is sometimes important and useful as instruction about sexual conduct. Yet much that is taught does not seem directly useful as sexual knowledge. To understand the importance of Kaguru initiation lore, one must go beyond the content, though that is important as an encyclopedia of the Kaguru social world. One must also appreciate this material as a means to create an adult, speculative mind. The acts of learning can themselves create a new sense of adult empowerment and responsibility through training in how to speak and exchange problematic information and opinions. These claims for the importance of Kaguru initiation lore will be clearer after I have recounted a body of such material. What we should bear in mind is that the deeper importance of this literature goes beyond its more obvious content and involves how, not just what, a Kaguru thinks and how a Kaguru learns to express these views to others.

Before examining these Kaguru initiation texts I first sketch out the situation in which initiates learn such material. We must keep these conditions constantly in mind to appreciate how and why such ideas and values are so readily embraced and so indelibly held by Kaguru.

The ideas conveyed in this oral literature are clearly more readily absorbed within the intensified isolation of a boys' initiation camp or in the constricted seclusion of a girls' puberty house than in everyday life. In these restricted surroundings, abstracted from quotidian affairs, a young Kaguru is particularly vulnerable to the arguments and suggestions of others. His or her sleep is disturbed. The initiate is forbidden the ordinary body care of grooming and bathing and is consequently kept uncomfortable. While the initiate may be enjoying more protein than usual, the routine of eating is dictated by the officiating elders, who make sure that the initiate is less indulgently catered to than by his or her mother. At initiation nurturance is important, but this is done according to a pace and schedule different from what the initiate is accustomed to. At no time is the initiate left alone but instead is constantly subjected to the comments and interference of older mentors. Everything that a boy or girl initiate does falls under the semblance of routine that may appear to be established during this initiatory period but is then repeatedly broken by seemingly arbitrary orders or restrictions imposed by her or his supervisors. This prevents the initiate from taking any new set of relations and procedures for granted.[1]

The impressionable state of a male initiate is further intensified by the pain of his recent circumcision, prompting considerable fear of more harm and violation.[2] In the case of a Kaguru girl, menstruation itself constitutes a shocking change for which few Kaguru girls are adequately forewarned. This is because girls have received little or no detailed information about menstruation prior to its onset. Kaguru describe young girls as alarmed, even horrified at the first blood. It is only after the shock of seeing the blood that a Kaguru girl can expect any frank, reassuring, and informative discussion of her own sexuality. In addition, some girls are also cut, although even without such wounding they would be fearful and vulnerable to the intimidations of elders, even when these are outwardly solicitous, as they often are for girls.

While boys and girls first encounter their publicly acknowledged adult sexuality in different ways, these contrasting experiences within the girls' instruction house and within the boys' circumcision camp are unsettling. Both involve situations of considerable psychic disorientation that make the initiates particularly receptive to the inculcation of crucial social beliefs and values. These two initiatory processes contrast in the sources of the disorientation they produce. In both cases, the source is physiological, but it is induced by an external operation for boys, whereas it is mostly inherent physiologically in girls. Elder men create a traumatic situation by a violent physical assault on the most guarded and valued part of a boy's body. Further infliction of discomfort becomes an important feature of much of the rest of a boy's indoctrination, through his being hazed. In contrast, most of a girl's fear and dismay springs from her own bodily workings and the fact that no one has earlier prepared her for this. Elder women react only after the shock of menstrual bleeding has driven a girl to seek help from them. Then elder women emphasize how to control and make use of such disturbing changes. The menstruation itself, more than any minor cutting, is what is said to upset a girl most.

The numerous Kaguru initiation songs (*sinyimbo*) or riddles (*figonho*) I present below were provided almost entirely by men, although I sometimes asked women about such matters, including the meanings of songs that I had already collected. I have every reason to believe that wives repeated some of these songs to their husbands and vice versa. It was agreed by all Kaguru with whom I spoke, men and women, that most songs were known to both genders. What is not clear is whether a few other songs were known by only one gender and were never disclosed to me. My own belief, and it is only a guess, is that all or most of the initiation songs are known to both groups. What I cannot be sure about is whether important rituals performed by women in seclusion remain unknown by me, and this consequently limits my interpretation. All of the material I present is known to both groups. What appears significant regarding Kaguru men's and women's interpretations of such material is how the two genders view the same material. While there were a few differences amongst informants as to how to decode the meaning of a particular song, these did not seem to reflect gender. Instead, these seemed to reflect differences in knowledge, individual imagination, or personal background. Where gender mattered was in the kind of moral meanings that were attached to such decoded interpretations. For example, both men and women would agree that a saying alluded to hiding menstrual blood, to the loss of fertility with old age, to the dangers of childbirth, to the dangers of adultery, or to a male's problems in achieving an erection. Differences would not usually arise at such a shallow level of decoding. Instead, differences stemmed from the fact that males and females view such matters as menstruation, childbirth, adultery, aging, and potency differently.

TELLING ABOUT SONGS

At initiation Kaguru girls and boys are taught *(kuwekufundwa)* how to behave properly as adults, as social beings, who can be held responsible for their actions. Kaguru say that people behave properly out of both fear *(chogoho)* and shame *(chinyala):* fear about the punishments they might suffer from others on account of what they have done or failed to do, and shame on account of being thought bad or mean-spirited by those whose respect and approval they value. Much of what Kaguru are taught involves duties *(milimoya)* associated with the work *(mulimo)* of maintaining a home that is viewed as the essential building block of society. This is problematic because a home is grounded on duties that are social but also on passions and desires that are not readily domesticated. This is because the key relation in the home is between a man and a woman, a husband and a wife, who are united by common social needs and interests and by sexual craving *(kuhelekela, kusulumila).* Initiation is aimed at teaching Kaguru girls and boys how to manage this copulation *(kusola)* or lying together *(kugona)* in a proper manner. One of the first problems for instructors to make clear to initiates is that proper behavior must always distinguish sharply between kin *(wandugu)* and others, between those with whom sexual relations are either proscribed or at least modified along certain conventionalized lines (as with affines and cross-cousins), and those outsiders *(wageni)* toward whom one might possibly speak and act seductively *(kuduwa)*. It is essential that no one make a serious mistake in confusing these relationship categories, either explicitly or by implication.

The main way that conduct and information are taught at initiation is through repeated singing *(wekwimba)* of songs *(sinyimbo)* that are also riddle sayings *(figonho)*. These contain the teachings *(amafundo)* of adulthood. All these riddles and songs embody manifold sides of Kaguru thought in poetic, imaginative, highly memorable forms. In learning such material Kaguru young people become immersed in the "associational clusters" (Burke 1957: 18) that constitute Kaguru belief. These materials represent a compression or amalgam of the feelings and images of the Kaguru view of the world (Beidelman 1986: 5, 30–31). The key to this process of instruction lies in differences between the obvious meaning of a song, if indeed its meaning is clear at all, and its deeper or hidden meaning. During the days that an initiate is confined, she or he is taught many songs. After learning a song, the initiate is asked what it means. Of course, the initiate at first never succeeds in providing a satisfactory answer to the question. In the process of explaining *(kugula)* the real meaning *(ulawilo)*, the instructor openly explores those topics of sexuality that were previously never freely discussed, at least not between knowledgeable elders and their ignorant juniors. Talk that was once forbidden is now not only allowed but encouraged. An initiate learns how to express such matters in appropriate adult terms.

To appreciate the impact of these sessions of instruction, one must understand that these are almost certainly the first occasions at which a Kaguru boy or girl has been allowed to discuss sexuality with a Kaguru adult in any kind of meaningful way. Of course, a young Kaguru picks up some sexual information simply by being around adults and amongst peers and by listening to what they say and watching what they do. But such information can be garbled and incomplete, especially since it cannot be questioned or discussed at that time. Few proper Kaguru would discuss sexuality freely with a child before initiation. When such candid and helpful advice and, more important, social empowerment to speak openly of such matters are finally obtained, these will come only from elders of one's own gender.

The initiation songs tend to pose sexual issues in a disguised and metaphorical manner. The young people's mentors explain the real meanings of these songs and respond to the questions the songs prompt, often employing blunt, even crude language to explain matters. Earlier a child would have been teased and rebuked for speaking in this way, and no grown-up would have used such words except in a jocular and teasing manner to some other adult.

We should consequently view this instruction at initiation as constituting a truly radical change for young Kaguru, not only on account of any physical alterations that have occurred that prompt keener interest in sex, but also on account of changes in social discourse that profoundly separate children from adults. After initiation, Kaguru males and females may indeed now speak about sexual matters within properly defined social situations. Yet, conversely, now they can expect to suffer serious punishment (fines, verbal abuse, fights, ostracism) if they openly speak of such matters with inappropriate people or at inappropriate times. Children and anthropologists may make such verbal mistakes and expect only mild rebuke or disdain, but initiated adults have no excuse. Adults who do observe such proprieties have a right to respect, whereas children and anthropologists are at best affectionately tolerated and at worst avoided or scolded.

THE SONGS OR RIDDLES

In the previous chapter I related the songs and sayings that were integral to the female and male initiation activities themselves. These clearly are associated with particular points in the activities I have indicated. No such order or sequence pertains to the songs recounted below. These are presented in whatever order they come to mind to the mentors instructing the novices. As each mentor is not present all day every day (mentors work in shifts so that they may tend to their other responsibilities), some songs may even be repeated. This is all to the good because Kaguru believe that it is only by constant repetition that anything is learned and remembered. Some of the instructors themselves are still learning, refreshing or expanding their repertoire of such material. Some older instructors who have attended many initiations know such material well. Some younger men have attended few ceremonies and still defer to elder men, who have a surer grasp of both the oral literature and the ceremonial procedures. In part this is due to age, but it is also related to the character of some instructors. Some women and men attend initiation because they must, since their close kin are being initiated, but others attend because they enjoy these occasions. Over the years, some Kaguru will have attended a far greater number of initiations than others. Some will eventually acquire reputations as real habitués and consequently experts at initiations. I suppose this could be considered an avenue to power and influence, but Kaguru never spoke of such experts as having any political or economic influence, though such knowledge is respected. Not all Kaguru adults possess anything like the same store of knowledge about the procedures and oral literature associated with initiation. Because of this, Kaguru recognize that there may be differences in how such ceremonies are conducted and how such literature is interpreted. It is not that some Kaguru are necessarily right and some wrong, but some know such things in more detail and with deeper insights. Initiation activities serve as learning occasions not only for the young novices being initiated but also for some of their mentors as well. At the initiations I attended, the mentors ranged in age from elders in their fifties and sixties to young people who themselves probably had been initiated only a year or two before. These young people were often as eager to repeat and learn procedures and songs as the initiates themselves. These were the apprentice experts and initiators of the future. Initiations are therefore both occasions that transform children into adults and occasions that consolidate and encourage knowledge for young adults as well.

Initiates learn songs in a manner similar to the way an anthropologist might learn a native text. The initiate repeats it until he can sing it by heart (anthropologists can tape or transcribe).[3] Then the novice is asked what the song means. The obvious meaning of the song is rarely considered to be its real meaning. Usually the song is a coherent but metaphorical allusion to some other level of meaning. Less often, the song seems to make little sense at all.

This may be for two reasons. Sometimes songs employ archaic or exotic words.[4] Sometimes texts are so condensed that they make no sense without much explanation. In any case, the novice invariably fails to supply the requested inner meaning. Indeed, many novices never even try. The instructors then proceed to explain the "real" meaning of a song. This exposition serves as a springboard for wider commentary upon a particular topic such as copulation, menstruation, or sexual etiquette. These explanations allow discussion between a novice and instructors. They give a novice the chance to ask a whole series of questions on previously perplexing points. Or the songs may raise questions the novice had never thought about before.

To facilitate my account of these initiation songs I have divided them into four broad topics: initiation, adult sexuality and its related themes of sensuality and copulation, menstruation, and pregnancy and childbirth. There is nothing in Kaguru tradition determining this categorization. These are not taught according to topic but jumbled up, so a song about menstruation could follow one about copulation or one about childbirth.

In my presentation I first provide the Chikaguru text and then an English translation. I follow these with the deeper meanings provided by my informants. I then expand upon that indigenous explanation, setting it within a broader context of Kaguru society and culture. This further exposition would, of course, be unnecessary for Kaguru young people, who obviously are already immersed in that background. Unfortunately, with increased Swahili education and sometimes with much time spent residing away from home in boarding school, more such background explanation is now sometimes needed by young Kaguru as well.

INITIATION

Some songs first taught at initiation are not riddle songs but refrains that may be repeated throughout the initiatory learning period. The five I record below were collected with other songs taught at boys' camp. While the rest of the songs recorded in this chapter are learned by both girls and boys, these five are probably learned only by boys, although I cannot be sure. The first three would be appropriate for either girls or boys, but the last two seem more appropriate for boys alone since boys far more than girls are harassed during initiation. There seems to be no comparable intergenerational antagonism between Kaguru girls and women.

Tutula wana mkanyisa!
Teach the children well!

   This refrain is repeated often at the times when the novices are being drilled in the initiation songs and their meanings.

Kulanga mutemi nani nyalesi chambila ulanga!
The chief in the sky who holds the stars above!

   This refers to the fact that it is sexuality that makes the world go around. Sexuality is the chief (*mutemi*, "leader," "guide") of people and their affairs. Kaguru repeatedly remind the initiates that what they are learning at this time is the most important knowledge they can and will ever acquire. Without such knowledge the children may not succeed in becoming successful parents, and without offspring they and their kin groups have no future and certainly no afterlife since they will have no one to remember and propitiate their spirits.

Chali ukaya, chali walelengwa, chejile kuno chejele kuno chigola singo.
When we were home, we were only children, but here we got knowledge.

   Before the novices were initiated, they were still children, persons not jurally responsible for their acts. Their misdeeds were the concern of their elder kin. If they wronged outsiders, their kin were held responsible.

With initiation novices gain knowledge that conveys personal and social responsibility. Now they themselves may be pressed into litigation and must assume the payment of damages for their acts. Their new knowledge brings adulthood, but it also conveys new dangers since as adults they must now reap the consequences of their decisions and deeds. For this reason, novices should pay careful attention to what they are taught.

Kongolo! Kongolo! Sija muliga ukaya!
Ing'inako mwiko! Sija muliga ukaya!
Ibabako mwiko! Sija muliga ukaya!
Ikolodyo mwiko! Sija muliga ukaya!
Awanghunga mwiko! Sija muliga ukaya!
Never! Never! I won't be abusive at home!
My mother is prohibited! I won't be abusive at home!
My father is prohibited! I won't be abusive at home!
My mother's brother is prohibited! I won't be abusive at home!
My initiators are prohibited! I won't be abusive at home!

This song emphasizes the complex relations and feelings between generations. One of the important lessons to be learned at initiation is the acceptance of awareness and the means to verbalize feelings in socially empowered ways. The teachings at initiation are supposed to make the novices aware of their responsibilities to conceal and repress hostilities. These tensions, rooted in the authority of the household and kin group, serve as paradigms for relations that are broader and even more enduring: the future relations between the novices themselves and their own descendants and between themselves and the ancestral dead, whom they must propitiate (see Fortes 1965). Before initiation a child would be punished for insolence and abuse toward an elder relative but would not face any kind of possible jural punishment. After initiation, serious misbehavior of this sort would result in actual litigation, although Kaguru pointed out to me that most people would try to avoid taking this into court because of the shame *(chinyala)*. Punishment would more likely be exacted at a family or village moot. For Kaguru, *maligo* (abusive or dirty language, language that is out of place) toward those whom one should respect constitutes an offense as serious as or perhaps even more serious than physical assault. For Kaguru, words are dangerous for two reasons: First, they may expose matters that should never be made public, sexuality and witchcraft. Second, words, if shouted in rage, may be witnessed by others and then easily transmitted through gossip beyond the place where they were uttered. At least a physical assault, awful as it may be, is not always public, and even when witnessed it may not always be clear what the causes behind it are. The badness of *maligo* is its capacity (and facility) to make the hidden aspects of deep social resentments open and consequently vulnerable to hostile outsiders. The song begins by singling out three primary figures of authority and respect amongst one's immediate kin: one's mother, father, and maternal uncle.[5] It ends by including the novice's instructors at initiation, who are serving as surrogate parents in moral indoctrination. It is said that Kaguru should remember these instructors and show respect toward them throughout their lives. (Of course, I refer to the elders in charge of such instruction, not to the young hangers-on who are not that different in age from the novices themselves.) What is left unstated in the song is why such admonitions should be necessary in the first place. Implicit in this is reference to the stern regime and occasional harassment imposed by the initiators. Authoritarian elders have sent the novices to these difficult initiation schools. Like Hamlet, they are being cruel in order to be kind. The song warns these young Kaguru that although authority may seem oppressive when experienced by those on the receiving end, everyone should in time mature and have offspring and then stand in the same position. Then the sense of it all should be clear. Ultimately, all living Kaguru stand in comparable subordinate positions toward the ancestral dead, who punish and reward, protect and harm, in ways that may at times also prompt feelings of anger and resentment as well as gratitude. These feelings should no more be voiced than one should voice annoyance at one's living elders; without the dead one would not have been born at all, nor could one bear future offspring.

Wadodo nyenye mwandiga mwakaso. Malusimimbi nawikila munda.
My little ones abused me last year. I held back my anger until now.

This is taught to the initiates but actually describes the feelings of the initiators. This implicitly reminds the initiates of all their past misdeeds and sassy behavior. For this they are now being harassed by those in charge of their instruction. Their past, undisciplined behavior was presumably due in part to their lack of initiation. The initiates are led to realize that when they complete their initiation, they will themselves become both examples and disciplinarians to young people.

The rest of the songs in this section all seem to be equally well known by both genders and to apply equally to both.

Mutema mbata temela mwitumba, ya Musingisi ng'haneka mbata.
You cut the stubble in Itumba, but in Musingisi no one sees the stubble.

The hidden meaning of this song is that while one can readily see that circumcised men have been initiated, initiation is by no means so clear for women, on whom the cutting may leave few or no marks. The nature of the minor cutting on girls usually is such that it would be difficult for men to be sure that this had been done, at least during any casual sexual encounter.

Kaguru go on to point out that this song highlights further, deeper differences between men and women. Through initiation men are unambiguously altered socially, whereas women are not. Initiated males are expected to embark upon the roles of husband and father and consequently become jural heads of households. These males are thought to have changed socially (morally) as markedly as they have manifestly been altered physically. In contrast, initiation is thought not to alter females in any radical moral way. They remain jurally some type of minor. The first truly significant change for women, menstruation, has taken place within their own bodies independent of any external change to their genitals. Initiation may help women understand this change, but it does not produce any striking physical mark. Kaguru women agree but interpret this differently. Women observe that their power, their importance, derives from their fertility, from their essential capacity to bear children and reproduce their matrilineage. No rite or ceremony can convey this. It is inherent in their beings as women (though, of course, such capacities are vulnerable to the powers of the ancestral dead, to witchcraft, cursing, and sorcery).

The imagery employed in this song is based on the Kaguru dichotomy between mountains or upcountry, portrayed by the Itumba Mountains, and low areas, portrayed by the Musingisi River valley. This associates women with the fertility and perduring moisture of valleys, not only on account of their reproductive capacities, but also because of menstruation. Men often boast that circumcision permanently removes feminine, unclean moisture from their genitals whereas women, on account of periodic menstruation, remain moistly polluting until menopause, despite any operation. The imagery of cutting stubble also suggests clearing for planting, establishment of order during the cycle of cultivation, or clearing overgrowth on graves in order to propitiate the dead, who bestow fertility. No such clear establishment of order may be assumed for women. Men may speak of this song as underscoring male superiority, but women sometimes observe that their fertility and their deep nurturant bonds with their children cannot be constrained by jural rules; in this sense women are not fully subjected to the kinds of arrangements made by men who claim to control them. This need not be a sign of weakness; it can be considered a sign of women's enduring strength, their vital power to perpetuate matrilineages and nurture infants, a power that cannot be appropriated by men.

Chalinganila na wanya ukaya fidege fosa kuhamba hee!
Singo ya nghanu sina na hambo![6]
Like everyone else in the village, all the birds are decorated, hee!
The head of the wildcat has no decoration!

The song seems to refer to the contrast between circumcised youths and women (or perhaps uncircumcised males). I assume that the birds are initiated youths, whereas the wildcat refers to a sexually voracious woman or an undisciplined youth. The wildcat is a favorite Kaguru image of undisciplined sexuality. Kaguru themselves were not helpful in explaining this song.

Mulungu wana toga dimusweko chilonganage ngani simalika.
God's children cast off clothing in order to finish matters.

This song reminds initiates that they are initiated (cast off their clothing) in order to become adults, to consummate their purpose in life by being able to engage in sexual intercourse and have children. The phrase "God's children" (*mulungu wana*) should remind the initiates that they are like other humans, that is, other Kaguru, and their initiation is an inevitable social process. Today some Kaguru employ a comparable Swahili term, *wanadamu* (children of Adam), to refer to an inclusive human category when they are philosophizing or pontificating. The image of casting off clothing suggests both a sexual encounter and social transformation. One sheds one's clothing at initiation not only because of the operation

Figure 15. Kaguru wife, dressed up for her photograph. Photograph taken at Berega in 1957.

that will be performed but also because one then changes one's status. The initiates will don new clothing when they emerge from the confinement and dance their new status. Finally, they will lose their clothing with death, the ultimate transformation into ancestorhood. Kaguru are buried in a simple new cloth or hide, and the death attendants are given the old garments. At initiation, the novices' old clothing is given to their instructors. In both cases, the old garments are given as payment to those who assist transformation.

Dina diwangala musingo dibwa dyetu.
Our dog's neck has a collar.

This refers to the loose skin that should be left on the neck of the penis after circumcision. It points out the transformed appearance of the penis when it is properly cut. Kaguru say that there should be some loose skin on a circumcised penis in order to facilitate friction in copulation. The choice of a dog to stand for a penis is consistent with other Kaguru imagery relating genitals to biting animals or pecking birds.

Koloina! Chose choligana, chose.
Koloina! All will be the same, all.

I was told that Koloina is a proper name, though I never encountered this elsewhere in all my years with the Kaguru. The deeper meaning of this song is that the initiate should be reassured about recovery. There has been a painful cutting, but the novice will get well and be able to enjoy sexual life.

Chinyanda-nyanda!
Chanyanda kumutwe chasapilima chimala matimba.
Scrape! Scrape!
The shaver on the head sometimes finishes off the earrings [earlobes?].

Many of the songs employ an initial onomatopoeia, as this one does. The song refers to circumcision. The Kaguru have many occasions to shave the head, including initiation. Here, the glans is compared to the head. The foreskin is removed, and while this may appear to be a horrendous act, the initiate should realize that it is really no more shocking than the grooming that people ordinarily undertake. Such was the interpretation that men gave me. To compare circumcision to a slip or accident may seem inappropriate, but we should recall that Kaguru legend credits the origin of circumcision to an accident. While I personally find this a somewhat alarming song, Kaguru insisted that this was meant to be reassuring. I think they were making fun of me.

Chijoka chia, chijoka kasinde chiluma ng'ombe chaya mukasinde.
That small snake, the small snake from the reedy spot, bit the cow and returned to the swamp.

The small knife carried in the instructor's equipment bag is used to cut the uninitiated but then is returned to the bag. This song points out the periodic, repetitive nature of circumcision. One's initiation, which appears so important and unique, is just like the earlier initiation of one's father, one's grandfather, and, if one is fortunate, one's son.

Filingeyele cheleka dikoba no mwaka ukwija cheleka dikoba.
The bean plant bears a pod and next year it bears a pod.

A male has a foreskin, and when he fathers a male child, it too will have a foreskin. This song, like the preceding one, reiterates the periodic nature of initiation. A shortsighted person might look at initiation as a process separating a novice off from the rest of society. Another might see it as separating a novice off from juniors who remain uncut. The longer and more searching view should see the overarching unity that initiation implies. It is a rite linking every generation and one in which the understanding and knowledge of past generations are perpetuated by being passed down to those who follow. In this sense, initiation expresses the historical continuity of Kaguru life.

Kulanga kudya kwalamile duma, wahasi wose wanala madandu.
Above there is a leopard, yet below there are spots everywhere.

When a boy is circumcised, his genitals (a wild animal) are cut while he sits on an animal skin, which becomes splattered with his blood.

Nghanga yudya mulimbika sunji ne mwana nae mulimbika sunji.
That guinea fowl hides that thing and the child also hides it.

The guinea fowl, a game bird that hides in the undergrowth on the ground, is a frequently employed image for the female genitals. Both the bird and the child (presumably its offspring) are said to keep something hidden *(mulimbika)* inside *(sunji)*. At the most superficial level this verb, *kubika,* conjures up all kinds of female associations since one of the basic features of women's initiation is hiding *(kubika)* from the gaze of men those things that women do and those things that women are. When asked, men and women both said that the deeper meaning of this song refers to the clitoris *(iligi)* hidden inside a woman's vagina and which a woman's daughters will also possess. My own view is that the clitoris may also suggest the fact that a woman's sexuality is, in part, not clearly disclosed in the way that a circumcised penis is disclosed and that with arousal a woman may disclose sexual aspects of which a man is not ordinarily aware. In any case, this song, like the preceding ones, stresses the continuity in sexuality from generation to generation. What is perhaps ironic in this and some of the preceding songs is that such blatant mention of sexuality in a way that connects a parent and child is ordinarily considered gross and repugnant to Kaguru. Yet in these songs, as in initiation itself, it is this common sexuality that accounts for the continuity of life and society and therefore constitutes the highest good. For young Kaguru, having elders engage them in such discussion is a remarkable new experience.

SEXUALITY

The largest number of songs taught to boys and girls at initiation involve instruction about their sexual organs, about how men and women have sexual relations, and about the dos and don'ts of everyday relations between the sexes. These constitute a rich characterization of how Kaguru view sexuality.

Lwandamila mwikolongo lugugu, lwandamila hee! Lugugu!
Running along the valley are reeds, running along, hee! Reeds!

The song refers to the onset of puberty. The reeds *(lugugu)* grow in the low, damp places, as hair grows on the genitals. For Kaguru, the genitals are associated with what is low *(hasi)*, and the pubic hair obscures the genitals' features, especially on women. Pubic hair signals maturity, but the most fastidious Kaguru are said to shave or trim it.

Chamukakata chibago cheilolo chikakatulagua na nwenya mugunda.
The stiff grass of the valley is dug up by the owner of the garden.

Every adult has body hair *(ujoya)* on his or her genitals. While a relative or friend will shave your head for you, only you yourself should shave your genitals. Even though this side of grooming is not ordinarily noticed by others, a conscientious person should take care in grooming his or her genitals. While Kaguru often told me that this should be done, those young Kaguru men I saw bathing had not shaved their pubic areas.

Nheme lukutyo nghakutile mhimbi. Mhimbi sa mwetu sina mhango nhali.
I cut a stick to poke the hyraxes. Our hyraxes have no deep cave.

This means that no matter how long or large a man's penis may be, a vagina will always be able to accommodate it. Kaguru men say that the point of this song is that boys should be reassured that they can always manage to satisfy women. I believe that Kaguru men also find that this song sustains their own image of themselves and of women. Men might have large penises and therefore be sexually powerful and impressive, and women, having their own sexual appetites, may welcome any penis, the larger the better. Yet Kaguru women do not find such assertions always impressive. One woman laughingly told me that Kaguru women were hard to please and that men needed all the physical equipment they could muster in order to please them. This fits other women's comments to me that sometimes a woman cannot be satisfied by one man and that men delude themselves into thinking they are such great lovers. Sometimes such comments by women seemed to be merely ribald jesting, but at other times they struck me as sharply antagonistic. Several times I heard women publicly abuse and shame men by referring to their supposed impotence or small penises. The song probably reflects male insecurity in the face of women's demands as much as it proclaims any male dominance.

Kwigongo wangi wolimwa, wangi wamalale.
At the hill, some is cultivated and some is reedy (fallow).

I was told that this song is of Gogo origin although I was given no reason why this is so.[7] The song means that some semen is ejaculated at intercourse, but more remains for other occasions. Kaguru compare intercourse between men and women to cultivators clearing land and growing crops. My own view of this interpretation is that it seems unconvincing, but I could get no further explanation.

Malangilisi gemita mwigenge galangi lila ng'holongo sikoga.
The people on the riverbanks see the valleys being washed away beneath.

Kaguru consistently maintained that this song means that when men copulate with women, their testicles do not enter the vagina. This ridiculously obvious observation struck me as information hardly worth conveying to initiates, but no other interpretation could be gained. The sexual imagery of river valleys being equated with vaginas is fundamental to Kaguru thinking. The image of erosion and flood is meant to express male force and domination.

Magegemela galewela imhango mwaka ukwija galewela imhango.
Starlings perch by the cave and next year they perch by the cave.[8]

The meaning of this song is the same as for the preceding one.
Kaguru sexual metaphors frequently associate birds with genitals,
especially male genitals. The cave metaphor is probably a universal
image for women's vaginas.

Chimudodo chilimo, chidodo chitunge dilenga chitunge ne dikami.
The small, small mouth makes milk and water.

This song explains that the penis is capable of both urinating and ejac-
ulating semen. Kaguru sometimes describe semen as a kind of nurturant
milk. Semen not only produces children but is thought to foster the maturation of girls, who should have frequent intercourse if they want to
develop a full, feminine figure.

Mang'ina sena mahusi-husi, galonda mbolo gabaka mafuta.
Your mothers are conniving to take a penis and anoint it with oil.

Women are said to lubricate men's penises with oil before intercourse.
Some Kaguru say that a woman should pass down her oil container to her
daughter. It is as much a material embodiment of her personhood as a
bow and arrow or a shotgun is for a man. Castor oil facilitates the receptivity of women. It is also a means of blessing a person, as in bestowing a
name. Any part of the body that is well oiled is thought to be more sexually attractive. At dances women often oil much of their bodies so that
they glisten alluringly.

Some men and women interpreted this song as meaning that women
are always conspiring to have intercourse and that consequently they are
perpetually concerned about how they look. Kaguru of both sexes generally concede that women often use everyday situations as potential scenes
for seduction. (But then so do men.) How this is interpreted varied
greatly. Some men said that women are sexually voracious and therefore
cannot be trusted. They should be carefully watched so that they do not
commit adultery. This kind of expression fits the stereotype of women as
always having to be under the supervision of some male, though men also
are often described as randy and unfaithful. Most of the women I asked
did not seem to find this song's imagery to be objectionable. They said

the song portrayed how insufficient one man would be in meeting the sexual needs of some women. They said that if a man did not try hard to keep his woman sexually happy, she had every right to look elsewhere. According to this view a polygynist has a hard row to hoe. The image of women as unruly and sexually demanding sometimes seemed to amuse women, who teased and insulted men about this. Some women mockingly observed that many men are sexually inadequate to being the men they pretend to be.

Nhema mutogo nigalile yaya nghona si yaya, yaya wamiyangu.
I cut the *mutogo* tree to carry the nurturer, and if not that nurturer, then my neighbor's.

This means that a man is circumcised so that he can copulate. If he is not provided with a wife, then he may copulate with someone else's. The *mutogo* tree *(Diplorhynchus mossambicensis)* provides a strong, elastic wood that is sometimes carved into a shoulder yoke for carrying two loads at once, often water. The *mutogo* therefore resembles a penis to which two testicles are attached. This song parallels the preceding one in that it too warns that sexuality must be fulfilled, if not licitly then otherwise. What is important to recognize in the way these songs are interpreted is that for Kaguru sexual looseness is usually viewed as harming men, not women. Sleeping around jeopardizes men's claims over children and their control of women. It is not seen as especially threatening to women. This is more than merely androcentrism. Women's rights in their children bear no relation to men's negotiations, and neither do those rights in children that men do hold as mother's brothers on account of matrilineality. It is men as husbands and fathers who should fear promiscuity.

Mang'ina senu magona lungata chana cha mhanya chasa kusonyola.
Your mothers lie on their backs while the rat's child comes to taste.

Everyone's mother has sexual urges, and indeed one came into being on account of these urges. This song calls attention to and prompts discussion of an initiate's mother's sexuality, something ordinarily utterly forbidden. Much of the great force of this and some of the preceding songs lies in uttering the forbidden. These occasions at initiation are the only times such sexual comment on one's parents' sexuality is allowed without involving implications of serious insult, curse, or witchcraft.

A person should never (outside initiation) publicly mention either a father's or mother's sexuality. A person should not even touch a bed on which a parent has sat or slept.

Chipongo-pongo, chitui che duma! Leka cho ngoka nghamema wongo.
Gaping, gaping, the head of the leopard! Let it be like that, for it never fills up.

The vagina is a gaping, threatening mouth of a ferocious predator. It is insatiable. Kaguru (even women) sometimes speak of females as man-eaters *(makala)* (see Beidelman 1964d: 11–16).[9] What this signifies to men and women is complex and probably different.

Some Kaguru men worry as to whether or not they can satisfy their sexual partners. Such thinking probably accounts for some Kaguru saying that adulterous sexual relations are often more pleasurable than licit ones with a spouse. Fears about managing or expressing sexual satisfaction are said at times to inhibit carefree copulation. For example, trouble may start if a woman lets herself go and expresses enormous sexual pleasure in orgasm. Her husband may also worry if she repeatedly pesters him to copulate, for he may then wonder whether he has managed to satisfy her. Or he may get suspicious if she suggests some new turn or twist to what they do sexually. Such behavior may prompt a husband to ask himself such questions as these: Where did she learn about these new sexual things? If she enjoys sex so much, can I alone satisfy her? If I do not satisfy her, will she turn to someone else? Will she even be telling me the truth when she assures me that she is sexually satisfied? Such doubts sometimes lead to contrary results. Sometimes a husband may become roughly aggressive in his sexual approaches or may treat his wife coolly. Either way a wife may respond by concealing her true feelings and needs and may not then enjoy sexual relations with her husband as much as she otherwise might. A woman is better off covertly seeking a lover elsewhere than she is putting her husband's masculinity in jeopardy by complaining about his performance. Both husbands and wives have a moral right to expect regular sexual relations, except when certain prohibitions are in effect regarding mourning, illness, breastfeeding, menstruation, and other factors. Those who fail to copulate regularly with their spouses may be verbally abused by the offended spouse or divorced. Either Kaguru spouse is justified in seeking divorce and return of bridewealth if the other refuses to have frequent sexual intercourse.

Some Kaguru playfully told me that those involved in adultery need not worry about women's possible sexual insatiability or about men's need to perform extremely well. With adultery the main goal is temporary sexual gratification because you do not have to worry about any enduring faithfulness from a lover, especially one married to someone else. Besides, some women and men mischievously added, the very fact that people commit adultery goes to prove that some men are not good lovers while others must be terrific. Otherwise would not everyone be faithful and satisfied within a home? Accusations of adultery appeared frequently at the monthly sessions of local courts. Adultery by a husband is no grounds for any complaint by a traditional Kaguru wife. Adultery is traditionally defined as having sexual relations with any woman for whom one has not paid bridewealth. Husbands receive adultery fines for their wives; fathers receive such fines for their daughters.

Some Kaguru men's fears about sexual inadequacy appear to be reflected in Kaguru's frequent mention of vagina dentatae. As Lederer observes, castration may be a concern amongst some insecure men (1968: 220). Kaguru women may metaphorically castrate men by publicly complaining about men's failure to provide sexual satisfaction.[10]

In terms of sexual enjoyment, Kaguru credit both sexes with ordinarily wanting and deserving the pleasure of orgasm. Kaguru recognize that male orgasm and consequent ejaculation are more easily attained than is female sexual satisfaction. Kaguru acknowledge that some men may fail to bring their lovers to orgasm. Yet it is acknowledged that it is to men's disadvantage and shame not to do their best to please and satisfy women. I never heard remarks by Kaguru that any men or women did not enjoy sexual relations in principle, and a lack of pleasure in sexual relations seemed to be usually blamed on the inadequate potency of men.[11]

Chifuko chanyu cho mulomo ngubwi chambike mboga na kuhombolela.
My pot with the covered mouth cooks food and makes it soft.

After orgasm a man's penis becomes limp. The imagery here reflects many powerful sexual associations. Cooking and eating food have strong sexual implications. The cooking pot embodies a woman's role as an attentive housewife and mother. That it is covered *(ngubwi)* may refer to the genitals being concealed or to the woman being covered (in the Western sense of stock breeding). Concealing is thought to be a feminine activity. While one can interpret this song positively in terms of a woman as a source of sexual satisfaction and fulfillment for a man, the song also clearly points out that ultimately a woman softens a man, that she domesticates him. All Kaguru believe this.

Dimachi doboya dititu ku meso dyanbike mboga mulile muhala.
The one with an ugly, dark face cooks food that tastes sweet.

Even an ugly woman can be an enjoyable sexual partner. Again we find the alimentary imagery of sexuality. The reference to dark *(titu)* is not due to European influence. Kaguru assured me that they have always considered extremely dark people to be less attractive than those with reddish brown complexions. *Titu* can also refer to that which is hidden and impenetrable, a close-faced person or mysterious, dangerous medicine.

Kaguru observe that no nubile woman need lack a lover. This probably also meant that in the past, when polygyny was more frequently practiced than today, few such women would lack husbands. When I lived in Kaguruland, extremely ugly, deformed, and feeble-minded women had children even if they were not married. At that time, I knew many Kaguru women who did not want to be married and share a house with some man who would try to boss them around; these women all, however, said they welcomed children who would help them work and who would care for them in old age. In a society that traditionally sets enormous value upon children, in or out of wedlock, no adult woman is likely to die a virgin. Kaguru sometimes say that the eye (aperture) of the penis is blind, that is, that when a man gets sufficiently randy, he will sleep with anyone, even someone unsuitable to marry—a concern expressed in many Kaguru stories as well as in initiation songs.

In this song the sweetness of food refers to the fun and pleasure of sexual intercourse. As Loizos points out, copulation is often play and may then not really aim at conception, a seemingly obvious point that is often neglected in much ethnographic literature (1980: 235).

Heyoo! Nhela mhembele yahala ukali we ng'ina!
Woi ihala ukali we ng'ina!
Hey! The fierce rhinoceros impaled Mother cruelly!
Oh, it stabbed Mother cruelly!

The rhinoceros is often mentioned in relation to sexuality. The animal's dangerousness is the attribute emphasized. Sexuality involves danger, for it often leads people to break social rules and sometimes to show a serious lack of proper feeling toward others. One's own parents' sexuality is particularly dangerous to oneself, and under normal circumstances (outside the initiation camp) reference to it constitutes a terrible wrong comparable to witchcraft and cursing. This song's aim is to make the initiate aware that the same ferocious emotions and drives that are now stirring in oneself also stir in one's parents. This is the essence of how life goes on, a theme repeatedly touched upon at initiation.

Dikopokopo, difusi dya yawa, leka dikopoke na mutima wela.
Squish squish, the vagina of the mother, let it squish and the heart is pleased.

Uninhibited sexual intercourse often produces unattractive sounds that may be embarrassing, but one should enjoy it and not worry. Copulation should be pursued despite any fleeting inhibitions. The unattractive sound is here associated with women and relates to their dangerous moistness. Of course, it is very difficult to do anything at night in a Kaguru house without being overheard by others in the home. Often one can even hear many sounds in neighboring houses. Kaguru children gain their first ideas about sexual intercourse by overhearing sounds in the dark from their parents' bed. This is one of the reasons given for sending older children to a girls' or boys' house.

Selemu, selemu, selemu, selemu, chisala chokusajila.
Crunch, crunch, crunch, crunch, the grinding stone grinds.

This song repeats the message of the previous one, warning lovers not to feel inhibited. The verb *kusajila* (to grind flour) is a euphemism for sexual intercourse. Both copulation and grinding make useful products, offspring and food.

Dikunjumwalu digosi dititu dikola nyumba ne migamba.
The male dark bird supports the house and the roof poles.

The man's penis pleases woman and produces offspring, thus ensuring the cohesion of a household. The *kunjumwelu* is a very small, dark bird, probably a finch. It is here associated with the center pole *(nguso)* of the house, which is also dark due to blackening from the hearth smoke. The small bird is mentioned with the *di-* prefix, ordinarily added only to a large or important object. This oxymoronic prefix implies that while the penis (bird) may appear to be a small and hidden thing, not even spoken about politely, it actually is important, the pivotal tool of a household. The center pole is sometimes explicitly compared to a penis in contrast to the stone hearth beneath it, which is associated with a woman.[12]

Kolodyodyo, kwega, kwega mukila mutali, kwega, kwega.
The black flycatcher, pull, pull its tail to get it long, pull, pull.

If you play with a penis, it becomes enlarged and erect. We also see again here the imagery of the penis as a black bird. The word *kolodyodyo* actually means "your mother's brother," but it is also a nickname for a bird. The word *mukila* (tail) is also a euphemism for penis.

Kunondwa kwina fituli fyejete. Kunondwa chimonga chakutwangila ndoboya.
In Nondwa there are two mortars. In Nondwa one is for pounding by the penis.

There are two orifices, the anus and the vagina. A man should penetrate only the vagina. Pounding flour *(kutwangila)* is a common euphemism for sexual intercourse, and correspondingly a mortar is a euphemism for a vagina. *Ndoboya* is said to be an archaic word for "penis." As an alien ethnographer I did not learn many details about what people actually do sexually, but I know that some sophisticated Kaguru associate anal intercourse with Muslim Arabs who have shops in Kaguruland.

Bed is the supposedly proper place for two persons to have sexual intercourse, not outside in the bush. Presumably sexual intercourse in bed is likely to be licit whereas intercourse out of a bed is almost certainly adulterous. To have sexual intercourse in the bush is to behave like an animal. Still, many Kaguru are said to be unfaithful there, where they cannot be so readily seen or heard. Going to the gardens, fetching firewood and water, traveling to markets or court, and even attending beer clubs all provide excellent opportunities for Kaguru women and men to meet secretly. Kaguru were constantly gossiping about whom they saw away from home acting suspiciously, as though they were involved in some sexual liaison.

Chimhoka changu mhandile kwigenge.
My plant planted in the riverbank.

This affirms the value of sexual intercourse. The metaphors of cultivation and planting reflect this from the perspective of a man impregnating a woman (riverbank).

Tema dyo muyombo! Nheme dyo musani! Chigakongheke chilange dikwake.

The wood twig of the *muyombo* tree! I cut the *musani* tree! Let's rub them together to see which one flares up.[13]

For Kaguru, kindling a fire clearly alludes to sexual intercourse. In making fire with firesticks, Kaguru use an active stick of hardwood and a passive stick of soft and easily combustible wood. The passive stick, the one drilled, is the female. The imagery is complex. The male stick ignites the female one, at least to the extent that it casts sparks onto the tinder lying on the bottom stick. The fire is associated with women, with food and the hearth, and with their capacity to nurture. Yet for Kaguru fire making conveys a sense of aggression and domination in that fire consumes and burns. Making fire is a task that men perform in order to please women since fire is necessary for women to perform their duties at the hearth. While most women could make a fire with firesticks in an emergency, using firesticks is supposed to be a male task. Today, of course, Kaguru use matches or borrow burning embers from a neighbor.

Mang'ina senu mahusi-husi, galonda duma goha kuluhengo.
Your mothers are crafty, they took a leopard to tie in the corner of the house.[14]

My informants were divided as to what this song might mean. The majority interpreted this as meaning that women often conceal lovers from their husbands or fathers. A few men suggested that the song means that before one's circumcision one's mother may at times see one naked but that after one is initiated this must never happen. Of course, a song can hold several meanings for singers, but this second interpretation strikes me as unconvincing because even before initiation an older boy would avoid any hint of sexual immodesty toward his mother once he becomes at all aware of what sexuality involves. Yet some of this modesty may reflect modern Christian influence; early visitors to Kaguruland describe boys going about naked until at least seven or eight. In contrast, little girls were reported to wear pubic coverings soon after they learned to walk.

Usiku woile we nghwale. Jogolo kautenda wakwe.
The night was the francolin's. The cock then made it his.

The song expresses a man's sexual domination of a woman. The francolin, a game bird that tends to hide in undergrowth, is associated with women. The cock (domesticated bird) prevails over the francolin (bird of the bush). The fact that some species of francolin have red legs and feet has led some Kaguru to associate them with women, comparing this red in the lower body to menstruation. A Kaguru story associates domestic animals with men and their wild counterparts with women.

Maswaga nghena luma ng'ombe. Muhando alatumula.
The lizard did not bite the cow. The red snake bit it.

This means that the testicles do not enter the vagina, only the penis. Kaguru were not helpful in explaining this further.

Kunyika huya kusina nhungu setu, singi simapinga.
In the bush there are our calabashes, some full, some half full.[15]

Some men are having no sexual intercourse, and consequently their testicles are full of semen, while others are frequently copulating, and consequently their testicles are only half full, but all these men are capable of fathering children.

Mashine yuyu kema mushashoni, chimonga kasa chimalile chalo.
That locomotive stands in the station. One came to finish the business.

I received two different interpretations of this song. The first came from a female informant and the second from a male, but I have no reason to believe that men and women would find either interpretation unacceptable. The first interpretation is that a man may have an orgasm before a woman does, but that ideally both should have one together. This does reflect an important concern of women, that men be considerate lovers. The second interpretation is that a woman bears a child but her ordeal is not ended until she has expelled the afterbirth as well.

Ing'holo kona ilapa yona miyangwe.
The bleating sheep saw their comrade.

If a person meets a prospective lover, that person's genitals will become excited and tumescent.

Kufisalambwa kufilenga fyelu, fingi fyakunywa fingi fiusungu.
Don't lap up white liquid. The one is for drinking, the other not
for drinking.

While the penis emits both urine and sperm, it is important that a copulating man makes sure he has urinated beforehand so that he does not
urinate instead of ejaculate. This interpretation struck me as rather far-
fetched, but while I was doing fieldwork informants insisted that one man
in a nearby village had been humiliated by being accused in court of just
such a slip. I asked whether this might also be making some allusion to
oral sex; Kaguru claimed to be horrified at the idea.

Sungula gwegwe, taga digaladlyo! Notage ule kongelo dya wana?
You, hare, toss your scut! How shall I do this to deceive children?

Some men brag and pretend to be very masculine, but when they actually have sexual intercourse with a woman it sometimes turns out that
they are impotent. Other informants claimed that the song refers not to
impotence but to sterility. In either case, the message is that some men
cannot "deliver the goods." Certainly many Kaguru women were ready to
agree with this interpretation. What is important here is the fact that during sexual intercourse the burden of adequate performance falls upon the
man. Can he achieve and maintain an erection, and can he copulate well?
Women can lie there silently or they can even pretend to enjoy themselves,
but, as some Kaguru remarked, a man cannot fake his work. The choice of
a hare (*sungula*) as the seducer in this song relates to the fact that Kaguru
consider the hare to be the epitome of clever deceit. My own view is that
such a man would be harelike if he succeeded in seducing a woman but
knew that he was infertile. There would be nothing clever about seducing
a woman and then being humiliated by being found out to be impotent.
Some women said that a sterile man should not waste a woman's time,
even if he has a wonderful sexual technique, because women want to become impregnated. While some Kaguru women said this, I am sure that a
good lover would be welcome and, as everywhere, is not easy to find. After all, Kaguru recognize that even postmenopausal women deeply enjoy
sex. I was repeatedly struck by how often and how openly old women
talked about sexual matters, especially at beer clubs and dances. If anything, older women can joke about sexual matters in public in a way that
would not be considered proper for younger, still fertile women.

Digwami tali hadumila langa mwaka ukwija hadumila langa.
The tall bamboo does not touch the sky nor will it touch the sky
next year.

No matter how long or large a man's penis may be, it is never so large
that it cannot be accommodated by a nubile woman's vagina. We have
already encountered another version of this song.

Chalawe, Chalawe, mutemi wa Lusega, nhembo saloka saleka Chalawe.
Chalawe, Chalawe, chief of Lusega, the elephant passed by but
spared Chalawe.

When a woman gives birth, much is expelled from her vagina, but her
clitoris, though it may extend from the folds of her labia when she is
aroused, is not lost at childbirth. This seems a ridiculously obvious assertion. What Kaguru seem to be emphasizing, however, is that initiates be
made aware of how the clitoris behaves when a woman is aroused and
that it is important for the woman to be properly aroused. Chalawe is a
proper name itself associated with emergence. Lusega is a place in
Kaguruland.

Chagendanyaga na mulalmu Itumba. Chadya singhowo kanyima mupunga.
We were traveling with an affine in Itumba. We ate bananas but you did
not give me rice.

You may be traveling with a comrade, and while you are traveling
alone, he is with his wife. When you reach a village at night, he is able to
sleep with his wife while you must sleep alone. This song seems at first so
simple that it has little point. It does, however, allow instructors to expand upon the problems of observing various restrictions concerning sexual relations. Obviously one should not have sexual intercourse with just
anyone. An affine well illustrates the difficulties involved. If a man is an
affine, then he is sleeping with one of your kin or you are sleeping with
one of his. This shows how sexual relations may establish important ties
between previously unrelated people. Yet because of these sexual (affinal)
relations, many people who might originally have been able to sleep with
each other are now forbidden as sexual partners. Affinity neatly illustrates
the fact that many of the restrictions one must observe regarding sexuality stem from social conventions that must be learned and which may require genealogical consultation. Initiates are warned that one should not

let one's sexual urges jeopardize the stability of carefully engineered social relations and that certain seemingly attractive sexual possibilities actually involve dire consequences. Had a person committed adultery with the wife of a traveling companion who was only a friend, this would have been treachery, but it would not have been considered a serious misdeed by any of the kin of those involved. But having sexual intercourse with a person who is in some way affinally related not only sets two kin groups at odds with each other but also generates serious mystical dangers that can be removed only by complicated purificatory sacrifices to the offended ancestral dead. Such sexual relations between affines mystically endanger not just the two sexual partners and the deceived spouse but all close kin on both sides as well, including the offenders' children.

Chitololondo chinyama chidodo mwaka ukwija chinyama chidodo.
The small finches provide little meat and next year there is little meat.

If a woman is left to herself by her husband and is not penetrated regularly, her vagina will shrink and become like that of a small girl. The Kaguru metaphor of genitals and birds is repeated. (Kaguru are willing to eat most birds, but clearly the little, elusive finch is not worth the effort of hunting or trapping.) So too is the association between sexuality and food. The most important theme is that women must have sexual relations frequently if they are to remain subdued. Kaguru men believe that women whose sexual cravings are not regularly met will seek satisfaction adulterously with other men. This song supports the image of men struggling to satisfy women. Conversely, it presents women as persons who may at times become frustrated by not securing what is their just reward and fulfillment. A man who cannot satisfy his wife should not complain about her.

Isungwe-sungwe mutemi miyangu hona nghulonga yenamile hasi.
Ashamed before the chief when I speak, my comrade looks down.

When a man has committed illicit sexual relations with some woman, he may be brought before an elder of a matrilineage or the head of a government court in order to be denounced and to be made to pay compensation. At such a time, the offender just looks down in shame and can say nothing to excuse himself. If the elders could truly search the man's feelings and thoughts, then they would find that the man's penis was hanging limp, but it had not really changed its nature. A man may apologize regarding his sexual offenses, but his sexual drives remain, and the next time they are stirred the man will be just as sexually aroused and consequently just as foolishly rash as he was when he got into trouble earlier. The song enables the instructors to point out to the initiates that a person's sexual drives are indeed powerful and can lead one astray, even against a person's own common sense and best interests.

Mugunda we isanga chimala mbeyu no mwaka ukwija chimala mbeyu.
The garden in sand ruins the seeds and next year it ruins seeds.

Ipande digono chimala umwaka ukwija chimala.
The worn-out pipe is no good and next year it is no good.

Both these songs have the same meaning, that it is a waste of a man's time to copulate with a postmenopausal women. In actual fact, this is obviously not the case if one's aim is sexual enjoyment. What this song illustrates is the persistent Kaguru idea that sexual relations make no sense if they do not produce children. Indeed, I had considerable difficulty trying to explain to some Kaguru that some European women and men would take precautions not to cause conception during intercourse. Some Kaguru did agree that young girls might not want to become pregnant before they got married, especially if they had been converted to Christianity or were still attending school. It is also believed that a woman who is still nursing an infant should not become pregnant because this would harm her capacity to provide milk to her present child. It is said that women who are nursing who do become pregnant (even though nursing inhibits conception) are selfish and inconsiderate toward their living children. Some women may be embarrassed to have conceived under such circumstances (though they can always blame this on their inconsiderate husbands' importuning), but I never heard it suggested that a woman would want to abort such a pregnancy. In general, no one could imagine that anyone who was married would not want to produce as many offspring as possible. To want to prevent conception or to abort a child were the sort of inexplicably perverse motive that must be some sign of witchcraft. As the song suggests, having intercourse with a woman who cannot bear children is not wrong but it is certainly a waste of a man's sperm.

Chitunda chidya chitunda Seigwe, mbidukile kuno nyagwa na Seigwe.
That hill is Seigwe's hill, and if I turn away from there I still meet Seigwe.

If a man wants to copulate with a woman, he should have no problem because there are willing women everywhere. In the song a man is on a journey presumably heading for a hill where a fellow named Seigwe resides. Even if the traveler changes his direction and goes elsewhere or even if he gets lost, he will presumably encounter Seigwe. In short, all roads lead to the same destination. Another implication of this view is that women are ever ready and willing to receive men as lovers. In one rather bizarre Kaguru lawsuit (see Beidelman 1961d: 11–14) dealing with alleged rape, many of the men attending court insisted that it was true that a man would be having unauthorized intercourse with a woman if he had not paid for such rights, but the issue of consent by the woman involved would be beside the point. Consequently, for Kaguru rape was traditionally not a crime different from adultery. What struck me most during various Kaguru court cases involving sexual misconduct was the prevailing Kaguru assumption that most women would not refuse most offers for sexual intercourse if an opportunity arose. I do not believe that this is so, but it is a sociological fact that women gain social advantages with children regardless of who the father may be. Clearly this psychological untruth asserted by Kaguru men reflects a certain jural reality that works for women and against men.

Dinghununghunu dijila dya mphwani, dyoile na nghwalo chimala madole.
The well-trod road to the coast would ruin people's toes if it were rough.

If the vagina were dangerously abrasive, there would be no male whose penis would not be injured. The song assures initiates that most adult, healthy males have sexual intercourse with women whenever they can, and this includes women with whom men have no jural rights to such relations. Men should try to live up to this stereotype.[16] This is a macho song asserting men's and women's sexual needs.

Musebelele unyala kumakungo kwisina kwakwa unghali mijolo.
The *musebelele* tree is dried up at its branches but is still green at its base.

When a man ages, his physique may well deteriorate, but he is able to enjoy sexual intercourse and father children until he is quite old, far older, comparatively, than is the case for women. It is important for Kaguru men to remember this if they are to engage in polygyny. Given the demands of bridewealth, it is only quite elderly men who are likely to be polygynists.

Mang'ina senu myenda ya chitambi ng'hona ikulala konga kumapinde.
Your mothers' bordered cloths are worn at the edges.

When women age, they do so first in terms of their sexual fertility. A woman may appear quite attractive but may have already reached menopause. *Myenda* are cloths that are wrapped around the waist. *Myenda ya chitambi* are cloths associated with the Swahili that have a colored design worked on the edge. Consequently, when they begin to fray with age, their distinctive design is the first thing to go. Instructors note that women may appear more sexually fertile than they actually are, in that their faces and bodies may look good even after menopause. The full meaning of this song seems to be ambivalent. On the one hand, the song asserts that men may be wasting their time having sexual intercourse with older women if these men's purpose in having intercourse is fathering children. On the other hand, the song also asserts that women do not cease being sexually attractive and worth seducing if pleasure and not children is the aim.

Itumba kudya kuwalima mphange muke luselo mulume luselo.
There amongst the farmers of the garden in the Itumba Mountains the wife twists and the husband twists.

Women and men writhe and twist when they copulate. People should not feel embarrassed or surprised at the ways people seek sexual gratification. Whatever position or movement gives pleasure is worth doing.

Pula dya ng'ombe dyali munakano mwaka ukwija dyali munakano.
These days the nose of the cow is damp and next year it is still damp.

A woman's vagina is always moist no matter when. As the initiate learns, especially the boy initiate, the moistness of the woman's genitals, especially during menstruation, accounts for the fact that her genitals are regarded as perpetually polluting. Moisture also denotes fertility. For Kaguru vaginal moisture is also associated with sexual receptivity, here meaning that women are always supposedly willing to be penetrated by men. They are sexually voracious. As is the case with many of these songs, this can be interpreted either as alluding to the fact that women have a driving need for men's sexual attentions or as meaning that men are hard pressed to meet these demands. In either case, this moisture is what provides society with its means to produce new members. Lying behind these different stereotypes of women's sexuality is the fact that women's fertility remains the central key, the *fons et origo*, of Kaguru social structure and that Kaguru men are divided in terms of the implications this has for their power as fathers and brothers, whereas fertility works more consistently for women's power as mothers and sisters.

Mpululuji mutiwa mulwanda na unoga muno hautemwa jengo.
The *mpululuji* tree of the river valley is good but should not be cut for lumber.

Even though your sibling of the opposite sex is attractive, you should never have sexual relations with that person. Here sexuality is doubly tied to the fecundity of river valleys and to the construction of homesteads. Kaguru have prohibitions against certain types of sexual relations. The most stringent of all are the prohibitions against sexual relations between those standing in a "sibling" relationship, people of the same generation within the same matriclan or people of the same generation with fathers of the same matriclan. Sexual relations between such people are tantamount to witchcraft and traditionally were punished with death. Yet Kaguru feel deep fascination and concern with sibling sexuality. A man's sisters will produce his lineal heirs. A woman's brothers' children will be the major competitors whom her own children must face for their lineal inheritance.

Kaguru never spoke to me about any desire to have sexual relations with a mother, actual or classificatory, but they often joked or fantasized about incestuous relations between a youth and his sister. Kaguru insisted that there was no hard-and-fast rule against a father having sexual intercourse with his daughter. Such conduct was thought to be sordid and stupid, but it violates none of the rules against clan incest. I encountered rumors of one such case that provoked snide gossip (see Beidelman 1971c).

Muhimba sugulu uhimbe digoya unghahimbisa kotula imbwisa.
The digger's stick pokes slowly and carefully because if you dig roughly you will break it.

If you copulate with a small woman, you had better insert your penis slowly or you may injure her. The metaphor of cultivation is clear. So is the allusion to Kaguru machismo. This song somewhat contradicts a previously reported song that described Kaguru women as sexually commodious and insatiable caves. In earlier times when large supplies of iron were scarce, some Kaguru employed a wooden digging stick rather than a hoe. This was a long stick with a fire-hardened, pointed tip. A hole was poked in the cultivated soil and then the seeds kicked in. The comparison with a penis is one Kaguru make.

Dimachikobwe dyengile chisima dyasa kulawa dyang'unhule meso.
The intruder entered blind and came out with beady eyes.

Some informants explained this song as describing how the penis has no eyes when it enters a vagina, but that the child it begets can see. Kaguru say that in a way the penis has an eye, an aperture, but that it does not carefully see, that is, discern. It finds a sexual target but does not consider whether that target is appropriate or not. When the penis is aroused, it acts blindly, simply jutting out to enter whatever is handy.

Other informants explained that the song simply means that an intruder is entering a dark hole. They argued that the inner meaning of the song is that a child is begat as an unseeing fetus in a hidden, unseen place but that it begins to see after it is born.

Both interpretations contrast the inchoate character of a fetus at conception with the growing consciousness and individuality that it attains after birth.

Mele ya mphene yalimusungunho yasunyunhila kuchihembe chimwe.
The goat's milk circulates, circulating to a horn.

Kaguru believe that repeated sexual intercourse accelerates the maturation of girls. A lover's semen is like nurturant milk that circulates through a girl's body and feeds the growth of her breasts (horns) and buttocks, the two protruding areas whose development is viewed by Kaguru as a sign of her sexual maturity and attractiveness. Traditionally Kaguru did not stress virginity for girls, so such intercourse was encouraged to help girls develop. It was, however, important that such sexual relations be deferred until after a girl's initiation. This song represents what Christian missionaries consider the worst side of initiation teaching, a song that encourages what the churches consider immoral behavior.

Chibudi-budi, chabudi baha chali chiwaha nichitowa mbaso.
Chibudi-budi, avoiding her, but were she larger I might knock her down.

Chibudi is a woman's name. The *chi-* prefix is an affectionate diminutive, relating to the fact that the woman referred to in the song is not large. The root *-budi* refers to avoidance, and therefore Chibudi is the name of a person in some way associated with some kind of avoidance. A young girl might be attractive, but men must avoid her until she is initiated. The basic message seems straightforward. The most revealing aspect of this song is its use of the verb *kutowa* (to strike) as a term for sexual intercourse. American expressions such as *knock up* and *fuck* (deriving from *strike*) would relate to this. While this song may at first appear to advocate restraint by men, its general tone reinforces typical aggressive Kaguru male stereotypes about the macho meaning of penetrating women.

Dibudi-budi dijenga nyumba dileka nyumba digona mulango.
Dibudi-budi has built a house and yet left the house to sleep at the door.

Dibudi is a proper name but also (as in the previous song) alludes to avoidance. The prefix *di-* conveys a sense of largeness. The sense of a growth in size is part of the play on the name and its association here with expansion due to sexual arounsal. The house refers to a vagina. The song is said to mean that a woman has a clitoris that appears concealed by the folds of her labia, but when she is properly excited by a lover it will become visible.

Dipela dia iwaha bwete amba mudodo koditowa ninyi.
That baobab tree is big for nothing because even though you are small you can strike it down.

Dipela dia wa chaka hata mudodo kolowela ng'onde.
That baobab tree is big for nothing because even a little one can climb it.

The two versions of this song have the same significance. In the first, Kaguru are told that no matter how large such trees may be, men fell them by a combination of setting fires around the base and cutting with axes. In the second song, Kaguru are told that such a tree can be easily scaled. Kaguru drive pegs into the side of such trees so that they can set beehives in them. The inner meaning is that any woman, even a mature and seemingly formidable one, can be seduced by a much younger male. Boys are encouraged to believe that once they have been initiated, they can entertain hopes of having an active sex life. They must now conquer the very inhibitions that they were earlier taught in order to keep them in their place as modest, shy children.

Mutalawanda no mabiko yetu no mwaka ukwija no mabiko yetu.
The *mutalawanda* tree is our remover and in the year to come it is our remover.[17]

This means that if a man has sexual intercourse with a woman, subsequently the couple's genitals should be wiped clean by the woman. She is supposed to take on the postcoital pollution. She does this by wiping their genitals with her hand and then wiping this onto her lap. The tree figures in this scenario as a source of leaves that could be used to wipe the body after defecation or sexual intercourse. The song itself strikes me as abusive toward women. Unfortunately, the interpretation I have came solely from men since I lacked the courage to ask any women informants about this aspect of copulation once I was given the initial interpretation.

What comments I did receive from Kaguru men regarding sexual relations tended to assert aggressive, macho conduct. For example, some men claimed that they would try to have sexual relations with women while lying on their right side and consequently forcing the woman to lie on her left side. This would incommode men's own right sides and leave women with only their right hands free. This would constrain women into using their "proper" or eating hand for play in sexual intercourse, whereas the men would use their "unclean" left hand.[18] I assume that in actual practice Kaguru copulate in all kinds of positions and that this description merely reflects male wishful thinking.

Chibwa chijelu nyangaya nacho no mwakaka sa nyangaya nacho.
I walk with the small white dog and another year I again walk with it.

Males walk about with sperm in their bodies all the time. They are always ready and able to propagate children.

Wadodo nyenye musame ukilawa mwija fikamisa mhela mukahembe sikihoma na kisajanga sikiyonesa kunduyng'hu wao.
Youngsters, never go out early in the morning or you will encounter a rhinoceros stabbing and cutting up, exposing red body parts.

Wadodo nyenye mpelaje kilawa mhali kwagana mhela mukahemba sikihoma na kisajanga sikiyonesa kundung'hu wao.

Mwana nyenye sameni ukilawa mwija mufikamisa mhela mukahemba sikihoma sikisajanga sikiyonesa noudung'hu wao.

This is the first song in which I present three versions of the Chikaguru text. All three versions have the same basic meaning, so I have provided not three translations but only one. The Chikaguru wording is so different in each that I have presented all versions.

The rhinoceros is said, like many other fierce, wild animals, to represent the genitals. The redness suggests danger for Kaguru even though one would be hard put to find anything red exposed when Kaguru copulate. Initiates are told that the song warns them never to enter their parents' house when they think the parents might be having sexual intercourse. Once the initiates have returned to their home villages, they must reside in a different house than their parents (although they may have already done so before). After initiation they must be particularly circumspect and wary about any actions that might lead to some suggestion of sexuality in the presence of their parents. Before their initiation they were also forbidden such conduct, but slips were forgiven as the thoughtlessness of children. After initiation one cannot take refuge in an easy excuse. To emphasize my point I note that Kaguru parents are said to disinherit their children by standing naked before them and calling attention to their genitals by hands and words. (I never heard of anyone actually doing this.)[19]

Hamwamba hadya hadimile nhenje napulapula, sinaona hondo.
Out there the antelopes [?] have been feeding and cavorting, but I have not seen any tracks.

I had difficulty translating this song, especially the word *nhenje*, which my word lists indicated as "cricket" or "cockroach" but which informants described as a small antelope. Informants agreed that this song warns boys not to go to that part of a river where women (game animals?) bathe. Even though water leaves no trace of genitals, the place would have been imbued with femaleness and therefore should be avoided. Men who have come into contact with female genitals should bathe before resuming other activities. Women who have been sexually involved with men should do the same. Traditionally males and females bathe in different parts of a stream, men upstream from women so that they could not come into contact with any menstrual blood, though I was told that women did not bathe when they menstruate.

MENSTRUATION

Since a large number of initiation songs are devoted to the subject of menstruation, I have placed these together in one section.

Chising'yagilo, ng'homela ngili yangu. Mwaka ukwija ng'homela ngili yangu.
We heel, kill my warthog. Next year kill my warthog.

A modest woman should always take care to conceal her menstrual blood from others. Sometimes she may have taken insufficient precautions and some falls to the ground. Then she should quickly cover it by grinding it into the soil with her heel. The motif of a wild pig is a popular reference for women's initiation and fertility. It also has associations with the ancestral dead (see Beidelman 1964a).

Nghengele lilaa, nghengele lilaa! Saa nane! Imwanywa nawasungu. Chamunsongoli chomuikuyu gombo! Saa nane! Imwanywa na wasungu.
The bell rings, the bell rings! Eighth hour! Known to Europeans. The doves with long tails quarrel. Eighth hour! Known to Europeans.

I failed to secure a clear interpretation of this song. All that I could learn is that it is thought to refer to menstruation. The only suggestion I can make is that birds are regularly associated with genitals and that a number of birds mentioned by Kaguru have red legs, perhaps referring to menstruation.

Wachikangaga ndosele wanangu, nolasa ule gongo dina miwa?
The Wachikangaga (swamp-reed people) help my child to ford, but how can I carry them when my back has a thorn on it?

I had difficulty translating this song. *Kangaga* are tall reeds. Presumably Wachikangaga are inhabitants of the tall reeds or beings associated with tall reeds. Kaguru sometimes name matriclans after locales, but there is no such matriclan amongst Kaguru. The thorn is said to refer to the onus of menstruation and indicates that a woman cannot perform certain kinds of duties or offer certain kinds of assistance because she is menstruating and is therefore polluting. A menstruating women would ordinarily avoid bathing or crossing a stream.

Ng'hangagange yudia mudongele no njila yasa panguka kadya mukongoni.
That otter walks on the path, but when it leaves the path, it eats at the lair [sleeping place].

Another version of this song substitutes a small wildcat *(chikanu)* for the otter. The wild animal in the song (otter or wildcat) refers to a sexually active woman. Kaguru gave two interpretations of this song. Some said that it means that a couple might be traveling together, but if the woman begins to menstruate, she must go off the path to secure means to tend to herself. She would probably look for some leaves to absorb the blood. Subsequently, she should travel behind the man. Others said that the song refers to a man and woman meeting on a path and then going off into the bush to copulate.

Mudali-dali mulila we sange. Mukoma sange no mulila kwage.
Hop, hop, the track of the wood rat. If you kill the wood rat, its trail is gone.

There were two interpretations of this song. The more prevalent and convincing is that a woman menstruates monthly but ceases to do so when she becomes pregnant. This interpretation reflects the Kaguru association of genitals with wild game animals (Kaguru hunt and eat wood rats) and the Kaguru comparison of hunting and killing with successful coitus. The other, less convincing interpretation is that a person can have a lover and/or a spouse, yet despite becoming very attached to each other, one is sure to die before the other.

Chibawa masada chihindile ng'ombe, ng'ombe sakwetu chitula madewa.
Let us pluck the fruit to tease the cows, and our cows break their byre.

When women menstruate, they use old cloth or leaves to absorb the blood. Here, women's menstrual blood is compared to livestock breaking out of their pen. Even though menstruation is recognized as vital to fertility, it is associated with disorder.

Finjuli-njuli fidege fya langa fyadile ng'huyu milomo midung'hu.
The twittering birds in the sky ate the figs, and their beaks are red.

When women menstruate, flies sometimes eat the blood spattered on the ground, causing their mouths to become red. This rather repulsive song is meant to warn women to take care to cover up any blood they may shed at menstruation. This is partly because it is shameful for this blood to be seen, but, more important, such blood is polluting to others and could be taken and used by witches and sorcerers wanting to harm the woman.

Chisinyagilo ng'homale ngili yangu no mwaka ukwija ng'homele ngili yangu.
The game track killed my warthog and next year you will kill my warthog.

When women menstruate, they sometimes drop blood onto the earth where they are standing, and if they do, they conceal it by surreptitiously spreading earth over it with their feet. The image of female sexuality is equated to a wild animal, to game, both by the mention of warthog *(ngili)* and by the game track *(chisinyagilo)*. Kaguru and related peoples associate porcine creatures, both wild pigs and warthogs, to women.

Dikwe-kwe-kwe dikila dye mamba dyagomelesa mwija kululenge.
The swishing of the crocodile's tail made someone return who was going to the river.

When a woman menstruates for the first time, this may occur when she is on her way to the river to bathe or to fetch water. If this happens, the girl will become upset, and instead of going on to the river she will rush home to ask her kinswomen where the blood is coming from. Then these women will tell her all about maturation *(ukulu)* and they will want to celebrate that their girl has grown up to become a nubile maiden *(kukukla kwa mwali)*.

Chitongo chia migambile ng'hajenge, ning'hali yanja, ng'hungwi kaukula.
I prepared that site for building, but before I could build, a small owl cried out.

The singer seduced a woman, but before he could actually sleep with her, he found that she was menstruating, so he had to abandon his plan. Here sexual intercourse is equated with the erection of a house. Kaguru affirm that sexual relations and the children such relations produce are essential to a household's stability. The small owl *(ng'hungwi)* is a very inauspicious bird (*ndege,* "bird," "omen"), sometimes termed a witch's bird. Here menstruation is compared to an evil omen, to something not to be flouted. The cry of the owl is said to signal misfortune (see Beidelman 1963c: 48). Amongst Kaguru a menstruating woman should not lie on the same bed with a man, not even her husband.

Inghwale yuyo magulu madunghu imwana naye magulu madunghu.
The francolin has red feet, and so does the child.

   A woman of childbearing age menstruates, and so will her daughter when she comes of age. Some species of francolins have red feet, making this game bird resemble a menstruating woman. Kaguru associate game birds in general with women.

Mutowa nhungwa ntowelage hasi muchibamamba yolila mwandende.
Drum beater beats on the hand drum, but the stony place gives forth an ugly sound.

   One should beat rhythm on a drum, not on a rock. The meaning is that menstruating women should be careful where they go so as not to bleed on some spot that does not allow concealment. If one bleeds on soil or sand, these can be readily turned over to conceal the splotch. If one bleeds on something solid and smooth such as stone, one cannot conceal the pollution, and that is both shameful and dangerous.

PREGNANCY AND CHILDBIRTH

Many Kaguru initiation songs portray pregnancy and childbirth, the proper culmination of all the instruction that the young initiates receive.

Muke mtumba musisile munda, yeja tumbulwa masila munane.
Mother's brother's wife has a slender belly, yet if it is cut open, one finds eight fetuses.

   Even a small woman stretches to hold a child during pregnancy. The reference to the wife of a mother's brother (*mtumba*) is puzzling but seems to suggest hostility, as do many of the songs. Such a woman's sexuality should not properly be mentioned. In the case of younger men (sisters' sons) such talk would suggest witchcraft. Traditionally a nephew would inherit such a woman after his mother's brother died. Consequently, to mention her sexually while one's uncle lives is to imply an interest in her and hence a hope that her husband, one's uncle, would die. A boy and his sister would be likely to feel ambivalent emotions toward such a woman since she would be the mother of important competitors against their own matrilineal claims to this elder's wealth.

In previous songs we encountered obscene remarks about initiates' parents. Initiation presents young Kaguru with a new challenge regarding their relations toward their elders. In one sense they are now entrusted with carrying out the traditions and needs of their kin groups, which are headed by elders. In another sense they are now, as newly constituted adults, ready to stand in competition with their elders for control of people and goods. I believe that much of the abusive, unpleasant tone of initiation reflects a new awareness by both generations of these changing relations. Ambivalent speech characterizes much that is spoken at all phases of Kaguru pivotal rituals of changing social status, funerals and weddings as well as initiations.

Chigologodyo mwanda mulujuwea mwaka ukwija mwenda mulujuwa.
The lizard basks in the sun and next year it basks in the sun.

A pregnant woman enjoys basking in the sun. When women become pregnant, they often become self-indulgent and express needs that they otherwise would not. Within limits these should be indulged. Everything should be done to encourage a woman's pregnancy to develop safely and normally.

Kolo dya baba fuga-fuga ng'ende ding'hofia njila yohinja nani?
Father's sheep rushes to go, for if it dies on the way, who will flay it?

A pregnant woman should hasten to a midwife when she goes into labor. Even if a woman were to die in childbirth and not give birth, the child would have to be cut out of the dead woman before she could be buried. Birth should develop according to its full course. Indirectly the song compares the delivery of a child to the culmination of proper herding and tending of an animal that is finally to be enjoyed (eaten) (compare Beidelman 1964d: 11–16).

Kusawa-kusawa, singo ya ng'hanu yandekelesa matanga kusesa.
Gaining, gaining, the wildcat's neck did not help the cucumber to peel.

Both a man and a woman throw themselves readily into sexual inter-course, especially the man ("neck of the wildcat" refers to the penis), but he turns out to be no help to the woman when the child is born. Men may copulate with a light heart for it is women who ultimately suffer from the results. This is a familiar theme in many cultures and drew vig-orous assent from Kaguru women.

Kunyika kuyu kutonyila fula, yakululisa fileuwa fowele.
It rained there in the bush and washed away the maize stalks.

The blood of childbirth is so great that it is thought to wash away the afterbirth. The genitals are associated with the bush, and the blood of birth with rain. The association of human fertility with agricultural fertil-ity is a common theme in Kaguru culture. Still, as Kaguru themselves concede, in an expression reminding one of Medea's famous lines com-paring childbirth and war, the blood of childbirth exceeds the blood of men's battles.

Kumhwani kudya nakwaila fyose, wingi wa nhemo na nlemele.
I earned everything at the coast but left some axes behind.

Another version of this refers not to the coast but to Gogo country to the west. The meaning of this is that a child is born fully formed except for its teeth. A child born with teeth would be considered a monstrosity *(chigego)* and slain (see Beidelman 1963c).

Mafula gose kutonya, kutonya fula dya mhili chimola magenga.
All rain is rain, but the rain of February breaks the riverbanks.

This song resembles an earlier one. Menstruation is nothing when compared to the blood spilled at childbirth.

Dyo mukongolo dyambile magenja dyo munangali dyowa matenyanga.
The *mukongolo* tree falls and is caught in the hands, but the euphorbia is left to smash.

The *mukongolo* tree is valued and used for lumber, but the euphorbia tree is useless for wood, being used only for its sap to provide a fish poi-son (or poison for other purposes less legitimate). When a child is born, the midwife holds the child but discards the afterbirth.

Sana dya ng'hwiga mugona wima dikwija biduka mwasi ulilungu.
The child of the giraffe sleeps upright but toward the end of the month it
turns upside-down.

The fetus is carried upright in the womb, but it turns around shortly
before birth so that it may emerge properly, headfirst. Kaguru regard
children born in breech presentation as *figego* (monstrously unpropitious)
and kill them.

Muke mutumba kwilaga mwitembe! Nokwile ule fula ikutonya?
Mother's brother's wife, climb on top of the house! How can
I climb up when it is raining?

A menstruating woman pollutes all that she contacts and therefore
should observe various prohibitions separating herself from some people
and tasks. Such a woman should never place herself physically above
other people. For this reason no Kaguru woman should ever go on top of
a house, even if she is not menstruating. People must climb on top of
houses in order to repair roofs, but only men are allowed to engage in
such tasks. The choice of a mother's brother's wife for this song probably
relates to the theme of ambiguity and ambivalence I mentioned earlier.

Mwija luwaha ndewelage somba nghona sikulema sangulila uko.
You come bringing fish for me, or if you cannot, then cut them up.

If a baby cannot be delivered, then it should be dismembered, drawn
out of the woman, and buried. This should be done even if the woman
herself is already dead. Kaguru regard pregnancy as a process that must
be brought to a conclusion, even if, as in this case, it comes to nothing.

*Machigunguli no ukobo wao wasola nyama watagila musanga. Musanga nao
utagilagwa nyama watagila musanga. Musanga nao utagilagwa nyama noile
na mage ng'ende nghalonde.*
The people of Chigunguli are bad. They take meat and throw it to the
ground. Meat is thrown to the ground and I cannot take it.

I had difficulty with this translation and am not sure it is correct. It is
said to be a song sung by a dog, which bemoans the fact that midwives
bury the placenta and blood from birth and do not allow dogs to eat
them. Kaguru are extremely careful to dispose of all such materials in
order to prevent them from being used for witchcraft. A midwife usually

gives the umbilical cord to the mother or maternal grandmother, who often keeps it until the child is older. It is carefully hidden and buried eventually. Today Kaguru women often give birth in hospitals and dispensaries, and many are uneasy as to how the waste materials from birth are disposed of.

Chana cha manya cha maganja kwela meji nailehi naila nwame.
The child of the rat, the palms of its hands are clean. He has washed with water from the Wami River, and I washed in the Wami.

When a child is born, it is usually much lighter in color than it will be when it becomes grown. No matter how light it is, the palms and soles of the child are paler than the rest of its body. The song expresses the fact that children resemble adults and that birth replicates the population. The imagery of the rat (genitals) and the Wami River (women's fertility) is consistent with other Kaguru sexual metaphors.

Kunyika kudya kwafiya nhwiga. Yagugumuye no usinga wayo.
There is a dead giraffe on the plain. It is buried with its hair.

A person may carefully tend his or her hair throughout life, but when that person is dead, grooming no longer matters. This song only indirectly relates to childbirth in that many women did die at such times. The term *usinga* is not Chikaguru but Swahili. It refers to long, straight hair and here refers to the long tail hairs of the giraffe, which are frequently used to make fly whisks for distinguished people.

Ugogo kudy kutonyila mfula yakululusa figua fyo uwele.
There in Gogo country it rained, and the rain beat down the millet stalks.

When a woman gives birth to a baby, a great deal is expelled, not only a baby but useless afterbirth (here, the stalks of the grain).

Ng'endang'endage nghingi so uwame nhgelesage Wame choulonga.
Let me walk along the banks of the Wami River and hear what the Wami will say.

One day a man's wife is ready to give birth to a child, but the husband is not allowed to stay inside with his wife. Childbirth is an occasion exclusively for women. Consequently, the husband must pace about and worry outside the house where the birth is taking place while the midwife and

Figure 16. Kaguru mother and child. Photograph taken at Berega in 1957.

others attend to matters indoors. The Wami River is an obvious image for fertility and birth. It is a watercourse that floods spectacularly during parts of the rainy season, when it becomes quite menacing, just as childbirth can be menacing. A watercourse with its connotations of both fertility and dangerous flooding is an excellent image for women's fertility.

Inghwembe yudya ng'howembaga bwete, hona yekuwemba kema mumakungo.
That hornbill did not cry out at all, but cried when it perched on a branch.

Mapungu-pungu madege go wulanga kutima hasi na kutowa mhungu.
The bateleur is a bird of the sky, but it cries out below and makes a noise.

These two songs have the same inner meaning. Both mean that a child does not cry while in the womb but makes much noise as soon as it is born. The word *nhembe* derives from a Ngulu term. It refers to a type of hornbill thought to cry only when perched, not when it flies. The bateleur eagle soars very high in the sky for hours on end. It soars so high that it could not be easily heard if it did cry out. Both birds have associations with birth and initiation. The bateleur figures in rituals of emergence after a child is born. The hornbill is sometimes compared to initiated girls. Some male hornbills seal up the female inside a tree while it incubates its eggs. This is compared to female Kaguru, who are confined inside the initiation house.

Chikwaju chia chikwaju makwache hamba chikwachuke habena kungo.
That tamarind tree is full-bearing, and though it is full-bearing, no branch breaks.

When a baby is born, it might seem to be large given the great inconvenience experienced by the pregnant woman, but in fact it is a small creature that can be readily held by the midwife. I found this explanation difficult to relate to the explicit text, but Kaguru insisted that this is what it meant.

Dindewa dia dija na mutuka fodilawile disome chitabu.
That chief came in a motorcar and left reading a book.

While a baby is within its mother's womb it is silent, but as soon as it is born it begins to cry. The imagery here eludes me and was not explained by informants.

Chiloko chidya chalokela mphene, mudimi naye yalokele baho.
The route by which the goats passed, the goat herder also passed there.

The afterbirth comes out from the same hole as did the child itself.

Chamunyang'anyi chaulaje nhembo, nhembo muwaha hokufaga bwete.
Chamunyang'anyi killed the elephant, but the elephant died for nothing.

A woman may die while she is pregnant, and in such a case the child is not usually able to be born. The woman's pregnancy has been for nothing. The elephant is often mentioned as an allusion to a profoundly menacing and destructive force. For example, often when a person dies, old people tell children that the deceased has been taken off by an elephant *(nhembo)* or a great beast *(digoli)*.

Mutowa mgobo towa ulengele, maso ya mbogo yalikumugongo.
Shooter of the buffalo, shoot carefully, for the buffalo's eyes are at its back.

If you beat a pregnant woman, you may injure the fetus. I could not find any sense in the imagery employed other than the notion of another being existing behind a first. The imagery of a man as a hunter and a woman as wild game is obvious.

Chisawe yuya muleka mwitongo no mwaka ukwija mulekwa mwitongo.
That which was abandoned on the plateau will be abandoned next year.

The woman delivers (expels) the placenta, which is buried. The people attending the birth then go off with the woman and child, but the placenta remains there in the earth.

Dibinubinu itambi dyo mpela amba dibinuche mitondo dyo goloka.
Sticking out, the baobab's branch, and tomorrow when it is in bud it will stretch.

A pregnant woman has a distended belly, but after she gives birth, her belly returns to a normal size so that you would never guess she had been pregnant. This is like the small baobab bud that later grows into a huge branch.

Hamba dya mbogo mahimbila hasi no mwaka ukwija mahimbila hasi.
The buffalo's horn is buried in the ground, and next year it is buried.

When a woman gives birth, the midwife takes the child but buries the placenta. This is done at every birth. It is important that the placenta be buried secretly so that it cannot be dug up and used by a witch or sorcerer trying to harm the mother and child.

Fidege fyose fitaga matagi, inghulumbisa kataga dye ng'andu.
All birds lay eggs, but the *ng'hulumbisa* bird lays remarkable eggs [metal eggs?].

All birds lay eggs, but the bat *(ichindebwa)* bears offspring alive, like humans and four-legged animals. The *nghulumisa* is said to be a forest bird, probably an oriole; "bat" is said to be the secret meaning of this term. I could not determine any reason why such a bird and a bat might be linked together. Furthermore, I found nothing in this song to explicate human childbearing. Still, informants insisted that this was indeed a proper initiation song. I remain perplexed.

Mutega mphelu moyo wa muchanya no mwaka ukwija moyo wa muchanya.
The heart of the trapper of mice is worried, and in the year to come his heart is worried.

When a couple conceive a child, they both worry about whether that pregnancy will come to term normally.

Chimile mugongo wa nhembo chisonya iyee heya hee.
Fidege fose fitaga.
Matagi chisonya hee heya ahe!
Inghulumbisa kataga dye ng'andu!
Chisonya iye heye ahee!
The sunbird stood on the elephant's back.
All the birds lay eggs.
Eggs of the sunbird!
The oriole lays exceptional [metal?] eggs.
The sunbird!

I was told that this song related to pregnancy and the birth of children, but I could secure neither a convincing translation nor any deeper meaning.

CONCLUSION

The preceding songs represent a central feature of what Kaguru value about the initiation of adolescents. Yet just what these signify is complex. At the most obvious level these songs relate information about sexual behavior: how adult Kaguru should comport themselves in sexual liaisons and how they should look after their bodies, especially their sexual organs. Kaguru initiation provides songs and backup information that should enable young Kaguru to negotiate their way through the ever-changing difficulties and intrigues of adult life. Though important, this substantive information represents the least interesting aspect of Kaguru initiation lore.

Other aspects merit more complicated explanations. These include how such lore reinforces deeper Kaguru loyalties, values, and beliefs, often couched in metaphorical, even poetic terms; how this learning experience itself provides young people with a new sense of social entitlement as adults; and finally, most important of all, how such learning, manifest in speculation, wordplay, and even something close to debate, provides young Kaguru with a striking new and stronger sense of personhood and even individuality.

The very form and style of Kaguru initiation lore emphasizes a poetic form of expression. Metaphors, onomatopoeia, complex analogies, manifold allusions, puns, and unusual and even archaic terms appear constantly. Young Kaguru were earlier told stories and taught simple word games such as riddles, but they were never before confronted with such a wide array of oral literature, nor were they ever made to think about and use complicated expressions for such a sustained period. The initiation schools of Kaguru oral literature constitute the first and greatest experience most Kaguru have of confronting the creative heritage of Kaguru culture, the traditions passed down from the ancestral dead. The form of this lore, poetic speech, is particularly apt for cataloguing the complex variety of Kaguru experience. Metaphors, which carry meanings across semantic domains, provide rich and suggestive bridges between landscape and settlements, between climate, terrain, and gender, and between the attributes of plants, animals, and tools and the qualities of persons and social activities. This diffuse interpenetration of meanings has a seductive staying power. It engenders memory. Such poetic expression facilitates the construction of Kaguru experience, and it provides a vivid fabric for memory, anchoring various moral ideas in a rich ground of feelings associated with reassuring and confirmatory everyday experiences. Kaguru remember these songs and legends vividly and continue to take pleasure in reciting them because these witty and colorful forms of expression endow everyday activities and surroundings with richer and more complex meanings. For Kaguru this is the most memorable form of language that they have yet encountered. For many, no subsequent verbal expressions ever equal these, much less surpass them. Kaguru emerge from initiation schools with a new sense of the beauty, interest, wit, and scope of their language, which they are repeatedly told embodies their true, ethnic identity as Kaguru. Today Kaguru, even educated Kaguru who have begun to lose touch with their native language and customs, recognize that such expressions and ideas have a seductive and reassuring power.

Kaguru initiation establishes a new sense of social empowerment for young Kaguru. Kaguru children are constrained in what they are allowed to express about sexuality and even the adult relations stemming from it. They are often aware of many sexual sides of the social life around them, but they are discouraged from ever expressing their ideas or feelings on such matters, at least with other adults. During and after initiation young people are no longer denied such expression. In this sense initiation is not so much a revelation of any secrets (though some things Kaguru young people learn may well be new); rather, initiation grants young Kaguru the new right to express such matters and to enter into the give-and-take of social commentary along with other adults.

During their seclusion young Kaguru are actually afforded a freedom of sexual discussion that will in some ways never again be equaled. During initiation they speak freely with elders in their parents' generation. After they emerge from initiation, though they may converse and even joke about sexual matters just like other adults, they will now, like all other Kaguru adults, be constrained in their speech with their parental generation. Later, they in turn will also be constrained in how they may speak and act toward the generation of their own children, nieces, and nephews. Adjacent generations of Kaguru, especially Kaguru kin, ordinarily—except for the brief time of initiation—observe considerable respect and reticence on all sexual matters. For these reasons the sexual openness at initiation represents an extraordinary time of solidarity within one gender and across generations. It builds a strong and memorable sense of male and female unity.

Empowerment here relates to the idea of secrecy. Kaguru repeatedly maintain that initiates learn many secrets about sexual behavior and attributes. This is clearly unlikely. We have seen that Kaguru children are familiar with many sides of adult sexual life; they may even have more knowledge of what goes on at initiation than Kaguru admit. It is acknowledgment that confers empowerment. Expressions of secrecy simply cover a social convention whereby the uninitiated young are denied all rights to express any thoughts or feelings about adult sexuality. Initiation confers the gift of recognition, acknowledgment that the novices now know and consequently may now speak and act as adults.

Kaguru initiation develops certain personal mental and verbal skills that will benefit Kaguru all their lives. Besides encouraging a sense of gender solidarity and a sense of ethnic identity, initiation encourages personal speculation, analysis, wordplay, and questioning, all skills that help Kaguru reach their individual social goals. In an earlier book (Beidelman 1986), I pointed out how Kaguru stories encouraged them to understand the workings of social relations, how to imagine the manifold motives, schemes, and ploys in social affairs. Kaguru storytelling teaches motives and plots, but it provides no interactive skills. What the numerous texts and, more important, the endless questioning and answering during the weeks of instruction teach is skill in speech and behavior. Kaguru learn about framing questions, explaining problems, using puns, allusions, and metaphors, and many other verbal skills. They also learn how to comport themselves in ways expected by an assembly of adults whose eyes are constantly upon them. They are now noticed as apprentice adults, not children whose errors are excusable or even at times funny, and they are encouraged to recognize the rich possibilities of the Kaguru language. These verbal abilities can be further honed and refined over a lifetime. Skills one learns as a novice during one's own initiation can be repeatedly developed as one subsequently serves as a teacher and helper at subsequent initiations. Of course, such skills are utilized and developed constantly during everyday life. Yet it is at initiation that a Kaguru first and most impressionably finds herself or himself center stage as a performer expected to demonstrate proper, mature sociability. Never before initiation have young Kaguru found themselves as recognized social performers before an assembled audience of others.

In this third, verbal and analytical sense, initiation develops Kaguru individualism. Yet how these skills in language and comportment are developed and how they contribute to a sense of self necessarily vary with Kaguru. Initiation is generally described by Kaguru as rites producing ethnic unity, common meanings and values, a sense of responsibility, and continuity regarding an ancestral heritage. Yet just what any Kaguru girl or boy makes of these gifts passed down from elders, these traditions and skills passed down from the dead, inevitably varies. All Kaguru learn these lessons, but we should not assume that all learn them equally well. Initiation then serves to distinguish Kaguru from one another, or at least it can, as well as it creates common bonds of understanding and responsibility.

CHAPTER 8

Conclusion
Person, Time, and Ethnicity

That moral centaur, man and wife . . .
> Lord Byron, *Don Juan*

Composed that monstrous animal a husband and wife.
> Henry Fielding, *Tom Jones*

"It is easier to accuse one sex than to excuse the other," says Montaigne. It is vain to apportion praise and blame. The truth is that if the vicious circle is so hard to break, it is because the sexes are each the victim at once of the other and of itself.
> Simone de Beauvoir, *The Second Sex*

Horses *saillent*, donkeys *bauduinent*, dogs *couvrent*, pigs *souillent*, goats are *boucsies*, bulls *vétillent*, fish *frayent*, cocks *cauchent*, cats *margaudent*. . . . But what do men do to women? They *do it*. Do what? They just do it.
> F. Béroalde de Verville, *Le Moyen de parvenir*

The study of an ethnic imagination may not be so subversive of modern African states as is generally believed; it may be constructive.
> John Lonsdale, *Unhappy Valley*

Kaguru believe that their thoughts and customs stem from what their ancestors thought and did. Kaguru further believe that what they think and do today is what their children and children's children should also do and think. It is such beliefs and customary activities that define being Kaguru. In this sense, Kaguru social memory is one with social reproduction. Social memory or reproduction is epitomized by the initiation of Kaguru boys and girls. For anthropologists, this rite of passage prompts three broad, interconnected questions.

The first and narrowest of these questions asks how rites of passage relate to other features of Kaguru society. Is it true, as most Kaguru maintained, that initiation explains Kaguru society to its members? If so, these ceremonies would provide a means for outsiders such as ourselves to comprehend Kaguru.

The second question asks how an account of Kaguru initiation might illuminate studies of rites of passage among other peoples. Answering this would also provide insights about related themes of age, gender, and sexuality.

The third question asks what Kaguru initiation may tell us about rituals and symbols and how these influence knowledge, values, feelings, and beliefs.

RITES OF PASSAGE AND KAGURU SOCIETY

Kaguru repeatedly told me that rites of initiation, and indeed all comparable rites of passage, work to maintain their supposedly unchanging tradition (*umoto*, "custom"). Yet allegedly enduring traditions actually embody transmutable beliefs and practices that are precarious constructs maintained against undermining time and changing influences. Traditions are not as unchanging or uniform as Kaguru describe them. Different Kaguru describe varying details and interpretations of rituals. Nor are Kaguru rituals as unique to Kaguru as they maintain. Much that I encountered among Kaguru resembled traditions I found or read about among neighboring peoples. Even the tradition of Kaguru ethnicity is more problematic than they acknowledge.

The Kaguru sense of identity and continuity that I encountered during my fieldwork was the result of a notion of unity that had gradually coalesced and grown over the years. In the past, Kaguru in different areas of the mountains, plateau, and lowlands appear to have considered their differences to be greater than they do today. In the colonial era, British administrators encouraged the congeries of people in present-day Kaguruland to begin thinking of themselves as one people in contrast to their neighbors. They gave Kaguru chiefs and other leaders a tribal administration and encouraged Kaguru to think they had a unique culture, different from that of neighboring peoples. They discounted the ways Kaguru language and customs resembled those of neighboring matrilineal peoples. Similarities to the patrilineal Gogo were even more strongly denied. Each ethnic group was argued to have its unique ways, which merited its being treated on its own by European colonialists.[1] As a consequence, Kaguru increasingly saw language and formal ceremonies as crucial in fashioning a necessary ethnic identity. Kaguru initiation of adolescents was the most prominent means, but rituals, including those at birth, marriage, and death, and the myriad customs and etiquette surrounding the activities of quotidian life all contributed to such a cultural world (compare V. Turner 1962a: 145).

Distinctions between society and the wilderness (what society is not) are at the root of Kaguru identity. These, in turn, have deep associations with gender so that ideas about male and female underpin Kaguru ethnic memory and identity. We should not, however, see these associations as sharp and fixed. Kaguru sometimes associate men with social rules, with contractual arrangements, and they associate women with less disciplined feelings and forces. Yet Kaguru also associate women with the heart of the home, with the hearth, with cooking and nourishing, all stabilizing features of society. In contrast, Kaguru associate men with the bush, with hunting (mastery of the wild and the creatures in it), and with clearing of overgrowth, but also with the drawing of magic from the plants, animals, and stones embodying the powers of the wilderness. Thus Kaguru women and men embody both order and disorder, stability and transformation. Kaguru express different moral or cosmic valences by focusing on different terms of space—domestic, communal, and wild.[2]

Kaguru rites of passage illuminate these complexities and subtleties by means of ritual movement and comportment in different arenas of space. Such rituals involve a repertoire of both order and disorder, stability and transformation, which oppose and complement each other. Kaguru rites focus on containing or harnessing time, and to do that one must embrace both containment and flow, boundaries and their dissolution. My study here emphasizes rituals of initiating adolescents, but these should be considered not in isolation from all other rites containing or controlling time but rather in tandem with them.

RITES OF PASSAGE AND KAGURU IDEAS ABOUT MEN AND WOMEN

The fundamental dichotomies manifest in Kaguru concepts about the social and the wild relate to dichotomization of the two sexes. I review this Kaguru material by comparing it to points made long ago by Rosaldo (1974) in a well-known and often criticized essay. There she contrasts men's and women's public and domestic lives, picturing women as bound more to children and a narrower set of associations (ibid.: 23–24). For her, women display continuity in their experiences (which she claims are similar before and after marriage), whereas adulthood confronts men with a break in behavior (ibid.: 25). Women are also said to develop more-personalized relations than men (ibid.: 26). For Rosaldo, womanhood is a given whereas manhood is achieved (ibid.: 28). For her, women are dangerous when they are barren or widowed because then they stand outside the roles of wife and mother by which they are ordinarily incorporated into society (ibid.: 32).

I know that many feminists now consider Rosaldo's essay outdated. I have selected it as a convenient point of departure, not to criticize Rosaldo or to claim she represents current analyses but to illuminate some perennial difficulties one may face in generalizing about the implications of gender for social roles rooted in kinship. Despite criticism, especially by some feminist anthropologists, Rosaldo's essay remains useful since the ambiguities at the source of its difficulties remain unresolved. It illustrates the fact that any and all attempts to dichotomize gender and sexuality inevitably obscure even as they may illuminate. Subsequent efforts to improve upon Rosaldo have not surmounted this impasse.

Rosaldo's observations make sense yet are misleading. This is because the distinctions that gender so readily leads us into making are, as is sexuality itself, rooted in ambiguities and paradoxes that make analytical dichotomies problematic. For example, Kaguru men dominate public oratory, ritual, debate, and formal exchange, but these men's affairs inevitably involve the outcomes of women's fertility, labor, and loyalties. Kaguru women's deep power and influence with their children are sources of contestation between these women's brothers and husbands. Much of Kaguru public debate between men implicitly parallels earlier arguments held indoors between men and women. It is true, as Rosaldo maintains, that Kaguru women's lives display a continuity of tasks far more striking than what confronts young men whose new duties as responsible, initiated adults open up novel spheres of ritual and debate previously closed to them. Yet continuity also pervades the lives of men. Young Kaguru men remain dominated by elder male ritual leaders well into middle age and are therefore little freer than women in making important jural decisions. While Rosaldo's contentions are supported by the fact that Kaguru women's routines are much the same before marriage as after it and by the oppressing experience of many young, newly wed women who enter the alien and unfriendly villages of their husbands, she is undermined by the fact that the main oppressors in such villages are also women (a husband's other wives, his mother, his sisters) and not men, and by the fact that, as a consequence, in-marrying women face greater loss of social continuity than men, who often continue to reside among their kin. Kaguru women frequently are described as tied to their offspring through affectual ties that transcend contracts and obligations set by men, but it is through these feelings that women become formidable protagonists in the jural contentions of men and even become manipulators. Rosaldo's argument that masculinity is achieved whereas femininity is a given closely resembles remarks made by Kaguru themselves about the differences between the purposes of male and female initiation. Yet Kaguru women are never considered proper women if they bear no children, and this fertility is repeatedly associated with women's individual moral character and achievement and not simply axiomatic to their gender. Motherhood is achieved, never automatic. In contrast, while Kaguru fatherhood is always achieved in the sense that it requires payment of wealth, actual procreation is often not accomplished by a legal father, a fact that sometimes demoralizes a man. In these senses, too, Rosaldo is misleading to suggest that women are dangerous mainly when falling outside the brackets of motherhood and wifehood. This tells us only part of Kaguru's anxieties about gender and sexuality. Barren women may be sources of anger and disruption, and widows may gain new opportunities to elude men's controls. Yet Kaguru also insist that women are most powerful and therefore dangerous because they bear children and that this is what leads women's husbands and brothers to contend for women's loyalties and what opens up men to manipulation by women. Many of these manifold ambiguities and contradictions are reflected in the complexities of initiation symbols and texts.

In contradiction to Rosaldo, Kaguru would probably agree with Beauvoir that men's lives are socially more varied than women's, whose daily tasks reflect a routine strikingly similar throughout much of their lives. Yet Beauvoir and Kaguru recognize that biological changes undergone by women through time are more radical than those confronting men, and to some extent this counterbalances the supposed cultural monotony of women's quotidian affairs (1974: 639–40).

Skewing of sexual fates, as evinced by Rosaldo's and Beauvoir's remarks, recalls Lange's observation about Rousseau. She notes that he makes arguments similar to those made by modern feminists who sometimes equate self-interest essentially with men (1981: 267) because men are supposedly less trapped in their bodies than women, whose weakness and nurturant capacities impede them. Both Rousseau and such feminists are wrong, though apparently due to opposite motives. Both men and women are caught in their flesh, and both are also caught in society and culture (compare Beauvoir 1974: 810). On account of both bodily and sociocultural reasons, self-interest is a universally held motive. What differentiates women from men is not the degree of self-interestedness but ways that self-interest is voiced or framed. In the Kaguru case, women's self-interest often coincides with that of their children rather than with that of men (their husbands, brothers, uncles, and fathers). Kaguru construct a mystique of feminine altruism and supportiveness that holds as long as women are considered as mothers rather than wives or father's sisters. Kaguru initiation songs explore these evaluative possibilities and repeatedly play on self-interest.[3] Kaguru oral literature criticizes both men and women, providing a rich catalogue of deceit, manipulation, and cleverness. Kaguru initiation defines gender for Kaguru but provides imagery that sustains subtle, polyvalent attributes of and judgments about it.[4] Gender provides terms for morality in general, for, as Lonsdale observes for Kikuyu, "where most labour was recruited by marriage and procreation, civic virtue required proper gender relations" (1992: 327). Kaguru initiation promotes Kaguru ideas about ethnicity and gender, but ever-changing modes of ritual and the motives and feelings evoked in initiation songs perpetuate diverse and shifting definitions of identity.

RITES OF PASSAGE,
ANTHROPOLOGICAL CONCEPTS, AND SEXUALITY

The concept of *rite de passage* applies to a wide range of symbolic changes, including ceremonies of birth and naming, marriage, and funerals as well as initiation at adolescence. These manifold changes in Kaguru life repeat and reinforce common beliefs and values. Initiation of adolescents is only one of many rites defining Kaguru identity. A cursory survey of anthropological writings indicates that most publications concerned with *rites de passage* emphasize the initiation of young people into adulthood. My study here is concerned with initiation, but it also deals with all kinds of other ritual changes of person among Kaguru. My approach indicates that earlier works on initiation would have been more useful had they incorporated more materials from a broader range of life crises and quotidian life.[5]

One of the earliest surveys of ethnographic literature on initiation of adolescents (Webster 1932) came to conclusions similar yet opposed to those I draw here. Webster believed that "these mysteries may be regarded as the most conservative of primitive institutions and as the chief means of preserving that uniformity and unchangeableness of customs which is [*sic*] a leading trait of primitive society. The ceremonies, coming at puberty, soon succeeded in repressing every favorable intellectual variation and in bringing all the members of the tribe to one monotonous level of slavish adherence to the tribal tradition" (1932: 60).[6] For Kaguru, such customs articulate and confirm tradition and hence ethnicity, but they are manifold in their meanings, especially in the associated oral literature and symbols reflecting quotidian life. In this sense, initiation continues and expands upon earlier childhood training (in stories) that encouraged social imagination and a sense of alternative possibilities in individual conduct and strategies for survival and success (Beidelman 1980a, 1986). Furthermore, initiation provides orientation toward understanding other rites and ceremonies yet to be encountered by novices as adults, such as marriage, naming of children, propitiation of the dead, and funerals. Consequently, Kaguru initiation provides a unifying ethnic vision that perdures over a lifetime and enriches many future changes in a Kaguru's life. Yet initiation allows Kaguru to entertain multiple perspectives and interpretations within that vision. This multiplex character of initiation is possible on account of these rites being built up from the manifold experiences and cues of everyday Kaguru routine.

Despite these wider features that anchor Kaguru initiation within the broad lifetime of a person, from birth to death and beyond, the overwhelming theme in initiation is sexual. Unfortunately, the anthropological literature on African initiation, especially that involving sexuality, reflects recent Western thinking that is far from how Africans such as Kaguru view such matters.[7] This has muddled our evaluation and understanding of the sexual thinking of non-Western peoples. Gradually, Western understanding of reproductive organs and associated attributes has gone from considering relationships in which masculinity and femininity are fitted within a hierarchical cosmos to a world of relationships of incommensurable differences, much like differences between species (Laquer 1990: 149). Our present scholarly perspectives on women and men are the givens of modern, liberal thinking, but they provide little help in understanding how other peoples thought or think, since such peoples are more ontological in their claims (ibid.: 8). However I may think about gender, I must change that thinking if I am to understand what traditional Kaguru are trying to teach about sexuality and gender at their initiations. Their messages, complex, ambiguous, and paradoxical, are rooted in a global, hierarchical view of the world and society in which sexuality and gender reflect very different moral and substantial modes of being from my own. Those ideas and values about sexuality and gender cannot be separated from other cultural categories and spheres of experience and judgment. This may seem an obvious pronouncement, but we must keep this in mind to appreciate the need to ground Kaguru sexual meanings within their broader quotidian affairs.

Ideas about initiation and change in personhood center around sexuality, gender, and age. The world's cultures have portrayed such differences as involving asymmetry and inequality (Sanday 1990: 2). This reflects a wide range of local assumptions about psychological processes (Heald 1982: 17) and about biological differences. Within any particular society these are further enhanced, made complex and manifold, through various symbols: "Mystery is used to make a social statement about separation, about the meaning of categories, about the autonomy of sexual capacities" (Schloss 1988: 92). It is the manifold details of everyday life that enhance Kaguru imagination of sexuality, gender and age.

Kaguru initiation (indeed, initiation of adolescents everywhere) is concerned with sexuality. Yet, as Laquer notes, "almost everything one wants to say about sex—however sex is understood—already has in it a claim about gender" (1990: 14).[8] Sex and gender are inextricably related, yet the lineaments of gender as it is constructed in any particular society cannot be derived simply from sexuality. Gender ideology turns out to be part of the total ideology of a society (Schlegel 1990: 39) and as such requires searching consideration into spheres of action and thought beyond the domestic and sensual. Kaguru initiation involves a revelation of ways to act, think, and feel. "Sex is the secret which is needed to be both discovered and controlled" (Weeks 1985: 144).

While Kaguru initiation is paideutic, this takes a form, to quote Money, of "sexosophy" (1980: 43), a philosophy of gender, sex and eroticism. Kaguru beliefs are founded upon certain "sex-irreducible roles" (ibid.: 137). What differentiates Kaguru beliefs from ours as analysts is that the Kaguru do not make any clear contrast between "phylographic determinants" (biologically inherent attributes) and "culturistic" ones (ibid.: 10). Kaguru equate culture with nature in the sense that they envision their culture and society as grounded in the inevitable (natural) realities of the cosmos. Yet they recognize an ability of culture to expand and play upon the ordinary capacities of gender. For example, Kaguru men assume nurturant roles during some periods of male initiation and women assume domineering, aggressive roles during some parts of female initiation, even though Kaguru tend to associate nurturance with women and domineering authority with men.[9] These contrasts illuminate how analytically difficult it is to reduce gender differences to neat dichotomies. The interplay between these factors is what lends power and mystification to the force of gender attributions. "The nature of sex . . . is the result not of biology but of our needs in speaking about it" (Laquer 1990: 115). That speaking is always contended and unresolved. The Kaguru material underscores how fruitless it is to try to construct firm social dichotomies characterizing men and women in the ways that Rosaldo and many since her have tried to do. Such categorization is suggestive but remains always and necessarily debatable and unresolved because those who hold such ideas need and want them ambiguous.

What is not debatable is that initiation deeply involves the human body and that discussion of men's and women's bodies involves power. That power involves the various labelings and judgments that some now term "gender." While gender may be culturally defined, it remains debatable even on cultural terms because it is rooted in intractable and complex embodied sexuality (Laquer 1990: 13–16).

Initiation marks changes in Kaguru personhood but also achieves these transformations (cf. Heald 1982: 16). To do so, Kaguru disrupt everyday life, their social habitus, but at the same time draw symbolically on that routine (cf. Jackson 1983a: 334). Some anthropologists describing African initiations emphasize the constructive harmony of rituals (c.g., V. Turner 1967: 33). Others emphasize these rituals' disjunctive violence (e.g., Heald 1986: 75). The Kaguru material shows that one should neglect neither of these two essential aspects of initiation. Each complements the other. Such rituals sometimes present the socially obligatory as desirable, attractive, and comforting, while at other times societal demands are fiercely expressed through fear and bodily pain.[10]

Violence and pain are powerful forces at the initiation of adolescents.[11] Among Kaguru, the violent cutting and related hazing of men are accompanied by many days of more supportive oral indoctrination and by healing and nurturing. For Kaguru boys, the very men who hurt them are subsequently those who heal, tend, and feed. Women initiators appear even more supportive in the case of girls' initiation. For Kaguru, then, initiation combines both positive and negative sanctions of a dominant and pervasive social order. Pain and nurturance are artfully combined: punishment followed with reward, intimidation wedded to seduction, admonition tied to assurance, denial bound to satisfaction, confinement of the novice coupled with promises of new freedom for the future adult. Successful socialization amalgamates contradictory/complementary sentiments and motives that cannot be simply labeled as positive or negative. The complexity and opacity of Kaguru rituals of transition are illustrated by the imagery of death. Metaphorical death portrays transcendence of the past in order to assume a new form of being (cf. V. Turner 1962b: 85). For Kaguru, and doubtless for many other peoples, the seemingly negative term *death* is embedded with opposite meanings. Symbolic death at initiation gives birth to adulthood just as death of the living gives birth to the ancestral spirits. Such is the polyvalent sense of Kaguru gender, age, personhood, and thus Kaguru *rites de passage* themselves. To achieve such multiplex meanings the wide panoply of Kaguru experience and surroundings is repeatedly drawn into the rites and sayings of initiation. Only when viewed in such broad temporal terms can transformations take on opposite, double meanings.

UNDERSTANDING RITUAL, SYMBOLS, AND METAPHOR

It has been argued that ritual promotes comprehension by resolving ambiguities and inconsistences in experience, at least for a transcendent, ephemeral moment (T. Turner 1977: 56–61; Kapferer 1979: 5). For example, initiation of adolescents amalgamates images of males as both boys and men, as fathers and sons. Such blending is possible in the symbolic world of ritual theater and play, even if not in the actual world of social relations in particular quotidian space and time. Yet rituals also teach Kaguru a varied range of conventional behavior that they may strategically employ in different situations (compare Jennings 1982: 117–19). While rituals may promote integrative knowledge, their capacity to teach strategies and ploys may be equally important. Kaguru ritual accomplishes diverse ends: teaching how to behave, encouraging speculative skills, conveying information, and creating some sense of moral and cognitive cohesion.[12] Tradition need not be as holistic as some argue; it can be "a network of narrow paths across an indeterminate hostile environment" (Berger 1979: 203). The complex and precipitous world of the Kaguru requires constant improvisation and cunning, especially in social relations. Knowledge and skills taught at Kaguru initiation provide manifold and devious paths to social ends. Such rites may at times be ethnically and cosmologically integrative, but they also provide multiple perspectives and a sense of many choices regarding gender, age, and other circumstances. Those subject to these rites and those who perform them come away with imaginative cunning and skill, not just a sense of social solidarity. Kaguru initiation presents disruptions and challenges to conventional self-consciousness and at times a sense of experiment (Goffman 1974: 564). What is integrative, even amid expressions of diverse motives and ploys to take advantage of others, is voicing such modes and means in Chikaguru. Kaguru retain the songs and sayings of initiation throughout their lives, and today such expressions often represent the one broad body of customary lore that most remember in the Kaguru language itself. This oral literature, which all Kaguru I met vividly recalled, indelibly inscribes their ethnicity on the minds of Kaguru.

Kaguru *rites de passage* work to build Kaguru notions of ethnic identity and solidarity, yet I do not want to mislead readers into assuming that the impact of such rituals is uniform. Kaguru adherence to such rituals, their intense concern with what rituals may mean and do, derives as much from these rites' powers to provide varying, even contested interpretations of what Kaguruness means. It is because these rituals allow different and changing interpretations that they perdure and hold people's concern. Perhaps the best way to appreciate this is through considering the varying spatial arenas in which such rites are enacted.[13] For example, the separation of Kaguru novices into camps or indoctrination houses creates a ritual participation for those actors that is distinct from that of any audience who saw the cutting. At these camps instructors teach novices free of onlookers. Then, later, united through their common indoctrination, the novices as a group confront the villagers whom they left and who now become an appreciative audience to the accomplishments of the novices and their teachers. In the final dances after the novices' recovery, initiates and their village audience merge as members of one community as they repeatedly dance, sing, and salute one another. "Breaking frame" and the subsequent creation of new groupings create a double sense of difference and integrity characterizing Kaguru (and most) initiation (compare Goffman 1974: 345–77). These rituals began with aggressive cutting and manipulation of novices, reduced to cringing passivity by an assault on their genitals. This is followed by the dyadic give-and-take of instruction, in which novices gradually assume ever more active reciprocity in their replies. As they recover further and learn more, novices gradually reemerge into their villages, first as serenading beggars on the outskirts, then as proud performers entering a village, and finally as dancers among other dancers in a village's center. These processes convey a unity of shifting perspectives and motives, more like a kaleidoscope or a montage than a holistic, transcendental vision.

Kaguru legendary history provides a common thread for some of these Kaguru rites. Kaguru ceremonies frequently allude to the ancestors on their great founding trek and their establishing the first homestead.[14] Such legends contribute to the "comprehensive character" (Jennings 1982: 122) of ritual. Rituals themselves reenact these sagas over the generations to produce a historical sense, what Scheffler terms a "historical redemption" (1981: 433). "In the regular recurrence of a given rite, a sense builds up, in each new performance, of the prior performances that have taken place through the lifetime of the participants but, normally, beyond as well, to the time of the ritual's origins nearest the commemorated historical event" (ibid.). Such repeated enactments give tradition substance. This ethnic, historical continuity contrasts with the changing perspectives of motives and strategies previously mentioned.[15] Certainly a Kaguru, to survive, must develop great inventiveness, an imaginative flair, a sense of bricolage, in order to cope with the myriad challenges of his or her difficult physical and social environment. Yet this divides more than it unites. For Kaguru, continuity is provided by ethnic stereotypes perpetuated through rituals, especially at initiation. Language, domestic etiquette (epitomized in notions of cuisine), and sexual rules are all embedded in Kaguru legends of origin. These provide Kaguru with a sense of relatedness and continuity but also differences between clans and the places where they settled. This is the nearest Kaguru rites and ceremonies come to the integrative, holistic model promoted by some anthropologists.

RITUAL, SYMBOLS, AND THE BODY

Bryan Turner claims that "the body is at once the most solid, the most elusive, illusory, concrete, metaphorical, ever present and ever distant thing—a site, an instrument, an environment, a singularity and a multiplicity" (1984: 8). Barkan claims that "in the life of primitive man, the self, and hence the body, is the only wholeness which can be grasped" (1975: 8), though confining his assertion to "primitives" seems wrong.

Kaguru ritual repeatedly demonstrates that "the body will be projected into the world, and the world will be introjected into the body" (Schilder 1950: 123), that "words are carried over from the properties of bodies to signify the institutions of the mind and spirit" (Vico 1968: 336). Symbols everywhere are rooted in the bodily senses and body imagery, and even more so in this study of Kaguru *rites de passage*, which focus on modulating and defining the embodied personhood as it alters through time. While I have presented the body as a source of symbols, the body itself requires symbolic work in order to exist socially (cf. Schilder 1950: 287). The body undergoes constant change, not only through aging but also on account of constant comings and goings through its openings and surfaces. The body's boundaries are constantly subject to change (cf. Bakhtin 1984: 319).

The body requires incessant ritual work to be maintained in its sociocultural form. Repression of some directions in our drives, particularly sexual, adds powerful reinforcement to those directions that are still allowed (cf. I. Richards n.d.: 55–56). Ritual symbols arise from needs for social control and needs to express drives whose complete gratification would result in a breakdown of social order (V. Turner 1967: 37). Certainly Kaguru ritual (and, indeed, the pervasive round of Kaguru everyday etiquette) restricts the modes of food consumption, the freedom to express wants, feelings, and emotions verbally, and the choice of objects to fulfill sexual desires. Yet Kaguru rituals and symbols—those of initiation, but also those as diverse as conduct making up joking relations or constituting proper "table manners"—allude openly or implicitly to what is forbidden or unseemly as well as to what is recommended or allowed. The repression of some forms of sexuality and alimentation provides a repertoire of libidinous Kaguru symbols that are utilized to express sexy, aggressive, or antisocial motives, through jokes, seduction, insult, intimidation, sorcery, and witchcraft.

Kaguru rituals, and especially initiation, emphasize bodily comportment and develop a sense of facility and security by putting initiates through various routines of movement: stressing polite comportment; encouraging proper tone and rhythms of voice, especially in responsive songs and riddles; and providing further instruction about dancing and singing. Kaguru novices emerge from initiation with new gravity and poise in their demeanor. There is no other period in a Kaguru's lifetime when her or his every move and word are so likely to be scrutinized and criticized as during the weeks of indoctrination as a newly initiated novice.[16]

Both anthropology and art criticism have a long history of interpreting symbols. Those most recently influential in art history stem from Panofsky (1962: 5–11; cf. Hasenmueller 1978: 296–97); those in anthropology come from writings by Victor Turner (1967: 50). Such approaches are reflected in my own analyses, especially as related to the decoding of iconic meanings. But neither Panofsky nor Turner nor most scholars following their leads have drawn interpretations much beyond decoding hidden meanings. Few relate meanings to the detailed routines of daily life or to a broader matrix of social activities and structure. Analyses restrict symbols to ideas rather than relate them to actions and groups.[17]

SYMBOLS' ROOTS IN QUOTIDIAN LIFE

In appraising the power of folk knowledge of preliterate peoples, Ginzburg notes that such knowing's strength is rooted in the concrete, in avoidance of abstraction, characteristics that many modern intellectuals have underestimated and have seen as weakness (1986: 115). Such knowing is grounded in a multiplicity of sensibilities, whereas with literacy, modern people have tended to overrely upon the visual (ibid.: 107–8). The evocative power of symbols stems from their ties to multiple sensations in everyday affairs, to the seeming trivia of ordinary living. "Life has always been reconstructing man from outside inwards" (Musil 1979 II, 2: 128). The order of the ordinary, the seductive repetition of daily routines, inform the words, symbols, and gestures that are sometimes marshaled for special occasions. "Art begins when a man re-evokes in himself emotions and *thoughts* which he has experienced under the influence of surrounding reality and expresses them in definitive images" (Plekhanov 1950: 8). It has sometimes been argued that special occasions, the *rites de passage* that form the benchmarks of our lives, provide the emphases that give meaning to such changes. Yet it is the engulfing security of everyday affairs, the reassuring regularity of small tasks and familiar surroundings, our socioculturally constructed habitus, from which we draw meaning to our experiences. "Patterns of body use are calculated with metaphors which in effect mediate the world of material objects and the world of ideas and sentiments. But there is always a very real connection between the physical deposition of objects in the material environment and the social or temperamental disposition of people" (Jackson 1983b: 133). If certain rites and ceremonies are remarkable, it is because they induce us to reflect upon everyday meanings and think upon the order of our experiences, whereas most of the time we are immersed in such activities and experiences without any sense of reflection. "Such metaphors are thus the verbal correlates of patterns of social interaction and bodily disposition within the *habitus*, and this may explain why metaphors of self refer universally to such immediate elements of the *habitus* as house, animals, plants, and in modern societies, machines" (ibid.: 136). Everyday Kaguru actions such as cooking, sweeping, fire making, or beer drinking are elevated and intensified in a ritual context. "What is evaluated is not so much the content of the performance as the skill with which the performance is achieved, how well the everyday is enhanced and transformed into something more than everyday" (Karp 1987: 141). This resembles Goffman's view of how ritual idealizes the styles of the everyday: "Life may be an imitation of art, but ordinary conduct, in a sense, is an imitation of the proprieties, a gesture at the exemplary forms, and the primal realization of these ideals belongs more to make-believe than to reality" (1974: 562).

In rituals and songs at initiation, action is reflected upon and knowledge consolidated by being reinforced through bodily engagement while tuned to the specialness of what one is doing (Jennings 1982: 115–16). In habitual activities Kaguru retain a profound sense of continuity and tradition. Berger puts this eloquently for peasant farmers everywhere: "The very great variety of these routines and rituals which attach themselves to work and to the different phases of a working life (birth, marriage, death) are the peasant's own protection against a state of continual flow. Work routines are traditional and cyclic—they repeat themselves each year, and sometimes each day. Their tradition is retained also because it appears to assure the best chance of the work's success, but also because in repeating the same routine, in doing the same thing in the same way as his father or his neighbour's father, the peasant assumes a continuity for himself and thus consciously experiences his own survival" (1979: 207–8). Sometimes, even some disordering or distortion of these symbols encourages us to be aware of this order and structure. Such an argument is at odds with V. Turner, who argues against the irreducibility of symbols to components from secular life. Certainly Turner's counterargument that symbols must be grasped in their "specific essence" is pretentious double-talk (1962b: 86).

Few would argue with Wallace that ritual involves the intents of its performers, the stated aim of the rite, and a set of assertions or assumptions about the nature of the world in which those intentions are to be realized. Ritual has a purpose, but that makes sense only in terms of a broader cosmology that defines such aims. We should keep in mind (and I think that Wallace and others fail to emphasize this sufficiently) how closely these two aspects of ritual are linked. That seemingly passive backdrop of a world, which supposedly provides a stage for ritual, a cosmologically mapped arena, is defined by ceaseless and infinite activity. Such everyday behavior is echoed or intensified by assertive ritual acts (Wallace 1966: 237).

RITUAL, SYMBOLS, AND LEARNING TO IMAGINE AND REFLECT

Discussing Panofsky's approach to symbols (an approach that I have already admiringly cited), Hasenmueller describes iconology, the decoding or interpretation of symbols, as a "philology of images," an explication of possible meanings secured through exercising our imaginations and through considering an immense set of past activities that inform objects, gestures, and words —the sum total of our past experiences (1978: 296–97). Symbols are informed by our myriad, quotidian experiences, but each of us selects from that manifold past, drawing upon and rejecting different aspects of that experience in order to construct meanings that work for us on different occasions and in different situations. We also try to make such meanings work for or on others. We seek to have these interpretations accepted by others or, less pleasantly, seek to impose them. Symbols involve matters both expressed and repressed: "In a Symbol there is concealment and yet revelation: therefore, by Silence and by Speech acting together, comes a double significance" (Carlyle 1896: 199).

Rituals, particularly the kinds of ritual that I have reported for the Kaguru, provide an important opportunity for persons to develop their imaginative and reflective capacities regarding many sides of their culture and society. This is an interpretation opposed to the French sociological tradition. For example, Durkheim and Mauss contend that where emotions are generated in a group setting (and for them rites and ceremonies invariably generate emotions), beliefs and customs resist critical examination and reflection (1963: 88). Carrying on that tradition, Lévi-Strauss takes a similar view (1963: 69). Even recently, Kratz claims that ritual masks doubts generated in male-female relations (1990a: 467).

An important reason for my arguing that rites and ceremonies prompt imagination and reflection is the fact that so many Kaguru rituals are closely associated with songs, sayings, and stories that provide fertile inducements to speculation. The very way such oral literature is presented and taught at initiation encourages critical reflection and imagination. Such thinking resembles the playful "manufactured clarities" that Goffman credits to self-interest and self-justification: "Moreover, what people understand to be the organization of their experience, they buttress, and perforce, self-fulfillingly. They develop a corpus of cautionary tales, games, riddles, experiments, newsy-stories, and other scenarios that elegantly confirm a frame-referent view of the workings of the world" (1974: 563). Thoughtfulness can be taught to initiates, but the distance from such messages achieved by an instructor or by an audience to the rites of others may also facilitate reflection (Kapferer 1979: 8; cf. Goffman 1974: 87–158).

The wordiness of Kaguru initiation should not be seen in modern Western terms. We would do better to keep in mind Kirk's cautionary reminder that in many preliterate societies, words have their own deep archaeology of meanings and that some adepts ponder words for their revelatory etymology, for the ways in which words' "true" meanings, that is, the deep and wide range of associations we take from them, reveal and generate further meanings (Kirk 1974: 58, 113–14, 135–36). This is a kind of word magic, not in terms of a simpleminded misuse of terms but rather in the capacity skillfully developed in poets and dramatists. At its crudest, we encounter this in the puns and wordplay that illuminate many of the points in Kaguru initiation songs. "Puns remind us both of our mastery and our task of control over language: this is their primordial ambiguity. We are always in danger of punning" (Redfern 1984: 123). This is because "all speech contains a great deal of unconscious, additional, or implied meaning that comes from the nearness of words to one another where many relations exist that need not be explicitly stated" (Frye 1982: 59). Wordplay reveals the facility of language, implicating both its utile and deceptive aspects. Such play "outwits the force of habit" (Richards n.d.: 244) and facilitates a "mental promiscuity" or "flexible mind" (Zerubavel 1991: 90). It suits "the arbitrary nature of the mind" (Redfern 1984: 6); wordplays "make us stretch our minds and double our attention" (ibid.: 24).

"Wordplay suits natures that are neither preponderantly straightforward nor esoteric. Its realm is that of the sly, the glancing, the teasing, the oblique. It is neither virile nor epicene, but androgynous: the area where man and woman overlap, the area of congress" (ibid.: 26). Indeed, wordplay is sexy, and at initiation Kaguru are made aware of the many possible implications of terms. They are taught the Wittgensteinian "family resemblances" that allow the games of verbal sparring, innuendo, and seduction (cf. Hughes 1977: 725).[18] Above all, a great deal of what is taught to Kaguru young people, first in riddles and stories and then more intensively at adolescence with initiation, is funny: "If there were no pleasure in the appreciation of the absurd, if there were no fun in playing with ideas, putting them together in various combinations, and seeing what makes sense or nonsense—in brief, if there were no such thing as humor—children would lack practice in the art of thinking, the most complex and most powerful tool of all" (Levin 1957: 921). Finally, we should recall that the very term *infant* in English derives from the Latin for "one who cannot speak," and education out of infancy involves the growth of facility and art in speech.

I have emphasized the manifold meanings of words. Yet symbols too are open to multiple interpretations. Water, blood, wilderness, fire, and other motifs assume varied, even opposite meanings, in different Kaguru rituals or as themes in stories and songs. As Kris wrote (long before V. Turner), "One cannot speak, therefore, of the meaning of any symbol, but can only specify its range of responses and the clusters into which these tend to be grouped" (1953: 244). Meanings can exclude or inhibit one another; they can form associated clusters or they can stress their ambiguity itself, depending upon how they are employed (ibid.: 245–57). In this sense Kaguru women and men might assign somewhat different valences to the same symbols, for example, sometimes appraising wildness as independence and sometimes as rebelliousness, or sometimes appraising fluidity as continuity and at other times as instability.

The skills Kaguru learn with symbols and words are needed to maneuver adroitly in Kaguru affairs. Everyday machinations of family, kin, and village give-and-take require ceaseless skill and wit. For example, unlike Maasai, Kaguru do not praise manly force and outspokenness. *Plain*, *blunt*, and *open* are not adjectives one employs to praise a Kaguru's social bearing. Like John Berger's French peasants, Kaguru envision a world "to which they are forced to pledge their actions as a series of ambushes. Ambushes of risks and dangers" (1979: 203). Kaguru set high store by crafty speech and deeds. Their facility at innuendo, double entendre, and insinuation is impressive. Crafty speech and sharp but hard-to-detect manipulation are important resources in

250   THE COOL KNIFE

a society such as theirs, made up of small settlements linked by complex and problematic cross-cutting loyalties of kinship and affinity. Their most florid side appears in Kaguru joking relations, their darkest in fears of sorcery and witchcraft. If Kaguru initiation teaches Kaguru how to grow up, then skill and reflection regarding the intricacies of meaning and expression count high in measuring successful adulthood. These, as much as sexual realities, are conveyed by Kaguru elders at initiation.

At the broadest level, all societies entertain "contested concepts" (Gallie 1964: 157–91). In the West we dispute the meanings of notions such as beauty, democracy, and justice. Gender and the attributes and behaviors appropriate to it are also contested concepts, especially for a society such as that of the Kaguru, where kinship and marriage provide essential avenues to security, esteem, and immortality. Gender is a "story" that conveys "a dominant sense of alternative possibilities" (ibid.: 26). For a concept such as gender to be contested, one must recognize rival uses of that concept. There are "different messages of authority and inauthority" (Karp 1987: 142) where Kaguru debate the claims and needs of women and men, old and young, kin and strangers. Kaguru initiation, as stories of childhood did earlier, teaches the "philosophical imagination" (Gallie 1964: 194–95) necessary to construct the social perspectives of others. This is not necessarily to cultivate sympathy or generosity toward others; rather it may facilitate Kaguru imaginative skill at "reading" and thereby influencing others in order to reach one's own goals and survive. Kaguru conform to Berger's characterization of peasants: "Peasant life is life committed to survival. Perhaps this is the only characteristic, fully shared by peasants everywhere" (1979: 196).

FINAL REMARKS

Unamuno believed that "we live in memory and by memory and our spiritual life is at bottom simply the effort of our memory to persist, to transform itself into hope, the effort of our past to transform itself into our future" (1954: 8–9). Our words are recollections (Halbwachs 1991: 173). Recently, A. Weiner has renewed our anthropological concern for memory as it is worked out through things imbued with cultural significance and personal identity (1992: 1–19). For Kaguru, remembering who they are has gained increasing importance and poignancy as they have been beset by hostile outside forces preaching change and absorption into a larger, more anonymous world.

For Kaguru, the primary means by which they remember who they are, the means by which they celebrate their language, customs, and beliefs, is the initiation of young people. This recognizes the power of kinesthetic experience to enforce memory (Bateson 1958: 225). "Patterns of significance and symbolic import are thus prefigured in the imaginative patterning of our bodily experience. And such patterns are often the bases of memory" (Johnson 1991: 79).

That Kaguru have chosen sexuality as the theme on which to play out their primary expression of their memory and identity should not surprise us. Sexuality constitutes a central theme in accounting for society itself, for "sex—far from being the most recalcitrant of forces—has long been a transmission belt for wider social anxieties, and a focus of struggles over power, one of the prime sites in truth where domination and subordination are defined and expressed" (Weeks 1985: 16). Sexuality is deeply implicated in kinship and consequently permeates most features of Kaguru life. It constitutes both a primary resource and a constant challenge to order. Sexuality provides a primary mode and need for interacting with one another (see Padgug 1989: 22–28). Kaguru initiation begins with bodily mutilation and incapacitation and concludes with the acquisition of verbal dexterity and physical skill in dancing, where Kaguru perform with and for the pleasure of one another. "The human mind is naturally inclined by the senses to see itself externally in the body, and only with great difficulty does it come to understand itself by means of reflection" (Vico 1968: 236). The body provides a powerful and ready tool for introducing imaginative thought. It is both an object of cultural attention and a means of cultural communication. Kaguru sensibly make it the focus of ethnic memory and identity.

"Beliefs are held by individuals as isolated bits, as it were, and not as entire systems" (Evans-Pritchard 1952: 122). In this sense, we should not expect Kaguru initiation to provide an inclusive and consistent credo of Kaguru values and thought. Neither the rituals nor the oral literature associated with initiation encompasses all Kaguru beliefs and values. What they accomplish is a forceful and appealing introduction to mature understanding by explicitly teaching young people the skills of feeling and thinking about what they know. Rituals, sayings, and songs work at making Kaguru aware of words, actions, gestures, and different times and spaces. Such awareness enables persons to define themselves and to perceive and define others. "Sexuality is as much about words, images, ritual and fantasy as it is about the body: the way we think about sex fashions the way we live it" (Weeks 1985: 3). Initiation stirs Kaguru imagination, and "morality is imagination" (Musil 1979 III: 430).

Initiation does not teach Kaguru to be nicer people, more obedient to Kaguru rules, or more loyal to kin and neighbors, though it presents the complexity of some rules and relations in challenging and seductive ways—challenging because no clear and definitive answers are provided, seductive because these ideas are cloaked in the reassuring blanket of everyday life. Many of these messages are open to several interpretations or even contradict one another. What initiation teaches young Kaguru is to think more deeply and more sophisticatedly about other people and about themselves, and to do so with reflexivity and emotional distance. It confronts young people with a world of possible choices, and that is the beginning of some adult sense of both morality and social opportunism. Initiation teaches Kaguru what it means to be human (Kaguru) in that they are indelibly impressed with their own inextricable involvement with others, most obviously in fulfilling their newly recognized sexual identities, epitomized not only in the pain and harassment that elders inflict on novices but also by the nurturance, comfort, and instruction that follow and which novices feel they have earned by their suffering. Punishments and rewards constitute equal parts of Kaguru initiation, but rewards conclude the sequence and consequently appear to justify and surmount suffering.

Initiation and indeed all *rites de passage* provide lessons not just for Kaguru novices but also for all others involved. Such ceremonies provide continuing and repeated messages for the instructors and audience as well as for those explicitly being instructed. In Kaguru initiation young people are reminded that their own experience replicates those of generations who preceded them and future generations to follow. "Inexhaustibly committed to wrestling a life from the earth, bound to the present by endless work, the peasant [Kaguru] nevertheless sees life as an interlude. This is confirmed by his daily familiarity with the cycle of birth, life, and death" (Berger 1979: 200). Kaguru *rites de passage*, especially initiation, are special occasions, times recalled vividly and nostalgically throughout a Kaguru's lifetime. They constitute repeated memories of personal identity and achievements in a lifetime career. As such, they are experiential landmarks that Kaguru carry within themselves (Halbwachs 1991: 175). Kaguru associate such memories with home, in this case their homeland and especially their village, the only place where such rites should be conducted and a space redolent with the myriad symbols utilized (see Bachelard 1969: 30). The most remarkable thing about such Kaguru rites is that what they are built upon, what gives them their vividness and continuity, is not something outstanding or special, but the shared, pervasive, yet humdrum pulse of everyday experience.

The importance Kaguru accord their rites of ethnic identity should redirect our sense of what is and remains important in identity over much of Africa. Ethnicity has too often in recent times been given a bad name by social scientists of Africa who see this only as a source of division frustrating national unity. In a brilliant and eloquent essay, Lonsdale (1992) remarks on the failure of scholars to give due credit to "moral ethnicity." This has been neglected while "political tribalism" has been a topic of ceaseless academic and political attention. This more negative form of ethnicity is an opportunistic ethos of political intrigue and oppression that constitutes divided communities responding to external competition based on fear, greed, and lack of generosity in understanding. This is an ethnicity born of the divisive oppression of a corrupt and biased state that plays off local groups against one another.

Defending ethnicity in Africa is a currently unpopular exercise, especially among American academics. Yet this is what my volume has set out to do. What I have described here for the Kaguru is no mere account of Kaguru age, sex, and gender, though that is important. Nor has this been simply an account of Kaguru stereotypes of their particular ethnicity, though ideas about sexual and familial character and duties about language and communication and etiquette, and nurturing, are immensely important to Kaguru. And while this study has also been an extended rumination on Kaguru sense of place (their space), on how Kaguru ground their memories and identities in their land, which they intensely value, that too is only another facet of the central and pervading topic of my concern. My study has been an odyssey in search of the lineaments of Kaguru moral ethnicity, of how Kaguru define the meanings and purposes of people's social life. This is in terms of Kaguru families, kin, and communities, groups meaningful through a changing yet continuing tradition of Kaguru being people whose humanity is uniquely Kaguru, not Tanzanian, not African. "Moral ethnicity creates communities from within through domestic controversy over civic virtue. It ascends from deep antagonisms to the very forces on which political tribalism thrives, class closure and overbearing state power" (ibid.). For these reasons the African national state has seemingly opposed or at least discouraged supposedly backward Kaguru traditions. Those Kaguru traditions constitute the moral ethnicity of the Kaguru people, and such ethnicity "is the only language of accountability that most Africans have; it is the most intimate critic of the state's ideology of order" (ibid.). Ethnic identity has continued to afford new means for Kaguru to unite both against ethnic outsiders and against abuse by local neocolonial politicians (Beidelman 1961c). This Kaguru ethnic/ethic tradition is creative yet conservative, stabilizing yet open to contention and negotiation. It is grounded on a playful and pervasive skepticism about the ambiguous and ambivalent motives and meanings generated by social order. The more a student of Kaguru society appreciates the complexity and polyvalence of what Kaguru tradition teaches, the more she or he can appreciate the Kaguru's keenness on preserving tradition in the face of over a century of inroads by missionaries, supposedly enlightened educators, and meddlesome provincial and national politicians. The cool knife of Kaguru education has cut Kaguru off as ethnically different from their neighbors. Yet it has given them poetic skills, insights, meanings, values, and identities that make them valuable to know and to work with, even at times all the wiser across cultural boundaries because they know and value who they are. Above all, the very reflexivity and flexible imagination underpinning Kaguru moral ethnicity seem surer and more valuable grounds for finding new directions in sociability and accountability than the more artificial and alien cant that doctrinaire outsiders have sought to impose upon Kaguru and similar colonized peoples.

Notes

PREFACE

1. While Lévi-Strauss is renowned for popularizing the nature/culture dichotomy in an-thropology and further associating this with gender, this distinction derives from Rousseau, though such ideas are actually rooted in the thinking of a wide range of French writers in the Enlightenment (Bloch and Bloch 1980). This nature/culture di-chotomy has long attracted the attention of feminist anthropologists (e.g., Ortner [1972].) MacCormack 1980 surveys this enduring but misleading dichotomy from Rousseau through Lévi-Strauss to Ortner. As my book was going to press, Ortner pub-lished an extensive revision not only of her 1972 essay but also of much of her subse-quent thinking on related issues; I was unable to incorporate it into this text.

CHAPTER I. INTRODUCTION:
PROBLEMS OF RITUAL, GENDER, AND IDENTITY

1. I entitled my earlier book on the Kaguru *Moral Imagination in Kaguru Modes of Thought* (Beidelman 1986) because of this.
2. This led Wollstonecraft to describe Rousseau as "this partial moralist" (Wollstonecraft 1985: 154), explaining that Rousseau was interested in degrading women to a subordi-nate relationship just as he degraded his uneducated mistress Thérèse le Vasseur (ibid.: 294–95).
3. Schwartz's defense of Rousseau is feasible by assuming a sociohistorical context to his world that would more appropriately apply to traditional Kaguru (1985: 144–45). For both Rousseau and Kaguru, women would be taught "this desire of being always women . . . the very consciousness that degrades the sex" (Wollstonecraft 1985: 199).

4. Ginzburg claims that for the modern bourgeoisie, novels have replaced initiation rites as a source of such information (1986: 115).

5. The quotidian reveals rudimentary and essential aspects of society. A comparable view is reflected in Giovanni Morelli's theories for attributing paintings to old masters by idiosyncratic patterns that they were unaware they displayed (1892). Morelli concentrated on renderings of ears, toes, nostrils, and other seemingly trivial forms: "An artist's personal instinct for form will appear at its purest in the least significant parts of his work because they are the least laboured" (Wind 1969: 40). Reik informs us that Morelli inspired Freud to develop a theory of subconscious behavior in dreams and slips of the tongue (1946: 2–36; Ginzburg 1986: 96–102). Structuralists from van Gennep to Lévi-Strauss have promoted similar analyses.

   Notions comparable to contemporary ideas about habitus as a basis of symbols go back to Durkheim and Mauss and indirectly to Rousseau. Many anthropologists have sought meaning in the subconscious. Sapir tried to explain the complexity of symbols as due to "deeper and deeper roots in the unconscious" (1934: 494). This seemed a way to explain a symbol's "actual significance being out of all proportion to the apparent triviality of meaning suggested by its mere form" (ibid.: 493). Today the everyday ubiquity of a symbol is seen as an attribute of its power.

6. Levine characterizes preliterate societies as rife with ambiguous, overlapping rules (1985: 30–35); this seems ethnocentric. All societies display characteristics that are essential to their flexibility and survival. Yet humans must remain calculable for morals to be applied (Nietzsche 1956b: 189–90).

7. By *deconstruct* I mean the ability to speculate about the manifold contexts that change terms' meanings. I mean the ability of Kaguru to recognize the ludic range of possibilities that a perceptive person may draw from words, gestures, and symbols. In mentioning deconstruction I have not "passed from that [role] of ratiocinative thinker to that of louche voyeur *(louche voyeur)*, for whom a night with a text is better than a night on the town, thinking has replaced Aristotle and Plato as role-models with Sade and Genet, and 'the invitation of philosophy is to lick with Lacan, slaver with Barthes, guzzle with Kristeva, tease awhile with Derrida'" (Bradbury 1987: 74). An example of unprofitable deconstruction of anthropological texts is Clifford 1988; compare Beidelman 1989a.

8. "Handling and use by able minds give value to a language, not so much by innovating as by filling it out with more vigorous and varied service, by stretching and bending it. They do not bring to it new words but they enrich their own, give more weight and depth to their meaning and use; they teach the language unaccustomed movements, but prudently and shrewdly" (Montaigne 1965: 665).

9. Winkler observes that women know two cultures, that presented by men as the hegemonic version and that experienced by themselves (1990: 174). In an account of Greek poetic imagination Winkler suggests methods by which we might understand the ways women picture male accounts of beliefs and values yet also entertain their own related but different views (ibid.: chapters 6 and 7).

10. "The more emotions we allow to speak in a given matter, the more different eyes we

can put on in order to view a given spectacle, the more complete will be our conception of it, the greater our 'objectivity'" (Nietzsche 1956b: 255).

11. The reciprocity of honor, shame, fame, and interpersonal give-and-take constitutes the contradictory motives of Homeric social life (Beidelman 1989b).

12. These views of Plato parallel those of Rousseau, who, like Plato, admired Sparta, was critical of expressive culture, and sought to expunge it from education (see Barber 1978: 79, 89).

13. Febvre reminds us that visualization remained underdeveloped as late as the seventeenth century, when sound, smell, and touch dominated sight, and recitation and aural imagery permeated thought and imagination in France (1982: 423–42). As with Homer, these supported "a total technology of the preserved world" (Havelock 1963: 44).

14. Arguments have been made claiming that the inherent force of things affects meanings held by those who use those things (Csikzentmihalyi and Rochberg-Halton 1981: 43–45, 53).

15. "Early societies were convinced that their continuance was guaranteed solely by the sacrifices and achievements of their ancestors and that these sacrifices and achievements [were] required to be paid back. Thus a debt was acknowledged which continued to increase, since the ancestors, surviving as powerful spirits, did not cease to provide the tribe with benefits out of their store" (Nietzsche 1956b: 222).

16. *Secret* derives from the Latin *secretus*, the past participle of *secernere*, "to set apart," "to discern." It is related to notions of criticism and intelligent discrimination. For a useful discussion, see Bok 1982: 6–10, 286; see also Beidelman 1993.

17. We see them in the Latin term *memor* (mindful), linked to the Greek *martus* (witness), hence *martyr* and *merimna* (solicitude, anxiety).

18. If Lienhardt underplays commitments to groups, then Parkin presents a conversely exaggerated picture. He argues that for the Giriama of Kenya, personhood is the reaction to crises and threats from outside, from others, and neglects the interplay between different self-interests and group norms. He presents a development of person couched more in crises than in the quotidian (1991: 215–16).

Riesman (1986) provides a survey of writings on personhood and the life cycle in Africa. This is valuable as a bibliographic reference but not analysis.

19. Beauvoir writes that a woman's body "promises no precise conclusion to the act of love; and that is why coition is never quite terminated for her; it admits of no end. Male sex feeling rises like an arrow; when it reaches a certain height or threshold, it is fulfilled and dies abruptly in the orgasm; the pattern of the sexual act is finite and discontinuous" (1974: 442); "because no definite term is set, woman's sex feeling extends toward infinity; it is often nervous or cardiac fatigue or psychic satiety that limits woman's erotic possibilities, rather than a specific gratification; even when overwhelmed, exhausted, she may never find full deliverance" (ibid.). These assertions seem dubious (though revelatory of the author's sexual experiences); they correspond to remarks Kaguru women and men made about women's sexuality.

20. This contradicts the traditional sociological view that we should seek precision in

labels, a view inherited from Durkheim's methodology (1952: 41). Terminological precision may facilitate analysis but does not correspond to how people ordinarily think.

21. This led Aquinas to equate the *venator* with the seeker after knowledge and truth (Ginzburg 1986: 131–32). Hunting is not the only Kaguru sexual metaphor of domination. Kaguru say that a polygynous man and his wives resemble a bull and a herd of cows.

22. Solanas provides a useful antidote to this downbeat account: "The female's individuality, which he [the male] is acutely aware of, but which he doesn't comprehend and isn't capable of relating to or grasping emotionally, frightens and upsets him and fills him with envy so he denies it in her and proceeds to define everyone in terms of his or her function or use, assigning to himself, of course, the most important functions—doctor, president, scientist—thereby providing himself with an identity, if not individuality, and tries to convince himself and women (he's succeeded best at convincing women) that the female function is to bear and raise children and to relax, comfort and boost the ego of the male; that her function is such as to make her interchangeable with every other female. In actual fact, the female function is to relate, groove, love and be herself, irreplaceable to anyone else; the male function is to provide sperm" (1968: 45).

23. It is useful to distinguish between patriarchal societies (premodern societies), where male authority dominates but essential, integral roles are played by women, and masculinist societies (modern societies), where women have been denied acknowledgment of their essential socioeconomic roles, if indeed they are provided any (see Ehrenrich and English 1978: 18).

24. This is what they seem to be stating; they may mean to state that men and women have fairly similar understandings of how a system is constructed and how it works, but that men and women then proceed to assume different judgments as to what this signifies. They simply may want to observe that men and women have different experiences of life. Clarity of English is not their strength.

25. Terence Turner takes van Gennep seriously (1977); I postpone comment on his essay until note 28.

26. Van Gennep believed that seemingly trivial customs, folktales, and etiquette reveal deeper patterns of a society's structure. In this he resembles Morelli, Freud, and Lévi-Strauss (see note 5 to this chapter). Niederer (1990) points out how van Gennep's model of rites of passage extends into quotidian life. Niederer fails to show that this is not only in form but also in content, from sacred to secular, from special to everyday, from congregation to person.

27. For such reasons Senn describes van Gennep as a structuralist, implying that he resembles Lévi-Strauss in applying structuralist analysis to social organization (his study of totemism), to belief and symbols (his study of rituals), and to popular culture (his study of folklife and folklore in France). In the last decades of his career, devoted to French folklore and popular culture, van Gennep sought to apply a tripartite model comparable to the model he used in describing rites of passage. This reflects his conviction that human affairs, thoughts, and physical living conditions reflect profound, unitary processes of classification (Senn 1974: 233–38).

28. Terence Turner assumes that ritual both embodies and/or reflects two levels of social relations that it mediates, the egocentric (subjective) and the sociocentric, the interactive and the integrative, "vertical" and "horizontal" levels, structural levels of discrepant power and generality (1977: 60–66). Turner argues that such transcendence characterizes the liminal phase (ibid.: 68), and thereby "rituals are able to serve as mechanisms for exercising such control because they directly model, in their own structures, the hierarchical mechanism of control that forms an intrinsic part of the structure of the situations in question. The structure of ritual action, in other worlds [*sic*], directly embodies its own principles of effectiveness" (ibid.: 62). This view is advanced and elaborated upon by Kapferer (1979). The symbols in rituals supposedly transcend limiting categories, transforming everyday, differentiating perceptions and experiences into a unified system. This is temporarily envisioned as conveying a deeply reassuring sense of holism. Turner and Kapferer claim van Gennep fell short in his analyses of *rites de passage* because he concentrated on the process of change but failed to give sufficient (if any) attention to actual transformation, meaning how ordinary categories and roles are merged and conflated in ways that facilitate a more unitary sense of reality. Turner's main point is that "formalized ceremonial or ritual behaviors are essentially to be understood as hypostatizations or models of common features of the structure and dynamics of social processes" (ibid.: 59). Such activities are related to the beliefs and doings of the members of the society in which they take place, but they are not hypostatizations. Hypostatizations are bases or underlying principles, and such rituals are not the principles or meanings of a society. They may reflect some of these, at best providing perceptual closure or holism within restricted, assorted sectors of social life, but that is a limited working sphere, however important. From this perspective the case for terming rituals "models" seems stronger.

Turner grounds his analysis in no ethnography. Kapferer provides sparse ethnographic illustrations. Kapferer's arguments owe much to Goffman's work on frame analysis, which I too find useful (1974: 124–55).

I cannot argue that inclusive, global rituals do not exist in any society, but I know of no convincing global examples of these from my own ethnographic research or readings. At best, one might argue that a political ritual such as a coronation or the Swazi royal first-fruits ceremonies (Beidelman 1966b) presents some sense of inclusiveness because it is associated with a prevailing polity. As an example from a New Guinea society, the ceremonies described by Gell for the Umeda may appear global, but they actually involve direct imagery of only half the society, males (1975).

CHAPTER 2. CONSTRUCTING ETHNICITY: IMAGINING KAGURULAND AND KAGURU PEOPLE

1. My figures on population derive from the East African High Commission's 1957 census, taken while I was in the field. From my own observations I estimate that such figures underreport the actual numbers (East African Statistical Department 1958). Today's figures must be double the 1957 ones, given the high birth rate in the area and the fact that few Kaguru emigrate.

2. I was immensely pleased when a friend who had visited Tanzania a few years ago told me that some Kaguru had used Kaguru stories presented in my publications as bases for skits critical of the political status quo.

3. By "social world" I mean something which is perhaps now an old-fashioned concept in anthropology: a "world view," "a characteristic attitude of purpose or obligation toward that which is confronted" (Redfield 1952: 33), what Bateson terms *eidos* (1958: 220).

CHAPTER 3. KAGURU PERSONAL STRATEGIES OF
KINSHIP AND THE FAMILY

1. General accounts of Kaguru life are available in Beidelman 1967a: 36–35; 1971b; 1986; Beidelman and Winter 1967: 134–203. Bibliographical information is in Beidelman 1967: 73–88; 1969; 1974a; 1981a; 1988a.

2. This is expressed by the fact that father-daughter incest is not a traditonally actionable offense for Kaguru but considered simply a sleazy and stupid business (see Beidelman 1971c). In contrast, all matriclan incest constitutes heinous, unredeemable offenses, with that between siblings and between mother's brother and sister's daughter being the most horrible. Kaguru assured me that mother-son incest was not possible.

3. Kaguru believe that such a paternal tie must not be reduplicated within a generation. The tie may be maintained by widow inheritance or sororate. In widow inheritance, the wife is likely to be beyond childbearing age. Young widows often return to their kin for remarriage. The sororate is likely if the first wife died childless. It is less likely when the deceased had grown offspring. It was encouraged where a matrilineal sister could take care of her deceased kinswoman's young.

4. In a speculative essay grounded in careless reading of ethnography, Rosen (1973) suggests interesting relations between the matrilineal Bemba's prohibitions and conflicts between the domestic household and matriliny. Her arguments suggest how deeply "the matrilineal puzzle" affects ritual. Neither Bemba nor Kaguru speak in such terms about these customs. Somersan (1984) unconvincingly tries to link the symbolism of reproduction and the afterlife to matriliny.

5. Paulme notes the enduring attachment of women to their natal kin at the expense of their husbands' kin (1963: 3). "A married woman always has two homes and owes a dual allegiance" (ibid.: 6). Her account shows bias from working exclusively with patrilineal peoples and from not recognizing that the central relation in most African women's social strategies concerns children and not their husbands.

6. From a woman's view, marriage to a cross-cousin would be a likely advantage, whereas men undertake such marriages because they are too poor to pay bridewealth. A father's sister's daughter or a mother's brother's daughter might be offered to a youth at reduced payment. In consideration, the new husband would have to reside with or near the benevolent elder kinsman and render brideservice. In such cases the wife continues to reside among familiar kin while her husband is an outsider. Or a youth might promise a benevolent elder control over bridewealth from his future daughters. Whatever the case, the youth's authority over his wife and children would be curtailed and this would give his wife more freedom. If a youth moves into his wife's natal village, her indepen-

dence from him would be even greater. In a matrilineal society a woman is sometimes less well off married to a mother's brother's son than to a father's sister's son because in the former case her brother cannot readily defend her against her father-in-law (van Baal 1975: 93). "Preferential marriages" favor elders and wives but never benefit husbands much at the early stages of the union before a male accumulates wealth and influence and repays his elders.

7. Joking kin provide links to the problematic supernatural world of the ancestral dead, and hence to fertility, since offspring are ceded to the living from the dead and since the benevolence of the ancestors must be ensured for rain and productive fields and livestock. Joking kin provide ritual services at funerals and ancestral propitiation; father's sisters and grandparents figure at birth and naming ceremonies for children, and grandparents provide instructions about sexuality, customs, and genealogical, clan, and district histories. Much has been written, especially for central and eastern Africa, about the equivalence of alternate generations (cf. V. Turner 1955). The key role of grandparents instructing the young provides a conservative brake against change by endowing tradition with a character older than parents' experience (cf. Marc Bloch 1964: 40–41). Grandparents and grandchildren are uninterested in the contemporary events that absorb parents (Halbwachs 1980: 63). Teaching by the old, what classical Greeks termed *geroia*, ensures (conserves) social memory (Connerton 1989: 39). Such elderly teaching characterizes Kaguru initiation.

8. "Motherhood is the basis of all kinship and in a structural analysis of kinship women necessarily must be seen in the perspective of motherhood because it is this which lays the foundation for the permanence of the intergroup relations commonly referred to as kinship. A father is expendable, but there is no kinship without motherhood" (van Baal 1975: 79).

9. Csikszentmihalyi and Rochberg-Halton observe that middle-class American mothers devote more psychic effort to maintaining affect in a home than do fathers. They ask whether this may be unfair to women since it frees men for more-rewarding outside pursuits. Such arguments might seem misplaced to Kaguru, whose highest priorities are parent-child bonds, which women are here strengthening. Kaguru women may well see their own high psychic input into familial relations as deeply rewarding, not only affectually but in terms of power. It is women's main strength against male authority (1981: 168–70).

CHAPTER 4. SPACE AND MEMORY: RITUAL, ETHNICITY, AND PERSONHOOD

1. A shorter version of this chapter was published earlier as Beidelman 1991a; see also Beidelman 1972a.

    Michael Jackson's recent work also at times develops themes and issues close to those of my concern (1983b, 1989). I differ from him, however, in two ways. I do not see the kinds of profound divisions between non-Western and Western thought that he does. Nor do I see African societies as being as benign as he does; rather, I see them as concerned with domination, subversion, and betrayal as well as with solidarity and peace, much as we ourselves are. A collection of essays edited by Shirley Ardener contains many provocative illustrations about gender and space but is considerably limited in its insights by being restricted to one gender (1981). For relevant passages in Mauss, see 1979a, 1979b, 1979c, and in Wittgenstein see 1963: 36; 1969: 28, 30; n.d.: 11). Some may find my neglect of Foucault odd, but no convincing case can be made for his grasp of the concept of space (Hirst 1985). Nor do I consider Moore's study of the Marakwet of East Africa, which is a clumsy and insensitive exercise (1986; Beidelman 1988b). Parkin's study of the Giriama of East Africa is subtle and complex reportage of social space, but he is far more concerned with broader structural issues than with the quotidian (1991; compare Beidelman 1994).

Wilson provides a survey of some writings on domestic space, especially the house (1988: 57–78) and the village (1988: 74–116). While often sensible, most of his observations strike me as merely repetition of others' ethnographies and conclusions.

2. Zerubavel sees the examination of spatial divisions as the best opening into a wider consideration of social categories in general (1991: 6).

3. Myriad everyday activities and experiences inform and construct our system of beliefs and values. This view owes much to both Wittgenstein and Mauss. Not surprisingly, my interpretation resembles arguments earlier advanced by Bourdieu, whose ideas derive from these same two predecessors. Unfortunately, Bourdieu's perceptive ethnographic accounts and analyses of everyday space and time among the Kabyle of northern Africa are diminished by a lack of any coherent account of Kabyle social organization and by a mass of turgidly written, obfuscating theory that seems to reduce the central features of Kabyle society to a mere dichotomy of gender (e.g., 1977: 89–95).

4. When I write of Kaguru ethnic identity, of their sense of being one people with a common language, customs, and history, I am writing about what Kaguru professed when I resided among them during the colonial and early postcolonial period (1957–1968). Much historical material reported by those Europeans who first encountered the Kaguru suggests that earlier Kaguru did not think of themselves in such a cohesive, neatly bounded sense. It appears that many sides of Kaguru ethnicity in the 1950s and 1960s, including their legends of clan and ethnic origins, were in part elaborations responding to European colonialists' expectations that they would deal with unified, "tribal" groups, preferably ones with a standardized language, persuasively regular beliefs and customs, and a political hierarchy, even though the earlier inhabitants of what is now Kaguruland lacked all these desiderata.

5. Needham points out that the sets of oppositions that constitute a system of beliefs and values are "in practice an odd-job notion seductively masked by the immediacy of a spatial metaphor" (1987: 228; cf. Doxtater 1984: 9). This immediacy derives from our bodily predicament in space. Long ago Kant observed that "our geographical knowledge and even our commonest knowledge of the positions of places would be of no aid to us if we could not, by reference to the sides of our bodies, assign to regions the things so ordered and the whole system of mutually relative positions" (cited in Tuan 1977: 36).

6. Hart rightly argues for the primacy of space over time as an explanatory mode: "One is distracted *from* time, but *in* space. Distraction within space is constitutive of the appre-

hension and understanding of things in place and of ourselves with them" (1973: 37); "since it is in place that a thing is first 'really' expressed. That says, in short, that things have their place in metaphors, that placement is incorrigibly metaphorical" (ibid.), by which he appears to mean that it is connective and synthetic. For this to "take place" requires doing, not only in quotidian life but above all in ritual, which will inform that life: "In not a few ancient tongues, the root meaning of 'to make' or 'to do' is to place (Greek, *tithenai*; Sanskrit, *dadhati*; Old Slavic, *deli*), so that to front a fact would be to be placed by what is in place, to come to belong to what belongs in the full range of its reference" (ibid.). All this is highly suggestive; Hart would, however, have made his argument clearer had he gone on to indicate the difference between space and place, place being familiarized, social, morally situated space (Tuan 1977: 73).

7. In the 1970s, after I left the field, massive government-enforced villagization of previously scattered Kaguru homesteads threatened traditional Kaguru culture. Apparently these policies were never carried out all over Kaguruland and today are no longer pursued, but they do indicate the potential for external undermining of Kaguru society.

8. For Kaguru, "uncircumcised" might mean that such outsiders do not practice circumcision (this assumption applies to none of the Kaguru's immediate Bantu-speaking neighbors), that outsiders are not cut in the Kaguru manner (applying to the Maasai and Baraguyu), or that even though physically undistinguishable from Kaguru, circumcised outsiders were cut without proper ceremonies and instructions (see Beidelman 1964b). Thus, some Kaguru would debate whether Kaguru circumcised in a mission hospital were truly circumcised at all. To be openly witnessed by other Kaguru as having been initiated is the only way to confirm true circumcision.

9. "If human sociation is *conditioned* by the capacity to speak, it is shaped by the capacity to be silent, although this becomes obvious only upon occasion" (Simmel 1950: 249n.).

10. As Lewin noted, speech is a form of "social locomotion" (1936: 49) whose spatial context is always significant. (For a useful survey of how this complexly relates to gender, see Gal 1991.)

11. "Cooked meat represents above all the overcoming of putrefaction. Together with the fermented drink it constitutes the principle of banquet, that is to say, the principle of primitive society" (Bachelard 1964: 103).

12. "Collective food as the conclusion of labor's collective process was not a biological, animal act but a social event. If food is separated from work and conceived as part of a private way of life, then nothing remains of the old images: man's encounter with the world and tasting the world, the open mouth, the relation of food and speech, the gay truth" (Bakhtin 1984: 281–82). "In the act of eating, as we have said, the confines between the body and the world are overstepped by the body; it triumphs over the world, over the enemy, celebrates its victory, grows at the world's expense. No meal can be sad: sadness and food are incompatible (while death and food are perfectly compatible)" (ibid.: 282–83). "There is an ancient tie between the feast and the spoken word" (ibid.: 282). Furthermore, for Kaguru a feast always has hosts, and their hospitality reasserts their proprietorship of the space they open to their visiting guests (compare Wilson 1988: 71–97).

13. "The house is a geometry, a series of relationships between objects rather than a collection of objects" (Wilson 1988: 17). It is in this sense that our culture has developed the term *focus*, deriving from the Latin word for hearth, the dwelling place of the Roman household gods. The Kaguru seem to draw an implicit analogy between house space, the body, and the generation of social organization, as demonstrated by the fact that the words *nyumba* (house), *tumbo* (belly or womb), and *mlango* (door) may be used to refer to a household or lineage segment.

14. The term *lugha* may simply reflect a different use of the alien Swahili term *lugha* (speech, language). If that is so, then the term would probably derive from the fact that communal or village speech is ordinarily exercised in this space.

   Tuan suggests that open space tends to suggest "hopeful" or positive affect (1977: 123). Certainly Kaguru associate open social space with moral openness and reciprocity, and they associate confining space such as the inside of a dwelling with more selfish, unsociable sentiments.

   Privacy is mainly defined in terms of differences between houses (households) (compare Wilson 1988: 179).

15. I have written my ethnography in terms of traditional Kaguru settlements composed of separate houses. I have not described Kaguru stockaded settlements formed by contiguous housing units making one structure. Such dwellings were traditional in some areas, especially during the precolonial era of raiding, when such settlements afforded better defense than did congeries of separated buildings. At the time of my fieldwork such settlements of connected dwellings prevailed in western Kaguruland, where I did not do much work. Yet space appears to be allocated there in a manner that is ideologically comparable to what I describe here.

   Today the Tanzanian government has destroyed traditional Kaguru settlements in many areas in order to enforce collectivized settlements. This seems sure to undermine many aspects of traditional Kaguru culture.

16. Rykwert argues that a true home requires neighbors and that homes in preindustrial societies always implied neighbors who could provide part of the stage on which social performances could take place. For him, personhood is possible only in such neighborly spaces where houses are homes (1991: 56–57).

17. Blacking is right: "Dance and the performance arts are especially interesting because they are areas of human life in which the most individualistic people are willing to suspend the sort of decision-making that they use for most tasks, and because they seem to express and are invariably claimed to express, the ethos of a society's collective life" (1985: 88; see also Allen 1985: 37; Jackson 1983a: 338). Tuan observes that "music and dance free people from the demands of purposeful goal directed life, allowing them to live briefly in what Erwin Strauss calls 'presentic' oriented space" (1977: 129).

18. Recently Parkin described a cultural heartland that is sparsely inhabited and pondered how unusual it may be for a sacred area to be uninhabited and rarely visited (1991: 11, 23).

19. Bachelard goes so far as to describe agricultural fires as purifying and compares the ashes to fertilizing excreta (1964: 104–5).

20. "Seasonal variation is but the expression of a translated landscape, a topographical image in its temporal dimension." There is an "interchangeability between landscape and temporality" (J. Weiner 1991: 8).

21. Kaguru learn myriad gestures that are appropriate to gender and age as well as serve to convey different feelings and intents. I see no reason to agree with Jackson that bodily gestures and stances are necessarily truer than words. Both are learned languages and are therefore means both to inform and to dissemble (1983a: 339). At best one might argue that verbal ruses are easier to pull off than bodily ones.

22. While this belief may seem primitive to some readers, they should remember that it was commonly held for many years in England (see Stone 1979: 248).

23. Sometimes a Kaguru spouse will commit such acts as disposal of a husband's weapons or shattering of a wife's cooking pot in order to indicate publicly that a relationship is finished. Since this implies a deadly curse, compensatory payments and purificatory ceremonies are required before a couple can resume cohabitation.

24. Tuan remarks: "Landscape is personal and tribal history made visible. The native's identity—his place in the total scheme of things—is not in doubt, because the myths that support it are as real as rocks and waterholes he can see and touch. He finds recorded in his land the ancient study of lives and deeds of the immortal beings from whom he himself is descended, and whom he reveres" (1977: 157–58).

25. Bourdieu's dichotomization of centripetal/female and centrifugal/male is too simplistic for the Kaguru material and perhaps even for the Kabyle as well (1977: 92).

26. In an ethnographically rich essay on Bachana funerals in Nigeria, Stevens (1991) points out that many contemporary anthropologists have wrongly restricted their consideration of rites of passage to initiation of adolescents. This may, as he observes, be partly due to a general analytical ignorance regarding classics such as van Gennep and Hertz.

27. "There are imaginations, not 'imagination,' and they must be studied in detail" (James 1948: 303).

CHAPTER 5. FIRST ENCOUNTERS WITH SEXUALITY

1. The only account of African initiation that considers information gained in childhood is that by Ottenberg (1989). He develops his arguments around a Freudian theory of "latency" (ibid.: xiii–xiv).

2. European medieval tradition provides an interesting illustration of comparable moral ambiguity (see Husband 1980; Bernheimer 1962). In the notion of the wild man Europeans explored the positive and negative aspects of socialization, reducing this duality to a highly ambiguous and ambivalent system.

3. Beidelman 1963a: 758–62. I have retranslated the Kaguru text, improving on my earlier version.

4. This reminds me of Leenhardt's observation: "It is aesthetics which puts a first coherence in primitive man's mind" (1975: xvi).

5. It was a Kaguru Christian who first informed me that a woman circumcises a boy in the Bible. Moses's wife, Zipporah, circumcised her son when no man was available to accomplish the task (Exodus 4:24–26). Also, as with the Kaguru, the Talmud describes

this as inept and eventually completed successfully by a man, Moses ('Abodah Zarah 27a). Some Kaguru are fond of comparing their customs to those in the Bible.

6. Certainly the old Bettelheimian theory that circumcision suggests that men want to resemble women (that is, bleed) would make no sense to Kaguru. Even though Brain (1988) worked with the neighboring, culturally similar Luguru (and therefore should know better), he continues to posit vagina envy as a theory behind the bloodletting of circumcision. His unscholarly farrago of disparate ethnographic snippets corresponds to nothing I could find in any East African thinking.

7. Beidelman 1965a: 22–24. I have retranslated the Kaguru text, improving on my earlier version.

8. Kaguru use the term *kuhasa* for forbidden sexual relations between persons affinally related, such as between a man and some woman to whom a close matrikinsman is already married or to a woman of the man's own wife's matriclan. Therefore, while it is desirable and proper for people of the two clans involved to have sexual relations, it is undesirable that such relations are duplicated amongst close kin, which would throw those kin into some kind of sexual or emotional competition with one another. Unlike actual incest within a matriclan, such relations may be cleansed through certain fines and rituals.

   Kuhasa also refers to sexual relations or marriage between *wahisi* (cross-cousins). Such unions are problematic in that they involve some irregular adjustments in the rules of bridewealth, brideservice, or residence. Some of the parties consequently emerge at considerable advantage and others at a disadvantage. Kaguru themselves say that one marries in order to convert strangers or enemies into kin. In *kuhasa* marriages, inimical kin are converted into affines: one kind of problematic kinship supplants another. Analysis of *kuhasa* neatly illustrates one of the basic arguments of this study: close examination of negatively defined customs, categories, or attributes reveals that they may exhibit quite opposite qualities or, mutatis mutandis, that relations which at first appear to be positive and unambiguous also take on some negative tone under deeper consideration.

9. For a comparison of Kaguru and Maasai (Baraguyu) grooming and its relation to sex and gender, see Beidelman 1980b.

10. To this day Kaguru male initiation is carried out only during the dry season. The story is, however, misleading regarding female initiation. While such ceremonies are more prominent in the dry season than in the rainy, this is because foodstuffs are more plentiful then and no one is working in the fields. Girls are necessarily initiated year round since this must be done as soon as a girl commences to menstruate. The ritual should never be postponed.

11. For that matter, it was only after I entered college that I appreciated the metaphorical etymologies of such basic English sexual terms as *cunt* and *fuck*, derivations which I suppose few Americans who use such obscenities actually know.

12. We know that classical Greeks also nicknamed the penis *peo*, "tail" (Vanggaard 1972: 62).

13. For an extraordinary compendium of American and other sexual vulgarisms, see

Schwartz 1988: 7–18, 53–60, 129–37. Richter 1987 is also useful but not as amusing or colorful. See also Sheidlower 1995, an amusing and thorough compendium.

CHAPTER 6. CEREMONIES OF MEN'S AND WOMEN'S INITIATION

1. My earlier remarks on Kaguru initiation appear in Beidelman 1967a: 48–49. There is an extensive literature on initiation among the matrilineal peoples culturally related to and neighboring the Kaguru. Unfortunately, most of it is devoid of proper analysis. Following is a listing of comparative ethnographic materials on initiation. For the Ngulu, see Beidelman 1964c; 1965b; 1967a: 65, 1981b; Cory 1944; Dooley 1936; Grohs 1980 (compare Beidelman 1981b). For the Luguru, see Beidelman 1967a: 32–33; Brain 1977, 1978, 1980; Mzuanda 1958: 119–40; Scheerder and Tastevin 1950: 260–63; M.-L. Swantz 1966: 131–32. For the Zaramo, see Beidelman 1967a: 20–21; L. W. Swantz 1966: 39–50; M.-L. Swantz 1966: 125–30, 1970 (compare Beidelman 1972b); von Waldow 1961. For the Sagara, see Beidelman 1967a: 52. For the Vidunda, see Beidelman 1967a: 25. For the Zigula, see Beidelman 1967a: 70; Grohs 1980. A general comparative account, though emphasizing the Zaramo, is Felix 1990; see also Beidelman 1991b. Other general accounts are Cory 1947, 1948, 1956, and Culwick 1939. Caplan 1976 provides a useful account of Swahili practices.

Felix provides illustrations of objects that he states are used in Kaguru initiation of adolescents or other rites. See particularly Felix 1990: 224, 306–7, 394–96, 410, 412–13, 480; Felix and Kecskési 1994: 69–70, 100, 223, 330–31; see also my comments in Beidelman 1991b.

In the sumptuous catalogue accompanying the huge exhibit of African art at London's Royal Academy of Art in 1995–96, a wooden carving said to be Kaguru (collected by Felix) is described in ways suggesting associations with Kaguru ritual practices that I never encountered or heard Kaguru mention (Phillips 1995: 155). I discuss these catalogue annotations here since any reader seeing them or the exhibit might wonder why I have made so little mention of ritual objects in my discussion of Kaguru initiation.

The carving is a wooden pole, notched at its top and decorated with two protuberances at one side, which probably represent a woman's breasts. The catalogue annotator, Zachary Kingdon, states that such "figurative poles" are "erected in meeting houses used by the 'secret' societies (now extinct)" that supposedly existed among Kaguru. I have never heard of or seen such meeting houses nor heard of any such "secret" societies either present or past. Kingdon goes on to describe such "figurative poles" as "also erected outside Kaguru houses, often under thatched shelters," which "served to protect the village from mystical dangers" (see Phillips 1995: 155). There are reports by early travelers and missionaries of thatched shelters protecting ancestral figurines and sacrifices given to them, but I never saw any such figures or posts during my fieldwork. In general, ancestral propitiation takes place outside the boundaries of Kaguru settlements.

Kingdon also asserts that figurative poles "may have served to help protect and ritually empower female initiates during their seclusion within the initiation hut" (ibid.). I have no evidence to prove or disprove that special initiation houses were ever erected for women or that such poles were utilized in them. I saw no such poles during my fieldwork and women were initiated in ordinary dwellings. Kingdon's assumption appears to be based upon the fact that old figurative poles are said to have been collected from Kaguru and these closely resemble poles from other areas of Tanzania where such initiation houses are said to have been erected (see Felix and Kecskési 1994: 223). Kingdon goes on to assert that "figurative poles and other objects (male symbols) were frequently carved with female imagery to create ritually powerful conjunctions of male and female symbols. Such artefacts were used in a variety of ceremonial contexts" (ibid.). I know no evidence to prove this for Kaguru. Kaguru explicitly associate center poles of houses with the penis and sometimes endow spears and sticks with male attributes. Kaguru are not inclined to endow any and every long object with male attributes, and they appear loath to combine or conflate male and female attributes in one object. They regard any physiological implication of hermaphroditism with horror. Consequently, this statement by Kingdon seems unfounded. In any case, none of these poles illustrated in various publications appears to be a center pole. A center pole protrudes beyond the top of a roof and its tip is often decorated like a fancy knob; it is not notched. In contrast, all of the "figurative poles" at issue are bifurcated or cleft at the top. Such cleft posts occur in most Kaguru houses; they are not solitary center poles, however, but posts supporting horizontal crossbeams. Kingdon fails to consider the top notch on the post as a device for holding a beam but instead believes this "may represent the traditional divided hairstyle which is a motif common to much of the figurative art of the matrilineal peoples of north-eastern Tanzania." Such a motif, sometimes reduced to simple bifurcation, does characterize some heads on abstract female figurines collected in this area. Without seeing such poles in use or without comment from Kaguru, we cannot know much about them.

I have devoted a long endnote entry to a single account of one illustrated object said to relate to Kaguru girls' initiation. The aim of my discussion is to show that we cannot know anything about what Kaguru objects mean outside what Kaguru themselves do and say. Since Christian missionaries early on stamped out most public use of Kaguru figurines and other carved objects, we have little to go on as to what any such surviving objects symbolize. I found almost no such objects among the Kaguru with whom I worked. Objects attributed to Kaguru may be found in museums; some of these were acquired shortly after initial colonial contact. Recently many more have begun to surface in various American and European public and private collections. We have very little information about exactly where such Kaguru objects came from, and none of those who have recently shown such objects, such as Felix, has provided any information about the circumstances of where and how they were acquired and whether Kaguru spoke about their use or age. Consequently, though I know that Kaguru "ritual objects" are reported and illustrated in collection catalogues and exhibits, and I have myself seen such exhibitions, I have no grounds for an informed discussion. Kaguru did not employ such objects in any of the ceremonies I witnessed, and on the few occasions when I came across carved objects in Kaguruland (Beidelman 1991b), Kaguru were unwilling to admit that they were used or of interest. While my writings consequently provide little help to those interested in interpreting Kaguru "art objects," even those said to be related to initiation, at least I have not contributed to the fanciful speculation that passes for analysis in some art catalogues.

2. For a useful comparative case see Worthman 1987.

3. It is remarkable how little any culture makes aesthetically of human genitals. Societies provide praises of noses, eyes, hands, feet, breasts, and, less frequently, buttocks, but the genitals are usually either ignored or described with coarse humor. Verlaine appears to be one of the very few important Western poets willing to give the genitals extended, serious praise. Gustave Courbet's *L'Origine du monde* is the only impressive portrait of the vulva by a great Western painter. This was commissioned by a Turkish diplomat and later owned by Jacques Lacan; it was seemingly parodied by Marcel Duchamp in *Étant donnés* (Faunce and Nochlin 1988: 177–78). Not surprisingly, Courbet's work has often been criticized. In more recent times, Robert Mapplethorpe has presented the penis as beautiful, which may account for some of the savage reactions to his works (Howard 1988: 155, 158); cf. Looby 1995. Thorn also presents a user-friendly account (1990). In contrast, Leonardo thought the genitals of both sexes to be repulsive (Mathé 1978: 29). The Japanese seem among the few artists to find the genitals hilariously funny visually. One of the few poetic yet philosophical accounts of the penis was published by Gonzalez-Crussi (1985). For a humorous account of the penis in contemporary popular culture, see Miller 1995. Verlaine (1965) appears to be the only major modern Western poet to confront the genitals and their activities openly. To find such carefree candor elsewhere one would have to go back to Lord Chesterfield or Catullus, both of whom often lurch from the affectionate to the scabrous. I disqualify Martial as simply and deliberately obscene. Going back further, I refer the reader to Henderson 1975, Rousselle 1988, and Richlin 1992, which amply demonstrate that the Greeks appreciated and excelled at expression of such matters.

4. One's close kin must sponsor such rites. In a typical Kaguru clan legend a "lost" male child is sent back at adolescence to his natal kin for circumcision before he can be absorbed by the new group into which he will marry (Beidelman 1970).

5. During the colonial period Christian missionaries and some Christian converts advocated the blessing of initiations by clergymen. Missionaries were unable to condemn circumcision out of hand because Jesus himself had been cut, but they condemned the sexual instruction provided at such occasions as well as the dancing and drinking essential to confirm such changes.

  At the times I did fieldwork, most of the mission medical staff were women, including the surgeon. Being circumcised in the mission hospital in a feminine environment only made Christian male initiates' humiliation worse, even if a male dresser might do the actual cutting.

6. As with many languages, Chikaguru employs the term *ng'ombe*, which does not specify the sex of the animal. I translate this as "cow" but mean any bovine creature.

7. *Chisonya*, a small drab bird, also called *chinindi*. This is almost certainly the oxpecker (*Buphagus erythrorhynchus caffer*), familiar to anyone who has observed East African game or livestock.

8. Children may have spent some nights encamped in the fields shortly before harvests

guarding crops from baboons and other pests. If so, these camps included elder kin who would tend a fire and cook. These could include women. These preharvest camps were familiar and casual affairs, relaxed and fun, far from the harsh and scary separation of boys from their villages that is emphasized at circumcision.

9. Turner and Blodgett 1988 provides one of the few accounts of how such changes are manifest in African initiation.

10. I have no direct knowledge of the objects utilized in Kaguru initiation other than the medicinal horns and beaded ornaments used by the initiator, and the disposable straw garb worn by the initiate novices at *kugongola*. Felix, however, presents examples of various objects (fly whisks, stools, dolls, staves, masks, ceremonial axes) that may have been used at initiation. Unfortunately, no such items appeared in use during my stay with the Kaguru (Felix 1990: 224, 306, 323, 332–33, 376, 394–96, 410, 474–75; Beidelman 1991b).

11. Compare this to my report of female initiation (*guluwe*, "wild pig") among the Kaguru's neighbors to the east, the Ngulu (Beidelman 1964c).

12. Eliade (1965: 42) made this point many years ago, but the Kaguru material suggests that he was wrong to assume that these smaller numbers of initiates necessarily lead to any marked restriction in complexity. The songs, rituals, and instruction provided Kaguru women appear complex and extensive. While girls are indeed usually initiated singly, many women assemble for the rites, and several hundred men and women come to the dances and feasts marking a girl's recovery.

13. I write of the 1950s and 1960s, when I did fieldwork in Ukaguru. With more recent government-enforced consolidation of settlements many Kaguru again live in larger communities. This would allow resumption of the older pattern of group initiation of young people, although I have no idea whether this has ever occurred.

14. As Wollstonecraft observed, the education of women is always subordinated to some corporal accomplishment. She saw this integral to women's subservience (1985: 104–6).

15. As Norman Douglas wryly remarks: "Although his outfit left nothing to be desired, they did not succeed in making him rise to the occasion. You cannot do so—at least not everybody can—when other people are laughing all the time" (1967: 48).

16. When I did fieldwork in Ukaguru in 1957–61, 6 percent of all married Kaguru women lived in polygynous unions while in the more remote and less missionized mountain areas the proportion reached 18 percent. I assume that polygyny has continued to decline in subsequent years.

17. The gap in age between that of parents and that of their first initiated child may be changing. Kaguru repeatedly told me that boys are now initiated at an earlier age since there are no longer good economic or political reasons to encourage delays when elders might seek to exploit boys as dependent minors. Though I have no proof, it seems likely that the Kaguru diet has improved in recent decades; if so, this would also make it likely that both sexes now reach sexual maturity at an earlier age.

18. Erikson argues that American children exhibit striking differences in their commitment to space and structures and that these differences reflect gender, although, being a Freudian, he seems to envision these as inherently sexual. He describes boys erecting

externally oriented structures and inclined to destroy what they have constructed; in contrast, girls are disposed to play in enclosed spaces and to be occupied with arranging interiors, and they show no sign of destroying edifices. Erikson seeks to relate this to male and female sexuality, even to the nature of the genitals themselves. Typical of his rash ahistorical and acultural assertions, he bases these on one play group in California involving older children who have clearly been highly socialized (1963: 102–6). I mention this example in our culture only because it does oddly parallel the Kaguru material on male and female initiation space.

19. Considering Swahili initiation, Caplan (1976: 26–27) describes girls' initiation as "confirmatory" and boys' as "transformational." This is a perceptive observation but too simple. Kaguru do say that boys' natures are more sharply changed by initiation than are girls'.

   The boys' stark removal into the wilderness emphasizes the initiators' assault on the earlier status of the novices. Considering a parallel situation, medieval pilgrimages, Rothkrug aptly notes that distance and danger eloquently convey a sense of the supernatural while also undermining personal autonomy (1979: 50–51).

20. The idea of semen nurturing a woman's body has also been held in the West. For a long, piquant view from the eighteenth-century English herbalist and astrologer Ebenezer Sibley, see Waller 1977: 251. For Kaguru, semen is a kind of male milk.

CHAPTER 7. LEARNING ADULTHOOD: INITIATION SONGS

1. The harassment and hazing that I experienced during army boot camp in the infantry repeatedly reminded me of what Kaguru youth experience during initiation.

2. While doing fieldwork in East Africa, I witnessed male circumcision several times among the Kaguru, among the neighboring Ngulu, and among the Baraguyu. The initiates always appeared very apprehensive, and while none cried out, the initiates' bodies were rigid with pain.

3. I did not possess a tape recorder during my fieldwork. Texts were collected in two ways. Some were transcribed by me as they were sung by various men and women gathered specifically to provide such material to me. Others were collected by literate Kaguru assistants. Kaguru informants repeatedly provided explanations of what the hidden or "real" meanings of such texts might be. Conditions were too chaotic at initiations for me to collect texts at those times.

4. Sometimes the words to be translated were not very difficult but stemmed from the languages of neighboring peoples. The boys and girls being initiated were far less sophisticated than the instructors, so it was not difficult to present instruction in arcane terms. Today with the rise of Swahili and the decline in the use of Chikaguru as a vernacular, some educated children even regard some ordinary Kaguru phrases as difficult. Unfortunately, a few terms in the songs remained difficult for me to translate.

5. The father's sister is not mentioned. Kaguru did not explain why. My explanation is that father's sister has little positive power over her nieces or nephews. Her interests are popularly defined as opposed to one's own. A father's sister's blessing is sometimes

sought, but this is mainly to gain reassurance that she is not resentful or hostile. Her children's interests (as one's father's heirs) are at odds with one's own, and she has no important reason, other than love of her brother, to wish one well. In contrast, one's mother, father, and mother's brother all have well-recognized claims on one's labor and wealth and consequently have good reasons to associate their self-interest with one's own. I never heard Kaguru characterize father's sisters as sources of meaningful support or dependable concern, only as possible hidden and resentful enemies who should be respected out of concern for one's father but not relied upon.

6. I cannot determine the hidden meaning of this song. My interpretation derives from my understanding of other, related songs and texts. It is not derived from specific comments by Kaguru.

7. Neighboring Gogo, Ngulu, Sagara, and others initiate girls and boys and intermarry with Kaguru at the borderlands. Consequently, these ethnic outsiders attend Kaguru initiations in some areas. There is good reason to assume that some songs circulate between these ethnic groups. I found similar songs among Kaguru and the Ngulu to the east; there is no reason to doubt that Kaguru share songs with Gogo to the west.

8. *Magegemela* refers to the long-tailed glossy starling, *Lamprotornis* spp.

9. Beauvoir's characterizations of femininity strike me as dubious, but I cite them as uncannily similar to views expressed by Kaguru. She says of a woman that "her body promises no precise conclusion to the act of love; and that is why coition is never quite terminated for her; it admits of no end. Male sex feeling rises like an arrow; when it reaches a certain height or threshold, it is fulfilled and dies abruptly in the orgasm; the pattern of the sexual act is finite and discontinuous" (1974: 442). "Because no definite term is set, woman's sex feelings extend toward infinity; it is often nervous or cardiac fatigue or psychic satiety that limits woman's erotic possibilities, rather than a specific gratification; even when overwhelmed, exhausted, she may never find full deliverance" (1974: 242).

10. Lederer is probably right to dismiss Freudian notions about women's alleged penis envy as "an invention of and a legacy from the 19th century" (Lederer 1968: 214–17); it seems alien to Kaguru thinking. Lederer is wrong to see frigidity rather than barrenness as the "universal" problem of women, regardless of culture. Unquestionably the single greatest sexual concern of Kaguru women is barrenness.

11. I did not learn whether Kaguru (like many premodern Europeans) saw female orgasm as a sine qua non of conception (Laquer 1990: 199).

12. The old Norman English word *potence*, referring to a supporting center pole, would be a perfect translation for *nguso*, were that English word not obsolete.

13. I assume that *muyombo* (*Brachystegia* spp.) and *musani* (*Combretum* spp.) are not the only woods used in fire making, but they are often the ones employed in making firesticks. I could not determine which was associated with male and which with female.

14. An alternative version of this song substitutes a sheep *(ng'holo)* for a wildcat *(nghanu)* or leopard *(duma)*.

15. An alternative version of this song substitutes Gogoland (Ugogo) in place of the bush *(kunyika)*.

16. Most informants maintained that all Kaguru men are keen to copulate with women whenever they can. A few admitted that some men might be impotent. After I had known Kaguru for six or seven years some admitted that a few men were homosexual, but they insisted that such Kaguru had learned such sexual proclivities from outsiders, Europeans and Arabs in towns and markets. A few Kaguru men enjoyed homosexual relations, but this was considered an unusual and secret pattern. This would not deter such men from marrying or fathering children. Even if such a man was a poor or ineffectual lover, his wife would still be able to become pregnant by others. For Kaguru, marriage is so important that sexual proclivity would not be a decisive factor in preventing it. I found even less willingness to discuss homosexuality among women. It was conceded that at girls' initiation women might teach initiates how copulation takes place by simulating it, either with an initiate or with one another while an initiate watched. I have no idea whether such reports were true, merely fantasies by male informants, or a case of my being put on by mischievous friends. The important difference remains that a Kaguru man unstirred by women would have difficulty achieving an effective erection whereas a Kaguru woman could become pregnant during an encounter in which she was indifferent (frigid or homosexual) or even hostile (rape). In contrast, a man must in some sense always have some psychic commitment to a sexual partner if he is to perform. This may well be hostile and unaffectionate, as in rape, but it must in some way stir his sexual imagination.

17. *Mutalawanda* is probably *Markhamia zanzibarica*. It is used for firewood and its leaves may be used to wipe things clean in lieu of a cloth.

18. Lévi-Strauss (1966: 145) cites this practice but carelessly misreads the ethnographic report and gets matters reversed for women, thereby missing the point.

19. At first I did not believe how strongly Kaguru took this prohibition about avoiding parents' sexuality and how it was obeyed even by young children. Then one day when I was staying in a Kaguru home with mischievous and inquisitive children, I lamented that I was worried about leaving my camera unattended. My host told me to put it on his and his wife's bed along with other valuables. My things were untouched during all my stay.

CHAPTER 8. CONCLUSION:
PERSON, TIME, AND ETHNICITY

1. When I first arrived in Ukaguru to do fieldwork, the local colonial commissioner told me I was welcome because my findings about traditional customs would facilitate his task. (We had very different ideas about how neutral researchers should be, so that by the end of my fieldwork he was no longer speaking to me.)

2. As Gray points out, both genders may be associated with nature, and presumably with culture as well (1979). While a very different society and culture, the Foi of Papua New Guinea are nicely shown to express their total culture in memorable moments of life crises in J. Weiner's study (1991). Weiner is particularly perceptive in relating ritual and symbols to space.

3. Lange notes how privacy of the family privatizes Rousseau's ideas of social relations.

Rousseau associated manipulation with women whereas both men and women are adept at it (1981: 264). Lange appears more perceptive here than Rousseau.

4. Lederer describes men's fear of women (1968: 4–6). Certainly each gender fears the other on account of the dependence yet difference between them. Such fear and dislike relate to resentment over loss of autonomy. Lederer cites many authorities to show that men and women are supposedly morally different (ibid.: 92–94). This may be the case for many societies, including the Kaguru, but this is because the two genders occupy different social situations, not because of any inherent characteristics.

5. Unfortunately, Bryk's judgment made many decades ago still applies: explanations as to why initiation takes the forms that it does still "furnish a splendid example of the versatility of human extravagant imagination, and are at the same time, a document of the ambivalent validity of casuistic argumentation" (1934: 92). Bryk surveyed the varied and contradictory explanations provided in his own day for why adolescent boys' (ibid.: 92–187) and girls' (ibid.: 288–99) bodies are mutilated and found these quite contradictory, muddled, and unconvincing.

6. Social analyses of initiation have not improved greatly since Webster. In a recent anthropological survey of initiation of adolescents Paige and Paige note that all basic explanatory theories of such ritual assume that the "real" purposes behind such practices are seldom if ever grasped by the participants (1981: 3). It is unfortunate that such callow functionalism still persists among anthropologists. The Paiges' catalogue many bizarre and dubious theories developed to explain initiation (ibid.: 1–78), but their own explanations are no better.

   Few would dispute the Paiges' contention that reproductive ritual is related to politics if by that they mean notions of morality and power. It is, however, doubtful whether surgical operations on the genitals demonstrate kin bonds because they imply trust, a strange argument advanced by the Paiges (ibid.: 257–58). After all, deception, harassment, and obfuscation are prominent in some of these rites, at least as practiced by Kaguru, so one has little reason to assume that initiators always inspire confidence. At best one can agree with Sanday that multifaceted changes are exhibited throughout the life cycle of both genders (1990: 8–9), though she fails to provide useful illustrations of this.

   Generalizing work such as that by the Paiges (1981) is vitiated by approaches that extract data out of cultural and social contexts in order to make superficial comparisons. The worst offenders of this sort, armchair psychologists, produce hotchpotches of ethnographic tidbits set adrift from their contextual moorings (e.g., Paige and Paige 1981; Schlegel and Barry 1979, 1980; Brown 1963, 1969; Whiting et al. 1958; Cohen 1964; Child and Child 1993: chapter 8). Such writers rely on the notoriously unreliable Human Relations Area Files (HRAF) or G. P. Murdock's World Ethnographic Sample. Rarely are such works produced by anyone who has demonstrated ethnographic skill and consequently is able to evaluate the sense of such varied reportage. These represent the crudest forms of functionalist determinism and slovenly comparative analyses. Norbeck et al. 1962 provides a useful methodological critique of this messy material, and Young 1962 provides a sociological analysis far more convincing than Whiting's hypothesizing.

7. I have made no attempt to survey the vast literature on the topic of initiation. I have cited what seems to me to be representative or useful. Some works may display enormous and far-ranging erudition, but this in no way guarantees any value, for example Rancour-Laferriere (1992). One of the best-known recent ethnographies of initiation displays such unconvincing accounts of one gender (women) at the inflation of the standing of the other (men), along with such an overreliance on violence as an explanation, that I discount it (Bloch 1986). Probably the best accounts of initiation of adolescents in continental Africa are Droogers 1980 (compare Beidelman 1982a); Heald 1982, 1986; Kratz 1990a, 1990b, 1993, 1994 (compare Beidelman 1995); Ottenberg 1989; Richards 1956; and Turner 1962a, 1964, 1967 (compare Beidelman 1968).

8. One could simplemindedly accept Diderot's witty view of how men and women are physical inversions of one another (1956: 140–41; Laquer 1990: viii); or one might say about sex's relation to gender what Simmel said about sex's relation to marriage: "This element is not sufficient to realize the form" (1950: 132n.).

9. Can one lightly dismiss Money's flat assurance that there seems to be a pervasive biological bias toward female nurturance (1980: 5)?

10. It may be that Frank's glib characterization is apt and a parallel exists between psychotherapy and initiation by which rituals construct "enduring modifications in the patient's assumptive world that will enable him to function more effectively" (1961: 75). Even if this is so, it is only one aspect, not their essence.

11. Among East Africanists, Heald has stressed how violence at male initiation evokes a future predisposition for violence by men (1986: 75). I am not convinced that the violence of genital mutilation of women and men necessarily creates particularly aggressive adults. In any case, her account is unconvincing on other grounds (Beidelman 1990).

12. An anthropological bias toward an integrative model of ritual is as old as Durkheim and Robertson Smith. It is possibly reinforced by researchers influenced by Freudian and social psychology. One may gain some idea of how hoary and pervasive these notions are by considering such diverse but well-known writers as Festinger (1962: 1) and Wallace (1966: 239–42), who both argue for the attractions of unitary models in dispelling cognitive dissonance.

13. Kapferer (1979: 7), inspired by Goffman, writes of how varied rituals use space to modify the roles of actors and audience by providing changing foci of perception. His argument anticipates my own.

14. By now readers may have noticed that I use the terms *ritual* and *ceremony* in an overlapping manner. For me, ceremonies are particularly elaborate affairs that invariably contain rituals. When ritual actions qualify as ceremony seems arbitrary to me, though certainly contemporary Kaguru weddings, cutting of initiates, and funerals are ceremonies, as are the welcoming-home celebrations of recovered novices. Formalized greetings between two Kaguru or formal ways by which one visits another's household or eats with strangers are not ceremonies, but they do seem to be kinds of rituals.

15. Writing of French villagers, Berger remarks: "The peasant's ingenuity makes him open to change, his imagination demands continuity" (1979: 208).

16. Jackson has promoted an anthropology of body sense, noting that many anthropologists have overemphasized thoughts about body imagery and symbolism to the

detriment of grasping how the body conveys its own meanings through its movements, bearing, and motor skills (1983a).

17. The meanings I have found in Kaguru symbols are greatly based on what Kaguru themselves said. Yet my analyses spring from my need to translate Kaguru explanations and meanings into sociological terminology and therefore inevitably appear different from what Kaguru would say. Furthermore, my need to explain as a Westerner is different from a Kaguru's. A Kaguru needs no explanation of many symbols because he or she already finds these self-evident. Consequently I, unlike Kaguru, must detail Kaguru quotidian life and surroundings. There are, however, features of my analyses that go far beyond Kaguru explanations. An anecdote illustrates some of the difficulties involved in such cross-cultural decoding. In an early essay (1961a) I analyzed a Kaguru story about hyena and hare in such a way that I concluded that Kaguru males may profit socially by the deaths of maternal kin. I am convinced that this is unquestionably demonstrated by the logic of Kaguru social organization and the personal motives it generates. Yet no Kaguru would ever acknowledge my arguments since that would question one of the highest values in Kaguru social life, the allegiance and affection between males and their maternal elders. When I mentioned my theory to Kaguru, they vigorously rejected it. The violence of their rejection might be interpreted not as a sign that I was wrong but as a reflection of the degree to which my analysis touched a tender spot in their social thinking. One can never know whether my analysis was perceptive or wrong, any more than a patient can prove that a psychiatrist's analysis that she or he rejects is off the wall or simply so painfully accurate that it cannot be acknowledged. In the long run, then, the value of any social analysis must depend upon two things: how well the analyst has utilized all of the data, and how persuasive (attractive) the reader finds the argument. The best statement I know on this topic is Victor Turner's (1964: 27–29).

18. Needham makes similar observations regarding how we may approach categories of kinship (1975).

Bibliography

By necessity, by proclivity, —and by delight, we all quote.
R. W. Emerson, *Quotation and Originality*

My quarrel with him is that his works contain nothing worth quoting; and a book that furnishes no quotations is, me judice, no book—it is a plaything.
Thomas Love Peacock, the Rev. Dr. Follicott in *Crotchet Castle*

Allen, J.
    1985   The Category of the Person: A Reading of Mauss' Last Essay, pp. 25–45 in M. Carrithers, S. Collins, and S. Lukes (eds.), *The Category of the Person*, Cambridge University Press, Cambridge.

Anderson, Benedict
    1991   *Imagined Communities* [1983], revised edition, Verso, New York.

Ardener, Shirley (ed.)
    1981   *Women and Space*, St. Martin's Press, New York.

Aronson, Elliot, and Judson Mille
    1959   The Effects of Severity of Initiation on Liking for a Group, *Journal of Abnormal and Social Psychology* 59: 177–81.

Bachelard, Gaston
    1964   *The Psychoanalysis of Fire* [*Le Psychoanalyse du feu*, 1958], Beacon Press, Boston.
    1969   *The Poetics of Space* [*La Poétique de l'espace*, 1958], Beacon Press, Boston.

Bakhtin, Mikhail
    1984   *Rabelais and His World* [*Tvorschestvo Fransua Rable*, 1965], Indiana University Press, Bloomington.

Barber, Benjamin R.
    1978   Rousseau and the Paradoxes of the Dramatic Imagination, *Daedalus* 107, 3: 79–92.

Barkan, Leonard
    1975   *Nature's Work of Art: The Human Body as Image of the World*, Yale University Press, New Haven.

Bateson, Gregory
    1958   *Naven*, second edition, Stanford University Press, Stanford.

Beauvoir, Simone de
    1974   *The Second Sex* [*Le Deuxième sexe*, 1949], Vintage Books, New York.

Beidelman, T. O.
    1961a   Hyena and Rabbit: A Kaguru Representation of Matrilineal Relations, *Africa* 31: 61–74.
    1961b   Kaguru Justice and the Concept of Legal Fictions, *Journal of African Law* 5: 3–20.
    1961c   Umwano und Ukaguru Students' Association: Zwei stammespartikularische Bewegungen in einem Hauptlingstum in Tanganyika, *Anthropos* 58: 818–45. Republished in English translation as Umwano and Ukaguru Students' Association: Two Tribalistic Movements in a Tanganyika Chiefdom, pp. 303–26 in John Middleton (ed.), *Black Africa*, Macmillan, New York.
    1961d   Beer Drinking and Cattle Theft in Ukaguru: Intertribal Relations in a Tanganyika Chiefdom, *American Anthropologist* 54: 534–59.
    1961e   A Note on the Kamba of Kilosa District, *Tanganyika Notes and Records* 57: 181–94.
    1962a   A History of Ukaguru, Kilosa District: 1857–1916, *Tanganyika Notes and Records* 58 & 59: 11–39.
    1962b   Iron-working in Ukaguru, *Tanganyika Notes and Records* 58 & 59: 288–89.
    1963a   Five Kaguru Texts, *Anthropos* 58: 737–72.
    1963b   The Blood Covenant and the Concept of Blood in Ukaguru, *Africa* 33: 321–42.
    1963c   Kaguru Omens: An East African People's Concepts of the Unusual, Unnatural, and Supernormal, *Anthropological Quarterly* 46: 43–59.
    1963d   Some Kaguru Riddles, *Man* 63: 158–60.
    1964a   Three Kaguru Tales of the Living and the Dead: The Ideology of Kaguru Ancestral Propitiation, *Journal of the Royal Anthropological Institute* 94: 109–37.
    1964b   Intertribal Insult and Opprobrium in an East African Chiefdom (Ukaguru), *Southwestern Journal of Anthropology* 20: 359–92.

1964c   Pig *(Guluwe)*: An Essay on Ngulu Sexual Symbolism and Ceremony, *Southwestern Journal of Anthropology* 20: 359–92.

1964d   Ten Kaguru Texts: Tales of an East African Bantu People, *Journal of African Languages* 3: 1–37.

1965a   Six Kaguru Tales, *Zeitschrift für Ethnologie* 90: 17–41.

1965b   Notes on Boys' Initiation among the Ngulu, *Man* 65: 145–47.

1966a   *Utani:* Some Kaguru Notions of Death, Sexuality, and Affinity, *Southwestern Journal of Anthropology* 22: 354–80.

1966b   Swazi Royal Ritual, *Africa* 36: 373–405.

1966c   Intertribal Tensions in Some Local Government Courts in Colonial Tanganyika, Part 1, *Journal of African Law* 10: 118–30.

1967a   *The Matrilineal Peoples of Eastern Tanzania*, International African Institute, London.

1967b   Intertribal Tensions in Some Local Government Courts in Colonial Tanganyika, Part 2, *Journal of African Law* 11: 26–45.

1968   Review of Turner, *The Forest of Symbols*, *Africa* 38: 483–84.

1969   Addenda and Corrigenda to the Bibliography of the Matrilineal Peoples of Eastern Tanzania, *Africa* 39: 186–88.

1970   Myth, Legend, and Oral History, *Anthropos* 65: 74–97.

1971a   Kaguru Descent Groups, *Anthropos* 66: 373–96.

1971b   *The Kaguru*, Holt, Rinehart, and Winston, New York. Republished Waveland Press, Prospect Heights, 1983.

1971c   Some Kaguru Notions about Incest and Other Sexual Prohibitions, pp. 181–201 in Rodney Needham (ed.), *Rethinking Kinship and Marriage*, A.S.A. Monograph 11, Tavistock, London.

1972a   The Kaguru House, *Anthropos* 67: 1–18.

1972b   Review of Swantz, *Ritual and Symbols in Transitional Zaramo Society*, *Africa* 42: 356–57.

1972–3   Kaguru of Central Tanzania, pp. 234–42, Vol. II, and pp. 262–73, Vol. III, in A. Molnos (ed.), *Cultural Source Material for Population Planning in East Africa*, East African Publishing House, Nairobi.

1973   Dual Symbolic Classification among the Kaguru, pp. 128–66 in Rodney Needham (ed.), *Right and Left*, University of Chicago Press, Chicago.

1974a   Further Addenda to the Bibliography of the Matrilineal Peoples of Eastern Tanzania, *Africa* 44: 297–99.

1974b   The Bird Motif in Kaguru Folklore, *Anthropos* 69: 162–89.

1975   Kaguru Names and Naming, *Journal of Anthropological Research* 30: 261–92.

1978   Chiefship in Ukaguru, *The International Journal of African Historical Studies* 11: 227–46.

1979   Kaguru Oral Literature: Discussion, *Anthropos* 74: 497–529.

1980a   The Moral Imagination of the Kaguru: Some Thoughts on Tricksters, Translation and Comparative Analysis, *American Ethnologist* 7: 27–42.

1980b   Women and Men in Two East African Societies, pp. 143–64 in Ivan Karp and Charles Bird (eds.), *Explorations in African Thought*, Indiana University Press, Bloomington.

1981a   Third Addendum to the Bibliography of the Matrilineal Peoples of Eastern Tanzania, *Anthropos* 76: 864–65.

1981b   Review of Grohs, *Kisazi*, *Africa* 51: 880–81.

1982a   Review of Droogers, *The Dangerous Journey*, *Anthropos* 79: 609–11.

1982b   *Colonial Evangelism*, Indiana University Press, Bloomington.

1982c   The Organization and Maintenance of Caravans by the Church Missionary Society in Tanzania in the Nineteenth Century, *The International Journal of African Historical Studies* 15: 601–71.

1986   *Moral Imagination in Kaguru Modes of Thought*, Indiana University Press, Bloomington. Republished Smithsonian Institution Press, Washington, D.C., 1993.

1987   Circumcision, *The Encyclopedia of Religion* 3: 511–14.

1988a   Fourth Addendum to the Bibliography of the Matrilineal Peoples of Eastern Tanzania, *Anthropos* 83: 558.

1988b   Review of Moore, *Space, Text, and Gender*, *Anthropos* 83: 277–78.

1989a   Review of Clifford, *The Predicament of Culture*, *Anthropos* 84: 263–67.

1989b   Agonistic Exchange: Homeric Reciprocity and the Heritage of Simmel and Mauss, *Cultural Anthropology* 4: 26–59.

1990   Gisu Violence: A Hobbesian Account, *Current Anthropology* 31: 480–81.

1991a   Containing Time: Rites of Passage and Moral Space, or Bachelard among the Kaguru, *Anthropos* 86: 443–61.

1991b   Review of Felix, *Mwana Hiti*, *Anthropos* 86: 606–9.

1993   Secrecy and Society: The Paradox of Knowing and the Knowing of Paradox, pp. 41–47 in Mary Nooter (ed.), *Secrecy: African Arts of Concealment and Ambiguity*, Museum of African Art, New York. Republished in *Program of African Studies* (Northwestern University) 3, 5 (1992): 6–7.

1994   Review of Parkin, *Sacred Void*, *Journal of Religion in Africa* 24: 62–64.

1995   Review of Kratz, *Affecting Performance*, *Journal of the Royal Anthropological Institute* 1: 446–47.

Beidelman, T. O., and E. H. Winter

1967   Tanganyika, pp. 57–204 in J. H. Steward (ed.), *Contemporary Change in Traditional Societies*, Vol. I, University of Illinois Press, Urbana.

Bellman, Beryl L.

1981   The Paradox of Secrecy, *Human Studies* 4: 1–24.

1984   *The Language of Secrecy*, Rutgers University Press, New Brunswick.

Belmont, Nicole

1979   *Arnold van Gennep* [1974], University of Chicago Press, Chicago.

Berger, John

1979   *Pig Earth*, Pantheon Books, New York.

Bernheimer, Richard

    1962   *Wild Men in the Middle Ages*, Harvard University Press, Cambridge.

Blacking, John

    1985   Movement, Dance, Music, and the Venda Girls' Initiation Cycle, pp. 64–91 in Paul Spencer (ed.), *Society and the Dance*, Cambridge University Press, Cambridge.

Bloch, Marc

    1964   *The Historian's Craft [Apologie pour l'histoire*, 1952], Vintage Press, New York.

Bloch, Maurice

    1986   *From Blessing to Violence*, Cambridge University Press, Cambridge.

Bloch, Maurice, and Jean H. Bloch

    1980   Women and the Dialectic of Nature in Eighteenth-Century French Thought, pp. 25–41 in Carol MacCormack and Marilyn Strathern (eds.), *Nature, Culture and Gender*, Cambridge University Press, Cambridge.

Bloom, Allan

    1968   Interpretive Essay, pp. 307–436 in *The Republic of Plato*, Basic Books, New York.

    1979   Introduction, pp. 3–28 in J.-J. Rousseau, *Émile, or on Education*, Basic Books, New York.

Bok, Sissela

    1982   *Secrecy: On the Ethics of Concealment and Revelation*, Pantheon Books, New York.

Bourdieu, Pierre

    1977   *Outline of a Theory of Practice [Esquisse d'une théorie de la pratique*, 1972], Cambridge University Press, Cambridge.

Bradbury, Malcolm

    1987   *My Strange Quest for Mensonge*, King Penguin, New York.

Brain, James L.

    1969   Matrilineal Descent and Marital Stability: A Tanzanian Case, *Journal of Asian and African Studies* 4: 122–31.

    1977   Sex, Incest, and Death: Initiation Rites Reconsidered, *Current Anthropology* 188: 191–208.

    1978   Symbolic Rebirth: The *Mwali* Rite among the Luguru of Eastern Tanzania, *Africa* 48: 176–88.

    1980   Boys' Initiation Rites among the Luguru of Eastern Tanzania, *Anthropos* 75: 369–82.

    1988   Male Menstruation in History and Anthropology, *The Journal of Psychohistory* 15: 311–23.

Brandt, Elizabeth A.

    1980   On Secrecy and the Control of Knowledge: Taos Pueblo, pp. 123–46 in Stanton K. Tefft (ed.), *Secrecy*, Human Science Press, New York.

Briggs, J. E.
   1918   *In the East African War Zone*, Church Missionary Society, London.

Brown, Judith K.
   1963   A Cross-Cultural Study of Female Initiation Rites, *American Anthropologist*
          65: 837–53.
   1969   Adolescent Initiation Rites among Preliterate Peoples, pp. 59–68 in Robert
          F. Grinder (ed.), *Studies in Adolescence*, second edition, Macmillan, London.

Bryk, Felix
   1934   *Circumcision in Man and Woman*, American Ethnological Press, New York.

Buckley, Thomas, and Alma Gottlieb
   1988   A Critical Appraisal of Theories of Menstrual Symbolism, pp. 1–53 in
          Thomas Buckley and Alma Gottlieb (eds.), *Blood Magic: The Anthropology of
          Menstruation*, University of California Press, Berkeley.

Burke, Kenneth
   1957   *The Philosophy of Literary Form* [1941], Vintage Books, New York.
   1962   *A Grammar of Motives* [1945] *and a Rhetoric of Motives* [1950], Meridian
          Books, New York.

Caplan, A. P.
   1976   Boys' Circumcision and Girls' Puberty Rites among the Swahili of Mafia Is-
          land, Tanzania, *Africa* 46: 21–33.

Carlyle, Thomas
   1896   *Sartor Resartus* [1836], Atheneum, Boston.

Cassirer, Ernst
   1947   Kant and Rousseau, pp. 1–60 in *Rousseau, Kant, Goethe: Two Essays*, Princeton
          University Press, Princeton.

Chapple, Elliot D., and Carleton S. Coon
   1942   *Principles of Anthropology*, Henry Holt, New York.

Child, Alice B., and Irwin L. Child
   1993   *Religion and Magic in the Life of Traditional Peoples*, Prentice Hall, Englewood
          Cliffs.

Clifford, James
   1988   *The Predicament of Culture*, Harvard University Press, Cambridge.

Cohen, Yehudi A.
   1964   The Establishment of Identity in a Social Nexus, *American Anthropologist* 66:
          529–51.

Coleridge, Samuel Taylor
   1871   Table-talk [8 July 1827], pp. 289–90 in Professor Sheed (ed.), *The Complete
          Works of Samuel Taylor Coleridge*, Vol. VI, Harper and Brothers, New York.

Collier, Jane Fishburne, and Sylvia Junko Yanagisako
   1987a   Introduction, pp. 1–13 in J. F. Collier and S. J. Yanagisako (eds.), *Gender and*

Kinship: Essays toward a Unified Analysis, Stanford University Press, Stanford.
1987b   Analysis of Gender and Kinship, pp. 14–50 in J. F. Collier and S. J. Yanagisako (eds.), *Gender and Kinship: Essays toward a Unified Analysis,* Stanford
University Press, Stanford.

Collingwood, R. G.
1958   *The Principles of Art* [1938], Oxford University Press, New York.

Connerton, Paul
1989   *How Societies Remember,* Cambridge University Press, Cambridge.

Cory, A. [Hans]
1944   Figurines Used in the Initiation Ceremonies of the Ngulu of Tanganyika
Territory, *Africa* 14: 459–65.

Cory, Hans
1947   Jando, Part 1, *Journal of the Royal Anthropological Institute* 77: 159–68.
1948   Jando, Part 2, *Journal of the Royal Anthropological Institute* 78: 81–94.
1956   *African Figurines,* Faber and Faber, London.

Csikszentmihalyi, Mihaly, and Eugene Rochberg-Halton
1981   *The Meaning of Things,* Cambridge University Press, Cambridge.

Culwick, G. M.
1939   New Ways for Old in the Treatment of Adolescent African Girls, *Africa* 12:
425–530.

Delaney, Janice, Mary Jane Lupton, and Emily Loth
1988   *The Curse: A Cultural History of Menstruation,* University of Illinois Press,
Urbana.

Diderot, Denis
1956   *Rameau's Nephew and Other Works,* Doubleday Anchor Books, Garden City.

diLeonardo, Michaela
1991   Introduction: Gender, Culture, and Political Economy, pp. 1–48 in M.
diLeonardo (ed.), *Gender at the Crossroads of Knowledge,* University of California Press, Berkeley.

Dooley, C. T.
1936   Child-Training among the Wanguru: III. Moral Education, *Primitive Man*
9: 1–12.

Douglas, Norman
1967   *Some Limericks* [1928], Grove Press, New York.

Doxtater, Dennis
1984   Spatial Opposition in Non-Discursive Expression: Architecture as Ritual
Process, *Canadian Journal of Anthropology* 4: 1–17.

Droogers, André
1980   *The Dangerous Journey: Symbolic Aspects of Boys' Initiation among the Wagenia
of Kisangani, Zaire,* Afrika-Studiecentrum, The Hague.

duBois, Page
    1988   *Sowing the Body*, University of Chicago Press, Chicago.
Durkheim, Émile
    1949   *The Division of Labor* [*De la division du travail social*, 1893], Free Press, Glencoe.
    1952   *Suicide* [*Le Suicide*, 1897], Routledge and Kegan Paul, London.
    1956   *Education and Sociology* [*Éducation et sociologie*, 1922], Free Press, New York.
    1960   Rousseau's Social Contract [*Le Contrat de Rousseau*, 1918], pp. 63–148 in *Montesquieu and Rousseau*, University of Michigan Press, Ann Arbor.
    1961   *Moral Education* [*L'Éducation morale*, 1925], Free Press, New York.
    1977   *The Evolution of Educational Thought* [*L'Évolution pédagogique en France*, 1938], Routledge and Kegan Paul, London.
    1979a   A Discussion on Sex Education [*L'Éducation sexuelle*, 1911], pp. 140–48 in S. F. Pickering (ed.), *Durkheim: Essays on Morals and Education*, Routledge and Kegan Paul, London.
    1979b   Rousseau on Educational Theory [*La 'Pédagogie' de Rousseau*, 1919], pp. 162–94 in S. F. Pickering (ed.), *Durkheim: Essays on Morals and Education*, Routledge and Kegan Paul, London.
Durkheim, Émile, with F. Buisson
    1979   Childhood [*Enfance*, 1911], pp. 149–54 in S. F. Pickering (ed.), *Durkheim: Essays on Morals and Education*, Routledge and Kegan Paul, London.
Durkheim, Émile, and Marcel Mauss
    1963   *Primitive Classification* [*De quelques formes primitives de classification*, *Année sociologique* 1901–2 (1903)], Cohen and West, London.
East African Statistical Department
    1958   *Tanganyika Population Census*, Parts 1 and 2, East African Statistical Department, Nairobi.
Ehrenrich, Barbara, and Deidre English
    1978   *For Her Own Good*, Doubleday Paperback, New York.
Eliade, Mircea
    1965   *Rites and Symbols of Initiation* [1958], Harper and Row, New York.
Erikson, Erik
    1958   *Young Man Luther*, Norton, New York.
    1963   *Childhood and Society* [1950], second edition, Norton, New York.
Evans-Pritchard, E. E.
    1952   Letter to E. E. Evans-Pritchard from L. Lévy-Bruhl, *British Journal of Sociology* 3: 117–23.
    1965   The Dance [1928], pp. 165–90 in *Women in Primitive Societies and Other Essays in Social Anthropology*, Faber and Faber, London.
Falassi, A.
    1987   Festival: Definition and Morphology, pp. 1–10 in A. Falassi (ed.), *Time Out of Time: Essays on the Festival*, University of New Mexico Press, Albuquerque.

Faunce, Sarah, and Linda Nochlin
    1988   *Courbet Reconsidered*, Yale University Press for the Brooklyn Museum, New Haven.

Febvre, Lucien
    1982   *The Problem of Unbelief in the Sixteenth Century: The Religion of Rabelais* [*Le Problème de l'incroyance au XVIe siecle: La Religion de Rabelais*, 1942], Harvard University Press, Cambridge.

Felix, Marc L.
    1990   *Mwana Hiti*, F. Jahn, Munich.

Felix, Marc L., and Maria Kecskési
    1994   *Tanzania, Meisterwerke afrikanischer Skulptur*, F. Jahn, Munich.

Festinger, Leon
    1962   *A Theory of Cognitive Dissonance* [1957], Stanford University Press, Stanford.

Fortes, Meyer
    1965   Some Reflections on Ancestor Worship in Africa, pp. 112–44 in M. Fortes and G. Dieterlen (eds.), *African Systems of Thought*, Oxford University Press, London.

Foucault, Michel
    1980   *The History of Sexuality, Vol. I: An Introduction* [*La Volonté de savoir*, 1976], Vintage Books, New York.

Frank, Jerome
    1961   *Persuasion and Healing*, Johns Hopkins University Press, Baltimore.

Fried, Martha N., and Morton H. Fried
    1981   *Transitions*, Penguin Books, Harmondsworth.

Frye, Northrop
    1963   *Fables of Identity*, Harvest Books, New York.
    1982   *The Great Code: The Bible and Literature*, Harcourt Brace, New York.

Gal, Susan
    1991   Between Speech and Silence, pp. 175–203 in M. di Leonardo (ed.), *Gender at the Crossroads of Knowledge*, University of California Press, Berkeley.

Gallie, W. B.
    1964   *Philosophy and the Historical Understanding*, Chatto and Windus, London.

Gell, Alfred
    1975   *Metamorphosis of the Cassowaries*, Athlone Press, University of London, London.

Gilmore, David D.
    1990   *Manhood in the Making: Cultural Concepts of Masculinity*, Yale University Press, New Haven.

Ginzburg, Carlo
    1986   Clues: Roots of an Evidential Paradigm [Spie: Radici di une paradigma

indizidrio, 1979], pp. 96–125 in *Clues, Myths, and the Historical Method*, Johns Hopkins University Press, Baltimore.

Gluckman, Max
    1962   Les Rites de passage, pp. 1–52 in Max Gluckman (ed.), *Essays in the Ritual of Social Relations*, Manchester University Press, Manchester.

Goffman, Erving
    1959   *The Presentation of Self in Everyday Life*, Doubleday Anchor Books, Garden City.
    1967   *Interaction Ritual*, Doubleday Anchor Books, Garden City.
    1974   *Frame Analysis*, Harper, New York.

Gonzales-Crussi, F.
    1985   On Male Genital Anatomy, pp. 110–29 in *Notes of an Anatomist*, Harcourt Brace Jovanovich, New York.

Goudsblom, Johan
    1992   *Fire and Civilization*, Allen Lane, Penguin Press, New York.

Gray, J. Patrick
    1979   The Relationship of Males to Nature and Culture, *Anthropology* 3: 27–46.

Greene, Thomas H.
    1982   *The Light in Troy*, Yale University Press, New Haven.

Grohs, E.
    1980   *Kisazi: Reiferiten der Mädchen bei den Zigua und Ngulu Ost-Tanzanias*, Mainzer Afrika-Studien 3, Diedrich Reimer, Berlin.

Gurvitch, Georges
    1964   *The Spectrum of Time* [*La Multiplicité des temps sociaux*, 1961], Reidel, Dordrecht.

Gusdorf, Georges
    1965   *Speaking* [*La Parole*, 1953], Northwestern University Press, Evanston.

Halbwachs, Maurice
    1980   *The Collective Memory* [*La Mémoire collective*, 1950], Harper and Row, New York.
    1991   The Social Frameworks of Memory [*Les Cadres sociaux de la mémoire*, 1925], pp. 35–189 in Lewis A. Coser (ed.), *On Collective Memory*, University of Chicago Press, Chicago.

Hallowell, A. Irving
    1967   The Self and Its Environment [1954], pp. 75–110 in *Culture and Experience* [1955], Schocken Books, New York.

Hampson, Norman
    1991   A Guide without a Compass, *Times Literary Supplement*, 5 July: 23.

Harrod, James R.
    1981   The Bow: A Techno-Mythic Hermeneutic—Ancient Greece and the Mesolithic, *The Journal of the American Academy of Religion* 49: 425–46.

Hart, Ray
    1973   The Poiesis of Place, *The Journal of Religion* 53: 36– 47.

Hasenmueller, Christine
    1978   Panofsky, Iconography, and Semiotics, *The Journal of Aesthetics and Art Criticism* 35: 289–301.

Havelock, Eric
    1963   *Preface to Plato*, Harvard University Press, Cambridge.

Heald, Suzette
    1982   The Making of Men: The Relevance of Vernacular Psychology to the Interpretation of a Gisu Ritual, *Africa* 52: 15–35.
    1986   The Ritual Use of Violence: Circumcision among the Gisu of Uganda, pp. 70–85 in D. Riches (ed.), *The Anthropology of Violence*, Basil Blackwell, Oxford.

Heller, Peter
    1976   Nietzsche in His Relation to Voltaire and Rousseau, pp. 109-33 in James C. O'Flaherty, Timothy F. Sellner, and Robert M. Helm (eds.), *Studies in Nietzsche and the Classical Tradition*, University of North Carolina Press, Chapel Hill.

Helm, Robert M.
    1976   Plato in the Thought of Nietzsche and Augustine, pp. 16–32 in James C. O'Flaherty, Timothy F. Sellner, and Robert M. Helm (eds.), *Studies in Nietzsche and the Classical Tradition*, University of North Carolina Press, Chapel Hill.

Henderson, Jeffrey
    1975   *The Maculate Muse: Obscene Language in Attic Comedy*, Yale University Press, New Haven.

Hirst, Paul Q.
    1985   Power/Knowledge—Constructed Space and the Subject, pp. 171–91 in Richard Fardon (ed.), *Power and Knowledge: Anthropological and Sociological Approaches*, Scottish Academic Press, Edinburgh.

Horowitz, Asher
    1987   *Rousseau, Nature, and History*, University of Toronto Press, Toronto.

Howard, Richard
    1988   The Mapplethorpe Effect, pp. 152–59 in Richard Marshall, *Mapplethorpe*, Whitney Museum of American Art, New York, and Little Brown, Boston.

Hughes, John A.
    1977   Wittgenstein and Social Science: Matters of Interpretation, *The Sociological Review* 25: 721–41.

Husband, Timothy
    1980   *The Wild Man: Medieval Myth and Symbolism*, The Metropolitan Museum of Art, New York.

Hutton, Patrick H.
    1988   Collective Memory and Collective Mentalities: The Halbwachs-Ariès Connection, *Historical Reflections* 15: 311–22.

1993   *History as an Art of Memory*, University Press of New England, Hanover.

Jackson, Michael

    1983a   Knowledge of the Body, *Man* 18 (n.s.): 327–45.

    1983b   Thinking through the Body: An Essay on Understanding Metaphor, *Social Analysis* 14: 127–49.

    1989   *Paths toward a Clearing*, Indiana University Press, Bloomington.

James, William

    1948   *Psychology* [1890], Fine Editions Press, Cleveland.

Jeanneret, Michel

    1991   *A Feast of Words* [*Des mets et des mots*, 1987], University of Chicago Press, Chicago.

Jennings, Theodore W.

    1982   On Ritual Knowledge, *The Journal of Religion* 62: 111–127.

Johnson, Mark

    1991   The Imaginative Basis of Meaning and Cognition, pp. 74–86 in Susanne Küchler and Walter Melion (eds.), *Images of Memory*, Smithsonian Institution Press, Washington, D.C.

Kant, Immanuel

    1983   Speculative Beginnings of Human History [Mathmasslichen Anfang der Menschengeschichte, 1786], pp. 49–60 in *Perpetual Peace and Other Essays on Politics, History and Morals*, Hackett Publishing, Indianapolis.

    1988   Idea for a Universal History from a Cosmopolitan Point of View [Idee zu allgemeinen Geschichte in Weltbürgerlicher Absicht, 1784], pp. 415–25 in *Kant, Selections*, Macmillan, New York.

Kapferer, Bruce

    1979   Introduction: Ritual Process and the Transformation of Context, *Social Analysis* 1: 3–19.

Karp, Ivan

    1987   Laughter at Marriage: Subversion in Performance, pp. 137–54 in David Parkin and David Nyamwaya (eds.), *Transformations of African Marriage*, Manchester University Press, Manchester.

Kirk, G. S.

    1974   *The Nature of Greek Myths*, Penguin Books, Harmondsworth.

Kratz, Corinne A.

    1990a   Solidarity and the Secrets of Sight and Sound, *American Ethnologist* 17: 449–69.

    1990b   Persuasive Suggestions and Reassuring Promises, *Journal of American Folklore* 103: 42–67.

    1993   "We've Always Done It Like This . . . Except for a Few Details": "Tradition" and "Innovation" in Okiek Ceremonies, *Comparative Studies in Society and History* 35: 30–65.

1994   *Affecting Performance*, Smithsonian Institution Press, Washington, D.C.

Kris, Ernst
1953   *Psychoanalytic Explorations in Art*, Allen and Unwin, London.

Kundera, Milan
1991   In Saint Garta's Shadow, *Times Literary Supplement*, 24 May: 3–5.

La Fontaine, Jean
1985   *Initiation*, Penguin Books, Harmondsworth.

Lange, Lynda
1981   Rousseau and Modern Feminism, *Social Theory and Practice* 7: 345–77.

Laquer, Thomas
1990   *Making Sex: Body and Gender from the Greeks to Freud*, Harvard University Press, Cambridge.

Last, J. T.
1883   A Visit to the Wa-Itumba Iron-Workers and the Mangaheri, near Mamboia, in East Central Africa, *Proceedings of the Royal Geographical Society* 5: 581–92.
1886   *Grammar of the Kagúru Language*, Society for Promoting Christian Knowledge, London.

Lederer, Wolfgang
1968   *The Fear of Women*, Harvest Books, Harcourt Brace Jovanovich, New York.

Leenhardt, Maurice
1975   Preface, pp. xi–xxiv in L. Lévy-Bruhl, *The Notebooks on Primitive Mentality*, Basil Blackwell, Oxford.

LeGoff, Jacques
1992   *History and Memory* [*Storiae memoria*, 1977, 1979, 1980, 1981], Columbia University Press, New York.

Levin, Max
1957   Wit and Schizophrenic Thinking, *American Journal of Psychiatry* 111: 917–23.

Levine, Donald N.
1985   *The Flight from Ambiguity*, University of Chicago Press, Chicago.

Lévi-Strauss, Claude
1960   The Family, pp. 261–85 in Harry Shapiro (ed.), *Man, Culture, and Society*, Oxford University Press, New York.
1963   *Totemism* [*Le Totémisme aujourd'hui*, 1962], Beacon Press, Boston.
1966   *The Savage Mind* [*La Pensée sauvage*, 1962], Weidenfeld and Nicolson, London.
1974   *Tristes Tropiques* [1955], Atheneum, New York.

Lewin, Kurt
1936   *Principles of Topological Psychology*, McGraw-Hill, New York.

Lewis, C. S.
1990   *Studies in Words* [1960], Cambridge University Press, Cambridge.

Lienhardt, R. G.
    1985   Self: Public, Private: Some African Representations, pp. 141–55 in M. Car-
            rithers, S. Collins, and S. Lukes (eds.), *The Category of the Person*, Cambridge
            University Press, Cambridge.

Loizos, Peter
    1980   Images of Man, pp. 231–39 in J. Cherfas and R. Lewis (eds.), *Not Work
            Alone*, Sage Publications, Beverly Hills.

Lonsdale, John
    1992   The Moral Economy of Mau Mau: Wealth, Poverty, and Civic Virtues in
            Kikuyu Political Thought, pp. 315–504 in Bruce Berman and John Lonsdale
            (eds.), *Unhappy Valley*, Vol. II, Ohio University Press, Athens.

Looby, Christopher
    1995   Flowers of Manhood: Race, Sex, and Floriculture from Thomas Wentworth
            Higginson to Robert Mapplethorpe, *Criticism* 37: 109–56.

MacCormack, Carol P.
    1980   Nature, Culture, and Gender: A Critique, pp. 1–24 in Carol P. MacCormack
            and Marilyn Strathern (eds.), *Nature, Culture, and Gender*, Cambridge Uni-
            versity Press, Cambridge.

Mathé, Jean
    1978   *Leonardo da Vinci: Anatomical Drawings*, Miller Graphics, New York.

Matthew, St.
    1885   *Nsachilo Nswamu kwa Mattayo kwa Nongwa ya Kaguru* [translation of the Book
            of Matthew into Chikaguru], British and Foreign Bible Society, London.

Mauss, Marcel
    1979a   [with the collaboration of Henri Beuchat] *Seasonal Variations of the Eskimo*
            [*Essais sur les variations saisonnières des sociétés Eskimos: Études de morphologie so-
            ciale*, 1904–5], Routledge and Kegan Paul, London.
    1979b   Body Techniques [Les Techniques du corps, 1935], pp. 55–123 in *Sociology
            and Psychology*, Routledge and Kegan Paul, London.
    1979c   A Category of the Human: The Notion of Person, the Notion of the Per-
            son, the Notion of "Self" [Une Catégorie de l'esprit humain: La Notion de
            personne, celle de "moi," 1938], pp. 57–94 in *Sociology and Psychology*, Rout-
            ledge and Kegan Paul, London.

Mead, George Herbert
    1956   *The Social Psychology of George Herbert Mead* [1934–38], ed. Anselm Strauss,
            University of Chicago Press, Chicago.

Middleton, John
    1987   The Notion of Secrecy in Lugbara Thought, pp. 25–43 in Kees Bolk (ed.),
            Secrecy in Religions, Brill, Leiden.

Miller, Toby
    1995   A Short History of the Penis, *Social Text* 43: 1–26.

Money, John
    1980   *Love and Love Sickness: The Science of Sex, Gender Difference, and Pair-Bonding*, Johns Hopkins University Press, Baltimore.

Montaigne, Michel Eyquem de
    1965   *The Complete Essays of Montaigne*, Stanford University Press, Stanford.

Moore, H.
    1986   *Space, Text, and Gender*, Cambridge University Press, Cambridge.

Moore, Sally Falk
    1976   The Secret of the Men: A Fiction of Chagga Initiation and the Relation to the Logic of Chagga Symbolism, *Africa* 46: 357–70.

Morelli, Giovanni
    1892   *Italian Painting*, Vol. I [*Die Werke italianischer Meister*, 1880, original articles 1874–76], John Murray, London.

Morinis, Alan
    1985   The Ritual Experience: Pain and the Transformation of Consciousness in Ordeals of Initiation, *Ethos* 13: 150– 74.

Mtey, Robert
    1968   Mila na jadi za Wakaguru, *Nchi Yetu* 48: 6–8.

Muhando, Daudi
    n.d.   Untitled typed study of Kaguru, Sagara, Zigua, and other peoples [in Swahili], Morogoro Provincial Office.

Musil, Robert
    1979   *The Man without Qualities* [*Der Mann ohne Eigenschaften*], Vol. II, *The Like of It Now Happens* [*Seinesgleichen Geschicht*, 1930], Vol. III, *Into the Millennium* [*Ins taussandjährige Reich*, 1932], Picador, London.

Myerhoff, Barbara
    1982   Rites of Passage: Process and Paradox, pp. 108–35 in Victor M. Turner (ed.), *Celebration*, Smithsonian Institution Press, Washington, DC.

Mzuanda, C.
    1958   *Historia za Uluguru*, privately printed, Luguru Native Authority, Morogoro.

Needham, Rodney
    1975   Polythetic Classification: Convergence and Consequence, *Man* 10 (n.s.): 349–69.
    1987   *Counterpoints*, University of California Press, Berkeley.

Niederer, Arnold
    1990   Comportements ritualisés au quotidien, *Ethnologia Europaea* 20: 151–60.

Nietzsche, Friedrich
    1956a   The Birth of Tragedy [Die Geburt der Tragödie, 1892], in *The Birth of Tragedy and the Genealogy of Morals*, Doubleday Anchor Books, Garden City.
    1956b   On the Genealogy of Morals [Zur Genealogie der Moral, 1887], in *The*

Birth of Tragedy and the Genealogy of Morals, Doubleday Anchor Books, Garden City.

Norbeck, Edward, Donald E. Walker, and Mimi Cohen
  1962   The Interpretation of Data: Puberty Rites, *American Anthropologist* 64: 463–85.

O'Flaherty, James C.
  1976   Socrates in Hamann's Socratic Memorabilia and Nietzsche's Birth of Tragedy, pp. 114–43 in James C. O'Flaherty, Timothy F. Sellner, and Robert M. Helm (eds.), *Studies in Nietzsche and the Classical Tradition*, University of North Carolina Press, Chapel Hill.

O'Neil, John
  1985   *Five Bodies*, Cornell University Press, Ithaca.

Ortega y Gasset, José
  1986   *Meditations on Hunting* [prologue to Edward Yebes, *Veinte años de caza major*, 1942], Scribner's Sons, New York.

Ortner, Sherry B.
  1972   Is Female to Male as Nature Is to Culture? *Feminist Studies* 1, no. 2: 5–31.
  1996   *Making Gender: The Politics and Erotics of Culture*, Beacon Press, Boston.

Ottenberg, Simon
  1989   *Boyhood Rituals in an African Society*, University of Washington Press, Seattle.

Padgug, Robert A.
  1989   Sexual Matters: On Conceptualizing Sexuality in History, pp. 14–31 in Kathy Peiss and Christina Simmons (eds.), *Passion and Power*, Temple University Press, Philadelphia.

Paige, Karen Erickson, and Jeffrey M. Paige
  1981   *The Politics of Reproductive Ritual*, University of California Press, Berkeley.

Panofsky, Erwin
  1962   *Studies in Iconology* [1939], Harper Torchbooks, New York.

Parkin, David
  1991   *Sacred Void: Spatial Images of Work and Ritual among the Giriama of Kenya*, Cambridge University Press, Cambridge.

Paulme, Denise
  1963   Introduction, pp. 1–16 in Denise Paulme (ed.), *Women in Tropical Africa*, University of California Press, Berkeley.

Phillips, Tom (ed.)
  1995   *Africa: The Art of a Continent*, Prestel, Munich and New York.

Plato
  1968   *The Republic of Plato*, Basic Books, New York.

Plekhanov, G.
  1950   *Unaddressed Letters* [1925–27, 1936] *and Art and Social Life* [1912–13], Foreign Language Publishing House, Moscow.

Potash, Betty

1989   Gender Relations in Sub-Saharan Africa, pp. 189–227 in Sandra Morgen (ed.), *Gender and Anthropology*, American Anthropological Association, Washington.

Precourt, Walter

1975   Initiation Ceremonies and Secret Societies as Educational Institutions, pp. 231–50 in Richard W. Brislin, Stephen Bochner, and Walter J. Lonner (eds.), *Cross-Cultural Perspectives on Learning*, Sage Publications, Beverly Hills.

Rancour-Laferriere, Daniel

1992   *Signs of the Flesh: An Essay on the Evolution of Hominid Sexuality* [1985], Indiana University Press, Bloomington.

Redfern, Walter

1984   *Puns*, Basil Blackwell, Oxford.

Redfield, Robert

1952   The Primitive World View, *Proceedings of the American Philosophical Society* 96: 30–36.

Reik, Theodore

1946   *Ritual: Psycho-Analytic Studies*, Farrar, Straus, New York.

Richards, Audrey I.

1950   Some Types of Family Structure amongst the Central Bantu, pp. 207–51 in A. R. Radcliffe-Brown and Daryll Forde (eds.), *African Systems of Kinship and Marriage*, Oxford University Press, London.

1956   *Chisungu*, Faber and Faber, London.

Richards, I. A.

n.d.   *Principles of Literary Criticism* [1925], Harcourt Jovanovich, New York.

Richlin, Amy (ed.)

1992   *Pornography and Representation in Greece and Rome*, Oxford University Press, New York.

Richter, Alan

1987   *The Language of Sexuality*, McFarland, Jefferson, N.C.

Rieff, Phillip

1979   *Freud: The Mind of a Moralist*, third edition, University of Chicago Press, Chicago.

Riesman, Paul

1986   The Person and the Life Cycle in African Social Life and Thought, *African Studies Review* 29: 71–138.

Rivers, W.H.R.

1926   The Primitive Concept of Death, pp. 36–50 in *Psychology and Ethnology*, ed. G. Elliot Smith, Harcourt Brace, New York.

Rogers, Susan Carol

   1978   Woman's Place: A Critical Review of Anthropological Theory, *Comparative Studies in Society and History* 20: 123–62.

Rosaldo, Michelle Z.

   1974   Woman, Culture, and Society: A Theoretical Overview, pp. 17–42 in M. Z. Rosaldo and L. Lamphere (eds.), *Woman, Culture, and Society*, Stanford University Press, Stanford.

Rosen, Leora Nadine

   1973   Contagion and Cataclysm: A Theoretical Approach to the Study of Ritual Pollution Beliefs, *African Studies* 32: 292–46.

Rothkrug, Lionel

   1979   Popular Religions and Holy Shrines, pp. 20–86 in James Obelkevich (ed.), *Religion and the People*, University of North Carolina Press, Chapel Hill.

Rousseau, Jean-Jacques

   1954   *Confessions* [*Confessions*, 1782–1789], Penguin Books, Harmondsworth.

   1960   *Letter to M. d'Alembert on the Theatre* [*Lettre à M d'Alembert sur les spectacles*, 1758], Cornell University Press, Ithaca.

   1968   *The Social Contract* [*Du contrat sociale*, 1762], Penguin Books, Harmondsworth.

   1979   *Émile, or on Education* [*Émile, ou Traité de l'éducation*, 1762], Basic Books, New York.

   1986   *The First and Second Discourses, and Essay on the Origin of Languages* [*Discours sur les sciences et les arts*, 1750; *Discours sur l'origine et les fondements de l'inégalité parmi les hommes*, 1755; *Essai sur l'origine des langages*, written 1750–60?], Harper and Row, New York.

Rousselle, Aline

   1988   *Porneia* (1983), Basil Blackwell, Oxford.

Rustin, Michael

   1971   Structural and Unconscious Implications of the Dyad and Triad: An Essay in Theoretical Integration: Durkheim, Simmel, Freud, *The Sociological Review* 19: 179–201.

Rykwert, Joseph

   1991   House and Home, *Social Research* 58: 51–62.

Sanday, Peggy Reeves

   1990   Introduction, pp. 1–19 in P. R. Sanday and Ruth Gallagher Goodenough (eds.), *Beyond the Second Sex: New Directions in the Anthropology of Gender*, University of Pennsylvania Press, Philadelphia.

Sapir, Edward

   1934   Symbolism, pp. 492–95 in *Encyclopedia of the Social Sciences*, Vol. 14, Macmillan, New York.

Scarry, Elaine

   1985   *The Body in Pain*, Oxford University Press, New York.

Scheerder, R. P., and R. P. Tastevin
  1950   Les Wa Lu guru, *Anthropos* 48: 241–86.

Scheffler, Israel
  1981   Ritual and Reference, *Synthese* 48: 421–37.

Scheler, Max
  1961   *Man's Place in Nature* [*Die Stellung des Menschen im Kosmos*, 1928], Noonday Press, New York.

Schilder, Paul
  1950   *The Image and Appearance of the Human Body*, International Universities Press, New York.

Schlegel, Alice
  1990   Gender Meanings: General and Specific, pp. 21–41 in P. R. Sanday and R. G. Goodenough (eds.), *Beyond the Second Sex: New Directions in the Anthropology of Gender*, University of Pennsylvania Press, Philadelphia.

Schlegel, Alice, and Herbert Barry III
  1979   Adolescent Initiation Ceremonies, *Ethnology* 18: 199–210.
  1980   The Evolutionary Significance of Adolescent Initiation Ceremonies, *American Ethnologist* 7: 696–715.

Schloss, Marc R.
  1988   *The Hatchet's Blood*, University of Arizona Press, Tucson.

Schwartz, Joel
  1985   *The Sexual Politics of Jean-Jacques Rousseau*, University of Chicago Press, Chicago.

Schwartz, Kit
  1988   *The Female Member*, St. Martin's Press, New York.

Scott, Joan W.
  1986   Gender: A Useful Category of Historical Analysis, *The American Historical Review* 91: 1053–75.

Senn, H. A.
  1974   Arnold van Gennep: Structuralist and Apologist for the Study of Folklore in France, *Folklore* 85: 229–43.

Sheidlower, Jesse (ed.)
  1995   *The F Word*, Random House, New York.

Shklar, Judith
  1985   *Men and Citizens: A Study of Rousseau's Social Theory* [1969], Cambridge University Press, Cambridge.

Simmel, Georg
  1950   *The Sociology of Georg Simmel*, ed. Kurt H. Wolff, Free Press, Glencoe.
  1971   *On Individuality and Social Forms*, ed. Donald N. Levine, University of Chicago Press, Chicago.

1984   *On Women, Sexuality, and Love* [*Das Relative und das Absolute im Geschlechter-problem*, 1923], Yale University Press, New Haven.

Solanas, Valerie

1968   *S.C.U.M. Manifesto*, Olympia Press, New York.

Somersan, Semra

1984   Death Symbolism in Matrilineal Societies, *Ethnos* 13: 151–64.

Southall, Aidan

1972   Twinship and Symbolic Structures, pp. 73–114 in J. S. La Fontaine (ed.), *The Interpretation of Ritual*, Tavistock, London.

Spencer, Paul

1985   Introduction, pp. 1–46 in Paul Spencer (ed.), *Society and Dance*, Cambridge University Press, Cambridge.

Starobinski, Jean

1988   *Jean-Jacques Rousseau: Transparency and Construction* [*J.-J. Rousseau: La Transparence et l'obstacle*, 1971], University of Chicago Press, Chicago.

Stevens, Phillips Jr.

1991   Play and Liminality in Rites of Passage: From Elders to Ancestors in West Africa, *Play and Culture* 4: 237–57.

Stone, Lawrence

1979   *The Family, Sex, and Marriage in England, 1500–1800*, abridged version, Harper Colophon, New York.

Strage, Mark

1980   *The Durable Fig Leaf*, William Morrow, New York.

Swantz, L. W.

1966   *The Zaramo of Tanzania*, Nordic Tanganyika Project, Dar es Salaam.

Swantz, Marja-Liisa

1966   *The Religious and Magical Rites Connected with the Life Cycle of the Woman in Some Bantu Ethnic Groups in Tanzania*, Nordic Tanganyika Project, Dar es Salaam.

1970   *Ritual and Symbol in Transitional Zaramo Society*, Studia Missionalia Uppsaliensia 16, Gleerup, Uppsala.

Sydie, R. A.

1987   *Natural Women, Cultural Men*, New York University Press, New York.

Thorn, Mark

1990   *Taboo No More: The Phallus in Fact, Fantasy, and Fiction*, Shapolsky Publishers, New York.

Tuan, Yi-Fu

1977   *Space and Place*, University of Minnesota Press, Minneapolis.

1990   *Topophilia* [1974], Columbia University Press, New York.

Tuana, Nancy

1993   *The Less Noble Sex: Scientific, Religious, and Philosophical Conceptions of Woman's Nature*, Indiana University Press, Bloomington.

Turner, Bryan S.

1984   *The Body and Society*, Basil Blackwell, Oxford.

Turner, Edith, and William Blodgett

1988   The Carnivalization of Initiation in Zambia, *Play and Culture* 1: 191–204.

Turner, Terence S.

1977   Transformation, Hierarchy and Transcendence: A Reformulation of van Gennep's Model of the Structure of Rites de Passage, pp. 53–70 in B. Myerhoff and S. F. Moore (eds.), *Secular Ritual*, van Gorcum, Amsterdam.

Turner, Victor W.

1955   The Spatial Separation of Adjacent Genealogical Generations in Ndembu Village Structure, *Africa* 25: 121–37.

1957   *Schism and Continuity in an African Society*, Manchester University Press, Manchester.

1962a   Three Symbols of *Passage* in Ndembu Circumcision Ritual, pp. 124–73 in Max Gluckman (ed.), *Essays in the Ritual of Social Relations*, Manchester University Press, Manchester.

1962b   *Chihamba the White Spirit*, Rhodes-Livingstone Paper 33, Rhodes-Livingstone Institute, Lusaka.

1964   Symbols in Ndembu Ritual, pp. 20–51 in Max Gluckman (ed.), *Closed Systems and Open Minds*, Oliver and Boyd, Edinburgh.

1967   *The Forest of Symbols*, Cornell University Press, Ithaca.

Unamuno, Miguel de

1954   *The Tragic Sense of Life* [*Del sentimiento trágico de la vida*, 1921], Dover Publications, New York.

van Baal, J.

1975   *Reciprocity and the Position of Women*, van Gorcum, Assen.

van Gennep, Arnold

1960   *The Rites of Passage* [*Les Rites de passage*, 1908], Routledge and Kegan Paul, London.

Vanggaard, Thorkel

1974   *Phallós* [1969], International Universities Press, New York.

Verlaine, Paul

1965   *Men and Women* [*Oeuvres libres* 1867, 1890, 1904], Comet Books, London.

Vico, Giambattista

1968   *The New Science* [*Scienza Nuova*, 1725], ed. T. G. Bergin and M. H. Fisch, Cornell University Press, Ithaca.

von Waldow, A.
    1961   Mädchenzeichung bei den Zaramo, *Afrika und Übersee* 45: 292–306.
Vromen, Suzanne
    1987   Georg Simmel and the Cultural Dilemma of Women, *History of European Ideas* 8: 563–79.
Vyverberg, Henry
    1989   *Human Nature, Cultural Diversity, and the French Enlightenment*, Oxford University Press, New York.
Wallace, Anthony
    1966   *Religion: An Anthropological View*, Random House, New York.
Waller, Benjamin
    1977   *Encyclopedia of Esoteric Man*, Routledge and Kegan Paul, London.
Warren, Carol, and Barbara Laslett
    1980   Privacy and Secrecy: A Conceptual Comparison, pp. 25–34 in Stanton K. Tefft (ed.), *Secrecy*, Human Science Press, New York.
Watson-Franke, Marie-Barbara
    1992   Masculinity and the Matrilineal Puzzle, *Anthropos* 87: 475–88.
Weber, Max
    1968   *Economy and Society*, Vol. I [*Wirtschaft und Gesellschaft*, 1922], ed. G. Roth and A. Wittich, Bedminster Press, New York.
Webster, Hutton
    1932   *Primitive Secret Societies*, second edition, Macmillan, New York.
Weeks, Jeffrey
    1985   *Sexuality and Its Discontents*, Routledge, London.
Weiner, Annette B.
    1992   *Inalienable Possessions*, University of California Press, Berkeley.
Weiner, James F.
    1991   *The Empty Place*, Indiana University Press, Bloomington.
White, Hayden
    1972   The Forms of Wilderness: Archaeology of an Idea, pp. 3– 37 in Edward Dudley and Maxmillian E. Novak (eds.), *The Wild Within*, University of Pittsburgh Press, Pittsburgh.
White, James Boyd
    1984   *When Words Lose Their Meaning*, University of Chicago Press, Chicago.
Whiting, John W. M., Richard Kluckhohn, and Albert Anthony
    1958   The Function of Male Initiation Ceremonies at Puberty, pp. 359–70 in Eleanor Maccoby, Theodore M. Newcomb, and Eugene L. Hartley (eds.), *Readings in Social Psychology*, Holt, Rinehart, Winston, New York.
Wilson, Peter J.
    1988   *The Domestication of the Human Species*, Yale University Press, New Haven.

Wind, Edgar
    1969   *Art and Anarchy*, Vintage Books, New York.

Winkler, John J.
    1990   *The Constraints of Desire*, Routledge, New York.

Wittgenstein, Ludwig
    1963   *Philosophical Investigations*, Basil Blackwell, Oxford.
    1964   *The Blue and Brown Books* [1933–35], Basil Blackwell, Oxford.
    1969   *On Certainty*, Harper, New York.
    1981   *Tractatus Logico-Philosophicus* [*Logisch-Philosophische Abhandlung*, 1921], Routledge and Kegan Paul, London.
    1984   *Culture and Value*, University of California Press, Berkeley.
    n.d.   *Lectures and Conversations*, University of California Press, Berkeley.

Wokler, Robert
    1978   Perfectible Apes in Decadent Culture: Rousseau's Anthropology Revisited, *Daedalus* 107, 3: 107–34.

Wollstonecraft, Mary
    1985   *Vindication of the Rights of Women* [1792], Penguin Books, Harmondsworth.

Worthman, Caroll M.
    1987   Interactions of Physical Maturation and Cultural Practices in Ontogeny: Kikuyu, *Cultural Anthropology* 2: 29–38.

Yanagisako, Sylvia J.
    1979   Family and Household: The Analysis of Domestic Groups, *Annual Review of Anthropology* 8: 161–205.

Young, Frank W.
    1962   The Function of Male Initiation Ceremonies: A Cross-Cultural Test of an Alternate Hypothesis, *The American Journal of Sociology* 67: 379–91.

Zerubavel, Eviatar
    1991   *The Fine Line: Making Distinctions in Everyday Life*, Free Press, New York.

Index

abortion alien to Kaguru thinking, 210
administration, Kaguru local: under the British, 37–38, 234; under German rule, 34, 36–37
adultery, 200–201
adults, moral status of, 110, 265n2. *See also* initiation rites; males; women
affines: relationships with the groom, 97; sexual relations with, 208–9
age: male maturation amenable to tinkering, 135–36, 174–75; and prowess of males, 211–12
agriculture, 31; need for men, women, and children as labor, 54–55; in space and time, 90–91
akidas (political agents), use of coastal Swahili, 34, 37
alien people in Kaguruland. *See* outsiders
alimentation: failure to observe etiquette of, 122; and space, 81–83, 106
anal intercourse associated with Arabs, 204
ancestors: Kaguru customs and thoughts stemming from, 233–34; Kaguru origin legends, 77–78, 101–2
ancestral dead: access to, 110; attempts by Ukaguru Students' Association to include in themes, 45; bush as burial space, 89, 97–99, 102; rites to propitiate, 90, 102–4;

role in impregnation process, 60–61, 261n7; role in male initiation, 137; ties to children, 92, 110–11
Anderson, Benedict, 30, 31
animals: concepts of, 103–4, 120–25; elephant as symbol of death, 89, 95, 228; rhinoceros in sexual imagery, 202–3, 216–17. *See also* birds
Arabs in Kaguruland, 33–34, 204
artifacts used in Kaguru rites, 138–39, 267–68n1, 270n10
artisans, Ngulu people as, 39, 42
ashes, significance in initiation rites, 149–50

baboons, story of origin, 120–25
Bachelard, Gaston, 12, 105, 107, 129, 264n19
Bakhtin, Mikhail, 13
Baraguyu (people): female circumcision rites, 167; grooming practices, 170; relations with Kaguru, 39–40, 42, 48
Barkan, Leonard, 244
Bateson, Gregory, 49
beads: use during male initiation, 150; worn by newly initiated Kaguru females, 168, 171
Beauvoir, Simone de: on contrasting women and men, 17, 20–23, 178, 233, 237, 257n19, 272n9; on fattening women, 165

122, 127–28, 204, 266n12; of women in song imageries, 195, 197, 200, 203, 209. *See also* penis

geographic areas of Kaguruland, 31–32

German East Africa, colonial administration, 34, 36

gestures as social mannerisms, 91, 265n21

Gilmore, David D., 23–24

Ginzburg, Carlo, 245, 256n4

girls: Church Missionary Society views on circumcision rites, 36; initiation rites, 94–95, 113, 162–70; occupation of single girls' houses, 84–85

Gluckman, Max, 24

Goffman, Erving, 15, 248

Gogo (people), in Kaguruland, 37, 170, 197, 235, 272n7

Gonzalez-Crussi, F., 269n3

Gottlieb, Alma, 125–27

grammar, Kaguru, publication by Church Missionary Society, 35

grandparents, 63, 261n7

Gray, J. Patrick, 273n2

greed: baboons viewed as displaying, 122; prevention through proper bodily grooming, 123–24; and witchcraft, 110

grooming: following initiation rites, 170–72; and prevention of greed, 123–24. *See also* shaving

Gusdorf, Georges, 8

habitus and metaphors, 246, 256n5

hair: associated with simians, 121, 122, 124; Kaguru ideas about, 122–23, 225. *See also* shaving

Halbwachs, Maurice, 77

Hart, Ray, 262n6

Hasenmueller, Christine, 247

Havelock, Eric, 11–12

head coverings, 172

headmen. *See* leaders, Kaguru

hearth, household: as center of proper home, 81, 83; confinement of bride and groom, 96–97; extinguishing fire at death, 98; inaccessibility to unmarried men, 85, 161

hegemony, male, through institutions and beliefs, 19

Hehe (people), males as uncircumcised, 134

highlands, Kaguru self-identification as people of, 32

holism in Kaguru ritual practices, 26, 28

home(s). *See* house(s)

Homer, views of his poetic style, 10–11, 12, 257n11

homosexuality among the Kaguru, 273n16

hospitals as birthing locale, 225

house(s), 264n13; construction as joint local labor, 85; hearth and food preparation as center, 81, 83; innermost recesses associated with death and sexuality, 93; marital space as secret locale, 84; as place for preinitiation storytelling, 112; seclusion of bride and groom, 96–97; separate facilities for initiated boys and girls, 84–85, 161; as site for girl's initiation, 94–95, 164–70, 176–77; in spatial imagery, 105

household identity, natal: through birth rites, 92–93; through blood relationship, 57, 70

households, individual: effect on matrilineal ties, 58–59; promotion by missionaries and governmental officials, 63

hunting: as Kaguru sexual metaphor of dominance, 19–20, 101–2, 258n21; as mastery of the bush, 103–4, 235

identity. *See* ethnic identity

imagery: in initiation songs, 191–92, 197; use of fire, 12, 257n14; use of play, 12–13

imagination: as hinge of Kaguru education, 6, 179–80; and human drives in Rousseau's *Émile*, 4, 6; learning through rituals and symbols, 247–50; use of fire as imagery, 12, 257n14

impotence, 207

incestuous relations, 213, 260n2

Indirect Rule, use by British colonial administration, 37–38, 234

initiation, 2, 14, 251–52; of adolescents as constructing ethnic identity, 74–75, 76; attempts by Ukaguru Students' Association to include in themes, 44–45; behavioral responsibility following, 15, 110–11, 217; Church Missionary Society views toward, 36; differences for boys and girls, 94–95; as ethnicity confirmation, 30–31; as form of education, 3; identity with the landscape as fundamental reality, 43; meaning of rituals, 27–29, 259n28; meaning of symbols, 27–29; memorization in Kaguru education, 15–16, 257n17; personhood as key construction in Kaguru world, 15–16, 257n18; riddles, legends and lore learned during, 182. *See also* initiation rites; rites of passage; songs